C000228980

CREDIBLE AND
TRUE

CREDIBLE AND
TRUE

THE POLITICAL AND PERSONAL MEMOIR OF
K. HARVEY PROCTOR

Biteback Publishing

First published in Great Britain in 2016 by
Biteback Publishing Ltd
Westminster Tower
3 Albert Embankment
London SE1 7SP
Copyright © Harvey Proctor 2016

Harvey Proctor has asserted his right under the Copyright,
Designs and Patents Act 1988 to be identified as the author of this work.

All rights reserved. No part of this publication may be reproduced,
stored in a retrieval system or transmitted, in any form or by any
means, without the publisher's prior permission in writing.

This book is sold subject to the condition that it shall not, by way of
trade or otherwise, be lent, resold, hired out or otherwise circulated without
the publisher's prior consent in any form of binding or cover other than
that in which it is published and without a similar condition, including
this condition, being imposed on the subsequent purchaser.

Every reasonable effort has been made to trace copyright holders of
material reproduced in this book, but if any have been inadvertently
overlooked the publishers would be glad to hear from them.

ISBN 978-1-78590-001-3

10 9 8 7 6 5 4 3 2 1

A CIP catalogue record for this book is available from the British Library.

Set in Dante and New Johnston by Adrian McLaughlin

Printed and bound in Great Britain by
CPI Group (UK) Ltd, Croydon CR0 4YY

MIX
Paper from
responsible sources
FSC
www.fsc.org   FSC® C020471

For Terry Woods and Granville Proctor, of course

CONTENTS

PART 3

*'Someone must have traduced Joseph K.,
for without having done anything wrong
he was arrested one fine morning.'*

—THE TRIAL, FRANZ KAFKA

ACKNOWLEDGEMENTS

I would like to thank all those who have helped and supported me in the daunting task of writing this book including family and friends. I also wish to thank Joanna and Roseanna Lane for their assistance with editing and the technical aspects of the preparation of this book.

I am grateful to the Duke and Duchess of Rutland for their encouragement and Derek Laud for his unswerving assistance, advice and loyalty.

Many members of the media have diligently followed my involvement in the police scandal which has recently enveloped me and I am grateful for their commitment to maintaining the highest standards of journalism in the face of a very serious threat to the freedom of the press.

Those individual members of Her Majesty's constabulary who have expressed their good wishes have my whole hearted thanks.

In conclusion, I wish to thank my dedicated solicitors Raza Sakhi, Nabeel Gatrad and Dimple Patel of Sakhi Solicitors in Leicester for their personal and professional advice, counsel and wisdom.

I acknowledge without all their endeavours I would not have completed the task.

THE DOGS BARKED

I did not know I had been traduced. How could I? I had been living in the peace and quiet of the beautiful English countryside for many years. The pressures of metropolitan life had long since fallen away. Initially, I hated the silence. I had been surrounded by noise for most of my life. Silence had been worrying to me. It was not the comfort a 'townie' might seek in a rural idyll. Belvoir had been my home for over thirteen years. It was the longest period of time Terry and I had lived together continuously anywhere since we had first met in late 1973. We had settled in, away from the gaze of the media, which had been a big part of our lives. By 2015, we had been a family for many, many years. Adam had lived with us for ten years. He had moved in to escape Nottingham and its dangers, gangs, knife crime and heavy drugs. Adam had worked on the Belvoir estate doing driving and DJ work, especially for the ducal family that lived at the castle, whose outline towered above the surrounding farm land. At our previous home – Engine Yard Cottage – though much nearer to it, we couldn't see the castle, well, not clearly or without difficulty. At Barn Farm, where we had lived for the last two years, it was obvious on the sky line. The northern aspect of the castle was in full view. You could see the flag flying proudly atop all. This house was in the middle of farm fields, half a mile down a rough farm track with numerous potholes. Our nearest neighbour was half a mile away and to the nearest shop it was about three miles. We lived in our own world.

We all aged well at Belvoir. We had settled. I had a responsible job as the Duke of Rutland's private secretary. Terry had retired from the art world. Adam had grown up and he had found love with Charlotte, whom he had married in Belvoir Castle's chapel in August 2014. Their wedding breakfast had been at Barn Farm; fifty-odd people including Emma, the Duchess of Rutland, sat down in the barn/garage. Nearly 100 had attended our house a week before to celebrate their forthcoming marriage at a drinks party in the courtyard. The barn was technically in Lincolnshire and the house in Leicestershire. Our five-bar gate followed the county boundary. The family was complete with the birth of their baby daughter in November 2014. Adam, Charlotte and the baby had lived in a kind of apartment over our ground-floor home with bedroom, sitting room and bathroom. The house was sensibly arranged downstairs; an entry porch led to a sitting room, formerly a stable of over 100 years' duration for several horses, then a dining room and kitchen. Off the kitchen was a shower room. We had arranged for a large barn, accessed via the kitchen, to be converted into a beautiful down-stairs bedroom with high ceiling and sliding doors and windows into the garden, through which we could see the sun set in the west. Much of the original, exposed red brick had been retained at our request. The windows of the house were double-glazed and the home benefited from central heating and a splendid cosy wood and coal burner. When the winds blew, and they did, we were protected. If future infirmity called, we could be on one warm and cosy level. It was near perfect. It was a wonderful life, one which I planned and expected to enjoy unto death.

I had just been persuaded to cut back to a three-day week at work, plus the hosting of weddings and corporate events that were often at weekends. The truncated week was just about to start. Terry wanted to see more of me and I of him and of our beloved dogs. We were to enjoy our remaining days surrounded by farm fields and immense skies. Adam, Charlotte and the baby were to leave shortly for Spain. It was their long-planned intention to live abroad with their child for the first year of her life, if not longer. Terry and I planned to pop out to stay with them from time to time.

The first trauma had already occurred a week or two before. It meant that our family in the United Kingdom had been split asunder. It is unbelievable, as so much of my life has been unbelievable, and has not been mentioned before in the press or publicly – but more of that anon. So, it was just Terry and myself in the house with our dogs that Tuesday night. Our conversation turned to the historic child sexual abuse inquiry. Heavy subject you might think, but, for months, being dragged into this inquiry, possibly as a witness, had been the only real fly in the ointment. What would I do if I was required to give evidence? I had been at the centre of a homosexual scandal in 1986 and 1987. It was inconceivable that I would not be drawn into this inquiry's remit. I had nothing to say that would or could help. Only I and Terry knew that, but how to respond if I was asked to attend? I had more or less decided not to go. With nothing to say, why risk my personal security by appearing in London at a prearranged time in a prearranged location at the mercy of every fanatic on or off the internet? The inquiry was likely to be given powers to call witnesses on pain of imprisonment if they refused. Notwithstanding, I had decided to maintain my privacy and refuse to give evidence. How could I help when I had witnessed nothing and was sceptical that anything alleged had happened in or around Westminster? If it had, I knew nothing about it. By even attending, I reasoned, it would be a case of guilt by association. I wanted nothing to do with it. I would rather face imprisonment.

We argued about it and gradually drifted off to sleep listening, as we usually did, to the BBC World Service news programmes. In the morning I awoke, made tea for me and coffee for Terry and then went back to bed clutching biscuits for the dogs. Sushi, our Akita, who slept on the sitting-room sofa, had joined Duke, the boxer, on the bed. Duke tended to bark first. Sushi would then bark to show her support. It never happened in unison. It was Wednesday 4 March 2015. At 8 a.m., they barked. Shortly after, there was an insistent knock on the front door. It was not the knock of a burglar or plumber coming to steal or mend something; it was the knock of someone about to enter, come what may. It was a knock that was to catapult me back into the media spotlight. A spotlight I had shied away from for many years – twenty-eight, to be precise – not because I had anything to hide, but to protect myself and my privacy. At the time of my personal difficulties I had experienced intrusion into my private life for eighteen months – it had been the longest-running of scandals in the 1980s – and it had not been a pleasant time. When I was working at the castle, I had agreed to speak to the press only as 'a spokesman' for the castle, not under my own name. When the film cameras rolled at Belvoir, as they often did, the unwritten contract stated I was to be firmly *behind* the lens, never in front.

I pulled back the curtain – well, a large red and green silk bed cover from the shirt shop days in Richmond which we used as a curtain to give privacy on the door and window leading to the front of the house, where there was a gravel-covered courtyard – and saw a police van. I thought it must have been to do with the castle, so I put on a dressing gown and made my way through the kitchen, dining room and sitting room to the inner front door. There, a man in a suit with papers was now gingerly knocking on the front door. I would have done too if I had been him. Both dogs were snarling, jumping up at the door, a frightening welcome for friends. These proved not to be friends. 'Can you control the dogs?' was his first remark as far as I recall. This was not an easy task with strangers in the house – their house. They are both gentle giants, really, and soon, after my reassurance, they calmed down. The man nervously asking the question was Detective Sergeant Matt Flynn, who then announced that he was from the Metropolitan Police Murder Squad and, under 'Operation Midland', he had a warrant to search my house.

PART 1

CHAPTER 1

CHILDHOOD

I was born in Pontefract in the West Riding of Yorkshire on Thursday 16 January 1947. I am therefore a Capricorn, not that I take notice of zodiac signs, although I might be tempted to read my chart if waiting for a haircut or in a dentist's waiting room if all other reading material had been exhausted. Dog is the animal and fire the element for a person born on this day if we consider the very old art of Chinese astrology – both strangely appropriate for my life. I am a Yorkshire man and very proud of my northern roots. I speak the Queen's English, but I can just as easily put on my Yorkshire accent if I want to do so.

I came into the world on an extremely cold day during a spell of very wintry weather. There was apparently thick snow on the ground. Just before my birth, my mother Hilda (née Tegerdine) fell outside on the icy path in the back yard when feeding our chickens and, for fear of further falls or difficulties with my birth, one of my aunts, Florence, was drafted in to look after my mother during her pregnancy. It was a sensible precaution. Just before my older brother, Granville, was born nine years earlier, my mother had been getting off a tram car at a stop in Leeds when a large car had knocked her down as she made her way to the pavement. The driver of the car had broken the highway code at a tram stop, and this accident had put my mother in hospital – Leeds Royal Infirmary – for months. Along with a fractured skull, smashed pelvis and broken ribs, the bones behind her ears had also been broken and she had to have a splint in her mouth for ages. Mother suffered from headaches throughout her life as a result of the injury, always having a constant supply of aspirins to hand. She had been lucky to survive. Even more surprisingly, however, my brother – who she was expecting at the time – was born without a scratch. Physically, we have always been a tough family. Predictably, when my brother dropped me on the floor from his lap on the second day of my life, I just bounced as babies do.

On the day of my birth Granville had joined my father, Albert Proctor, in celebrations. Wartime rationing was still in place so it was a major, lavish treat when my father bought my brother a peach. It cost 7 shillings and 6 pennies, about 38p now, but then a handsome amount. My father was a master baker. He worked at a bakery shop in Pontefract, one that had made the jockey Gordon Richards's wedding cake. My parents liked horse racing and would place small bets on horses throughout their lives. With me it's only been the Grand National, if that. Greyhound racing was another of their favourite pastimes. They had a greyhound during the Second World War and before a race they would get it to drink beaten-up eggs in milk laced with brandy, which I am sure must have been against any doping rules at the time. Not long after my birth, the family moved to Leeds.

My father had a sister called Eliza and a brother called Jack. Also in his family were two sisters, Molly and Annie, the latter who went to Australia. He also had two great-aunts, Annie and Mary, and a great-uncle called Arthur. Annie and Mary were both in the rag trade in Leeds, and Mary spent most of her life in the city. Annie and her husband, Walt, who was an engineer and an ardent trade unionist, retired to Blackpool and bought a house from which they ran a bed-and-breakfast establishment at Bispham. I often visited them at their Leeds house, exploring their cellar where clothes were washed and wrung out to dry by hand. I played with toys they gave me, including a toy fort, and I once saw Annie nearly choke on a fish bone as a child. It put me off eating fish – with the exception of fish from fish-and-chip shops – until I went to university. I think my first time away from home overnight was in their B&B. I was transfixed by the illuminations. The hundreds of thousands of bright colourful lights and moving tableaux were wonderful. They were truly fascinating and during the day I played cricket on the sands of Blackpool with a bat made by Walt. Later, in my mid-teens onwards, when I attended Conservative Party conferences held in the Winter Gardens every other October, I would stay with them. Despite not being Conservatives, they were hospitable, kind, generous and supportive of my interest in politics. They gave me an insight into trade unionism and truly working-class, good and honest people. Annie was always partially deaf and her hearing deteriorated throughout her life. Sometimes her hearing aid would whistle as she adjusted it, and I remember she never drank tea or coffee, preferring aired water instead. She was a devout Christian Scientist, a dedicated follower of Mary Baker, and when Walt died she returned to Leeds to live with Mary, her sister, who had never married. As a Member of Parliament, when on visits to Yorkshire, I would always seek them out for a family chat and a cup of tea until just before both of them died in old age in their late eighties.

During the Second World War, my father did not serve in the armed forces. He was in a special position, being a baker. At night, however, he served his country as an air-raid warden. He recalled seeing German fighter planes flying down streets between houses or just above them, machine gunning as well as bombing. The evil witnessed by that generation, now almost died out, and their fortitude to withstand and overwhelm the aggressor will withstand the test of time and is the basis upon which our system of law and justice was reinforced.

My mother's family was larger. She had four sisters – Florence, Annie, Doris and Eva – and two brothers, James and Wilfred. They originated in Lincolnshire and were a tight-knit family. We were forever visiting each other's homes. My uncle James was a soldier in the Second World War and a semi-professional footballer. I recall looking at his war medals and it instilled in me an early interest in history. He was married to a woman named Jessie, who made my mother's wedding dress. Her four sisters were bridesmaids and their tinted black-and-white wedding photographs show their dresses to be a torrid, bright green/blue colour. Mother's dress was traditional white, with a very long train, and she carried lilies of the valley in her bouquet. I recall James and Jessie's wedding present, which was in the family for many years. It was a hand-carved Indian elephant, with real ivory tusks, about eighteen inches high, made from a single block of teak wood. It carried a timber log in its trunk, which wrapped around it and was controlled by its Mahout with a tiny separate hammer or small pole. In fact, I think it was supposed to be a *cheru kol*. My mother kept the hammer safe and occasionally fixed it in position, otherwise keeping it in her purse. So pleased were my parents with the gift, that when James and Jessie married, they too were bought a carved teak elephant, though it was not as big as ours. When I was about eleven or twelve and James died, he was laid out in the front room of his house and I think it was the first time I saw a dead body.

Of all my mother's relatives, I recall Flo the most clearly. She was a solid, down-to-earth woman who was tough and gentle at the same time. Apt to be clumsy, she had a very kind heart, which made it difficult to criticise her dropping of plates and other items of crockery. In early life, I grew up with her daughter Jacqueline. We were of a similar age and in due course, I went to her wedding in Leeds – to a journalist from the *Yorkshire Post*, a newspaper I have always much respected. When, in October 2012, I attended her funeral just outside York, I found it to be an uplifting affair – she had done much charitable work, had raised a family and lived a wonderful life. I remember leaving the wake having doubts about what I had achieved in my own time on earth, full of introspection.

I was given two Christian names – a bit unusual at the time, I think. I was named Keith after one of my brother's friends who lived on Sun Hill Lane in Pontefract and whom I never knew. I always thought I was named Harvey, my second Christian name, after a pooka, a mythical drinking companion in Mary Chase's play about Elwood P. Dowd. It had come out on Broadway in November 1944 and, in it, the alcoholic Dowd had invented a mythical drinking companion so that he would never have to drink alone. In his case, it was a 6ft tall, invisible white rabbit called 'Harvey'. The play was revived in 1949 and turned into a film with the famous American stage and screen star James Stewart playing the lead. In the early 1980s, I saw Stewart resume the role of Elwood on the London stage. At the conclusion of the play he received a thunderous ovation, as much for his life and for his screen presence as for the role he had just played that night, I imagine. He then left the line of actors and actresses and went to the back of the stage and brought forward the invisible white rabbit, who took a bow and received the biggest applause of the evening. In my life, I have often played the role of a 'pooka' to friends, but not invisibly. My mother more or less confirmed this origin of my name, but my brother instead thinks I was named after the retail store Harvey Nichols. He says I was nearly named 'Marshall' after another store chain, Marshall and Snelgrove.

Whichever is correct, I preferred from an early age 'Harvey' to 'Keith' – I do not know why. But I also had an affection for the initial of my first name, hence even my early school books have on their front cover the name 'K. Harvey Proctor'. It was my unfathomable choice, not that of my parents. It was not, as some inferred many years later, an affectation from 'J. Enoch Powell', since at the age of six or seven I had no knowledge of him. This sort of myth and fiction were to follow me throughout my life – I have never understood why. I suppose fantasy can be more appealing than truth to many, but the truth of my life has always been stranger than fiction and much of it has always been fantastical. I have no need of embroidery. As you will read, I believe my life has been an extraordinary one.

My early childhood memories revolve around being wheeled in a pram by the side of a river. I remember hearing the river's water rippling over the stones and pebbles in the shallow riverbed, and I think it would have been in Ripon, possibly the River Ure. My family had moved to Ripon from Leeds when I was three years old. I certainly recall visiting Ripon Cathedral and hearing the choir sing in those splendid surroundings. I have never been a habitual, weekly church-goer, but would regard myself as C of E – Church of England. I enjoyed the ritual rather than the spiritual side of church activities

– the colour, the aromas, the drama of it all. When I was a little older, the local church had frequent Saturday weddings and I would often stand and watch the arrivals and departures of brides and grooms, but I cannot recall ever entering the church itself. I also remember listening to Ripon's town crier, who was dressed in bright robes as he rang his bell and shouted his calls in the town square. All in all, throughout my formative, pre-school years, I was fortunate to grow up in a secure, peaceful and above all loving family.

We moved from Ripon to York in the early 1950s, where my parents bought two bakery and cake shops – one on Bishopthorpe Road and one in Clarence Street. In addition, we had a large house in Scarcroft Road, which is now a guest house. It had five or six floors and I soon had my own bedroom. My brother had his at the top of the house.

Granville, being nine years older, wasn't the playful brother. More distant in character, from a young age I knew him to be very artistic. He became a student at the York Art School and then went to the Royal College of Fashion Design, where he studied under Janie Ironside. Once he graduated, he worked for Susan Small and Riva as a fashion designer.

He was very good looking and posed for *Honey* magazine in the 1960s on a soapbox, with models wearing dresses he had designed. It must have been election time. He was inherently talented. He has an eye for colour, can sew impeccably, design, cut and make patterns. As well as making many of my mother's clothes, he helped to design and make Princess Anne's wedding dress and the red dress that Margaret Thatcher wore, which helped to cement, sartorially, her reputation as the Iron Lady. I have always admired him and his gentle, quiet and selfless character. Over the years, we have grown ever closer and I know I could not have survived the trials and tribulations of my life without him.

I have fond memories of living at Scarcroft Road from the ages of five to eleven. One night, a cloudburst resulted in our long but narrow, flat back garden being flooded to a depth of a foot or two. I took the opportunity of sailing my toy yacht, painted green and cream with white sails, off the back raised steps, and thereafter never set eyes on it again. It must have sailed down the garden and out the open back gate.

The River Ouse flooded regularly. The centre of York seemed to be often under water, as did the houses and streets behind our shop down to the river. As a non-swimmer, I kept well away. When I was about nine or ten, attempts were made to teach me to swim. We walked from school in twos, carrying our multicolour towels, across York to St George's Swimming Baths. I hated the swimming lessons, the awful smell of chlorine in the water and in the air. It made my eyes water. In the first lesson we held hands in a circle in the shallow end, sang the song 'Ring a ring a roses' and, on the lines 'Atishoo! Atishoo!', we were told to put our heads under the level of the water. The others obliged; I did not. As a result, I was informed I couldn't attend the second lesson. Subsequently I have been told I did not have to put my head under the water to learn how to swim. This experience haunted me almost every time I tried to learn the technique, however, and to this day, to my shame, I still cannot swim. I have tried many times and came close on occasion, but I was not successful.

As a boy I collected Bayko building kits rather than Meccano sets. They were very bright bricks, similar to Lego, but very British. I played endlessly with lead toy soldiers, sailors and airman, though tended to favour the ones wearing ceremonial dress rather than those in fatigues and in action poses. I preferred marching bands to warfare. I had a brilliant model of a gold Coronation coach with horses and outriders, I liked arranging re-enactments of military tattoos more than reliving the Second World War. My boyhood passion was for collecting Dinky Toys and I used to look forward to birthdays and Christmases for the gift of the inevitably well-made scale model of a car, lorry, bus or large vehicle, like the dark-green BBC television outside-broadcasting vehicles, that ended up as my present. I had all three of those broadcasting vehicles, and in all, I had nearly 200 Dinkies. I kept them in pristine condition, including their boxes, and cared for them solicitously for many years. For some reason – and I was not consulted – my father got rid of them when I was aged fifteen. I had the obvious railway set – Trix, I believe – but, alas, received it too early to really appreciate it. I had long since removed the track from the large board stored in the attic before I got really interested and could have benefited from it. I was never given a second chance, despite longingly looking at Hornby train catalogues in my early teens. I have had a lifelong hankering to have a model railway system at home and, in the absence of one, I have always loved train journeys, enjoying this mode of transport in many countries.

The first dog I had was a Yorkshire Terrier. It lived only a short time and, to conceal the hurt of its death from me – I was only about four or five years old – another Yorkshire Terrier was produced. It had a different name and a different sex but at that age I was gullible enough to continue to believe it was the same dog, miraculously cured and made better just for me.

If I played with friends, it was usually on Scarcroft Green, a large open area of grass divided by the odd path or two. The usual games included football in the winter and cricket and rounders in the summer. In team games, I seemed always the last to be chosen by the self-selected captains. Not that I minded; I was keen rather than skilled at sports. I only had one road to cross to get to the Green and it was a quiet road with little traffic. There was a *Doctor Who* TARDIS-like police box on the Green and I remember I went to it once to report some lost possessions that I had found there. Three months later, when they hadn't been collected, the items were sent back to me. They were of little value, but I rather thought the police good eggs for letting me have them. Honesty is the best policy, I have always thought. It was an age when children were free to play out in school holidays until just before sunset – there were no apparent risks. It was just natural that children could do their own thing in a way that would be inconceivable today. It must have been a halcyon age for child development.

The war was over and soon material things began to loom larger. My parents bought a KP black-and-white television set in 1953 that had a small, grainy screen which was set in a rather large wooden cabinet and, together with neighbours, we settled in for the day to watch the Coronation on 2 June. It was emotional to watch and I have been an ardent monarchist ever since, though more in support of the principle than the characters involved in the wider royal family. Of the many television shows that I watched in the mid-'50s, I think the best was *What's My Line?* with Gilbert Harding, David Nixon (also a splendid magician), Lady Isobel Barnett and Barbara Kelly. You had to be patient when things went wrong and I developed a taste for the potter's wheel and shire horses ploughing fields while we waited for the inevitable faults, integral to live television, to be put right.

Both my parents smoked; my father Capstan Full Strength or Player's Navy Cut. They went out to the occasional dinner dance; Father dressed in smart evening suit with black bow tie, my mother in a multi-coloured sequin bolero jacket over bright ball gowns, her centre-parting hairstyle for all the world looking like the

Duchess of Windsor's. I liked their New Year outings. I tried to stay awake to see the balloons, paper and card trumpets, drums and party hats that they brought home for me. Some were very impressive. They liked to party.

As a treat, I would be taken out for afternoon tea every month. My mother and I would go to either Betty's or Terry's Restaurant in the centre of York, both situated in a square together with the Mansion House and a branch of Barclay's Bank, which was to become, later, my bank for twenty years. I much preferred Terry's, with its dark wooden panelling, thick-pile carpets and gorgeous cream cakes, scones and toasted teacakes – the sort my father baked – oozing butter. However, my favourite meal was that of mushrooms on toast. They were served in a cream sauce – regretfully, I have never been able to replicate its taste – washed down with breakfast tea from a silver-plated teapot with the weak design feature that the handle always became too hot to hold. Waitresses were traditionally dressed in black dresses and white aprons and little white starched cotton 'tiaras' in their hair. Even when it was full and busy there was a quiet air of dignity which pervaded the whole room. Terry's also had a shop that sold thick chocolate biscuits, both milk and dark. They were adorable, scrumptious, and when the restaurant closed nothing could replace them or it. Betty's continues but it was not the same as its rival. Terry's was quintessentially English, now seemingly from a bygone age. I regret its passing. The simplicity of such a childhood in the 1950s gave no warning of the horrors that were to come.

Initially, school was just the other side of Scarcroft Green at the State Primary and Junior Schools. They were accommodated in late-Victorian/early-Edwardian buildings. There were two large schoolyards either side of the central building with a great assembly hall and classrooms off either side of it. A few hundred children attended each school and it had a warm, friendly environment. I enjoyed playing roles in nativity plays at Christmas, though I was always nervous and shy on stage. My brother made wonderful costumes, often fit for a king even though I might be playing the role of a shepherd. I lived near enough to the schools to go home every lunch time. I did not mix well with other children and kept myself to myself. I might have been regarded as stand-offish by classmates – I was certainly timid. When I was about eight or nine years of age, on my way home from school I was set upon by a group of lads, all about two years older than me. I ended up at the bottom of a heap on scrub land near the school. When the other boys got up, however, I found that I could not. My leg had been broken in several places. I was hospitalised and my leg underwent an operation to straighten it. I was in plaster and in a wheelchair for three months as my leg had to be kept straight. As a result I was treated to a longish holiday in Scarborough by my parents. I felt no animosity to those other boys involved, however, and merely vowed never to get myself into such a position again – reinforcing my shy nature and inherent nervousness around other children once more.

I was not a bright child. Rather, I was middling, occupying the place where you were not bothered much by teachers who instead concentrated on the extremes of the very intelligent and the very dull. I was neither and consequently was not stretched academically. It was no surprise to me, therefore, when I failed my 11-plus examination. I think my parents were hoping for better things from me. Nunthorpe Grammar School was at the end of the road and for that reason alone would have been ideal. Instead, I was allocated a place at Danesmead County Secondary School, near to Fulford Barracks; a twenty-minute bus ride away across York. I started taking more of an interest in reading, visiting York Library every Saturday, using its reference rooms and lending services. At this time, too, I started seeing the benefits of York as a cultural city. I visited its many museums and walked the Bar walls, popping into churches and, of course, York Minster and the Shambles. Alas, I was to stay at my first secondary school only two terms. During that time, I took on a deep dislike for cross-country running. It was too muddy, in my opinion. I learnt the forward defensive cricket batting stroke – I left before I learnt scoring strokes – so later on I might not have been able to score many runs, but I was difficult to get out. I did learn, however, how to write in italic script, thanks to a Mr James, our form master. Whenever I write properly with a real fountain pen, I do so with an italic nib. It is a lost art which I must regain.

My parents' bakery shops were wonderful. A repository of beautiful, warm, fresh crusty bread, delicious but solid cakes like chocolate éclairs, vanilla and cream slices, Eccles cakes, custard tarts – so tasty I would drink the filling mixture cold if there was any left. My father baked them all, along with wonderful fruit and nut birthday, Christmas and wedding cakes. Easter was my favourite for the simnel cakes covered with thick marzipan. My mother kept the customers happy and served in the shop. She was tiny in stature, probably about 5 ft 3 in. tall. She had great aplomb in dealing with the public and reps who called in at the Clarence Street shop, which I recall having beautiful cranberry-coloured stained glass in its inner doors as well as magnificent floor tiles. It didn't last long. Although a fantastic baker, my father appeared not to be a great businessman and may have lacked man-management skills. It was, however, great to go round the villages at weekends, especially at Christmas time, delivering bread to snowbound villages around the City of York. It was wonderful going out with my father or the van drivers on these missions. I felt, as he did, it was a good, solid, worthwhile career.

It was heavy work, lifting trays of dough bread into coke ovens day after day and one day he suffered a hernia. My brother stepped in for a while as he recuperated.

Often I would look out of the Bishopthorpe Road shop window to the activity in the street beyond. There was an old-style pharmacy on one side and a fish-and-chip shop on the other. I loved queuing up for portions of their produce served in yesterday's newspapers – something they are really useful for – and going home next door with a large bottle of Vimto, a perfect Saturday lunch combination. Opposite was a butcher's, a wet fish shop and a grocery shop in the Meadow chain where butter and other commodities were sold loose. The post office and cycle shop were popular, as was the greengrocer's. The dairy, where a horse and cart were based that delivered our milk, was positioned opposite a hardware shop where we bought paraffin for stoves in winter and magnificent Standard fireworks from the beginning of October each year.

A memorable sight each day was the wave of ladies in raincoats, head scarves trailing behind them as they cycled to and from work at the Rowntree's and Terry's chocolate factories near to the Knavesmire Racecourse site. There seemed to be hundreds of them and they made it difficult if not impossible to cross the road when they were in full flow for several minutes. Their new working patterns, increasingly going out to work rather than being housewives, made it difficult for my father to continue in business. The growth of convenience foods, especially steamed white sliced bread – essential for the working wife who might not shop every day – made many traditional bakers go to the wall. A man of my father's professional talents, with the ability to make traditional crusty bread, would make a gold mine now, but in the late 1950s it was the reverse. First the house on Scarcroft Road was disposed of, and we moved to live above the shop not far away. Even that economy measure proved fruitless and, in 1958, my parents bowed to the inevitable and closed the shop doors for good.

They had always wanted to live in Scarborough. It was a place they frequently took my brother and me for holidays – he was even named after a hotel there, The Granville Hotel, and so I said good-bye, for the time being, to York.

CHAPTER 2

UNIVERSITY

On my return to York in October 1966, I was nineteen and fresh from the triumph of A levels. Two As in History and Economics and a B in Geography had won me a place on a History degree course at the University of York. In fact, I was offered a place with only three Es, so I guess York really wanted me. I had reached the apex of my academic ability at A level, though I did not realise it at the time.

Much had changed by this time, and we were no longer the happy family that had left for Scarborough. When I was fifteen, my father left. We had no notice; no indication of the calamity that was to befall us. I had failed my 12-plus examination and was borderline at thirteen, only attaining entry into the High School for Boys grammar school through the headmaster, Mr Marsden, and our shared interest in chess, which became apparent at interview. I lost a year and was placed back in the second year's form, but I donned my black-and-red uniform with pride. I went to school one morning as usual, but when I returned home my father was not there.

He had worked in hotels in Scarborough as a patisserie chef, latterly at the Royal Hotel. We worried that he might have been the victim of an accident, fallen ill or worse. Mother just thought he would return later. I went to bed only to be woken late that evening with the news that he still had not come home. Mother and I put on our coats over our pyjamas and started to walk the streets of the town centre looking for him. It was a desperate and forlorn hope. Approaching midnight, a police patrol car stopped. The officers assessed the situation, made enquiries of local hospitals and drew a blank. They took us home. We soon found out that my father had decided to live with another woman but could not face my mother with the truth. Within a few days a letter arrived detailing his abandonment and I never spoke to him again. My parents got divorced and, unlike my mother and brother, I did not attend his funeral.

Although still nervous and shy, my social life had already taken an upward turn. At the very moment Tony Hancock was cogitating how to expand his social life from his East Cheam abode in 'The Blood Donor' in June 1961 – for him it was a toss-up between joining the Young Conservatives and becoming a blood donor – I determined to become a Young Conservative. The seaside hotel opposite our rented home in Grosvenor Road was run by a Conservative councillor called Norman Fuller. He made the necessary introductions and, two years earlier than normal, at fourteen, I joined.

I calculated that, as I was against state control, I couldn't be a Labour supporter and, although my parents were National Liberals after the war, I couldn't be a Liberal either. They seemed to say different things in different constituencies just to get elected. That didn't seem to be right. By a process of elimination, in a tri-party system, I must therefore be a Conservative, I reasoned. I knew, however, that I was a very laissez-faire Conservative and not stridently political.

It seemed to me the Conservative Party was a very broad church, and I was comfortable within its ranks. Friday nights thereafter were never my own. I met many people through the Young Conservatives (YCs) who became my friends. I remember them with the greatest affection now. Meetings were predominantly social, including car rallies and wine and cheese parties. Political content increased just before local elections when YCs were expected to deliver leaflets, man committee rooms and even canvass. By the time I went to university, I had helped at many council elections and by-elections and assisted the local Conservative MP Sir Alexander Spearman, a former Suez rebel in 1956 and a man who knew his own mind. I helped with his surgeries on Saturday mornings, visited Conservative Party regional and national conferences, and made my first speech at the Grand Hotel, the imposing chocolate-brown building overlooking the South Bay. My speech was on education – singing the praises of the tripartite system and generally becoming the blue-eyed boy of the blue-rinse set of women that dominated fundraising in the area. I helped to organise jumble sales, coffee mornings, lunches and dinners. I attended every council meeting, sitting in the public gallery, and got to grips with political intrigue. There was no part of party organisation with which I was not familiar. I was even involved in the parliamentary candidate selection when Sir Alec retired. The YCs backed Michael Shaw, the avuncular accountant who beat Fergus Montgomery (later to become an MP elsewhere and a political ally in the Commons).

At school, I had stood as a Tory candidate in the mock election in 1966. I was a prefect and, aided by some dramatic *James Bond* posters obtained from my local Odeon cinema, carefully altered by Bruno Santini, who later went on to become a theatre set designer, I was surprisingly elected. It put an end to my shy and retiring, introverted loner status. Now I was 'popular', and I was hooked. When I grew up I knew exactly what I wanted to be: an MP, specifically, the MP for Scarborough & Whitby. I was told then, at the age of fourteen, that if I really wanted it, more than anything else in the world, and if I was prepared to sacrifice everything else in life for that goal, then I would achieve it. I wish I could remember who gave me that advice. It turned out to be true, but the price was very high indeed.

I campaigned in the 1964 and 1966 general elections in Scarborough & Whitby. In January 1966, I went to help twice at the Hull North by-election. Toby Jessel, who later became Tory MP for Twicken-ham, was an energetic young candidate, but Labour held onto the seat. I recall being fed sandwiches and bananas by Joan Hall, who went on to be MP for Keighley, but then played the role of surro-gate mother to the helpers who flooded Hull, almost bringing the city to a standstill. Inevitably, political women have had a big impact.

The first was Freda, the secretary to the Scarborough Young Conservatives and to the redoubtable Jack Gamble, who was the Con servative agent. Freda taught me how to organise jumble sales and coffee mornings in my teens. She had fiery red hair and a strong and determined mind, which was softened by her love for amateur dra-matics and music. She tried to organise Young Conservatives into a musical troupe for the stage (without success on my part) and was a dab hand at organising car rallies where one followed a trail of questions to the correct destination. These were among my social activities from the age of fourteen to nineteen, when she was in her twenties. She had close professional relationships with sitting MPs, first Sir Alexander Spearman and then Michael Shaw and on return visits to Scarborough we would meet up to discuss political devel-opments, but also chat about other Young Conservatives and their marital statuses. My early political career was reliant upon people like Freda, who had a down-to-earth Yorkshire common sense that I hope I absorbed by being in her company, together with so many others in the Young Conservatives at that time.

Going to university was not an easy choice. To make ends meet, mother and I had established a very small bed-and-breakfast business in our house. Advertising was by way of a small vacancies sign in the window. The reverse side with 'No Vacancies' on it was rarely deployed. Paying guests helped to get us through the summers, while economical, meatless (yet delicious) stews provided fuel for the winters. Funds were very tight. I had to consider whether I could afford *not* to start working in 1966. I wondered whether I should try to get work in a bank and take banking exams. With my political contacts, it was definitely an option, but mother was adamant that I should go to university. It was one reason why York, being nearby, was a good option. I could get home in an hour by train, and it was also a way I could pursue and develop my interest in politics on a slightly bigger stage.

I had taken on part-time jobs in my school holidays. I worked as a postie – the term for a student postman – at Christmas, delivering bags of Christmas cards for the Royal Mail. I had worked in a supermarket in Scalby owned by a political friend of mine, Wilf Proudfoot. He was MP for Cleveland from 1959 to 1964 and then Brighouse & Spenborough from 1970 to 1974 and an ardent supporter of the Common Market. He was an incredibly down to earth guy, full of basic common sense, and I worked as a shelf-stacker in his family business. The first day I took to the tills as a checkout operator, I managed to fuse all the tills; so back to the shelves I went. I also worked as a barman at the Crown Hotel's Vaults Bar, the down-at-heel staff bar at the back, rather than the glossy, American cocktail one for customers. I remember every day at opening time (5.30 p.m. in those days of restricted licensing hours), a little old lady dressed in district nurse's uniform would cycle up to the pub, dismount and totter up to the bar and ask for her regular tipple of half a pint of Guinness served in a small tankard. Just before she took a sip, she would look at me from behind the glass and say, 'Purely for medicinal purposes, you understand', down it in one and waddle back to her bicycle. I witnessed, in that pub, two women fighting for the first time, and started to see the darker sides of human character.

One wintry Friday night, on my way home from a Young Conservative meeting, I was asked for a light by a man in his twenties on the approach to the Valley Bridge. I politely explained that I did not smoke, but he struck up a conversation with me anyway. When I was near to my house on the other side of the bridge and said good night, he suddenly drew a knife out of his coat and started to drag me away from my home. I was terrified; struck dumb and senseless. Eventually, my self-protective instinct kicked in; I decided I had to take action and I wrestled myself free, then ran up, even in deep snow, the side of a hilly garden to the door of a friend's house. I last remember the man running down the alleyway towards me to the front door brandishing the knife. It was like a clip from a horror film but it was real. I regained consciousness in my home half an hour later. Apparently my friend Diana and her mother heard banging on their front door – apparently my head being used as a battering ram – before calling the police. My attacker ran off. I was not stabbed, but a police doctor was called. It was either an attempted sexual attack or a robbery. The police identified the man from my description and it turned out he had been in the police station earlier that night for drunken behaviour. He had given a false address, however, and they were never able to find him.

It would be wrong to judge Scarborough by this account; it was just an isolated incident, and I enjoyed living there. It was where

I grew up to be a man, where I would gain my independence. As a Yorkshire man, I loved going to the Scarborough Cricket Festival every September. There I saw the cricketing heroes of the day – Trueman, Close, Illingworth, Bailey, May, Cowdrey and Dexter – as well as Yorkshire's First XI – usually the County Champions, T. N. Pearce's XI, the Tourists and Gentleman versus Players matches. Scarborough was also a tourist destination, and had great entertainments, such as Max Jaffa and his orchestra on the Spa, the open-air theatre with colourful, amateur musical productions with professional leads, cold nights fortified with hot soup and thick rugs and blankets. *The Battle of the River Plate* was recreated in Peasholm Park twice a week, its loud explosions often interrupting the cricket festival matches. In the Library Theatre, initially in a room above the public library, I saw Alan Ayckbourn act before he developed his writing skills and, later, I also saw his plays there. I went to see Frankie Vaughan at the Spa theatre and Ken Dodd, often at The Futurist Theatre, always over-running his time but no one worrying as they enjoyed his performance.

Jimmy Savile's mother lived on the Esplanade. It was the high coastal road above the South Bay and he was often to be seen at social and charity events at that time. My friends and I thought him decidedly odd even then and steered well clear of him, but without knowing exactly why. Another person to be avoided, although he was a local Conservative councillor and Alderman and later went on to be Mayor in 1970, was Peter Jaconelli. He was physically large and diminutive in height, with shiny, black hair and was very dapper, almost extravagantly so, wearing flashy rings, strong aftershave and an air of control. He seemed to me to be a rather greasy individual and had a fixed smile always on his face. He had a huge Italian ice-cream business in the town – it was very good ice-cream – and my friends and I also thought him odd but, again, we could never quite put our fingers on why we had formed that judgement. There were often nods and winks from those older teenage boys who worked for him in the summer – they all looked tough and dressed the same in tight denim blue jeans with their white jackets and were usually lads from the local council estates – but, with no actual allegation, such nods and winks were meaningless to me at the time. At school, pupils were divided: boys either came from private or from council houses, there were athletic or academic types, practical or artistic, but the beauty of the grammar school was that everyone mixed well.

I loved Scarborough's natural beauty – its beaches, cliffs, Italian gardens and other green spaces – and I revelled in the clearly defined seasons. I liked spring the most, with the large skipping event taking place every Shrove Tuesday, blocking the foreshore road. Even now I like to watch the giant waves break on the coast road between the two bays and the sea fog wrapping around the town with just the eerie, mournful noise blaring out from the lighthouse that keeps passing ships off the rocks. I raised funds for the Royal National Lifeboat Institution and for the Royal British Legion on Poppy Day as my introduction to charitable endeavour. As a child, it was a fantastic place to live and learn many attributes in life that would later facilitate social and political progress and ameliorate the nasty side of life just around the unexpected corner.

My dog was called Jewel, and she really was that. She was full size, not a miniature or a toy and would play in our rather large garden at York, then seemed to survive in a temporary top-floor flat in Scarborough before moving into our house in Grosvenor Road. The garden was on one side of the valley and I took her for walks but she gained all the exercise she needed running up and down the hill. It was the days when, if vets existed, and they did, I never met any; she was never ill. If pet shops existed, I cannot recall going to any. If pet food existed, I am sure it did, we did not buy it for Jewel; she ate what we ate. At night, she would sit by my side when I got in from school or after an evening out at the Young Conservatives, and we would watch television together. I talked to her and shared my hopes and fears with her.

In the early summer of 1966, I went to the University of York for my interview. I returned home to find my tearful mum at the door, saying, 'I think Jewel is dead. She had lifted the dog into a cardboard box, which was placed in the dining room. Jewel was indeed dead. She had done very well and must have been fourteen or fifteen years old. I kissed her, dug a very large hole in the garden and buried the dog, cover and box. I was upset, but consoled myself with the fact that Jewel had a long and loving life. I rationalised it that my childhood had well and truly gone; a chapter in my life had closed – university was the next stage, and it would be very different.

I also realised that my mother would be on her own, with no companion, so I determined that the first weekend I returned home from York in that autumn, I would not be going alone. I read in the York newspaper an advertisement for the sale of Yorkshire Terrier puppies. I bought one and returned home with her; this was Cute Collette. Mother was very pleased; the puppy took her mind off my absence and gave her an interest. It was good to have a Yorkie around again. I think that dog died in the late 1970s, again living to a good age.

My two history teachers at the time were very influential in my life. Mr Smith – 'Biff Smith' – an old, seasoned, classical liberal gave me a love of history. Mr Binns was younger and had more modern, analytical methods and ideas to help his students pass exams. They were the reason I was back at York.

I lived for my first year as a paying guest not a stone's throw away from my parents' old bakery shop on Bishopthorpe Road. It was no longer a bakery, but some of the others from my childhood remained, including the fish-and-chip shop. The geographical area all seemed so small in comparison with how I had remembered it.

My life revolved around the King's Manor, the HQ of the history department while the university was still being built at Heslington Hall. Originally the Abbot's House of St Mary's Abbey, it had been the seat of the Council of the North from 1539 until 1641. York council leased the building to the University of York, one of Sir Edward Boyle's plate-glass universities, and it was opened in 1963. It was an appropriately historic building in which to study history, therefore, and the common rooms were suitably palatial and, in the winter, warm. It was also centrally situated, within easy reach of a Chinese restaurant where our social graces were honed with a cheap three-course menu and mountains of monosodium glutamate. I also began to develop a taste for fish again, which had been ruined by my great-great-aunt's unfortunate experience with the bone.

Our history professors were Graham Aylmer – an expert on the sixteenth century – and Gwyn Williams – keen on the French Revolution. Dons included a wonderfully eccentric man called Dr Roger Mettam who used to dress for all the world like Rupert Bear. Indeed, one of his colleagues, on meeting him, once said, 'I do declare, it is Rupert Bear.' I remember his lectures were detailed and amusing. Keith Robbins, who ended up as a Vice Chancellor, was a historian of the appeasement period and he had interesting, if controversial, views on the subject. Dr Claire Cross taught religious history and looked prim and proper with her grey hair placed in a tight bun which made her look older than her real age. I was interested in history but never put the hours into studying I would have needed to gain a 2:1. At the time, however, my interests were elsewhere. Universities were not just about career development then; they moulded the whole soul.

I survived economically at York on a maximum grant. I could not and would not have gone to university without that support. I dislike the current student loan rather than grant system just as much as I oppose the huge increase in university students that necessitated the change in funding. I think too many people go to university. The arbitrary transformation of polytechnics to university status was also, in my opinion, a great mistake. Artificial supply to meet artificial demand created by politicians to rig short-term unemployment statistics has proved disastrous to our long-term educational system.

In my late teens, I dressed badly. I was not into clothes at all, unlike my brother, and I often existed on his hand-me-downs, which may have been suitable for him in swinging London, but were not for me. I should have cultivated a more traditional and appropriate dress sense earlier than I did. I was just not interested in how I looked. I was attending a liberal university with few rules as far as I can recall. No walking was allowed on the covered ways that joined the various parts of the university on campus – a sign, I thought, of shoddy and cheap building materials and design – and, although you could row on the man-made lake, which covered quite a wide stretch of the land, you were not allowed to punt, as this might place a hole in the lake liner and cause the water to drain away.

In my first week I went to the Freshers' Fair, where organisations vied with each other to get new students as members, so upping the level of grant they might acquire from the students' representative council. I looked out for the Conservative stand. There I met the charismatic John and Edna Smith, chairman and secretary respectively. He was a good-looking, dark-haired, ex-public-schoolboy. Edna, his wife, was tall, blonde and elegant in appearance, and both were extremely intelligent, articulate and persuasive – though I would have joined the Tories even if they had been dull. I wanted the university Conservative Association to be the natural extension of my Young Conservative days, but they also persuaded me to join the university's Monday Club. I joined the committees of both. Well, they ran in tandem.

Edna, more than John, gained my membership. She had a big personality and was a big character. She was a political mover and shaker and watched her husband's back. She watched mine too. She was a southerner, rather posh but extremely friendly, and provided me with an early encounter with the establishment elite. After university, they went to live in Brighton and raise a family, but in York, she was full of political intrigue and taught me the importance of keeping one's cards close to one's chest. We discussed how to deal with radical student unrest and how to fight off political attacks on the right. She was very influential in my university life and she was a good judge of character. It is a trick all would-be politicians should learn, but a gift too few these days seem to have mastered.

Also at university was Emma. She was a postgraduate student, beautiful in appearance with long, dark hair, a penchant for wearing brightly coloured, crisp trouser suits – all the rage in the 1970s – and a razor-sharp brain to match. As first treasurer and then secretary of the university Conservatives while I was chairman, she was my rock for dealing with all the early political difficulties. Emma was articulate and politically sound, and we talked a great deal about who to invite to York, how to organise meetings, how to deal with our left-leaning students' representative council and their unfair allocation of grants to political societies, and about the legal problems. Emma could intentionally distract an audience by blowing massive smoke rings across a room, which would linger and hover, impossible to recreate now with the ban on indoor smoking in most buildings, but then it was an art form in which she excelled. When I was president of the Debates Society she delighted at these diversionary skills. I was impressed with her ability, just with body language, to win an argument or a political point. She came to my graduation ceremony, as did my mother and brother.

Between Edna and Emma, I learnt two valuable lessons about performing on television. The first is always to appear upright on the screen. One's face must not be leaning backwards or forwards; you would appear to be slumped and lazy or stooped forward and too energetic as a result. To achieve perfection depended on posture. Whatever the type of chair, I learnt to stick my bottom into the back of it and then to sit as upright as possible. Your face would automatically get into the perfect position for the camera. The second tip was to do with one's hands and arms, specifically: try not to move them on camera. To a viewer it is very annoying to see a person on television gesticulating with their hands in front of their face. It distracts from the message. So the tip I have followed is the reverse of public speaking, where mannerisms are fine and essential – do not move one's arms and hands, and certainly do not let them get between face and camera. Most politicians seem oblivious of this tactic, and it is one of my pet dislikes to see an MP's point lost on television through the distraction of hands waving about in front of their mouth. I did not need to go on an expensive London media training course to learn these tips; I just listened to Edna and Emma, and they were right.

At the end of my first term, I was asked by John and Edna to stand for the chairmanship of both the Conservative Association and the Monday Club and, although opposed, I was successful in the ballot; my second public election battle had been won. Edna had fixed her friends to vote for me as chairman and so I remained for the remaining eight terms that I was at York – a record not likely to be surpassed. My academic career suffered, but I was committed to the time-consuming task of organising a speaker programme that was second to none.

Emma and I outwardly might have given the impression of being an 'item'. I certainly liked her very much and our friendship blossomed over the years. She had an older male friend who one might call a 'sugar daddy' type, all of twenty years older than Emma. I enjoyed her company a great deal, but my sexual reticence and lack of knowledge held back any consummation. Sex never crossed my mind. We spent a great deal of time together, and so I think we might have been regarded as a flamboyant couple around the campus. Others might have gained the wrong impression about our relationship, but it was not by design – we genuinely liked each other.

Getting Conservative MPs to travel up to York was not easy, even when the Tories were in opposition. It was a three-and-a-half-hour train journey. Emma and I travelled to the House of Commons once a term to use the green card system, requesting a meet in the Central Lobby so we could appeal to those MPs on our list of desired speakers directly to come to York. The technique worked and we held eight meetings a term, often on a Friday lunchtime, with the great and the good – and the not so good – in attendance. Among those who visited us were Julian Amery, Duncan Sandys (our last Secretary of State for War), John Biggs-Davison, Ronald Bell, Jonathan Aitken, Mervyn Pike and Patrick Wall, a local Tory MP. Iain Macleod was shadow Chancellor when he came to York. Diminutive in stature but enormous in oratorical ability, he was feared by Harold Wilson and gave a tour de force economic speech that had left-wingers at the university bemused. On another occasion, Harold Soref, a Monday Club member and MP for Ormskirk, made some injudicious remarks on immigration and on black people at a university Monday Club meeting. It rightly upset the Student Union and we apologised, for which he then sued me for libel. This was quite an achievement in my first year as chairman, I thought!

The mess was finally sorted out by the York Conservative Association-tion chairman, who was a solicitor. It was an early warning to me that a political career was never going to be easy. I was now a world away from the relatively carefree days of the Young Conservatives.

The Monday Club was a right-of-centre Conservative ginger group, which balanced out the left-of-centre Bow Group. With a left-leaning leader of the Conservative Party like Edward Heath, the Monday Club was popular in trying to drag the party back towards the centre. At this time, it was a mainstream political pressure group with many former ministers and a galaxy of MPs as members. The club was originally established to oppose Harold Macmillan's 'winds of change' ideas on Africa, but by the late 1960s it was a free-trade, free-enterprise, minimum-government organisation that chimed in with my personal views. That is what I sought to make of it. I had strong support for individual freedom and 'libertarian' views, par-ticularly on cannabis, though I did not smoke or take drugs myself. My strong belief in the nation state, with strong armed forces and good policing, did not seem to conflict. Controlling our borders was a part of this and so my ideas about immigration were devel-oped at university and influenced by Enoch Powell. I becoming more and more fascinated by politics and by politicians. I was eager to learn their trade.

I also had the opportunity to meet former Prime Minister and shadow Foreign Secretary Sir Alec Douglas-Home and his wife at York. The talk was held in one of the large science demonstration laboratories, so big was the expected attendance. He sat on a high stool as I introduced him and, not used to such an uncomfortable position, when he got to his feet he leant too heavily on the free standing lectern on top of the science bench. The lectern slipped in one direction, his notes in another and as he slid, his stool fell to the floor and his trademark half-moon reading glasses went at an angle across his face. It was quite a start and the left-wingers in the audience went wild with joy, laughing uproariously. He quickly collected himself and his thoughts and said, 'There are two things a politician should not lose: his notes and [he paused] his seat.' Often timing can be everything in a speech, and with that, suddenly the audience was laughing with him and not at him. He'd won them over and then presented his speech on foreign affairs without much further trouble. He was a very accomplished politician and a real statesman. Often today, MPs become statesmen too quickly, before going through the intervening stage of hard grind and experience.

It was not easy being a Conservative student at university in those days. University authorities, frightened of the left, often sided with left-wing demonstrations and sit-ins, whereas our meetings would be physically attacked. The National Union of Students was dominated by the left – indeed, Jack Straw became its president in 1969. He went on to become Home Secretary and Foreign Secretary under Blair, and was Lord Chancellor throughout Brown's premiership. He was not the most vehement of student activists, but several of those others who blatantly decried free speech at this time went into Labour politics. It was the height of student unrest throughout universities in the 1960s, during which period a Labour government was in power but not in control of their leftist-leaning students. Vietnam was always a flash point, as was student politics. Free speech was challenged everywhere by extremists, and certainly at York, where many of our meetings were the subject of threat and verbal and physical attack. On one occasion, when Patrick Wall, MP for Haltemprice, spoke, left-wing students threw beer, including the glasses, and invaded the platform. He and I were in mortal danger. Police were outside and we invited them in to get our guest away safely. The university porters were out-numbered. Still, the next day, the weak-willed university authorities criticised us for calling in the police and, in blatant appeasement of the left, even threatened to stop us from holding further meetings.

The Debates Union could be alarming too. Very early in my chairmanship of the Conservative Association, Jack Straw, then Leeds University president, visited York to debate. It was a time when, through lack of practice, I was a pretty bad public speaker. As Tory chairman, I was expected to speak and articulate our position on the issues of the day. Ill-prepared and lacking in confidence, I was persuaded to intervene in the debate. I trotted out some platitudes and said, 'We are at crossroads and we have two ways to go.' Someone then wisely pointed out that at a crossroads one in fact has four ways to go, including backwards, which prompted great laughter at my expense. I vowed then that I would always prepare well before I ever spoke in public again. Unfailingly, I have always done so, although it might not always appear to have been the case. Apparently off-the-cuff comments have been thought through beforehand if at all possible; speeches well-researched and practised and read out loud in front of a mirror. I also realised that it was simply a case of practice makes perfect, and so I tried never to turn down an opportunity to speak in public. Despite this, I was (and still am) very nervous of speaking to large numbers of people – an occupational hazard for a politician. I soon discovered, however, that if you were not nervous you were not caring sufficiently about your audience, you would not make a good, interesting speech. I listened to how others tackled the art of public speaking and quietly learnt the techniques.

Of course, apart from the university authorities, sometimes Conservative MPs didn't make it easy for us Association Tories who were just trying to do our best. We were not professional party agents, but our lunchtime Friday meetings were popular and the girls in the association would rustle up appetising ploughman's lunches. The bread, cheese and fruit came from the street markets of York in the morning and the soup from the university kitchens. These cheap lunches were an attraction as well as the speaker. When Sir Keith Joseph came to one such lunch, all was going well until he took a mouthful of soup: 'There's pork in this soup!' he declared in horrified tones, before going into a corner of the room in a deep sulk. We had inadvertently offended his deep Jewish sensibilities. Well, we had not been alerted to any culinary issues by his office and there was only pork in the soup because we had served the university's innocuous soup of the day. Initially, Sir Keith thought we had slighted him. Of course we had not. Once he came to believe this he shook off his shock and disdain and spoke well. He was very cerebral and I can only imagine he must have rationalised the situation, but we were always careful thereafter about what we served our guests. His office, I noticed, sent out a culinary list whenever he was invited to speak in the future.

I managed to place the university Conservative Association on the map early. Wilf Proudfoot had invested heavily in a 'pirate' radio station based on a boat floating off Scarborough in the North Sea called Radio 270. It was just outside territorial waters and Wilf offered me the opportunity to make broadcasts on the radio. We recorded Patrick Wall and made a programme. It was mentioned during Prime Minister's Questions (PMQs) in the House of Commons, gaining local and national publicity. Certain Labour Members were apoplectic in their rage. I once braved my fear of the sea by visiting the base boat and thanking the DJs in person, transferring from vessel to vessel in quite rough seas in the North Sea. It was a very small and a bit of a rust bucket, but it proved to be safe.

York had some great personalities as students, one of whom was Tony Banks, a member of the Conservative Association at the time who attended meetings. He became a Labour MP and Minister for Sport but at York he held wide views, which allowed him cheerfully to be friends with many in the Conservatives. It was a sadness that he died so young in 2006.

Christine Hamilton (or Holman as she was then) was the Conservative Association's social secretary in my final year. The title fitted her well. She was a social character in all regards and liked to party. As soon as I saw Christine, I thought she would be formidable and so persuaded her to enrol and join the committee. She was charming in personality, fluent in voice and a doer. (I'm of the opinion that you can divide people into 'doers' and 'sayers'; Christine was most definitely the former.) I thought in those days she was maybe a bit on the centre-left, but at York University a valuable asset to the association. We had wonderful events and the speakers and attendees both thrived on the arrangements Christine made, but she was a woman who also knew her own mind. I felt the best way forward was to let her get on with it. Christine was concerned about some of my views at the time, but we had mutual respect. She was always a charming and adorable woman. She continues to be a friend to this day.

She went on to work for another guest speaker, and great character, Sir Gerald Nabarro MP, whose facial hair was such a trade mark that when he spoke, the left turned up in force wearing fake handlebar moustaches. Why they also turned up with alarm clocks, though, I am not sure. The attempted disruption of the meeting failed, in any case, and he gave his usual robust, rousing comments. Christine later became his parliamentary secretary and married my very good friend Neil Hamilton. Later, in London, we got to know each other better. Our mutual friend Neil brought us together more. Then, as our lives took their separate courses, we saw less of each other, but we could and still can pick up the conversation as though it was yesterday we had spoken, when in fact it might be all of two years. Christine kindly included me in some of her public relations and television interviewing activity. I recall sitting on a sofa on a boat in front of the Palace of Westminster as she interviewed me, magnificently dressed with wonderful hair, not a strand out of place in the wind and the rain.

Neil and I had met through the Conservatives. We attended conferences together and meetings of the Federation of University Conservative and Unionist Associations (FUCUA), which in 1967 was followed by the Federation of Conservative Students (FCS). We went to weekend student meetings at Swinton College, Masham, near Ripon, and in London. Neil was a very intelligent, traditionally dressed, very amusing raconteur and a gifted speaker. I envied this natural ability and knew he would attain office. Our political paths were inter-woven. We supported each other in difficult times and, for both of us, in separate ways, our times were to get very dark indeed. Neil and Christine and I remain friends.

Although Edward Heath never visited the university as party leader when I was chairman – he was never invited – I did meet him at a York Conservative meeting. We shook hands. It was clammy, weak and unedifying and described his personality and his politics to a T. His small talk, too, was nearly non-existent. As a grammar-schoolboy myself, rather than ex-public school, we should have hit it off, but we did not. He was a very wet fish and I thought his speeches were dull and uninspiring.

Enoch Powell was so different. I had first heard him speak in the middle of the North York Moors as a Young Conservative, when he was shadow Defence Secretary. I didn't meet him that day but I observed how he spoke and how he formulated a speech, which had – shock horror in today's age of the sound bite – an introduction, a number of points in the middle and a conclusion. It was logical, whether you agreed with him or not. One night at the Royal Station Hotel in York, I met him. I introduced myself and he made a reference to Oxbridge 'proctors' – very cerebral. He recalled that we had written to him to come to speak. It was after his famous immigration speech at Birmingham, which the university Conservatives publicly supported. It was known as the 'Rivers of Blood' speech, but, as Michael Foot later commented, it was widely misunderstood as predicting actual bloodshed in Britain, when in fact he had used the *Aeneid* quotation concerning the River Tiber merely to communicate his own sense of foreboding. As with many of Enoch's remarks, I believe his warnings have been proved correct.

When he visited us, such was his notoriety in left-wing circles that it was deemed impossible to hold the meeting on university premises. We had to use subterfuge to safely drive him to a local hotel. A full police operation was required. It was quite exciting for novice students to be a part of it and a great achievement to arrange a 100-strong audience who, an hour before, had no idea of the actual venue. There was not a single demonstrator; they were all expending their energies at a duplicate venue the other side of the city. On entering the hotel, Enoch wanted to use the lavatory. Oddly, I thought at the time, he asked me to accompany him into the urinal area. He explained to me that he was concerned that, without a witness, someone could accuse him of doing something untoward with another male while there. I was genuinely puzzled and thought it was strange, but I do not think it odd now. I wish I had been as fastidious in my private life as Enoch was in his public one.

His speech was brilliant. He could really hold an audience spell-bound. It was not on the subject of immigration, which was a disappointment to many, but on dependence, independence and interdependence. It was a conceptual address.

Enoch Powell returned a year later to speak again, this time at a dinner. I sat him between Christine and myself and the conversation went as follows: During the greater part of the starter course I engaged Enoch in conversation. It was not that easy to keep him entertained but I achieved the objective. Christine took over and asked him what he thought the stance of 'moderate' students should be in universities. Enoch turned to her, eyes swivelling, smiled and said, 'My dear, what do you mean by "moderate"?' She had not expected that retort, not sure herself of a definition of 'moderate', and that ended the conversation for the first course. Then the beef was served. Eventually, she plucked up courage and tried again. 'Mr Powell, we do not seem to be able to talk about student politics, what do you think about the present position in Cambodia?' Enoch's eyes swivelled even more, and his smile grew wider, 'My dear, Cambodia is not in my constituency.' Conversation ended until the pudding course. 'Mr Powell, we do not seem to be able to talk about student politics or international affairs, surely you have a hobby we can talk about?' Enoch turned to her, eyes swivelling out of control, the smile stretching almost ear to ear, and replied, 'Yes, my dear, carpentry.' That finished the conversation for the rest of the dinner. Christine might dispute the detail, but Enoch was not being unfriendly, he just revelled in intellectual argument.

I'm firmly of the belief that Enoch Powell was the best leader the Conservative Party never had. He had a brilliant mind and an articulate manner in which he deployed his arguments. He was not a racist. He had spent much time in India and spoke many Indian languages, including Urdu. Indeed, he spoke many other languages too. He wrote poetry, had a fascination for history, and politics was certainly not the only string to his bow. He was incredibly well-read and had a classical background. He was the youngest professor of Greek in the Commonwealth and his military career, during which he rose to be a brigadier, was outstanding. His intellect could be frightening, even intimidating, sure, but he also had a gentle, romantic side to him. He became a Conservative MP for Wolverhampton South West and served in Harold Macmillan's governments as Financial Secretary to the Treasury and as Health Minister. He was shadow Defence Secretary when he was sacked by Edward Heath in 1968. He later left the Conservative Party and became the Ulster Unionist MP for South Down in 1974. He is often vilified now, but in the time I knew him he was immensely popular with the ordinary man in the street. He was one of the best parliamentary orators of the twentieth century and, in my opinion, stands on a par with Churchill. It was an honour to have met such a distinguished man and to have become one of his and Pam's, his wife, friends.

Apart from Conservative events, I did not socialise much with other students; student parties were not my thing. Almost as a reaction to the public position I held, I tried to keep my private life private. I was actually rather shy. I left my paying-guest residence on Bishopthorpe Road in 1967 to move to a comfortable but small flat in the centre of York at 33 North Street, next to All Saints' Church, looking onto the River Ouse and opposite the rear of the Mansion House. The previous tenants were John and Edna Smith and they said the tenancy went with my chairmanship. They found me a flat mate – the then very popular president of the Athletics Union. He was not politically interested, but we got on well together as a result of our different interests, which we discussed over coffee at night in the cosy sitting room. It had green walls and an open coal fire and we used to be able to hear the mice scuttling about under the wooden floorboards above us. We

39

were two of only a handful of students that were counted in Lord Esher's report on York as living within the bar (city) walls. Upstairs lived Mrs Joan Kennedy, a kind of grand caretaker for the owner, who I never met as he lived abroad. It was a very old house and, on the ground floor which we occupied, at the back it had a small, walled rose garden and at the front a long hallway sloping down to the blue front door. In my final Easter holidays there, the doorbell rang early one morning while I was asleep. It rang again. I went to the door but soon had to throw on all the brakes – it was two feet underwater! I looked out of the front ground floor bedroom window and saw that the ringing had come from the police, in a boat, who wanted to know if we, particularly Mrs Kennedy, were in need of anything. The water soon receded, though, leaving the mud to be swilled away.

Joan Kennedy was in her eighties and a great character. She was widely travelled, had lots of grey hair, was well-dressed and bespectacled. She had lived on a wheat farm in Canada and was always seeking company and conversation, which she had developed into an art form. Among others, she told poignant stories of her life in the First World War when, as a flapper girl, she had lived above the Star and Garter Public House on the south side of Putney Bridge in London. She would wake up in the morning, she would tell us, read the lengthy death columns, which nearly always contained the name of a close friend, a girl friend would join her, they would commiserate one with another over lunch and drinks then go out to the cinema to watch a film and try to cheer themselves up, only to repeat the process the next day. She described Putney Bridge and the churches either side of it, little knowing that I would spend thirty years of my life living on the north side of that same bridge.

She was very generous with her money, but wished to keep the 'right ideas' of social standing that had since long disappeared.

She would take us to lunch on Sundays, sometimes dinner, at the newly built Viking Hotel just opposite the church. She would pay, as she knew we were impoverished students, but she would slip her leather purse into my pocket just before we opened the door to cross the street. I would return it to her the moment the door closed on our return. On one occasion, to make up for the disturbance of the building noises as his hotel was being built, the hotel manager invited us to have lunch, which was a very agreeable gesture. On my subsequent visits to York, I would take Mrs Kennedy out for a meal. She loved to talk and reminisce, and I learnt the valuable art of listening from her.

My successor as chairman of the Conservative Association and Monday Club was a fellow Yorkshire man, Jonathan Denby. He was polite, dark-haired, well-dressed, articulate, efficient and into fast cars. He got on well with everyone and was the perfect candidate to continue what we had tried to build. He was interested in politics but I thought not likely to want to be an MP. We were to cement our friendship when we both lived in London, but for now it was handover time while I took my finals. I graduated with a 2:2.

My interest in politics paid off professionally. John and Edna Smith had ingratiated themselves in the national Monday Club and I had met most of the members of the National Executive Council either in London or in York. I had also helped to promote branches in other universities. And so, upon completing my university degree, I was invited to become the assistant to the director (or was it 'Assistant Director'? – my title caused debate) – on the princely sum in 1969 of £1,000 per annum. It would be a useful stepping stone to becoming a Member of Parliament. I gave myself a target of ten years to get into the House of Commons, and if I hadn't achieved it by then, I would move into the world of commerce. I was twenty-two years of age.

CHAPTER 3

LONDON

London was a great adventure and I first set foot in the metropolis with a mixture of fear and excitement. It was very different from Yorkshire. I had been to the capital before to attend meetings and conferences and on my 'speaker hunting' trips. I had visited my brother a few times and stayed with him at his flat near Great Ormond Street Hospital and had once stayed at 92 Cheyne Walk, the London home of Sir Patrick Wall and the address from which the 92 Committee of right-wing back-bench Conservative MPs acquired its name. Now I had to find accommodation for myself, and it would have to be a lot less grand than the palatial abode of No. 92 facing the River Thames. With a few university friends in the same predicament, I rented a grotty upstairs flat in Streatham. Its floor was sloping and mice were the major inhabitants. Thankfully, my stay there didn't last long. Through a contact in the Monday Club, I was found a paying-guest habitat in Carlisle Mansions, just round the corner from Westminster Cathedral. The bedroom was small and I had a shared kitchen to use. In due course Cyril Townsend, a fellow

Conservative, took up residence, but I was not happy. I was very lonely. One Sunday, I went into the streets of Victoria to try to cheer myself up. I thought I would go to the cinema – it was the sort of thing Mrs Kennedy would have done, so I thought it might work for me. In my naivety, I thought I would see a cowboy film – *Midnight Cowboy*! I left the cinema even more depressed than when I entered.

I am sorry that I may disappoint some of my readers by not commenting on my private sexual life, other than when it was dragged kicking and screaming into the public arena. I have always regarded my private sexual life to be just that – private – but I had better say now that, until I was twenty-three years of age, I had not had sex with anyone. I had managed to get through my entire school and university life without ever having experienced a sexual encounter. Life was so different in the 1960s. Homosexuality was only made legal between consenting males over the age of twenty-one in 1967. The heterosexual age of consent was sixteen. The law was inequitable, but at the time I did not stand up against this inequality because I did not wish anyone to know I was a homosexual. Although I had realised I was probably not straight by the age of sixteen, I did not know until seven years later exactly what being homosexual meant or what homosexuals did. I was an innocent in these matters when I first arrived in London. I had concentrated my mind and time on political advancement to the exclusion of all else, following the advice I had been given, and that had included sex. London proved a fast learning curve in this respect. Nonetheless, I was extremely nervous, timid, even apprehensive and frightened, by the whole idea.

Unlike many public schoolboys, I had no interest in young boys. I did not develop crushes on people younger than myself at school or afterwards. Indeed, I did not develop crushes on anyone and in fact, my first encounter of a sexual nature was in 1970, with an American who was nearly ten years older than myself. It was a civilised affair including dinner and drinks. Emotions were very mixed. Physically, it was not an enjoyable experience. The awkwardness of the activity was such that I wondered whether such a sexual experience had been worthwhile. It was mechanical and unsatisfying. I began to learn the difference between love and sex. However, it had occurred and I was grateful to my friend for introducing me to the mysteries of sex. My curiosity was at an end. I remained in touch with him for many years, purely as friends.

I did meet girls for dates and some accompanied me to dances, dinners and events and, although they might have wanted such relationships to blossom, I did not. I did not discuss sex with any of them and always tried to find excuses why overnight activity was not possible; the art of the 'white' lie to avoid causing offence or revealing to anyone else details of my private life.

After my encounter with the American, which endured a couple of weeks, I met young men my own age and continued to find gentlemen in their twenties to be of interest. I tried very hard not to mix sexual with political or professional interests. With very few exceptions, I think I have succeeded. I believe the number of my liaisons may have been greater than that for an average heterosexual but as I see it could be a part of being a homosexual. I am pleased that my relationship with Terry has lasted more than forty years – a lot longer than most marriages of the heterosexual variety. We are very good friends.

The Monday Club offices were in a down-at-heel office block opposite New Scotland Yard at 51–53 Victoria Street. It was walking distance from where I was living. Its three rooms were situated three floors up and, although there was a lift, I tended to bound up the stairs. The director, Freddie Stockwell, was an enigmatic former diplomat based for part of his career in Egypt. He was in his sixties, had white/grey hair and thick eyebrows and all the mannerisms of the White Rabbit in *Alice in Wonderland*. He was an archetypal civil servant, with a dry sense of humour, a slightly pompous streak to some and obsequious to others. I had met him before and looked forward to working with and for him. In difficult circumstances he taught me the merits of tact and diplomacy, traits I would require throughout the rest of my life, and, above all, politeness and grace. His wife Veronica was, and I had not come across one before, an alcoholic. She was also charming and elegant and very hospitable. Sometimes, when he disappeared from the office unexpectedly, I now realise it might have been to minister to her. He was a kind man, always seemingly in a rush, not exactly shaking his watch, but referring to it as though he could not believe what it was telling him.

In another office was the typist secretary, who for a while was a bubbly girl called Susie. She typed and organised mail distributions to the 2,000-plus national club members, as well as the university and regional branches. The large office in which I had a desk contained a long, highly polished old table around which meetings could be held, and a further desk where an elderly former banker would drop in almost daily to discuss the newspaper headlines. Maurice ran the fundraising together with Geoffrey Baber. It all seemed very ex-public school. Every other day we were joined by Brigadier Chapman, who had written a book about tanks in the First World War. He was rotund, with ruddy jowls and a great sense of humour. He wore a formal suit, shirt and tie – a military regimental one – and walking some of the way to the office from his Dolphin Square apartment was his exercise. He very occasionally invited Susie and me to lunch or dinner in his home and we enjoyed his hospitality and his many wartime stories very much. I certainly did not think our visits there would be relevant forty-five years later. They were convivial but not newsworthy and I doubt if he could have comprehended what was to be alleged in the years ahead.

I also attended a cocktail party at Dolphin Square given by Professor Hugh Ford, his wife and daughters, at their home there. Hugh was a science professor at Imperial College and he was a Monday Club member. He was a sophisticated, dapper and incredibly intelligent man. Dolphin Square seemed a good but expensive place to live in those days, with none of the connotations it was to develop and which wrongly hang round my neck now.

At the time, in the early 1970s, the Monday Club was a body which collected together right-minded, mainly professional people interested in patriotism and loyalty to their country. It was started in 1961 and I knew two of the four founding members, Ian Greig and Cedric Gunnery. It was not a fascist, racialist or extreme organisation. Far from it, as it contained more than fifty shadow ministers, MPs and peers. It was, while I was working for it, a respected Conservative organisation. Its members had a universal detestation of the views of Edward Heath. To the extent that it considered economic affairs, it was largely free market and free enterprise. It did have a markedly different approach to decolonisation of Empire to that proposed by Macmillan and others on the left of the Conservative Party, but debate in the '70s was in the main good-humoured. The club supported Ian Smith and it feared the winds of change in Africa would be detrimental to black and white alike. Who is to say that the inhabitants of Southern Rhodesia would not have had a more prosperous and peaceful existence if Mugabe had not become its president? The Monday Club supported the defence of the realm, our armed forces, the independent nuclear deterrent and the police force. It was patriotic. It had begun to realise that mass migration from the New Commonwealth and Pakistan in the twenty-five years after the Second World War was not in the country's best interests. It chimed with my own views, nurtured from Enoch Powell, who was never a club member, but who spoke at its meetings. I thought the Monday Club brought to the Conservative Party support which, without its existence, would otherwise be lost to the respectable right. I always felt that you should be a member of the Conservative and Unionist Party before you could be a member of the Monday Club. My basic loyalty during the 1960s, 1970s and 1980s was to the Conservative Party and no other.

For some it might have been regarded as a social club, and a very heterosexual one at that. There was wining and dining (which goes hand-in-glove with political action and organisation), but it was, at heart, a political entity. I make this point now as its role and ethos in those days was and is much maligned to its and, particularly, my detriment.

There were enough thinkers and writers in the Club at that time; my role was to help to organise both the regional and university clubs and some of the national events. I therefore travelled a great deal and attended meetings throughout the United Kingdom. These formative years were very important. I continued to speak and debate against the odds, even courting controversy from time to time. I travelled by train, often arriving home in the early hours of the morning, but on one occasion, having been to the south coast for a meeting, I missed the last train home and decided to hitch. I thought it was simply a question of standing by the side of the road, waving a thumb roughly in the direction one wanted to go and you got a lift. Wrong. It started to snow and there were no vehicles in sight. I walked into a village and a police officer had to wake up the owners of a local hotel, bolted and barred for the night, to get me a bed.

I was present in Cambridge on the night of 13 February 1970, when the Garden House riot took place. By coincidence, I was speaking at a political dinner in a nearby university college. Six students were subsequently found guilty of offences. It was one of the few episodes of student unrest there, but throughout the country if you were politically regarded to be on the right, you were fair game for the left to shout you down and deny you free speech. It was put to me on my return to London that I had started the riot – I had not. It was a protest against the Greek government and I was not involved in any way.

I think the terminology 'left' and 'right' was over-used at the time. I certainly did not set out to be 'right wing'. I considered myself to be at the dead centre of my political spectrum and political people or their opinions fell to the left and the right of me. It was for others to judge, but often that judgement in my case has been made irrationally, without all the necessary information being in the public domain. I hardly recognise myself, nor do my friends, from the caricature that is often painted of me. Above all else, I am true to myself, but human beings are complicated. To dismiss a person's views in a single word is wrong and preposterous. Still worse is the attempt to trash their whole life because of their beliefs.

I enjoyed my job and began the process of settling down in London. I moved to Putney and lived for a while with a university friend in a flat in a house in which Lewis Carroll was reputed to have lived on Putney Bridge Road. I got to know London geographically through the use of the underground train network. I knew the difference between a tube train running in a tunnel bored through London clay, and an underground train, travelling in a trench that was then covered. Many Londoners do not know the difference. Like a rabbit, I would pop up from a train to get to know the surface area around a station, only to pop down again to get home. It was many years before I learnt how all these individual areas I knew on the surface through my use of trains under London linked together.

In 1969, I visited an Italian hairdresser with premises in the same block as the Monday Club. Initially I was unhappy with wearing hair nets and having the obligatory blow dry, so popular at the time. But the two guys who ran it were very good at cutting hair. They used cut-throat razors and flashed them speedily to get the desired sharp-cut result. Much later, when I no longer lived in London, I would visit them. They had moved premises, just a block away by Artillery Mansions, and had a ladies' hairdresser's in the basement. I let them cut my hair for forty-six years and early in 2015 I visited again. One of the guys had died a few years earlier, but, then well into his seventies, the owner cut my hair and we discussed my problems. He was reassuring and genuinely pleased to see me on what proved to be the last time. Three months later, on the day I met with my publishers to discuss this book, I had a little time to spare and dropped into Victoria Street to get my hair trimmed. Sadly, the hairdressers had closed.

Through the Monday Club I met and got to know many people, whom I would continue to stay in touch with throughout the rest of their lives. G. K. Young was a merchant banker working for Kleinwort Benson in the City of London. He had been a member of secret intelligence and became deputy head of MI6, the Secret Intelligence Service (SIS) that works overseas. Despite his pro-Common Market stance, influenced by his banking position, we got on well. His views on immigration and defence and security made him an important figure in the club, as did his financial position in raising much-needed money. He was influential in the Society for Individual Freedom, becoming its chairman, and instrumental in encouraging Gerald Howarth to become involved in the administration of the society during exactly the same period as I worked at the club.

I had met Gerald during university days – he was at Southampton – and I knew him also through his membership of the Monday Club. He was particularly interested in defence issues and was a keen pilot. He was always good company with no edges – a clean cut, no-nonsense loyal Conservative who fully deserved his position later in life as a Defence Minister and, after his untimely removal from office, his knighthood. In our band of three – Gerald, Neil and I – all very close in those days, Gerald has been politically the most successful. He has an undeserved reputation for being anti-homosexual, but has always been solicitous to me personally in my trials and tribulations and his friendship, which continues now, is valued.

Later, I met Adrian Day. He worked at the Society for Individual Freedom after Gerald, was very interested in economics and, together with Pauline Russell, a Canadian friend of mine, he was a devotee of Ayn Rand. I lost track of him for a time, but he went to live and work in the West Indies and eventually I met up with him in Washington, DC on one of my visits to the States. He had married a girl from the USA and became an American citizen.

Another person I met through politics at this time was Bee Carthew, who sometimes used her maiden name, Muir. She had Scottish and French blood in her veins. I had met her through Monday Club conferences in London in the 1960s when I was still at university and it was through the Monday Club that we became friendly when I moved to the capital. I think her father was a journalist and she looked back on a time when journalists were well regarded. She despaired at the bad press our mutual hero Enoch Powell received. To the extreme left, she was an ogre figure, being personally friendly with Enoch and Pam Powell, secretary of the nearest thing to a fan club that Enoch would allow, Powellight, and in view of her unwise but transient flirtation with the National Front for just over a year.

When she lived in Twickenham, we would meet up for lunch or afternoon tea and go for long walks by the banks of the River Thames. It was with her on one such walk that I first noticed a 'fire mark' on an historic building. We had long chats about politics, friends and enemies – seemingly more of the latter than the former, though we never discussed them in personal terms, always political. She was definitely not 'politically correct' (few of my friends in my life have been), but she was not a racialist. She was the very antithesis of a fascist, more an old-fashioned patriot. Bee and I argued usually about tactics, how to achieve an end result, rather than the result itself. She left the Conservative Party several times during our friendship, which never affected our relationship but did cause heated disputes. It distressed me when she felt she needed to leave, but I felt it was more an adverse reflection on the state of my party than on her. I was always pleased when she re-joined.

She was above all a very civilised, articulate and cultured lady who was distressed at what she saw as the ruination of her country. She had a distinguished war service record fighting fascism and, in her work with military intelligence, she is reputed to have known more about Hitler's generals than Hitler did. She kept a card index on their activities, which included whereabouts, likes and dislikes. At the end of the war, she remained in Berlin working on the denazification of Germany. She was a Catholic and her flat was filled with books and icons. She had a long, romantic partnership with a Polish military officer she met in the war and, with French and Scottish blood in her veins, her ability to speak five languages fluently, and her firm grasp of European culture and history, it might be surprising to learn that she was passionately against our membership of the European Union, as it's now known.

After the war work ended, she worked for the *Daily Mail*, not, as might be imagined, in journalism, but in the exhibitions department. She helped to organise the Ideal Home Show. Because she spoke so many languages, she was the right person to oversee the foreign stands, which formed an important part of the exhibition. She was supremely professional, dressed impeccably and was a great standard-bearer for the exhibition. She very kindly invited me to the opening days of many Ideal Home Shows to have lunch, and always made a point of introducing me to those on the stands of the Asian, Caribbean and African countries, and the people who organised them. I noticed how well-regarded she was and how everyone involved treated each other with good humour. It is a far cry from how Searchlight and other left-wing organs perceived her and, I suppose, me. My friend was well-regarded by Enoch and Pam Powell, both of whom did not suffer fools gladly. Bee was also no fool. Bee helped many people with their difficulties and was slow to take up offers of help for herself in return.

The Monday Club was like a big debating chamber for political views. Its members frequently disagreed on the subjects of the day, most noticeably the Common Market. Fierce rivalries among essentially like-minded friends could be portrayed wrongly. The Hon. Jonathan Guinness, who became its chairman, was an ardent anti-immigration voice, but very pro-Common Market; Sam Swerling the same, but with strong corporate economic views. He was a lawyer and a straightforward, down-to-earth bloke. You could disagree with him, debate with him, but remain friends. As a former solicitor and law lecturer, he has kindly been in touch with me and offered his support and help. He was ever the gentleman and I am grateful to him.

There were divisions of opinion, which weakened the club's influence on the Conservative Party and inevitably tore the club apart.

I left its employment in 1971 as a result of a far more mundane matter, but a question of principle about which I felt strongly – the opening of mail. Freddie Stockwell had stepped down as director; Cedric Gunnery took on the role. He was ex-public school and the club's treasurer. I do not know why but we never quite hit it off personally. I think he tried to treat me as though I was his 'fag'; not of the homosexual variety, but as a public-school servant. He was a well-built, smartly dressed, cuddly type of person with slicked-back, thinning hair, concealing a sharp temperament and an inflated sense of his own importance. One of his early commands as director was that he alone was henceforth to open all mail, however addressed. I took a different view. If mail was addressed to me by name, not position, then I thought the named person should open that envelope, unless that person had given strict instructions to the contrary. I had always opened my own mail and the mail addressed to me was organisational and not politically significant. We disagreed and I resigned on a point of principle. It was strange how, when there was a plethora of political differences, the parting of the waves was over the mechanics of correspondence.

I went home and was shocked at what I had done. I do have a stubborn and unbending streak. However, it was not long before I was working again. Through contacts, I was appointed research assistant to the 1970s Conservative Parliamentary Group. It was that group of Tory MPs – including Tory grandees like Sir Derek Walker-Smith, Sir Robin Turton, Neil Marten, Enoch Powell, Richard Body, Roger Moate and others – who opposed Edward Heath's attempt to pass legislation to facilitate United Kingdom membership of the Common Market.

On the day that Heath signed the Treaty of Accession, I was in Brussels protesting peacefully and democratically. As Heath had ink poured over him by an angry woman on an unrelated matter, I was in a large crowd of British protestors baton-charged by the riot police. How much better our own police were, I thought.

Heath had pledged he would only take the country into this European organisation if he had the full-hearted consent of Parliament and the people. He had neither. He signed the treaty even before parliamentary debate.

I worked in a solicitor's office behind Marble Arch to try to ensure the legislation to take us in was defeated, and, if not defeated, then amended. The European Communities Bill was so drafted as to be unamendable. By that I mean one amendment carried in the Commons would have scuppered the Bill. It had to be passed in its entirety, without amendment if it was to give legal effect to Heath's signature on the treaty. The government majority was reduced to only four votes on one such amendment and on the Bill's Second Reading to a government majority of only eight votes. In Heath's eyes, this constituted 'full-hearted consent'. It was not. It is for this reason that the European question was to prove to be such a divisive issue within the Conservative Party for decades. It was not those parliamentary rebels who made it so. It was that the proponents of the ill-advised venture who had reneged on the 1970 election pledge in their mad-cap scramble to give up our parliamentary sovereignty in favour of European Economic Community. It has been masked in economic terms, but it has always been a political movement, an attempt to procure a federation and a very anti-British federation at that. We were an island nation with Commonwealth and trading partners throughout the world. We threw all that away for the tunnel-vision approach of limiting our horizons to just a part of Western Europe. The horrors of the Second World War, and the Cold War tussle between the USA and the Soviet Union, made certain Western

European politicians anxious to form their own superpower, just when the age of superpowers was about to crumble. My main contribution, working for this impressive group of MPs, was a critique of the Common Fisheries Policy, far less dramatic but just as important for our fishing communities and fishing ports. History shows that Scarborough and Whitby were decimated, as predicted.

I witnessed at close hand how parliamentarians could manoeuvre and campaign for causes in which they believed passionately. It was a great schooling for anyone with parliamentary desires and a love of parliamentary democracy and tactics. European regulations and directives would henceforth be incorporated into British law and there would be nothing our sovereign Parliament could do about it. We lost the votes in those debates but I thought we had won the arguments. The test of whether Prime Minister Cameron regains parliamentary sovereignty in 2016 will be whether he amends the legislation that allowed us to join in the first place. I was honoured to have played a small part in such historic debates. It would not, could not, however, be the end of the matter. Parliamentary sovereignty will be regained someday, and I hope I am alive to witness it.

Through the help of Sir Ian Mactaggart, I had moved home into a block of flats just on the north side of Putney Bridge. I was to live there for nearly thirty years. It was a red-brick mansion block of flats which had seen better days; the Art-Deco entry hall was shoddy and progressively deteriorated. The shops underneath varied – newsagent, chemist, florist, dentist, antiques and the offices of the Fulham Conservative Association. Sir Ian, who owned the block, had been their parliamentary candidate and also let them have, free of charge, two flats for their agents. Times were hard and they had need of only one flat for the sole agent. They rented the other one to me. It was a corner, front flat over an antique shop. Fulham was not the salubrious area it is now; the street had four pubs and drink-fuelled disorder occurred often. One night, a drunk decided to throw a brick through the antique shop window below me. I heard the noise as the brick rebounded off the window and rang the police. His second attempt failed but while I was talking to the police he succeeded – the police heard the crash of breaking glass over the phone. They arrived too late to arrest him but at least I recovered the few items he stole and left lying on the pavement. The street was also the home of the Fire Brigades Union and I was always amused by the sight of huge numbers of fire engines who would block the road at even the slightest sign of a fire, even smoke, to save their union headquarters.

My flat had two bedrooms, a small kitchen and bathroom and a large sitting room. I shared the flat and the rent with others over those early years. One was a man called Andrew, from Australia, who once affixed a political poster to the window in support of Gough Whitlam. I told Andrew if he did not take it down we would have a brick through the window – thrown by me from the inside!

This flat was the base from which I conducted my first campaign to get elected to Parliament. I had applied to join the Conservative Party's candidates' list but I had been selected for that rock-solid Labour seat in the East End of London named Hackney South & Shoreditch before my application was considered. There were two parliamentary elections in 1974; I fought them both.

I stood as a Conservative and Unionist Party candidate. I thought the link with the Unionists in Northern Ireland was sufficiently important to reflect it in my description. An East End Conservative and Unionist Association is an organisation to behold. Its officers and members were fervent Conservative supporters. They held meetings above a pub at Dalston Junction on the Balls Pond Road. The association secretary was a former teacher called Mary Watts.

She was efficient, dedicated, quiet, small, but firm and quietly spoken. She was in her seventies and had been a teacher in the East End, where she claimed to have taught the Kray twins ('bad boys' even then, she told me); they went on to become famous gangsters and the foremost perpetrators of organised crime in the East End of London during the 1950s and 1960s. If so, she would have been quite a match for them.

When I first became their prospective parliamentary candidate, the association thought they would impress their new 'find' by organising a swish, black-tie dinner. They certainly impressed with waitresses dressed, as I recall them, in Terry's restaurant-style attire, all black suits with white aprons. The chairman was a delightful Northern Irish Protestant man; his wife a southern Catholic. Just before they brought on the Brown Windsor soup first course, she whispered to her husband, heatedly, 'Go on, just do it.' Flustered, instead of standing up and saying grace, he got confused and proposed the Loyal Toast! At least those who smoked – in those days quite a few – could smoke throughout dinner. They were a very supportive group of Conservatives and looked after me, not just on that night but throughout the run-up to the election and the campaign itself. My agent was Frank Pike, a senior agent responsible for candidates in over twenty constituencies. He and his wife, Marion, were very helpful. They fully supported my views on immigration, as did the association. I was exactly the candidate they wanted, if not one Central Office would have preferred.

During the run-up to the 1972 party conference, I drafted a number of motions that the association submitted on immigration, race relations and voluntary repatriation, and on other subjects. Voluntary repatriation had been a plank in the election manifestos of Sir Alec Douglas-Home and Edward Heath but it had just not been implemented. One of these motions concerning these important but controversial matters was selected for debate by the conference delegates. This alarmed the party leadership. It further concerned them that, as their candidate, the association wanted me to propose the motion. I obtained not just the right to speak, but also a rather longer period of time to speak and deploy the case, and therefore more exposure as well. The association were delighted; I had an even better plan.

I talked to Jonathan Denby, who, having graduated from York, was now Enoch Powell's private secretary. Over lunch I suggested that I was prepared to give up my speaking opportunity in favour of the association's president, none other than Enoch himself. Would Enoch agree to propose the motion? Later that afternoon, I received the reply: he would be delighted to receive any such invitation. An exchange of letters cemented the coup, to which the association's officers enthusiastically agreed. Enoch took centre stage at the conference, to the fury of the organisers, and set up a direct challenge to Robert Carr, the Home Secretary. Jonathan and I were delighted with our manoeuvre.

Enoch and his supporters won the debate but inevitably lost the vote. The show of strength by those who foresaw immigration to be a never-ending concern to the electorate was noted. It is not often Central Office was put on the defensive and wrong-footed, but that was certainly one of them. Edward Heath never forgave me.

I cut my teeth politically in Hackney South & Shoreditch. I canvassed the tower blocks and the occasional run-down squares of houses which either were to be demolished or were to be gentrified thirty years later. I was out in Hackney every night of the week. I held surgeries, delivered leaflets and shook hands in markets. I was bitten by a black poodle dog; it actually belonged to a supporter and resulted in me waiting hours in a local hospital for the necessary tetanus jab. I met wonderful Londoners including a woman called Hilda Chapman, who gave me tea and biscuits whenever I was in the area. She was a Tory through and through, of the type at which Heath and Carr would have turned up their noses. They would have regarded her as a racialist, just as Gordon Brown came unstuck with an alarmed Labour voter on the subject of immigration in the 2010 general election campaign, calling Gillian Duffy a 'bigoted woman'. Hilda was no such thing, just a hard-working woman concerned for the dramatic changes in her country and its make-up, which the British people had not been asked about or consulted on by our so-called democratic politicians. She kept in touch until she died, after which her family continued to give me their support.

I was up against Ron Brown, brother of Lord George Brown, a former Labour Foreign Secretary. In the election campaign it was like fighting two MPs as Lord George supported his brother. I do not recall speaking to either of them. Notwithstanding the fact that it was a safe Labour seat, I managed to retain my deposit, a sign of manliness for a Conservative candidate in the East End. I had made a good shot at fighting the constituency and made many friends. Heath had gone to the electorate asking the country, in the wake of the debilitating, three-day week, who should rule the country? The public said if you do not know we had better have the other lot in and the electorate had given Harold Wilson a narrow majority of seats though not of votes by way of an answer. The association asked me to continue as their candidate as a further general election looked imminent; I agreed. Although a National Front candidate entered the fray in the October election, and the Tory vote dropped a bit, I still managed to maintain my deposit. Hackney South & Shoreditch was to continue to be my political base in the mid-1970s. It was an

area with which I have fond memories and I will always remember
the many kindnesses shown to me in those years by those loyal
Conservatives.

It was also during this period that I met my long-term friend Terry
Woods. I received a call in my constituency office from a man who
wanted to help in the election. I was sitting at an old, dusty, scratched
wooden table. I still have that table – I bought it from the association
just before they were to throw it out. It is an 1820s Regency drop-
leaf flame mahogany table and has been the venue for many a lunch
or dinner party, seating six comfortably and eight or ten at a push.
If only that table could speak! I arranged to meet Terry where he
had been staying in the Eton Mission with the Reverend Edwin Stark.
They had met at the Athenaeum gentlemen's club off Pall Mall.
He had wanted to help in the election and had telephoned an MP to
offer his assistance. The MP, in no need of help in his Tory strong-
hold, suggested Terry throw himself into the deep end and get in
touch with the Hackney Association.

I visited Terry, carrying, as was my usual style, voluminous papers
in plastic carrier bags, dressed in a hand-me-down long coat, dishevelled, drenched from the rain and sleet and tired from a day of
campaigning. He was well-dressed in a casual sort of way. I was
offered sherry, not my favourite tipple, and trotted out my main
political thoughts. I left thinking I had not made a good impression,
but a few days later Terry arrived at the office offering to be put to
work. He was not really interested in politics but wanted something
to do. The free post of one's election manifesto was crucial. He
stuffed envelopes, handed out leaflets and generally helped when
help was at a premium. We eventually lived together and still do.
We have had our arguments and disagreements, one leading to his
leaving for seven years, marrying a childhood girlfriend and having

two children, divorcing and returning. During his absence we saw
each other every other week. He is one of four children from Irish
stock but brought up in Leicestershire. He likes to drink, sometimes
in his life too much. He is clever, articulate, artistic and well-travelled.
He has stuck by me through many of the trials and tribulations of
my life – not many would have done that. It is odd how politics
brought us together but how the strains and stresses of political life
was to split us asunder. He and I, separately and together, have got
into many scrapes, but, forty years on, we respect and care for one
another and I think we will continue to do so to our dying day.

Just before and between the 1974 elections, I had worked for Roger
Moate, the MP for Faversham at the time, and then his brother
David. Roger had the idea of starting a parliamentary magazine.
It was the forerunner to the *House Magazine* and was called *Review of
Parliament and Parliamentary Digest*. I was the editor. It was a review
of the week in the Houses of Parliament and contained a flowchart
on the progress of legislation. Once a week I went from offices in
Blackfriars to printers in Shoreditch and then near Croydon and
proofread the week's edition, ensuring the journal was in the post
to subscribers over the weekend. It built up a circulation sufficient
for Roger to sell the company. For a short time, I worked in Wool-
wich, but then was told the new owners were to discontinue it.
David Moate involved me in his new antique business for a while.
He had a shop in Knightsbridge which was situated in a basement,
while a girl friend of his had a clothes shop above at street level.
I recall going to a number of auction houses with him to buy stock,
including many Victorian chimney pots. They were the only things
I remember selling.

I needed a proper job, however, and so applied for a position
with the British Pulp, Paper and Board Industry Federation. In the

afternoon after the election on Friday 11 October, I went to Plough Place off Fetter Lane, just behind the *Daily Mirror* buildings. To get there I caught the Underground to Temple and walked through streets obviously full of lawyers and barristers, less obviously full of journalists – two professions I was to be involved with incessantly in the future – to meet Rear-Admiral John Adams.

John Adams was a tall, dark, slicked-down-and-oiled, short-haired, imposing figure of a man. He had the amazing ability to recall names and faces, which people were always instantly charmed and put at ease by – an ability I have always found difficult to emulate. He was debonair, handsome, incredibly smartly dressed, always immaculate, and intelligent. Indeed, he would have needed to be. He had been involved with submarines, was captain of the Royal Yacht *Britannia* and had worked in the Ministry of Defence (MOD) under Denis Healey trying to promote 'through aircraft cruisers'. He had overseen an MOD report that had recommended 'through-deck cruisers' and was sacked for his pains. He was the Paper Federation's Director-General. We chatted about my career so far and he was very interested in politics, so we discussed the election campaign. He was particularly impressed that I had been up at my count in Hackney town hall until the early hours of the morning. He offered me the job as assistant secretary of the federation, which I accepted. We shook hands and I achieved my first and only proper job. I had not had to rely on anyone I knew. I had taken my first foot into the business world on merit, with no need of a personal contact or a friend to smooth the way. I was delighted and started work the following Monday.

My first secretary was a Sri Lankan, Sinhalese lady called Sonya. Those were the days when secretaries still typed on typewriters, but photocopiers had taken over from duplicating machines. Sonya wore the most wonderfully patterned saris of fantastic colours. She was a fast and efficient typist and very intelligent and she helped me to settle into my role. All reports had to be written and printed in a certain uniform way to please the Director-General – he was a stickler for detail – and Sonya showed me the ropes. We became friends. In due course, I was appointed secretary of the federation. The previous holder of the position went to work for Woolworths. He was a slight but precise man from whom I learnt much about administration in an office that employed sixty people and had large industrial relations and statistical departments. In those days, computers had to operate in air-conditioned rooms and what can now be stored on a laptop or mobile device took a sizeable room kept at a certain even temperature. I found the work fulfilling and enjoyable, and I found the company of others in such an environment stimulating and enthralling. Coupled with my party political work in the evenings and at weekends, I found life very busy.

For the Paper Federation, I built up an all-party parliamentary group and Frank White, a then Labour MP, was one of its keenest members. It meant constant visits to the Houses of Parliament, organising meetings and dinners and other events. The Labour government, with its pay and price control and its determination to run everything, including manufacturing industry, was forever holding sector meetings, so I was in the forefront of civil-service briefings, industry demands and trade-union representations. It was often exciting, intriguing and tiring. My interest in party politics sometimes had to be subordinated to the role I played for the federation. I learnt the ability to keep several different balls in the air at the same time as well as how to analyse situations in differing ways.

The annual paper industry dinner held at the Hilton Hotel was always an organisational challenge. It was preceded by a tasting lunch where Director-General John Adams and I tried various menus and wines. It was fascinating. John Adams had certain culinary requirements, acquired during his time on *Britannia* and the Queen's demands; for example, buffet food had to be 'forkable', meaning capable of being moved or separated with a fork – no need for a knife or a third hand. There had to be a little mustard in the vinaigrette and candles to illuminate the cuisine should be placed in the freezer beforehand so they burned more slowly; one had to be economical. La Ina sherry from Jerez de la Frontera was vital to accompany the first course. He recounted the story of attending a dinner, after which when he was asked, 'How was it?' He replied: 'At least the Champagne was warm!' The seating plans for these annual dinners were extraordinarily difficult to arrange, with several hundred guests to be seated in exactly the right location on tens of round tables. The menu, and the paper and board it was printed upon, had to be just the right weight and size. When I was invited subsequently to a political lunch or dinner as a guest, I knew just how much effort and thought normally went into organising such events. I managed to obtain some handmade cream paper from Turkey Mill with watermarks for my personal stationery – it was beautiful and added weight to missives I wrote. Again, I always considered life is all about attention to detail.

The Paper Federation was essentially a public-relations organisation to promote the British paper industry. John Adams was the ideal man to have in charge, as he was a natural communicator. The PR department was very important. It was headed by Jim Fobbister – an old-time PR man who came from Bulawayo in Zimbabwe. He was a devout Christian and had left Africa when the troubles started to protect his young family. He became a great friend. He helped me with the design of my election manifesto in 1979 and ensured it was a very professional product, full of photographs, that put across my message well. Alas, he died young and left a wife and two children. He was a person who, in life, it is a privilege to have met.

To assist the running of the parliamentary group, the federation employed a news agency in the House of Commons' press gallery, run by Robin Page and Philip Marshall. I met them regularly to discuss legislation and parliamentary business in their offices overlooking the square beneath Big Ben with the underground car park entrance and exit ramps. This was relevant to one of the horrors that was to come. The agency alerted us to any matters that might affect the paper industry. They were very professional and I maintained contact with them when I became a Member of Parliament. If only all members of the press at that time could have been as courteous, polite and accurate in their reporting as Robin and Philip.

In whatever spare time I had, in the late 1970s I would go to the theatre, cinema, opera and the ballet with Terry. On leaving *The Accidental Death of an Anarchist*, the internationally recognised play by Dario Fo, who later received the Nobel Prize for Literature in 1997, I bumped into a friend who said, 'What a lot of seditious nonsense that was.' My tastes were broad; we went to art galleries and recitals at Leyton House, the Barbican, the Royal Opera House and Wigmore Hall. A friend of ours, Jeremy, was a concert pianist. Terry had worked for Charles Trenet in Paris and knew him well; he was the French Frank Sinatra. I met him twice later. We went to parties and social events, usually organised by girls Terry knew and with whom I became friendly. We met many artistic and design-orientated people. Life was not all about work or politics. It was a good, rewarding time in my life and extended my interests.

My interest in food evolved; Terry was an excellent cook. I developed an ability to cook breakfast and make cakes – I guess taking after my father – though I have lost the knack now. Terry also taught me about the need to dress traditionally and my dress sense improved as a result: shirts and ties, coordinating not clashing, from Jermyn Street – Turnbull & Asser were the best – and grey, navy, pin- or chalk-striped suits, a blazer and a sports jacket were essential. I did not go as far as one of my parliamentary colleagues, Alan Clark, however. He told me once at 55 Park Lane, while we waited for others to arrive for a meeting, how he always wore the same make, colour and cut of suit, shirt and tie so that his appearance was always identical. He said that there were so many Tory candidates and back-bench MPs all wanting to make an impact on the party leader, she would notice him more if he maintained the same look in London. So, he always wore a navy-blue suit, pale-blue cotton shirt and solid, navy-blue tie. He was incessantly ambitious to climb the greasy pole and talked about it a lot; I was not. In the country Alan wore tweeds; I preferred urban life and avoided the country like the plague.

My political life ground to a halt. I did my best for the Hackney Conservatives and I continued accepting speaking engagements, developing my thoughts on immigration, the Common Market, Northern Ireland and the economy. I played a minor role in the referendum campaign on the Common Market, but my real desire was to gain re-admission to the Conservative Party's candidates' list, without which, however hard I worked in Hackney, they and I knew I would never be an MP.

I was called to meet a vice-chairman of the party, Marcus Fox, at Central Office in Smith Square. Marcus, a Yorkshire MP, had spoken to meetings of the Scarborough Young Conservatives when I was a vice-chairman. Notwithstanding what he thought of my political views, he knew that deep down I had always been a loyal, hard-working Conservative. For this reason, he allowed me to be placed on the list, but only for Hackney South & Shoreditch. He said that if I was selected for another constituency he would look at the matter again.

The process of applying for selection as a candidate was not easy. You had to know where there was a vacancy. I had to rely on word of mouth from friends and colleagues. I think I wrote to eighty or so constituency associations seeking an interview. I was unmarried, not rich, had no connections to speak of and was not a great prize. I was known for my principles and straight-forward political opinions, which I was able to promote through the Monday Club. I did not receive a single invitation to a selection interview, usually not even the courtesy of a reply. As one neared the date of a potential general election, one's first high aims disappeared, goals were lowered, and eventually logical despair set in – I wasn't going to be a MP. Then, out of the blue, I had a tip off about Basildon. It was a safe Labour seat (so was Hackney), with a majority of over 10,000 votes.

There had been a financial scandal involving the Conservative MP for Bournemouth East, John Cordle, and he resigned, leaving a vacancy and triggering a by-election. David Atkinson, who had been the prospective parliamentary candidate ('prospective' is the word used to stop election expenses having to be accounted for before the election has been officially announced) for Basildon in Essex, applied to be the candidate. He had a similar arrangement with the Basildon Association as I had with mine in Hackney, namely, he was not going to win in Basildon. He was allowed to look elsewhere and his good fortune presented an opportunity for me to move onwards if not upwards. David was successful, elected and served in the House until 2005. He had a wife and two children and died in 2012. The year before, he came 'out' as homosexual and entered into a civil partnership, though I did not know of his sexuality in the 1970s. I discussed the Basildon seat with him briefly before applying for the vacancy his move had created. I didn't know him before then, even though he had been National Young Conservative chairman, and I did not know him well when we were both in the House together either. It never occurred to me that he was an homosexual. In later police speak, I didn't 'socialise' with him.

I had spoken in Billericay on behalf of the Monday Club a year before the vacancy arose and impressed two or three of the local Tories. It had been one of the many hundreds of meetings I had undertaken during the 1970s throughout the country. I was invited to submit my CV and apply, which I did. It was 1977.

I caught the train down to Billericay, one of its five railway stations, for the first selection meeting. I think they had selected about fifteen people to interview. The constituency was geographically large, including Billericay and Wickford to the north and the new town of Basildon to the south, which covered Pitsea to the east and Laindon to the west. It had about 110,000 voters, almost twice the size of an average seat. I was driven to meet supporters in a pub and then on to the large home of Brian and Joy Edwards in the sleepy village of Little Burstead. Brian was a solicitor, solid and a pillar of the local Tory establishment. Joy was a very effective chairman (I do prefer the word even for ladies holding such a position) of the Women's Advisory Committee. I could tell they did not support my candidacy but treated me hospitably. I was interviewed by about fifteen people, many of whom were councillors. Derek and Lillian Greenfield and Peggy and Ron Marshall were present and they were to be some of my main supporters. It was very much a council-orientated association.

I made my short speech, in which I recall laying out clearly my views on immigration, the Common Market and free enterprise, defence and support for the police. Answering the questions was going to be the tricky part. In the main, the questioners wanted their candidate to be a mirror image of themselves. It was obvious that there were many egos in the room and to side with one against another was not sensible. So, I stuck to my principles. Councillor Gwen Jones from Ramsden Bellhouse asked a question I can still remember. She was a large lady physically and in her personality. She asked me who I would support as leader of the party if there was a vacancy, and both Edward Heath and Enoch Powell were not available. For any prospective candidate it was a trap – not that I think Gwen realised it. Whoever one named, the vast majority of the selection committee would want someone else. So, how to get out of it?

I answered:

> It has often been put to me that Edward Heath or Enoch Powell might be walking down a road and get run over by a bus. It has never been put to me that Edward Heath and Enoch Powell would be walking down the same road, hand in hand, and get run over together by the same bus.

Gwen and the others laughed at the thought, distracted, and I was off the hook and did not have to answer the deadly question. I was shortlisted; round one of selection was over.

My supporters were delighted and telephoned to discuss round two. This was to be a mass meeting of members of the association, for which I needed to be briefed on the constituency and its problems. Above all, they asked whether I could take with me a female partner as 'balance'. So on this occasion my views were likely to get support, but it was my marital status – single – that could be a problem.

I had a word with a very good friend, Fiona. She had a boyfriend who she went on to marry, but she agreed to accompany me to the 'big' meeting about two or three weeks later. She was a slim, good-looking girl, well-dressed, with impeccable manners. She was a great hostess and I had many wonderful homemade lunches and dinners at her Fulham Road apartment. I got to know her very well. Her support and presence gave me the confidence I might otherwise have lacked and it was bound to have impressed the members of the Conservative Association. I know it did from their later comments about her, and I kept being asked how she was and when she would attend this or that function.

The 'establishment' choice I think was Frances Chambers. Frances was on the other wing of the party to myself. She was accompanied by Clive Landa, who went on to be chairman of the Reform Group, a left-of-centre Conservative pressure group. Councillor Tony Ball, then association chairman, took them on a morning tour of the constituency to give her a steer before the 2 p.m. meeting. There were two other candidates, one possibly a London councillor. The hall was packed with 400 or more members present. I spoke well, with notes, but had memorised most of my remarks. I concluded that politically we were about to fight just as important a battle in the coming months as that fought by the brave pilots in the skies over the Essex country-side in the Battle of Britain. It was rhetoric that struck a chord with my audience. Questions went without a hitch. Fiona and I waited in a room at the back of the hall, drinking tea out of basic pale-green cups and saucers, eyeing the others and nervously wondering whether that sudden burst of applause for one of the other three doing their stuff meant they had stolen the show. Soon everyone had had their turn and the votes were counted: I had won more than 50 per cent of the vote on the first ballot. I was to fight the next general election.

It was an achievement to be selected; It was not expected I would win. My job was to work hard and long, substantially reduce

Eric Moonman's Labour majority and place myself in a good position to fight a safer seat in the following election. I was thirty years old. Conservative Central office confirmed that I could fight the seat – with my overwhelming victory at the selection gathering they could do no other. After all, I wasn't going to get in, was I? I had a feeling of intense pride that I had been chosen, that it was an honour to represent the party of which I had been a member for sixteen years. I had overcome opposition and I felt vindicated that I could stick to my guns on my political opinions, not trim to the prevailing winds, and still be victorious. The election itself would be another matter.

After the selection meeting, Fiona and I went to my home in Fulham. Terry cooked a wonderful supper, not perhaps realising these events would set us on a collision course. The balance in our lives had altered. I planned my political future; Fiona her engagement and her wedding. Fiona joined me for a number of engagements in London subsequently. A few years later, Terry and I went to her wedding on the Isle of Wight. As things happened, we stayed at the same hotel where she and the groom were on their wedding night and we joined them both for breakfast the next morning. Subsequently, after she married, I gradually lost touch with her, but I will always remember the way she helped me at the selection meeting with great aplomb and style.

At the time, it was expected of single male Conservative candidates that they should be accompanied to social events, certainly a selection gathering. That was the culture of the time and impossible to understand now. It contributed to the certainty of my advancement and I do not think that my supporters or constituents felt badly towards me as a consequence. I hope they did not. It was certainly not mentioned to me again.

CHAPTER 4

GENERAL ELECTION 1979

I t was Friday 30 March 1979, just before 3 p.m. I rang the press gallery of the House of Commons from my Paper Federation office looking over Plough Place and spoke to Robin Page. Two days before the Labour government had lost a vote of no-confidence in the Commons. There was to be a general election. It would have consequences for the paper industry, and for myself, and I needed Robin to brief me. Shortly into the conversation, I heard – over the phone line – a boom. Robin, in horror, described the scene below him. Although we did not know it at the time, Airey Neave had been killed. A magnetic car bomb fitted with a ball-bearing tilt-switch exploded under his 1979 Vauxhall Cavalier at 2.58 p.m. as he drove up the ramp and out of the Palace of Westminster car park. He lost his right leg below the knee and his left was hanging on by a flap of skin. He died in hospital an hour after being freed from the wreckage without regaining consciousness.

Robin and I talked for a while, him telling me of the rescue attempts being made beneath his window, until it became too difficult for either of us to continue and we terminated the conversation. Conservative leader Margaret Thatcher later led the tributes to Neave:

> He was one of freedom's warriors. No one knew of the great man he was, except those nearest to him. He was staunch, brave, true, strong; but he was very gentle and kind and loyal. It's a rare combination of qualities. There's no one else who can quite fill them. I, and so many other people, owe so much to him and now we must carry on for the things he fought for and not let the people who got him triumph.

Neave's death was to colour the entire 1979 general election campaign. It was strongly felt that Irish terrorists would attempt to sabotage the election, targeting candidates, however unlikely they might be to get elected. It was determined that all candidates were to have some kind of police protection and, in my case, it came in the form of two Essex police detectives. My opinion was not sought. They were to accompany me during the election campaign, especially when I was to speak at public meetings or appear at events where the time and venue was to receive advance publicity. I got to know them quite well and accepted their need to look under whatever car I was using or whatever stage I was to walk upon for any bombs. It certainly made one feel even more important. After all, this was a safe Labour seat, and I was not predicted to get elected. However, all eyes are on the candidate during an election; the association is disbanded. You, and your agent, are in charge of the conduct of your election in the constituency. You receive advice from Central Office on the political themes to be pursued on a certain day – best to avoid that advice – and on legal issues with reference to election law and expenses procedures – best to follow that advice.

I had spent the two years since selection in the pursuit of support and supporters. I had not declined a single invitation within the area. Every request from my association, or one of its ward committees, to speak was accepted. Every coffee morning, lunch, dinner, cocktail party, every retirement home, school, college, farm, business or work place that wanted me was assiduously cultivated. The Basildon New Town Development Corporation and its general manager Douglas Galloway kept their distance, obviously believing the incumbent Moonman was safe as their houses. The Labour-led Basildon district council disliked many of my views. My agent and her husband, Peggy and Ron Marshall, had placed at my disposal their caravan and virtually every Saturday we manned it in Basildon town centre, giving out leaflets, meeting residents and helping with any problems they might be experiencing; with a Labour council, there were quite a few. It was a time-consuming task, but gradually my name and views were getting around the town. I had been very busy and, of course, my full-time job at the federation, if anything, became more burdensome as I became the federation secretary. It left less and less time for Terry and myself to have quality time together. Strains began to show.

A candidate has to balance the rival factions within his association and we had our share of difficulties. I tried to act as a peacemaker between wards, between councillors and between personalities. I also had to deal with the press and promote my own, very direct political views without losing the support of the association as a whole. I thought there was no point in being a candidate, let alone a Member of Parliament, if you did not articulate your own opinions as well as those of the party you sought to represent.

In those days, canvassing and a good committee-room system on the election day itself were vital. To achieve that you needed foot soldiers. I arranged as many friends as I could to come into the constituency to deliver leaflets and canvass. I persuaded as many local people, including the Young Conservatives, to be active in the campaign. Peggy Marshall as my agent was wonderful – a font of wisdom and advice. Often, I would stay overnight at her house to save having to leave an evening event early to get the last train home, or so we could make an early start the next morning. Peggy and Ron were very hospitable. They knew the area so well, and who the movers and shakers were, and helped to locate venues, organisations and clubs where I could gain support. As well as this invaluable local intelligence, they were also very good at publicity. In the main, this came in the shape of posters affixed to key farm fences in the rural areas between the five conurbations, on stakes in gardens and affixed to windows around the constituency. If a poster was removed or damaged, it was replaced. You couldn't drive through the area without seeing my face, name and party affiliation; there were thousands of them. In such circumstances, it can be difficult to keep your feet firmly on the ground and stick to common sense. If anyone wished to vote Conservative they knew who they had to vote for without a doubt. It is a far cry from these days when, in some parts of the country, it is difficult to know there is an election taking place. Many of the councillors helped with their teams of supporters. They knew I had helped them in district council and county elections and returned the favour. Well, they had to – local elections were on the same day!

It was decided that during the three weeks immediately before election day on Thursday 3 May 1979, I would stay in the constituency. A very kind lady agreed to provide accommodation overnight in Billericay and I took my annual holiday from work to fight the election 24/7. The association offices above a shop in Billericay high street were turned into campaign headquarters. The adoption meeting over, held in the splendid Billericay Constitutional Club where I had many friends and supporters, I campaigned flat out. It was an impressive campaign – no stone was left unturned: we canvassed in the snow as well as the rain, much to the amusement of our opponents; wore royal blue rosettes; drove around the streets in cars with loudspeakers, creating an atmosphere of excitement; had magnetic backed posters that could be switched from car to car; and had a car with a large sun roof so I could stand upright, megaphone in hand, putting the message across: 'Vote Conservative – Vote Proctor'.

I was incredibly indebted to my supporters. All candidates say that, most noticeably in their speech on election night after the announcement of the ballot, but I truly mean it. They put their lives on hold for several weeks. I made friends with so many people in this period. The candidate has to appear confident, strong and personable; you might think that you will not win, but you must maintain faith. Many times, late at night, I thought it would all be for nothing, but I had to remain firm, committed and publicly optimistic – if privately sanguine.

So what of the policies? Mrs Thatcher had indicated she wished there to be a different form of politics after the election; we could not continue the decline experienced over the last thirty years. Political parties of whatever colour since the war had gone to the electorate, told them the dramatic reforms they planned, only to do U-turns within eighteen months once the Cabinet was courted by civil servants. Mrs Thatcher was to be different. Pay and price control had ripped the heart out of Labour. As neither workers nor employers could create inflation, even if they tried, they could not be expected to stop it. Only politicians with firm control over the money supply could do that. People might not have fully understood all the ramifications of such economic theory, but I was cheered and supported on the Ford tractor union picket line, where I stayed with them round their wood burners. Ford could afford to pay their employees more. Labour wouldn't let them. It was daft. Unemployment was rising. The Saatchi poster 'Labour isn't working' was devastating for Labour. The Tory 'right to buy' housing policy was also very effective. It was vital to winning over blue-collar, working-class voters in the new town of Basildon. People had aspirations of home ownership; it was a vital factor. People were fed up of the UK being seen around the world as a soft touch, losing influence and power. The Conservatives promised to defend the realm. Law and order was to be at the forefront of a Conservative government's programme. Terrorism, especially Irish terrorism, was to be dealt with firmly. Airey Neave was to have brought Ulster more into the United Kingdom family of nations, to be integrated. I felt it was so important that I deliberately stood as the official Conservative and Unionist parliamentary candidate.

There were issues that party leaders shied away from that I did not. I had long supported Enoch Powell's view that successive governments since the Second World War had allowed too many immigrants to come into the United Kingdom from the New Commonwealth and Pakistan – and that trouble was brewing. It had changed the population of our country in a dramatic way without any democratic support. I proposed an end to such immigration and, as the Conservatives had pledged before in previous manifestos, including those of Sir Alec Douglas-Home and Edward Heath, a policy of voluntary repatriation. I thought I was being realistic and not racialist. Enoch and I said that we dealt with the problem before us. If the immigration had been made up from a preponderance of white people on the same scale, problems would have been similar, but at that time it was not. Annoyingly for our opponents in all parties, these ideas were popular. In my own constituency, an odd Conservative councillor here or there was nervous of the line, though most were enthusiastically in support, as were association members. The electorate were overwhelmingly supportive; it was the political elite that was out of step.

One day during the campaign, I was walking around Basildon town centre when a couple in their sixties came up to me and said, 'We voted for you.' I replied: 'That is not possible, the election day is some way off.' 'No,' they responded, 'we voted for you in 1974 in Hackney South & Shoreditch. We were able to get out and away from the problems created by immigration, our friends, alas, cannot. We will vote for you because of your views on immigration.' They didn't blame the immigrants for coming into Britain, nor have I; it is the politicians who are to blame for letting them into the country in such numbers. I owed it to them, and the people in inner London I had met, to speak out on their behalf as a candidate. Knowing the risks, the attempts to brand me as a racist, I kept faith with those people.

Another issue aggravating my voters was bad railway communications to and from London. In the preceding months, people had faced disastrous delays and cancellations on the trains and commuters were out to take their revenge. I made a point of visiting the railway stations as often as I could during the campaign and speaking to travellers – they were to repay my interest in them.

I held several public meetings, often very well-attended. I failed to see my main opponent during the election and I cannot recall a debate of all the candidates, only a social event at the onset. I do not know if he took his re-election for granted, but he certainly went to more marginal constituencies to speak for his friends. I was not expected to win, so had no visiting speakers that I can recall to support my candidacy.

On election day, I awoke early, dressed in a smart, navy-blue suit, pale-blue shirt and blue tie, pinned on a large, blue rosette and did what candidates can do on election day – rally the troops. I thought we stood a chance; I was optimistic. It is so easy to think that when, on the night before, people were saying that I would make it. There were fifty or so polling stations, each with a committee room, in close proximity. A candidate could visit inside the polling station; a party worker could not. I tried to visit them all twice, thanking those who had worked all day to oversee the poll as well as my party workers in the committee rooms. It was a formidable task.

In the early evening, I recall my second 'run' through Basildon New Town. I was dismayed. Conventional wisdom held that a Conservative did not want to see high turnout of voters in the evening, especially in the areas perceived to be more Labour, as these were traditionally Labour voters. The schools, often used as polling stations, were besieged. Queues of voters stretched from school doors out of the school yard gates. I was downcast, inwardly sick and resigned myself to losing. I kept up appearances for my team, but I thought 1979 was not going to be my year. Still, it was a sunny night and we had all done our best. At the close of the polling stations at 10 p.m. I went to change my shirt and tie, freshen up and pen a few words of thanks to the returning officer and his loyal, hard-working staff and talk about the next time. I had a light supper, lovingly provided by my kind lady host, after which I could have fallen asleep.

My two detectives had spent the whole day with me and they knocked on the door at the prearranged time to take me to the count. They were tired too. Just one last role for me to play and one last event for them. They had become familiar, like helpful acquaintances but not exactly friends. I thanked them both profusely. They were young and both just wanted to end their duty, return home to their wives and sleep after all their endeavours of the last few weeks.

I know both of them would have put their lives on the line for me. I have often thought about them and how grateful politicians should be to the police that protect their very existence. We knew the count would be lengthy as local elections had taken place the same day and the parliamentary ballot papers had to be separated from local ones first. I think I arrived about midnight. Job done, the detectives went home after the final goodbyes.

It was a crowded sports hall and it very soon became apparent that it was going to be a long night. Many of my supporters had gone to the count directly; they wanted to see the black boxes opened, get a feel from the different areas about how we and they, if they were council candidates, had done locally as well as nationally. The Liberal candidate arrived first, then me with my agent and then, in a fanfare of camera flashes, Eric Moonman. His grin soon vanished.

Initial reports from our observers indicated that we were doing rather well in traditionally good Labour areas. They were straws in the wind. The same intelligence filtered through the Labour ranks. Then, a couple of hours later, the parliamentary ballot papers were counted. The piles of my votes gradually stretched ahead of those of my Labour opponent. His supporters started getting worried. It looked like a lead of about 5,000 votes, but votes still had to be counted. It was tense. The lead held to the end. Even on a big electorate, he knew a recount was out of the question. I had been elected. I was understandably pleased for myself but also for my party workers.

My majority, engraved on my heart ever since, was 5,180. I tried to stay calm. The swing, at over 11 per cent to the Conservatives, was the biggest swing in England in a seat which was gained from Labour. There was a moment, just a moment, when a flash of self-satisfaction crossed my mind. It did not last long; I had to make the victor's speech. I had to commiserate with the sitting Member of Parliament, thank him for his past work in the constituency and, to the cheers and boos of respected clans, I said I looked forward to a Conservative government. I thanked my agent and supporters. The television screens flashed up 'Basildon: Conservative Gain'. It must have caused mutual concern in both party headquarters in London. Labour realising they were going into opposition; the Conservatives that they had as a member someone who might be difficult, if not impossible, to control. After all, I was a real Tory. I rang Terry at home. He had been fast asleep but had just woken to see the same message flash on his TV screen. He was delighted and appalled in equal measure. Our life together could never be the same. My association officers and members were ecstatic, enthusiastic and delighted. There was a party to attend, one they deserved. But uniform police wouldn't let me leave until my 'escort' returned, and so back rushed the two detectives. They had gone to sleep early, only to be awoken by their wives to be told, 'You won't believe it … he's got in.' They drove me to the early-morning party in Little Burstead. Everyone was tired but my supporters just wanted to savour the moment that little bit longer. I went to bed about 6 a.m., but only for a couple of hours. By mid-morning, I was being driven around the streets thanking the voters for their confidence, then I went home for a good night's sleep. I had been elected just within my arbitrary ten-year deadline I had set myself on leaving university – I was thirty-two years of age.

CHAPTER 5

THE HOUSE OF COMMONS

I was sure something would happen next but I was not sure what. After all, I had been elected as a Member of Parliament. I had achieved my boyhood ambition from the age of fourteen. Strangely, in the same way, I had never had the ambition to become a minister, still less a Cabinet minister or, God forbid, Prime Minister. Not that I felt such drive for preferment wasn't an honourable aim, it was rather that it had never crossed my mind as it must have others of my vintage. I was not in the position of having to be careful who I dined with or what I said. I didn't have to consider promotion every day, nor weigh with whom I mixed or 'socialised'. For many with greater and higher ambition, they always had to consider their position and stance on issues to reflect party situations as they climbed the greasy political pole. Their determination to advance was their greatest weakness as seen by party managers. The apparatchiks in the party quickly noted who they could control and how. I had no such concerns. It is not that I would not have said yes to official preferment, it is just not something that drove me onwards. Nor was I prepared to sacrifice my independence in favour of rank. To be a good constituency MP – now there was my raison d'être.

The Whips' Office and its occupants were in place to carry through the government's wishes. They would use everything in their power not to disappoint whoever was the occupant of 10 Downing Street. Knowledge was influence and ultimately power; I must have been a puzzle to them.

I had told my supporters at my adoption meeting as a parliamentary candidate that I wished to be not just their Member of Parliament, but a 'good constituency Member'. That was code for 'if I am elected, do not expect me necessarily to become a minister, nor will I set my stall out for such advancement'.

Furthermore, I had set out my loyalties. I would be loyal to my party, which I had served as a member for more than half my life. Without party, Parliament cannot function and I would not be in a position to be elected, so how else could I regard my party but as a loyal member of it? Many Conservative Members of Parliament were not technically members of their party; they had not paid a subscription fee. I was a fully paid up member of the Conservative Party and always did pay my subscription dues in the twenty-six years I was in the party. But I told them there was a greater loyalty: to be loyal to one's constituents. Without them, I would be nothing. I had to be loyal to those who would be voting for me, as without their votes I would not be elected and, if elected, I would seek to represent to the best of my ability all of the electorate, whether they had voted for me or not. Yet, there was a greater loyalty still: I wished to sit in the national Parliament. I was a representative, not a delegate. Something might be in the interests of my constituency, but the national interest might outweigh local or regional concerns. The loyalty above all others, however, was that to myself: I had to be true to myself and my own opinions. Of course, I explained, on any issue before the House all these loyalties had to be balanced one against the others. If elected, I would seek to do my best. It never crossed my mind, being politics, that anyone would be loyal to me. I did expect, even without thinking about it, however naïve it might sound, that I would continue to have a modicum of privacy in my private life.

So here I was, waiting at home for a special document, possibly sealed with fancy language to confirm my position and request for me to attend the House on such and such a date. Instead, I received nothing. Should I ring anyone? I wondered, and if so, who?

I did receive a call, but not one I had anticipated. It was from the police, who wished to visit me at home to consider my personal security. They seemed pleased that I did not possess a car myself, but stressed the importance of carrying a mirror on a long pole to check under any vehicle I was to enter. Although no further assassinations had taken place during the course of the election, they looked carefully at the flat door on the first floor of my apartment block. They determined it needed strengthening. It should have a sheet of metal attached to the inside of the front door, thick enough to deter small-arms fire and security bolts to improve the door's ability to withstand being kicked inwards. It was only later, after the workmen left, that I noticed they had cut out a piece of metal for the letter box, at just about chest height.

One morning, I read in the *Times* newspaper that the House of Commons was to sit on 10 May. I thought I had better go along and see what I had to do. Of course, I had seen the Chamber of the Commons before, from the elevated heights of the Strangers' Gallery, but walking into it now, it seemed small and intimate. I queued up and took my oath of allegiance by swearing on the Bible, which used to be kept in the government dispatch box from which ministers spoke. As I passed by the sacred green leather benches forming the government front bench, I noticed the metal decorative corner pieces of the dispatch box, worn smooth by the nervous gripping of speakers' hands as they stood at the box, literally sweating over their next pronouncements.

Obviously, I felt a sense of pride and achievement, but my main feeling was that I had to get on with the organisational part of being a Member. I had no time to sit back and feel self-congratulatory; there was too much to do. The job – it was a job – was all-consuming. Its effect on my personal life was immediately dramatic. The amount of time it took up was immense. Together with constituency pressures, it meant my relationship with Terry was to come under stress. He had no interest in politics and never visited the Basildon constituency, unlike Hackney. He could not contemplate that my time was no longer my own and, to be honest, nor could I. There was too much detail with which to grapple. The first day was full of facts, procedures and bureaucracy; feelings of honour and self-satisfaction were to filter through, but much later.

I next looked for an office. They had not been allocated and would not be for some time as senior members in the previous parliament had first to be accommodated, and that took time and negotiation. At the Paper Federation, I had the luxury of my own office and my own secretary, so it was quite a shock to find nothing mirrored those essentials in the commercial world. I knew and understood the salary was not to be replicated and that I would take a cut in salary to do my new job. I knew also that I couldn't continue being the Paper Federation's secretary – it was too much of a full-time job to hope for that. In any event, I wanted to be a full-time MP – and I soon realised I had to be.

The first thing I did after taking the oath was to locate the post office situated off the Members' Lobby and pick up my mail. I was astonished that, in my first collection, I had over 200 items of post. With no secretary to answer anything and an eagerness to open the missives, I squatted at a desk in an open-plan area just off the Strangers' Gallery. It was peaceful and the desk had a supply of House of Commons stationery in various colours. Unlike Dame Irene Ward, I chose the blue. Irene was a doyen of the North East Conservatives and when she replied in the affirmative to an invitation to speak at York, we had been surprised by the red-coloured heading on the House of Commons paper. Apparently, the Tory Party colour in the north-east, when she was first elected, was red.

I opened my first envelope. It was from an old lady who lived in a residential area of Billericay. To paraphrase, she wrote, 'Mr Proctor, I have always voted Conservative and I voted for you and now you can do something for me. My street light outside my house has not been working for months. I am frightened to go into the street at night. Can you get it working, please?' I pondered the situation. This was the first letter. I wasn't sure how to proceed and, anyway, I had another 200 and more letters to deal with. I spied in the letter rack some cards. They were pre-printed acknowledgement cards informing a constituent that [the MP] had received your kind letter and would be dealing with the matter. In the absence of a secretary, stationery, office and a guide setting out how to be a Member of Parliament, I used one such card. Well, by the time I had opened the mail that day, I had used many of these cards. I was to realise in the months and years ahead that it took many hours to address what was going to be the happy treadmill of two bundles of letters a day. The enormity of the electorate of Basildon resulted in the heavy caseload I gladly had to bear. I looked forward to the mail and what it contained, while recognising that many of my colleagues thought it was for them just dreadful. It may have been Julian Amery who said to me once that the worst thing about being a MP was having to have a constituency and constituents. For myself it was the opposite, my constituency work was one of my favourite parts of the job.

Two days later, still without secretarial support, I opened the mail again. In the bundle was another letter from the lady in Billericay. Was I to be scolded for not acting on her defunct street light? Was she to advise me she would not vote for me again as a result of my dereliction of duty? No. 'Mr Proctor,' she wrote. 'I knew I was right to vote Conservative. Thank you for putting on my street light. I will always vote for you in the future.' I had done nothing. It seemed masterly inaction had a role to play in politics – I learnt that in my first week. I hoped all my political and constituency problems could be solved so easily; I learnt subsequently that they could not.

I needed a secretary, and found one in the shape of Lyn. She had worked at the Paper Federation but was not full time. I asked her if she would work for me and fortunately she said yes. In the eight years I was at the House of Commons, Lyn worked assiduously for me and for my constituents. She was magnificent: efficient, but kind and understanding. She had a relaxed but firm telephone manner, which both protected me and answered queries with ease. Her husband, Geoff, was a newspaper and magazine photographer. He had worked for, among others, Robert Maxwell's papers and was caught up in Maxwell's pension scandal. I liked them both. Lyn was vital to my parliamentary life and constituency affairs. Offices were found eventually for Lyn, which she shared with other secretaries, and a few weeks later I was allocated a desk.

Lyn was my parliamentary secretary for the eight years I was a Member. I could not have been as effective a constituency MP as

I was without her. She was efficient and courteous and polite to all who crossed my path professionally. Lyn was by my side in the good times and bad when I served in the House. We kept in touch afterwards and met up to discuss the 'old days'. MPs' secretaries are very underrated in the parliamentary system. I always liked Lyn and can think of no better person to have spent so much of my professional time with and salute the work she did for so many of my constituents.

I was to reside in the East Cloisters, which, in the heart of the Palace of Westminster, had been carefully restored and were full of stone and sobriety. Mine was an open-plan office, in the main peaceful and calm unless a fellow occupant was having an argument with an over-persistent constituent or an unbending civil servant. It was a great place to work. If you worked in a historical building it made sense to have history all around you and you certainly did there.

Near to my desk was the Members' entrance and Members' cloakroom, with its scrolling ticker-tape machine and the pink ribbons hanging from our coat pegs that tantalisingly begged the question: 'What are they for?', to which one would receive the rebuttal, 'That is where you hang your sword, Sir.'

The cloisters were perfectly located, within easy reach of Westminster Hall and, at the bottom of the Members' entrance staircase, the Members' lobby, post office, vote office and (past the statue of Churchill and the snuff box), the Chamber itself. It could not be better. I greatly regretted when I had to move, as, I imagine, so did all who had the privilege to work there.

It was not only geographically and historically perfect; it played host to a wonderful collection of Tory MPs. Life was never dull there. The desk opposite mine was occupied by Ivor Stanbrook, the MP for Orpington. He was polite and very helpful to a new member.

Ivor was a barrister, shared my views on immigration and had splendid contacts in Nigeria and, as a result, I was invited to social events organised by the Nigerian High Commission. He was a great Commonwealth man, but pro-Europe too. Personally, Ivor and his wife, and Clive, one of his sons (also a lawyer), were very friendly, and Ivor guided me through the early procedural matters with aplomb.

Dr Alan Glyn was the MP for Windsor & Maidenhead. He was a medical doctor (always useful to have a doctor in the House) and came across as much older than he actually was, his grey hair and moustache surrounding his spectacles. Alan was very proud of representing the Queen and was a tad eccentric in his manner, friendly if a touch aloof. Kenneth Lewis was also based in the cloisters. He was a left-of-centre, but personally a very affable, Member. Having been in the House for twenty years, Kenneth knew much of its tradition and procedure and he was generous with sharing his knowledge with a new boy, even one with whom sometimes he disagreed. He used to puff on slim cigars and worked hard for his constituents, but worried constantly about his expenses and his pension. He was very friendly with Richard Body and their desks were adjacent. Dick had been Member of Parliament for Billericay from 1955 to 1959, so knew my constituency well. He was also a fellow Europe sceptic and Enoch supporter, so inevitably we got on famously and he encouraged me throughout my parliamentary career. He always had time to talk over one of my constituents' problems and was full of advice, particularly on agriculture, on which he was an expert. A Quaker, he was a gentle friend and a doughty opponent and someone I respected deeply. Apart from myself, another new entrant in 1979 was Mark Lennox-Boyd, the Member for Morecambe & Lonsdale who became a whip and a Foreign Office Minister. He was always polite and friendly towards me, but he had ambitious eyes.

He was the son of a Viscount and somehow you could tell. His dry sense of humour coupled with constant smoking of small cigars and his aristocratic demeanour placed him in the very centre of the establishment. *Private Eye* wrote a piece on me within a couple of weeks, describing me as 'so far right wing as to be somewhere in the North Sea'. Well, as I said at the time, that depends on which way you look at it, and they went on to write equally misinformed pieces on other new MPs, heading the next column 'New Boy 2'. I guess I was their New Boy 1 and gave them the idea.

The unusual figure in our midst in the East Cloisters – apart from me – was Charles Irving. He was the Member for Cheltenham and chairman of the catering committee. I thought at the time he might have been homosexual, but it was not a subject we ever discussed. Indeed, it was not a subject that was discussed with other members, *ever*. Charles was witty and precise, with a sharp tongue, and his amusing, almost effete mannerisms disguised a strong-willed man when crossed. He was a wonderful storyteller and very generous with his time and his money. Charles would often help other Members who were troubled or in trouble, and his concern crossed party lines. Having the chairman of the catering committee in your daily sight was extremely useful. You could always get a table, always get a room for a meeting, a lunch or a dinner, and always received an insight into what was going on in and around the non-political aspects of the House. He knew the gossip and how to spread it, but he did it without rancour and with much good humour. His great friend was Janet Fookes, who went on to become Deputy Speaker. She certainly brightened up the cloisters on her frequent visits to consult Charles or to be escorted by him to dinner.

All of us in the East Cloisters batted for one another; we looked after each other's social interests and domestic needs, whatever our political opinions on the issues of the day. I can never remember us having arguments; we respected each other, and the others were helpful to a new member finding his feet. Not all, but most are now dead. I regret their passing and I am sorry that I did not attend their funerals as I would have wished, had I not placed myself in a political baulk position of which I shall describe, if not explain, later.

As one wondered around the House, the big 'beasts' of the Conservative Party would hove into view down a corridor. I had to pinch myself often initially to recognise I was walking the same corridors. Most, like Willie Whitelaw and Sir Keith Joseph, were incredibly solicitous to new members; the same could not be said of others. Edward Heath, former Prime Minister, never uttered a word to me in the eight years I was in the House. When he saw me coming towards him down a corridor, if he could not take a detour, he would lift his eyes (and his nose) high in grand disdain. He obviously felt about me exactly what I felt about him – only he could show it more openly. Like me, he was a grammar schoolboy (though he did not have the experience of three secondary modern schools first), but that is where the similarity ends. It is indeed strange that all these years later, and with no warning, I am catapulted into a situation, not of my making, where I am obliged to seek to defend him – not for his political views, which I continue to berate, knowing them well, but for his personal and private life, about which, at the time, I was ignorant.

In politics, I have always been more attracted to principles than personalities. The latter can be a distraction from the real business of policy decision-making based on principles long-held and developed. One woman who combined both, however, was Margaret Thatcher. When I became an MP, I saw her most nights of the parliamentary week. Without abusing the privilege, you could have a word with her quite easily in the division lobbies or within twenty-four hours if you requested a meeting and if she was in the country. I did not think she was right on everything, and I was prepared to rebel against her leadership if I felt she had become under the spell of the 'wets' or her civil servants. Much has been written about her; I did not think her *Spitting Image* creation was accurate, nor did I feel Alan Clark's admiration of her in a sexual way carried much weight in reality. Politically, she stuck to her policy guns. Unlike her predecessors, she did not commit her party to U-turns at the behest of the civil service. I have two particular memories of her, both to her credit.

During the Falklands War, whenever she heard of the death of a serving member of our armed forces, she did not sleep without penning a handwritten letter to their next of kin. I think that is to her eternal credit. I know subsequent Prime Ministers followed her example, but I do not think it was done quite like that before her premiership. I believe it was her maternal instincts that pushed her to do it.

She was also good at small talk and was sympathetic to the plight of her colleagues. Inviting members of one's party organisation and other important figures in your constituency to lunch or dinner at the Commons was an important social duty for any Member; for a new one it was mandatory. To have dinner in one of the restaurants of the House, for the guests to see who they could spot and identify – whether hero or villain – at the same feeding trough, and then to be in the Strangers' Gallery to witness the winding-up speeches and the vote was a perk a Member could give. A back-bench Member had few perks at his disposal but this was certainly one of them. One night I was committed to play host to two senior constituency Conservatives. However, the business of the House finished early, there was the customary dash to the Members' entrance to get away and yet I had to stay and entertain in the Harcourt Room (now the Churchill Room). I made my apologies to the two, who hid their disappointment well. They knew me, had no need to see me and the 'spotting' game was over as the restaurants were completely empty. We made perfunctory conversation, knowing the ability to walk into an empty Chamber at 10 p.m. was no match to the oratorical slogging match they had been looking forward to witnessing. Suddenly, there was a rustle of activity at a neighbouring table as waiters got it ready. They thought their job was done, just serving my guests and me. The Prime Minister and her husband Denis then walked into the restaurant and sat down at the table. Margaret ordered a whisky – 'and make it a large one', she said. Surveying the empty room and recognising my predicament, she immediately came over and started up a conversation with my guests and me and kept it going throughout dinner. My guests went from understandable disappointment to the height of ecstasy having Margaret's ear and being able to dine out for months on the fact that they had met with the PM. They were as eternally grateful to me as I was to the Prime Minister.

It is superfluous for me to express my admiration of Mrs Thatcher here, but it was based to a very large extent on the policies and thoughts she articulated and put into statute law rather than her personal skills of small talk, so woefully lacking in her Conservative predecessor. History will treat Mrs T much better than contemporary opinion. During my travels abroad, she was extremely well-regarded and foreigners I met were always jealous that Britain had in its first female Prime Minister a character they would have wanted for themselves. Her reputation will continue to grow and her premiership, which I was privileged to have been able to support for eight of her years in the House, will rank supreme alongside Churchill's wartime stint. If I could have served in any two parliaments in the twentieth century, I would have chosen those I was fortunate enough to have done so, between 1979 to 1987.

Getting to know the parliamentary niceties was important. It took time; some members never get the hang of them. Many of these niceties, I am told by former colleagues still in the House, have been swept aside; others the reformers want to ditch as soon as they see an opportunity. For example, I rather liked the voting system. It meant, by voting in person by walking into one of two lobbies, you could meet your colleagues, have a word with a minister, which might save a letter, get a quick answer to a nagging point, or whatever. Voting robotically from your office would be quicker, yes, but MPs would lose so much more time overall without that face-to-face time. It would, paradoxically, slow up the system. Early on, I was voting in the aye lobby one night when I literally ran into trouble. There are actually two votes taken on any division; one when you leave one of two large rooms where clerks sit at two high desks, and tick downwards against your written name on a list (the written vote that appears in Hansard the next day). But the result is required more urgently so other parliamentary business can take place. This counted vote is announced within minutes of the division bell sounding calling members to vote. It is achieved by four 'tellers' (usually party whips; two from each side) counting members as they leave the two division lobbies showing their full face. In the past, some members would dress their servants up in their cloak, hat and scarf pulled tight over their face, and send them in to vote in their stead, which saved them the hassle of leaving their drink in the bar. I am not sure parliamentary aides would not perform a similar duty for their masters now, should electronic voting ever materialise at Westminster. On this particular night, I followed Angus Maude, the Paymaster General, out of the lobby. Suddenly he stopped and bowed his head extravagantly, taking some time about it. I was not to know he had developed over many years in the House an elaborate, almost theatrical manner of 'showing his face' and I charged onwards, eager to show my own face and not realising Angus was standing in the way. I kicked him hard on the back of one of his legs, upon which, aghast, I apologised profusely. He grabbed my arm and pulled me aside. 'Young man,' he declared with a wry smile that immediately put me at ease, 'everyone in my political life has kicked me, why should you be any different?' and then walked to the government front bench.

Gradually ever so gradually, I started to get the hang of the place. In the same way as Badge Messengers in white tie and tails and police officers, delivered messages for Members on green cards around the place, got to know by sight and name all the new members, I tried to learn the names of other members' constituencies by heart. It is another sound practice that you refer to each other in the House as 'the Honourable' or 'Right Honourable Member for', and then insert their particular constituency. It is, as such, much more difficult to insult a part of a city, a whole town or county if you get angry with an MP in the Commons!

I started to think about making my maiden speech. It was conventional wisdom that you could not or should not address the House, even to ask a question, before this had been done, so it was important to get it under your belt. However, as there were many new members in the 1979 parliament and the Speaker had made it clear that he would only accept a few in each debate, it was going to take several weeks. I decided to ask an oral question before attempting a speech. I had already put down questions for written answer. It was 21 May and the question was about the paper industry – I was on safe ground. Even before I addressed the House, on 19 June, I had voted against the government concerning the competence of the European Community on aircraft noise. Only one other Conservative rebelled and that was

Neil Marten. I was castigated by my whip John MacGregor. I am not sure, but I might have been the first of the new intake of MPs to rebel.

I considered long and hard on what subject to devote to my first contribution to debate. When I left university, I might have guessed it would be immigration; ten years later, I had become very concerned about our membership of the Common Market. It permeated all our political life and seemed appropriate to address the subject. My maiden speech took place on 16 July 1979, just after 5 p.m. My mother and Terry were in the Strangers' Gallery and inevitably it was a proud moment. This is what I said:

> It is a privilege to make my maiden speech in this debate. It is a particular pleasure for me to speak after the Rt Hon. Member for Battersea North (Mr Jay) and my Hon. Friend the Member for Scarborough (Mr Shaw), the views of both of whom I respect very much indeed. It was in the Young Conservatives in Scarborough that I first cut my political teeth.
>
> I have the honour and privilege to represent in this House the electors of Basildon. It is a large constituency – the second largest in England and Wales – with over 103,000 voters. It is a very varied constituency. It has a new town, Basildon, with its associated residential areas of Laindon to the west and Pitsea to the east, and two more traditional towns well known in this House, Billericay and Wickford, to the north. There are several charming villages and farms in between, which must not be forgotten.
>
> The election result in Basildon on 3 May was notable. It was one of the best in England for the Conservative Party, with a swing of a little over 11 per cent. My grateful thanks were due to a hard-working agent, Mrs Peggy Marshall, and a happy and enthusiastic band of Conservative Party workers.

Many former Labour supporters voted Tory for the first time. They did so for numerous reasons. Of course, many wished to buy their own corporation or council homes. Many are already doing so, thanks to a Conservative administration. Many wanted improvements in the commuter service into London, on both the Liverpool Street Line and the Fenchurch Street Line. Many skilled workers were dismayed at the depressing of their differentials as a result of pay curbs and controls.

Many people, having fled from the problems created in inner London by New Commonwealth immigration in the 1950s, 1960s and 1970s, voted Tory because they did not want that self-same problem to follow them into the new town.

At this juncture, I pay a warm tribute to my predecessor, Mr Eric Moonman. He had been a Member of the House on two occasions – from 1966 to 1970 for the seat of Billericay, and from February 1974 until this year for the Basildon constituency. He was well known in this House for his work for many causes, particularly that of mental health. In the constituency he had the reputation as a good constituency Member of Parliament, and I hope to follow in his footsteps.

I also hope to follow in the footsteps of my Hon. Friends who have represented part of my constituency – the Hon. Member for Essex, South East (Sir B. Braine), the Hon. and Learned Member for South Fylde (Mr Gardner), the Hon. Member for Holland with Boston (Mr Body) and the Hon. Member for Brentwood & Ongar (Mr McCrindle).

There are three points that I wish to make, two of which I believe will command almost universal support and the first which may not. First, the gross community budget is too large and should be reduced. It should not be used as an engine to drive us into economic and monetary union, as set out in the documents before the House. I agree with the Right Hon. Member for Battersea North that we should not be seeking further sources of finance for the EEC until we have sorted out the CAP position.

Secondly, the community budget contains a grievous imbalance – and I refer of course to the common agricultural policy, which my Hon. Friend the Financial Secretary mentioned as absorbing 70 per cent of the budget. The Conservative Party is committed to radically reforming the CAP – and the sooner the better for the British taxpayer, consumer and farmer. I share the views of Rt. Hon. and Hon. Members who have spoken in the debate that our share of the net contribution to the EEC budget is too large. The financial mechanism of 1975 that was intended to reduce our contribution has been calculated in the preliminary draft budget, volume 7A, pages 513 to 517, at 68 million units of account, or some £44 million as against the deficit of over £1,000 million. That is peanuts; it is not good enough. It is a Conservative manifesto pledge that we shall reduce the burden that the community budget places on the public sector borrowing requirement and the British taxpayer. If unilateral action is required and nothing else, then unilateral action it must be.

I quote from an observation in paragraph 96 of the White Paper of 1971: 'Thus in the government's view neither our contribution to nor our receipts from the community budget in the 1980s are susceptible of valid estimation at this stage.' That was rather an understatement. It went on: 'And it is for this reason that the community declared to us during the course of the negotiations that if unacceptable situations should arise, "the very survival of the community would demand that the institutions find equitable solutions".' So they must.

In all these areas where change is required I believe that the government will have the full support of the House and the country. Whether ministers wear a velvet glove in preference to a mailed fist is of purely academic interest. At certain times both will be required. What our people seek are results.

If it is not trying the patience of the House too much, I shall close with some general observations on the current position of the EEC. Three options are open. There is federalism and economic and monetary union, leading to a single currency, common economic policies, common taxation and common external policies. That will lead inevitably to a supra-national State – a United States of Europe.

Secondly, there is a continuation of what we have now – the break-up and breakdown of the EEC in disagreement, mutual distrust and recrimination. Unless the EEC can get to grips with the large food surpluses, the CAP will collapse and with it the whole edifice of the bureaucratic structure of the EEC Commission. Some Right Hon. and Hon. Gentlemen may think that that time should not be long away.

Thirdly, a more positive view is that we should seek to establish a partnership of nation states, each sovereign and supreme. That would require the EEC to change its rules and role, its format and outlook, to reject the Treaty of Rome as outdated and old hat, and establish a free-trade area in Western Europe – as wide and diverse as possible. That is the sound and sensible approach – the middle way.

Some have supported federalism honourably because they believe that the nation state has had its day. I believe that they are out of keeping with the spirit of the age. The renaissance of the sovereign state and this, our independent Parliament, is at hand.

Sadly, those closing words are as apt today some thirty-odd years later.

My speech was followed by Russell Johnston, a fervent pro-Common Market Liberal. He very kindly said my speech was clear, assertive, but not aggressive in manner. Sir Ronald Bell also commented, saying generously,

> It gives me great pleasure to speak after my Hon. Friend the Member for Basildon. I admired his maiden speech greatly and agreed with it. I admire his confidence and the forthright way in which he expresses his opinions. The House looks forward to the day when he is no longer inhibited by the convention of not being controversial. It gives me special pleasure to congratulate him because for so long I have agreed with the views that he has expressed outside the House. I had always hoped that one day he would have the opportunity to express them inside.

Summing up the debate for Labour, Peter Shore said:

> It is my pleasant duty to open my remarks by congratulating the Hon. Member for Basildon on his maiden speech. We all welcome and appreciate his remarks about his predecessor, Eric Moonman, a colleague whom we all miss. Virtually all of us were enheartened by the Hon. Gentleman's approach, which seemed to me to be a healthy and a non-ideological approach to EEC affairs. His general message on the future of Europe, of national states co-operating for common aims where it is sensible to do so, and the way he turned his face against a supranational Europe, will find an increasingly resonant echo on both sides of the House. We look forward to his future contributions, especially on the whole question of the EEC.

Nigel Lawson replied on behalf of the government. He said:

> I begin by congratulating my Hon. Friend the Member for Basildon on his excellent maiden speech. I shall not comment in detail on the many points that he made about his constituency and the germane arguments that he put to the House about the matter that we are discussing.
>
> One of his remarks stuck in my mind. He said that the British people seek results in this difficult matter. That is right. It is not a question of discussing precisely the best negotiating tactic to achieve those results. At the end of the day, we shall stand to be judged by the people according to the results that we can achieve. What I have said about my Hon. Friend is more than a formality. I hope that we shall have the pleasure of hearing him on many occasions in future.

I went home that night thinking I had scaled the first obstacle in a parliamentary life unscarred. I was pleased. I was in my element. I had everything. I thought I might be rather good at the role I had taken on and that justified all the sacrifices I was making to be in it.

Parliamentary life predominated everything. I had no 'pair' – a Labour MP I could agree with not to vote on the perceived less important parliamentary issues – so I had to be at the House most times there was a vote Monday to Thursday. The piece of paper issued on a Thursday afternoon set out the following week's business and when the whips would like you to attend the House. Two or three lines underlining an item of business stressed the importance of your presence. With no 'pair', however, these mattered not a jot to me, the assumption was that I would always be there – and it was also assumed I would vote with the government. I was assiduous in my parliamentary duties and attendance and it meant my voting record was second to none in support of Mrs Thatcher's government, even including several members of the Whips' Office, who traditionally always had to be present in the House on whip's business. It did not mean I always voted the way they would have wished.

I was subjected to pressure from the Whips' Office on numerous occasions. To begin with, this took the form of the usual persuasive tactics – for example in the run-up to a vote on which I had expressed my intention to abstain or vote against a government measure (usually on immigration, the European Community or Northern Ireland). As the vote inched nearer, however, and if I was not the only dissenter, I would be asked whether I would like to see this or that minister to talk it over in his or her office, politely over a drink or, more impolitely, as a carpeting exercise, without. Occasionally, a whip would buttonhole you in a corridor and start shouting at you, presumably to try to embarrass you in front of others. They would then threaten to place you on a dull committee, where your time would be eaten up to no avail or insist you could not go on a long-planned trip abroad – often organised by the whips themselves.

On no occasion did any whip mention their office's alleged black book of misdemeanours, in which, supposedly, Members' private transgressions were listed for future use against them. If I had been so listed, I rebelled so often I am sure it would have been brought out and used on me. I am not saying the book, if it did exist, contained no reference to me – it might have done – rather it was never used as a threat. There were sufficient other threats in the early years – but not that. I never sought help from the whips on personal matters as far as I can recall, so I was not indebted to them in any way.

I recall arguing with Tristan Garel-Jones one afternoon in the committee room corridor when he was a whip. I was so incensed by a criticism he had of me and what I thought was unfair whipping tactics that I said, rather innocently, that if that was his position, I would refuse to vote with the government for a week – and not just the matter in hand. It was brinkmanship and he was both shocked and furious. He said that was blackmail, but I thought the best way to treat whips was to verbally attack them back if provoked. Tristan was in his early period in the Whips' Office and since then he no doubt refined his tactics and I think I gained his respect. In the end, I didn't carry out my threat. He was a tough cookie and he went on to be an important, albeit silent force to be reckoned with in the party and in the government.

There was one night, however, when matters did get out of hand. It was on a vote on Northern Ireland. I think it was 1982 and I had voted against the government and, after returning from the voting lobby, I sat in my place awaiting the continuation of business. My favoured seat was on a row one before the back and on a seat just below the gangway. There was always a rush to gain the seat you wanted and it was tradition that you placed a prayer card on the seat you desired on the morning of that day. If, by tradition, you attended prayers before start of business in the early afternoon, the seat was yours for the rest of that day. There was another tradition that seemed to take precedence, namely that a senior member of your party, maybe a Right Honourable, could arrive and shift you from the preferred gangway seat; some would even tear up your prayer card. On this occasion in 1982, it was late in the evening and I had not been shifted. I was leaning back, surveying Members moving around the Chamber, and suddenly, the government Deputy Chief Whip, straight out of *House of Cards*, rushed in swearing. He made a beeline for me and I still to this day do not know why. He shouted obscene remarks at me – of a heterosexual, not a homosexual variety

– and had to be physically held back from punching me. A Member can never be drunk in the Chamber, so let us say he was tired and emotional. He was John Stradling Thomas, MP for Monmouth. John had a perfect public-school mixture of utter charm and blatant thuggery; that night he did not show his charm. If he thought he might provoke me, he failed. I think I am mild-mannered at the best of times, and rarely get angry or rise to the bait. I was, however, shocked, and remember colleagues, more concerned than I, consoling me as John was dragged away by others. Fortunately for him, there were so many Members on their feet that the Speaker did not see the incident, or if he did he turned a Nelsonian blind eye. Neither John nor I mentioned it again.

My regional Essex whips were, first, John MacGregor and then John Major. Both were diplomatic. By the time John Major was in place, I was known for being an independently minded MP. He and I would discuss issues carefully and politely and I never felt threatened by him. As well as being of my own mind, I was also known, however, as someone who would always, without fail, inform the whips of my voting intention. The whipping system works only if they know what is to happen and the weight of opinion in the party on any issue. What they cannot abide is doubt. If they know they are to be defeated, they will put pressure on the minister in charge of a measure to withdraw it, rethink it or represent it. They cannot do that if party members try to conceal their intentions; I did not and was open with them. The pressure from the whips in my second parliament was a lot less stressful than in my first.

Despite the pressure, I certainly found the whips to have a compassionate side. Once, I returned from a visit to Gabon, in 1985 I think, with all the symptoms of a heavy flu. That day was Budget Day and I had to be present to vote on a three-line whip. In the evening I was on a committee dealing with the passage of a Bill. As time went on I physically deteriorated, my temperature rose and, although I wished to stay, the government whip on the committee sent me home. Three days later, I was admitted to the Hospital for Tropical Diseases with malaria and I was there for over two weeks.

I am credited with making the longest speeches in the House of Commons. It started at 11.49 p.m. on the evening of 7 August 1980 and I resumed my seat at 5.35 p.m. on 12 November 1980. That was a lengthy contribution, but there was a parliamentary summer recess in between; it was on an adjournment debate on the subject of financial assistance to opposition parties. A number of my colleagues and I had been kept up on successive nights in the summer of that year and, in revenge, we decided that we would talk out a motion tabled by the Leader of the House, Norman St John-Stevas, to increase the amounts paid to opposition parties. The increase, which was way ahead of the rate of inflation, would not be held off for ever, but we could at least delay it until the late autumn.

Mid-way through the adjournment debate, I was called to speak. While on my feet, my colleagues informed me that I had to keep speaking so that, when the time came for the vote, it could not be taken. I had prepared very little material, but my colleagues interjected in my speech to help me keep it going. Labour MPs were incandescent with rage but had to accept that their late-night activities, keeping us up night after night, had rebounded on them. The motion stood adjourned. It was not a filibuster as such and had not been planned but, rather, it 'materialised' as the evening wore onwards.

When the government motion was scheduled for further debate, I asked the clerks at the Table Office whether I could speak again. I was told not only could I speak again, but technically I was mid-speech and so held the floor. So, when we reconvened after the recess, I continued my speech. Hence my claim, technical though it is, to hold the record for the longest speech.

On most of the major issues facing the government – inflation, trade-union reform and the economy – I fully supported the government. On issues where I had little or no experience, I sought advice. One such matter jumped out at me from a constituent's letter I read in the Chamber during a vote. It requested more public facilities for breastfeeding. I looked around for inspiration and found it in the form of Edwina Currie sitting just in front of me. She kindly advised me to send a supportive response, which I did. On another subject, on which I had a little more, but still very private, experience – homosexuality – while I did not initiate reform, whenever a change or reform in the law came before the House, I supported it. I did not wish to be a hypocrite, but nor was I to be a frontrunner. With hindsight, and with regret, I should not have been so reluctant; the climate of opinion was very different to that of today. I was not involved in Section 28 issues as that legislation was introduced after I left the House.

The subject of my homosexuality burst into the mainstream media limelight, for the first time I believe, in 1981, when the strains of living with a Member of Parliament finally took its toll on Terry. He had never visited my constituency, but felt it and the House took too much of 'our' time and he left after a disagreement. Unfortunately, he made his views public. The tabloid press swooped. Non-political friends advised me to say as little as possible in response. I did not wish to discuss my personal life in or through the media, so I took their advice. As the long summer recess was about to start, I went abroad. No one in my constituency talked to me about it except the press. The issue went away, but I was badly bruised by the experience and had lost the friend I had relied on for seven years. Privately, we both suffered emotionally, but when the dust settled we saw each other every week and he subsequently married and had two children.

Later in that summer, I went to Berlin for a conference organised by the Konrad Adenauer Foundation. It was to take my mind off my private life, where there was now an emptiness. During the week, I walked through Checkpoint Charlie on an unannounced visit to East Berlin. It was intimidating walking in and out under the sights of tanks and sub-machine guns and bolstered my view later of how courageous Mrs Thatcher was in facing up to and, together with President Reagan, defeating the Soviet Union in the Cold War. I think she will always be remembered for that.

It was another war, however, that had more immediate impact on Parliament: the Falklands. During it, you felt the weight of history was upon you. It is not often that Parliament is called to sit on a Saturday, still less called to discuss going to war and then vote for it. Even more unusual, perhaps, was the occasion on which the backbench Conservative 1922 Committee hears from a senior Conservative statesman, on this occasion Lord Carrington, the Foreign Secretary, and then destroys him verbally in a single meeting. I was shocked at the ruthless demolition of such a senior figure, however deserved.

The Falklands War was waged and from then on, together with other Members, I would constantly be studying the ticker-tape machine to gain the latest news, often in the late evening. The death and injury impacted upon one forever. I went to the funeral of one of the youngest soldiers to die, at Goose Green, who was from my constituency. I was impressed at the pride and fortitude of his parents. I never questioned the decision to fight was absolutely the right one, but the price was very heavy. Years later, at Belvoir, I met Robert Osborne. Like his parents, he worked at Belvoir Castle.

He was in the Scots Guards regiment and lost a leg in the closing days of the war. He was a constant reminder of the commitment and bravery made by others when politicians decide on a certain course of action in the comfortable atmosphere of Westminster. He and his mother, Sheila, have always been very supportive towards me, especially in recent months. I am indebted to them both and I will always be thankful for the sacrifice he and so many others made on their country's behalf.

I am often criticised for my views on immigration and race relations and I will come to that thorny subject, but I think some do me a disservice by solely concentrating on that issue to the exclusion of other causes I took up in the House. I made many speeches on new town development corporation issues concerning housing and planning development. Another important matter I tackled was mental health reform. I was very honoured to sit on the special committee set up to consider the Committee Stage of the 1983 Mental Health Reform Bill. It was one of Norman St John-Stevas's reforms to allow certain committees to cross-examine witnesses before commencing the line-by-line reading of the Bill. I became very friendly with the mental health charity Mind and with certain psychiatrists. I also paid a visit to Broadmoor to meet a constituent to discuss his concerns, which I took up with a minister. He was reputed to be an arsonist and I met him in an interview room with a large, red, bell push on the wall. I just hoped I could reach it if there was any trouble. I need not have worried; he was articulate and polite and just wanted help. He was in the same ward as one of the Kray twins, but we didn't meet. Nor did I meet or see Jimmy Savile, who apparently had had keys for Broadmoor since 1968 and had the run of the place. I was in ignorance of his involvement in the establishment and certainly what was alleged years later.

Deliberation on the committee was intense, but it was satisfying to work on reforming legislation concerning the mentally ill. No such review had been conducted since 1959 and it initiated the long-overdue closure of many Victorian institutions where many poor souls spent decades of their life forgotten and untreated, out of sight and out of mind and, for politicians, with no vote. That I had a part in providing greater protection for the mentally ill is a proud memory for me. Henceforth, a second opinion had to be sought to detain a patient thought to be suffering from mental illness. It is a pity that the resources that were made available to National Health trusts around the country did not make their way fully into providing for greater resources for care in the community projects.

On immigration and race-relation issues, I was not afraid to say in the Chamber of the Commons what I gained a reputation for saying outside it, namely, that immigration from the New Commonwealth and Pakistan in the 1960s and 1970s had been at too high a level and that voluntary repatriation, and I stress the word voluntary, should have a role to play in reducing numbers.

In a debate on the immigration rules in 1980, I said:

> I am pleased to take up the remarks of the Rt. Hon. Member for Down, South (Mr Powell), who has spoken inside and outside the House on a number of occasions on this subject when politicians of both main parties have felt, like some Hon. Members tonight, that he would do best to be silent about the issue on which he speaks so well and so succinctly.
>
> The Rt. Hon. Gentleman began by saying that the House rarely debates this subject. He referred to the last full debate on immigration and emigration held on 24 May 1976. It is a pity that we do not discuss the subject at greater length. The fact that

we do not debate it at further length contributes to the fear that many whom we represent have come to associate with the issue. We are indebted to Her Majesty's Opposition for the fact that we have this debate, but we temper our indebtedness in the knowledge that they seek less rather than more control over immigration from the New Commonwealth.

I represent a constituency that has been little affected by immigration of large numbers of citizens from the New Commonwealth to our shores over the past three decades. However, many of the voters whom I have the honour to represent have experienced – many of their relatives are still experiencing – the problems in the inner cities that such migrations have exacerbated. We cannot turn a blind eye to present and future racial strife merely because we represent constituencies in the greener pastures of, for example, Mid-Essex.

Successive governments have heard the fears of black and white alike. They have witnessed the strains and stresses on the surface in our inner-city areas and in our urban conurbations. Both parties have responded by imposing successive controls on immigration, Alas, they may all be typified by the words 'Too little and too late'.

Racial harmony and avoidance of strife will be achieved only when the indigenous population see a fall rather than a rise in the total New Commonwealth population resident in the United Kingdom. Simply stopping the immigrant flow will not now, regrettably, be sufficient to bring this about.

[...] This subject and the fears of our people about it will not go away with the passing of these rules. The House will be driven to return to it. I hope that it will return to it before long.

On 15 December 1982, I took part in and was responsible for one of the few defeats of the government on the floor of the House. It was on the immigration rules. I spoke as follows:

> I wish to explain to the House why I signed the motion in the name of the Leader of the Liberal Party and why I intend, with regret, to vote against the government tonight.
>
> I did so as a sign of encouragement.
>
> After all, this is the first recorded act of the Liberal Party to oppose a measure the effect of which is to increase immigration from the New Commonwealth and Pakistan. [...]
>
> Much has been said tonight about manifesto commitments. I shall vote against the rules, because our party has made promises in successive manifestos, most notably in 1970 and in 1979, and they have all worn rather thin. I have begun to wonder whether anyone will believe us next time. In 1970, we said that there will be no further large-scale permanent immigration from the New Commonwealth. Since then, more than 560,000 immigrants from the New Commonwealth and Pakistan have entered this country legally. Since our manifesto commitment in 1979, more than 100,000 immigrants have entered Britain legally. Such is the betrayal of public confidence and faith.
>
> [...] I make no criticism of any individual immigrant from the New Commonwealth and Pakistan. If I had been in their position I, too, would probably have come to Britain. The blame rests not with the immigrants, nor with the indigenous community, which has been incredibly tolerant. The criticism is of successive politicians of both parties during the past thirty years. That is where the criticism should correctly remain.
>
> At a time when we are facing a breakdown of law, order and

authority, it is hardly helpful to the encouragement of good race relations to put still greater strain on the tensions that are to be found in our society, especially in inner-city areas where immigrant communities are concentrated.

I do not believe that these rules have the support of the British people. They are demonstrably detrimental to British interests. They will undermine our self-confidence and our identity. They are a disgrace and the betrayal of our promises is a greater disgrace. Such disgrace deserves defeat.

The measure was defeated by 290 to 272 votes. It was a significant defeat.

On 15 February 1983, when the matter returned to the House, I said:

I shall set out to the House immediately the premise upon which I base all my arguments. We have now and have had for many years too many immigrants from the New Commonwealth and Pakistan to be integrated peacefully in our society. Those who witnessed the riots in our inner-city areas, members of the public if not Members of this House, know full well the common sense of that statement. They will agree that enough is enough.

The House will not therefore be surprised to learn that I will be supporting the action of my Hon. Friend the Member for Orpington (Mr Stanbrook) and my Hon. Friend the Member for Chorley (Mr Dover) in the division lobbies tonight against these immigration rules.

[…] Why are we in this position? I believe that it is because the government do not wish to introduce primary legislation on immigration. That is why they fear the quota and the register and

indeed the demands of myself and others, which will increase in
the months and years ahead, that those who currently have the
right to come here will probably have to lose those rights if we
are to maintain law, order and liberty in this country. The consequences and the alternatives mean that that will be the better
of the two evils that will face us in the future. I regret that I shall
have to vote against my government tonight but I am consistent
to my principle and to my constituents on this issue.

The government won the vote by 261 to 298 votes. Numerous previous rebels got back into line; I retained my principles.

I also drew attention to the proportion of immigrant births in the
1980s that were to mothers of NCWP (New Commonwealth and
Pakistani) ethnic origins. I made the point that those percentages –
20, 25 and 30 per cent in inner-city areas and cities in the Midlands
and the north – if repeated over a generation (twenty-five years)
would inevitably produce the same proportion of the whole population. I was ridiculed for the impertinence to say as much; I have
since been proved right.

To speak on this subject as I did was not easy and the political
intelligentsia of the day derided me and others who did so. It was
all a question of numbers, yet we were called racists and smeared.
On 13 October, at a Conservative Party conference at Blackpool,
I proposed a motion on behalf of Billericay Conservative Association on immigration, voluntary repatriation and race relations.
I said controls of a tougher nature were required: 'It's not racism,
its realism.' The motion, which had been selected for debate by
conference representatives, was narrowly defeated. My speech was
well-received – probably Home Office civil servants and Conservative Central Office did not like it – and coverage of it was good.

A colleague of mine said he did not like a word I had said but that he thought it was a brilliant speech.

I think people who know me know also I have not a racist bone in my body and in my personal dealings I am more likely to discriminate positively in favour rather than against a person of another colour. In the words of Iain Macleod, in my life I have always been 'colour-blind rather than colour-prejudiced'. Looking back over my life, much of my personal heartache has been caused by my speaking out on this issue. For me it has always been a matter of principle to stick to strongly held beliefs, whatever the cost. I have not spoken politically for twenty-eight years on these matters. I believe I was right at the time and subsequent Prime Ministers and governments of both parties have spoken out more vehemently in support on the subject in a way I could never have done, but only when nothing could be done about it. Ex-ministers often speak the truth when they are unencumbered by office or bureaucrats. I have never understood why. Generations to come will wonder why a totally unnecessary problem was brought to our shores and why those who pointed to the problem at the time were so cruelly treated. If I was in the House today, I hope I would still have the fortitude to speak out on immigration matters as Europe, not just Britain, becomes overwhelmed by non-European migration. Our geographical advantage – of being an island – was squandered by generations of politicians after the Second World War. Genuine asylum seekers and refugees are one thing – we have a proud history of catering for those, Jews and Huguenots, for example – mass migration first from the New Commonwealth and now from anywhere in the world, but particularly from the Middle East and from North Africa, is quite another.

I was not surprised that the press, especially the Maxwell stable of newspapers, disliked me. I had, after all, defeated Maxwell's friend

Eric Moonman. He used his papers to gain his revenge. He disliked my views on immigration but knew that in my constituency and nationally they were popular. They changed tack.

The *Sunday People* alleged that, in PMQs, Mrs Thatcher had not given me the usual courtesy of the accolade 'My Honourable Friend' when answering one of my parliamentary questions. The inference the newspaper was trying to spread was that she did not like me. This was odd to me, as I had no knowledge of her alleged antipathy towards me – in fact just the reverse. So I did a bit of research. It was not always the case that the Prime Minister in answering a parliamentary question from one of her colleagues used the term 'My Honourable Friend'. Sometimes it wasn't said, did not need to be said and no inference as to the state of their friendliness or otherwise could be drawn from or inference implied from such an omission. When I looked at the relevant Hansard, the parliamentary verbatim record, it was clear. The Prime Minister in answer to my question had not only said 'My Honourable Friend', but had used the term at least three times during her answer, culminating in the statement: 'My Honourable Friend is absolutely right.' Sometimes Hansard is known for inserting courtesies which were not extended, so to be sure I listened to the audio tape. Hansard was right. My solicitor, who was by now my friend Jonathan Denby, contacted the newspaper. They issued a grovelling apology in the High Court and paid the costs of my action against them. They could do no other and did not countersue. It was an embarrassing climb-down for Maxwell. I went to hear the apology read in the High Court and a retraction appeared in the newspaper. They never forgave me and the consequences were to be dramatic and disastrous.

In 1983, the Falklands War over and opinion polls swinging towards the government, thoughts turned towards another general election.

Boundary changes had been in the offing for over a year. It was obvious that my large electorate would be split and, therefore, my constituency would be recast. These deliberations and outcomes can sometimes be prolonged and messy. It was finally agreed that the new town of Basildon in the south should form its own constituency. The rest would not come up to an electorate of 65,000 and would require more voters from somewhere, so it was agreed to take them from the eastern part of Thurrock in the wards of Stanford-le-Hope, Corringham and Fobbing, the Homesteads and Orsett. I had good relations in the area already, especially with a former docker, Ted Attewell who had become Mrs Thatcher's number one fan, his family and friends. Councillors on Thurrock Council were also very supportive. Local Conservative Associations were established to mirror the new constituencies. I am pleased, and very flattered, to say that both associations asked me to be their candidate. I was very honoured by the requests. As a sensible chap, I opted for the area where I had bought a house, the Billericay constituency, and one that was the safer seat. Not that I thought Basildon would not return a Conservative Member. I thought that, with the right candidate, although it would be close, we would 'gain' a seat; two Conservative MPs for the price of one. Having readily understood my decision without rancour, the Basildon selection committee met and gave themselves a choice between David Amess and Buster Mottram, Britain's number-one tennis star at the time. I was present. David won and went on to be a splendid MP and ambassador for Basildon New Town.

I had known Buster too. He facilitated my ability to say now that I once played tennis at Wimbledon on semi-finals day. He had kindly invited me to lunch during one Wimbledon Championship, after which he took me into the hallowed changing rooms where we met Ivan Lendl, who was to play that afternoon. There was time to take a walk before the start of his match and, as we did, we came across the Lawn Tennis Association's Junior Programme in action, two teams of children playing short tennis with a soft ball. Professional commentators had collected a large crowd and as they eyed Buster they mentioned him and persuaded him to play. He would only do so if I agreed to join him. We slipped off our city shoes and I did my best. I am sure the crowd had no idea who I was. Tennis was one of the few games I played at this time. I subsequently played tennis at Queen's Club on a number of occasions with the present Mr Speaker, John Bercow. I wonder if he has forgotten – but more of Mr Speaker anon.

So, Basildon had its candidate and I canvassed for David as much as I could. Not that I neglected my own new seat, but it was regarded to be safe. How the 'wets' must have hated the thought that I had gone from fighting the 'unwinnable' Basildon constituency to now having a likely very safe Conservative seat. As I say, though, I did not treat it as such. We had as good a campaign team in 1983 as we had in 1979. Once again, I stood as a Conservative and Unionist candidate. It was just as time-consuming, but I knew the ropes and enjoyed fighting elections. My election manifesto was professionally produced; this time the photographs were taken by Geoff, my secretary's husband. It was a quality product. I was now reasonably well known in the area and had already got to know the Conservative supporters in East Thurrock. Everyone wanted to see me; they all wanted a word, and I wanted to see them. With such support, the popularity of the Prime Minister following the Falklands, and my high profile on certain political issues, we achieved the wonderful majority of 14,615 and received over 53 per cent of the votes cast. David won, too, in Basildon New Town. The Conservatives were a shoo-in.

I had my fair share of hate mail during the election. Par for the course being a candidate or a Member, but I did object to burning pieces of paper being pushed through my house's letter box located in the front door and just behind a curtain. There was little damage from this failed attempt to set my home on Jacksons Lane in Billericay on fire and both my mother and I were out at the time, but the consequences could have been grave. The police seemed uninterested. In security terms, this was quite unlike the 1979 election. If there was protection it was virtually invisible, though matters were to change soon.

Before the terrible events of 1984 unfolded, I and two of my friends, Neil and Gerald, both Members of Parliament with me, were involved in the BBC's dreadful *Panorama* programme called 'Maggie's Militant Tendency'. Michael Cockerell produced a biased and untruthful account of our alleged links with foreign and far-right organisations in Britain and on the Continent. To my face he was friendly and complimentary. The programme was broadcast on 30 January 1984; my colleagues subsequently sued the BBC and won a famous libel action. My good friend Bee Carthew was a 'star' witness and, after her testimony, the BBC caved in. Why, one might ask, did I not sue?

The morning after the programme was broadcast, I was summoned to Conservative Central Office to meet John Selwyn Gummer, the party chairman. He wanted to go through the programme with me line by line. Before we did so, he drew to my attention the startling fact that I appeared on the broadcast wearing three different suits at what was purported to be the same meeting. He said, 'I know you to be many things, but a quick-change artist is not one of them.' My words had been as badly edited as my pictures. John was very friendly and supportive; he knew my record of support for the Conservative Party and for no other. He was a leading 'wet' but recognised that I was not the neo-Nazi or fascist pig *Panorama* had tried to portray me as.

I was less inclined to sue than the others, mainly because I knew how ruinously expensive libel actions could be. But my solicitor, Jonathan Denby, who was now in partnership in a shipping law practice in the City, discussed the programme with me and agreed not only to represent me legally, but, knowing the 'real' me, also to be my 'banker of last resort'; in other words, to fund the action.

I undertook a huge amount of research, demolishing with evidence each critical or malicious point, illuminating each falsehood and, as a result, huge numbers of files amassed at Jonathan's offices. It was very time-consuming and, for him, also very expensive. I understand his partners fell out with him and one of the issues, I believe, was his support for me. He called me in to see him several months later to say he was sorry, but he could no longer back me financially. I had no wealth and subsequently had to sue for peace with the BBC. Thankfully I did not have to pay any of the BBC's costs. I have never forgiven the BBC for the programme and since then have always insisted on doing live interviews with them to avoid this calamity being repeated. In any event, I am happy to wear the badge of being one of 'Maggie's Militant Tendency'. I thought she was a great Prime Minister and am happy to be counted as one of her praetorian guards.

I always tried to go to Conservative Party conferences. When I was an MP, I would go in a group from the constituency headed by the constituency chairman, my agent Peggy and senior ward chairmen and active party workers. We were a happy band and had enjoyed the 1984 Brighton conference. We wined and dined on the Thursday night until after midnight and then we walked to the sea front and decided what choice to make. Either we would go west to the Grand Hotel for one last nightcap in its splendid surroundings, look for who else we could see and meet, or to turn to the east and head for our bed-and-breakfast abode not so far away in Kemptown. Peggy had developed a bit of a headache; she wanted us to stay out but we agreed we would all go back to the B&B and get some rest. With Mrs Thatcher going to speak in the morning and a drive home afterwards, it was to be the usual important and tiring last day. We went east. Just before we got into the little B&B, some of us thought we heard a dull thump or muffled bang. We thought nothing of it and went to bed.

As we woke and made our way to breakfast the next morning, the full enormity of what had happened at the Grand Hotel left us pole-axed. The normal hubbub at breakfast was silent. No one spoke. The gravity of the situation was brought home to us not so much by the collapsed white hotel's frontage and shattered balconies, however dra-matic, but more by the poignant rescue attempts to get Norman Tebbit out of the ruins. Ashen-faced, covered in grey dust on a precarious stretcher, more like a ghost than a man, he was saved in the full glare of television. Five people were not, including the Honourable Anthony Berry, one of my colleagues and the gentlest of men. In mourning them, we mourned the passing of a different age. I never felt quite the same about politics afterwards. There were the brave words of not let-ting the terrorists win so reminiscent of today. In many respects, the terrorists did get their way by the use of the gun and the bomb; they changed government policy by force. I regret that they did.

Was my feeling induced by fear? I had been near to bomb attacks before – I missed one of the Harrods bombs by an hour or so. The Wellington Park Hotel in Belfast had its breakfast room blown up the day after I had breakfast there on one of my annual visits to Northern Ireland. A car bomb was placed under an office block near my apartment in London and the blast shook my flat windows. But this was different; I was not frightened for my own safety. I had paid yearly visits to Ulster even before I was a Member; I felt it a duty to visit and get the feel of the place if you spoke about Northern Ireland affairs. After all, I had been to Crossmaglen by car with Harold McCusker. My Conservative parliamentary colleagues flew into the army barracks and out again by helicopter. I had been with Harold to his constituency and our two RUC protection officers had become agitated, urging that we should leave quickly as an IRA gunman could be whistled up in ten minutes and we had already been in the Market Square for fifteen. No, it was not a feeling of fear. It was simply that a deep depression had set in, maybe about the threat to democratic deliberation and maybe a premonition that my parliamentary life itself was to self-combust, and that I had inexplicably reached my zenith. I had no reason to think so. Life was good and in all other respects I was expected, and logically could expect, to remain a Member of Parliament to a ripe old age, perhaps even to the present. I believed that I had, through years of hard work, earned it, and was sitting on a very safe parliamentary seat.

My inner thoughts were not outwardly obvious as the second parliament got into full swing. My interests widened; I worked with the electricity industry on a kind of parliamentary fellowship, visiting Dinorwig in north Wales, a hydroelectric plant, which stored power for peak demand, say at breakfast time, and used more electricity than it created. I also visited nuclear power plants in the UK and in France and had a general tour of the industry. While a nuclear power station was being constructed, I climbed down ladders within narrow pipes to see the skilled workmanship in its central core. It was very claustrophobic and physically demanding, especially climbing out of it, 40 feet up the same encased ladder. I relished these experiences very much. With my pulp, paper and board industry interests, I enjoyed industrial matters and they kept me busy, as did my constituency.

I was appreciating the House of Commons and felt I was now an experienced Member, better equipped to serve my constituents with their problems. I had mastered parliamentary procedure and I knew my way around. I did not believe I would become a minister, as I had acquired a reputation for common sense, sticking to my guns and not bowing down to the whips. I believe I had done this in a non-confrontational way. Yes, I had upset some in the party on immigration, but I think they knew I was no racialist. They also knew I could not stay silent on such an important issue. It may have been regarded as a quirk, but it was one that would keep me out of office. No Prime Minister could have tolerated the political taunts about me, yet I felt respected for my individual stance on this and other political subjects. I settled down to being what I had always wanted to be, and that was that wonderful, long-standing back-bench Member of Parliament. I might almost have succeeded, had my private life not got in the way.

CHAPTER 6

THE CONSTITUENCY

n 1979, I had such high hopes of being a Member of Parliament for the rest of my life. I had a good majority, was young and enthusiastic and not even contemplating boundary changes at that time. I considered the chances of a bright and long career in the House were reasonable, with only one thing to worry about – my constituency.

I set about ensuring that, whatever else was said, no one could criticise my work on behalf of my constituents. In my selection meetings, I had been asked if I would live in the constituency and had answered that I would buy a house there. London was my home, I had long lived there, but I knew I would require a base locally. My mother was still living in Scarborough; it was a family decision that she should come and live in Billericay in a house that was within walking distance of the high street and the railway station. My brother and I could watch over her better there than on our infrequent trips to Yorkshire. I would be there most weekends and some nights during the week. It was ideal. My brother made all her clothes, too, and they were always commented upon in very complimentary language. She was in her element, becoming a well-known figure on her daily shopping trips, and constituents and party workers would keep a watchful eye on her. While I was in London, however, it was in fact she who was my eyes and ears in the constituency. I often found people would tell her things that they would not say to me directly and she would store up information and then relate the stories to me, which was very useful. She also came with me to the many social events, the dinners, lunches and cheese and wine parties, that abounded. It gave her a new interest and a new lease of life. At home, she would keep my press cuttings in order and take other cuttings of interest she thought I ought to know about, which I appreciated greatly. She was very happy and contented and our arrangement meant I could be with her much more often.

I decided to hold at least three 'surgeries' a month. I wanted to be available to constituents to come and air their points of view, and usually their problems, on set and publicised days. Usually they were held on Saturdays. The first such surgery was in a room at Basildon council offices, which had all the feeling of a modular, prefab building. I was more used to the civic grandeur of Scarborough town hall, a wonderful Victorian building. In comparison, this down-at-heel planning mess lacked gravitas and dignity.

The council waiting room was flooded with people waiting to see me, maybe thirty or forty people. Many wanted to do just that – see their new Member of Parliament. They had no problem; it was simply a kind of voyeurism. All were welcome. I recall a young girl with baby was one of the first. She had a housing problem. She didn't have one – a house, I mean. As I couldn't give her the immediate answer she wanted, or rather a set of keys to one, she began to cry uncontrollably. I was nervous of the reaction on the rest of the supplicants in the waiting room outside, wondering what they'd think of me if they thought I had reduced such a young mother to tears. I waited but with no diminution of the tears and pressed for time, I had to show her out (still crying) while promising I would see what I could do. My agent Peggy said afterwards that there was a lot of twitching among those still waiting to see me.

Surgeries were also held in Billericay and in Wickford. It was in the latter that one of the strangest requests was made. I held my surgery there over an old people's day centre, where we could all have tea from the kitchen. On this particular Saturday morning, a very respectable lady, carrying a large handbag, and a one-legged man mounted the stairs to see me. As soon as they sat down she got out what I thought was an empty Nescafé jar from her bag. She explained that they had come to talk about the woman who lived in one of their adjacent bedsits. She kept rabbits; twenty rabbits, running loose around the woman's bedsit. Well, I could cope with that, after all, I had once visited a constituent who kept a lion in a cage in his garden – this issue was just about rabbits. She then opened the jar to show me the dead evidence of the flea problem that these rabbits had created. Quickly asking her to seal the jar, I turned to the man. He said the woman had not paid her electricity bill and lit her abode by candlelight. He was afraid a rabbit would knock over a candle and set fire to the building. He slept at night without his artificial leg and he was frightened he might not have time to strap it in place should there be a fire and be trapped in the building. Clearly, the woman needed help – so what had been done already? Oh, yes, a social worker had visited her, had gone away and then brought back carrots to feed the rabbits! The problem was eventually sorted with the help of the council, together with a different social worker, to agree that the woman would have only two non-breeding rabbits as pets and assisted her in catching up with her electricity payments.

Of course, the vast majority of the problems could be solved by the people themselves. I do believe I helped to show some of those people maybe a different way of looking at their difficulties. But many needed the help of the county council, the district council, the Basildon New Town Development Corporation and my help with ministers and civil servants. I was often their intermediary. This took time, voluminous correspondence, attention to detail and dedication. I did my best. I believe now, such work is done by MPs' aides; I made it my business to be involved with every case. I read every letter. Whether it was mercenaries in Angola or missing children abroad removed from their mother, the inability of fathers to see their children under court orders or whatever the painful problem was, I was attentive and receptive. If I was to be a glorified social worker, I could cope with that. It was everything I'd wanted to do since I first helped Sir Alexander Spearman to do similar work in his Constitutional Club offices, when I played 'Peggy's role' as a receptionist. It was this hard grind of helping constituents that had first drawn me into politics, and I knew that it allowed me the privilege and honour to express my own opinions on a wider stage.

In the early 1980s, I dealt with the strange case of a constituent's son who had been murdered by Peruvian Indians. He had been tall and blond and the local folklore on the side of the Amazon river where he and a friend had unwisely camped related to white giants stealing away the Indian's souls. This myth was sufficient to cause the locals to shoot him and his friend. It was desperately sad and I needed diplomatic endeavour with the Peruvian ambassador to get to the truth and to retrieve what was left of the poor young man's belongings.

At no time did I tire of holding these surgeries. They will have amounted to several hundred and, at the end, I continued to wrap up as many outstanding cases as I could and hand over those files that I had not had the time to bring to completion to my successor.

Organisations often visited me at the Commons. Groups wanted to visit the Palace of Westminster, to learn about parliamentary procedures, the history of Parliament and the role of an MP. Many Members would get tour guides to give their constituency groups a guided tour, though this was not my style. I wanted to conduct the tour myself. I mugged up on the history of the palace, attached myself to other tours so I could learn what was said by others and gradually learnt the ropes. I perfected a tour that lasted about ninety minutes, which included the House of Lords. As the group went into the Commons Chamber the odd person sat on a green bench and risked being shouted at by a badge messenger. These are gentlemen who would bring you urgent messages and green cards, requests to see you in the Central Lobby, into the Chamber while the House was sitting. The messenger would shout, 'If you want to take a seat here, you must first fight an election and win.' The miscreant would jump up in embarrassment. The red sword lines on the carpet would fascinate visitors – a hangover from the days when Members would carry swords. The lines were so that if anyone was rash enough to draw a sword, if they stayed behind their line, no one would be injured. I usually booked a room where my constituents could ask any questions they might have after the tour. It was often a room off Westminster Hall, again, full of history and significance. I know many constituents enjoyed their visit and learnt something new every time, as did I. I picked up 'vibes' in the constituency from these visits, too, which would have not been easy to note, but for the relaxed atmosphere of such an outing. The ambience of the building made even the most cynical person leave the place with a sense of awe. For me, the building had a continuing interest throughout my time there; I never tired of it.

The invitations to a new Member from the constituency came thick and fast. Douglas Galloway, the general manager of the New Town Development Corporation, made contact within a few days of my election to see if I wanted to buy one of the corporation's houses. His view of my budget way exceeded my pocket, but I was courted by him and his fellow corporation board members. He was a dry but courteous man, with great expertise in property development. I remember he always wore a dark-navy suit – perhaps he picked up a tip or two from Alan Clark. He was very helpful on the housing 'right to buy' issue and on the many new town issues that came up in Parliament.

Representatives of the major companies in the area also wanted to meet me. One of these was Carreras Rothmans, which had a cigarette-making factory in the new town. The company was initially started by a Spaniard, Don José Carreras Ferrer. They had a public-relations arm and they courted me. Although I was and am a non-smoker, I was perfectly happy for others to smoke if they wished. I might smoke a cigar every two or three months, but not more, and partly because I like the aroma after a good dinner. I was very much against the 'nanny state' interfering in people's lives, or their deaths, as long as the dangers were pointed out to people. In general, people succumbed to smoking-related cancers in their sixties and seventies. I urged the company to develop safer cigarettes that meant such diseases affected people on average in their seventies and eighties. I was not sure if that was possible, but I was certainly one of those who opposed the banning of cigarette advertising on libertarian grounds. It didn't seem sensible, if you wanted people to give up 'heavy' for 'lighter' brands, not to allow the publishing of information about which was which.

Ford Motor Company claimed I was their 'Mr Ford' after they had worked out that I represented more Ford workers than anyone else in the House. The Ford engine plant, the Ford tractor factory and Dunton Research and Development Centre were situated locally, and many of their Dagenham car-making employees lived in Basildon. They had invited me to attend their research centre on numerous occasions, but something had always cropped up in the House to prevent my visit. I eventually went to Dunton with some trepidation. After about an hour of my inane questioning about cars and engines on the visit, they were shocked to discover that I did not, nay, could not, drive. They were confused and stopped the visit, consternation setting in, upon which they immediately took me out to their test track, put me in the driver's seat of one of their cars with a Ford test driver, who proceeded to give me the experience of how to drive. They suggested I go every Saturday until I learnt, so eager were they for me not to be a non-driver. Time did not allow me to do this while I was a Member, but getting around the constituency without a car was less of a problem than might be imagined. People were always willing to meet you at a station and drive you to an engagement. While they did so, they had your undivided attention for anything they might want to bend your ear about. Often, ideas for parliamentary questions were born while en route to some function or other. I didn't pass my driving test until ten years after I left the House.

Not a week passed by without some interesting visit to a local factory, farm or commercial enterprise. In 1984, Gordon's built a new factory on an industrial estate in Laindon. I was invited round and introduced to the delights of their sloe gin. The landfill site at Pitsea, which was a nuisance to constituents, especially if the wind was in the wrong direction, warranted my attention. A food factory in Billericay showed me an amazing selection of culinary flavourings. There too was a shirt-making factory for supplying, among others,

Marks & Spencer. These visits were never boring and from them I learnt so much in such a short period of time. In my opinion, it is this ability to do so many new and varied things, that would have otherwise taken a lifetime to fit in, that is one of the great advantages of being a Member of Parliament.

I was invited to numerous sports events, too, where I was asked to present prizes and cups; I was made president of a judo club (and given the kit) and took part in a 24-hour snooker marathon for charity. Some of my younger constituents challenged me to go to a West Ham football match. I stood behind the goal and my hosts were impressed with my ability to stand and endure the rain with them.

I am proud to say that, while I was asked to open things, I was never to close anything. I remember there was a very good friend of mine, John Allsop, who was very interested in telecommunication equipment. When the government reformed British Telecommunications and liberalised the rules, John stood ready to act. Until the early 1980s, there were no mobile phones, and your house landline had to be rented from BT. John established the first mobile phone shop in London. I was impressed by his intelligence, commercial flair and drive, and arranged for Kenneth Baker, the Minister for Science and Technology, to open his shop in the Trocadero Centre in Piccadilly, London. It was in September 1985. The press was invited. On the same morning, there was a Cabinet reshuffle and Kenneth said he could not make it; he had been made Environment Secretary. John understood but insisted that he needed an opener and so I deputised at his insistence. I am, therefore, fairly sure I can claim to have opened the first mobile phone shop in the UK! In those days, the handset was as big as a brick and twice as heavy – but that was the start of the London Phone Company. John was loyal and helped me with my later trials and tribulations. Although younger than me, he would take me out for dinner and I would entertain him to lunch or dinner. I very much enjoyed his company and he gave practical support to me when I hit the rocks. He had a French partner and I received fantastic truffles and bottles of Chablis from a family vineyard. I do not know why, but, in his thirties, John committed suicide. I was in India at the time and I regret not being available for him to talk to me about any stresses he might have had in his life. It was a life that, from the outside, appeared to be full and prosperous. He was a very good-looking, funny and bright young man. I very much regret his early death, which was a tragedy for his parents and robbed me of a true and intelligent friend. In the mysteries of life, his death was the most mysterious. I felt diminished by his passing.

Through me, my brother was asked to redesign the uniforms of a marching band of girls named the Mayflower Corps. They were very competent and won many awards. After the Falklands War, I was asked by some of the girls if I could arrange for them to play and march on the harbour side by way of welcoming HMS *Hermes*, our aircraft carrier and command vessel, back to port. A number of the girls had become pen pals of the sailors on board. I had a word with John Nott, the Defence Secretary, and he thought it was a good idea. They put on a great performance and I was disappointed that parliamentary business meant sending my last-minute apologies, but they had a great time by all accounts when they visited the ship a few weeks later. The captain subsequently invited me to visit *Hermes* and I was given a tour, on which I was surprised to find Chinese laundry men sitting in front of an open fire in the centre of the ship. The captain gave me lunch and tea and, on leaving, as a memento, a plaque of HMS *Hermes*, which I still treasure. About ten years ago, on a subsequent visit to Cochin in India, I saw *Hermes*, which had been sold to India, recommissioned and sailing under its new name – INS *Viraat*. I was proud to say that, through my constituency connection, I had been on board.

The emergency services provided in-depth insights into their important work in the constituency. I spent several nights on duty patrols with the police and the fire and ambulance services. Once, I recall having to climb up a 100ft-high fire tower by ladder at Basildon Fire Station. From there, I stepped onto the turntable ladder, which had been positioned to the tower's side, showing a clean pair of heels (to save your toes being cut off when the ladder retracted), but without being told there was 'give' in the ladder. As soon as my weight touched it, it dropped away from me. Beneath me was the local paper's photographer, waiting for the action shot of the event that 'caused the by-election'. I think he was rather put out when I reached the ground in one piece.

All these events and visits were of interest to the local newspapers. I had an evening paper and several weekly local papers with which to deal; it was a love/hate relationship. I hope I was always polite and patient, but sometimes we had arguments. They were an important link between me and my constituents in the work I was doing on their behalf, in and out of the constituency, and sometimes they had excluded some important matter which was of concern. Democracy in action is fine to behold, but I felt it was not, nor should it have been, a cover for muck-raking over an individual's personal, private life. Nor because we mutually used each other to promote, analyse and explore what work I was doing as an MP was it any justification for them to say that gave them a right to report what I did or didn't do in my bedroom. Go down that road, and very few people would stand for election, and, what's more, they would not be candidates most people would want.

Invitations flooded in to speak at Rotary Clubs, Round Table, Women's Institutes, church groups, school sixth forms and just about every gathering imaginable. I genuinely relished the opportunity. I once attended a church-organised meeting of several hundred people on the thorny subject of Sunday trading. Dashing to Billericay, I had no time to change, having just landed at RAF Northolt following a trip to Norway and was late. I made my speech in full army fatigues in support of Sunday shop opening, much to the surprise of my church-going constituents. Most opposed my stance on Sunday trading, but they appreciated that I had appeared before them to make the case.

I spoke at a public inquiry to protect the green belt in the Thurrock part of my constituency. An attempt was made to build a large new town in the area, which was universally opposed by residents, and I had no difficulty in supporting my constituents. I knew there were plenty of brownfield sites in the East End of London; they should have been developed. There was no need to eat into the narrow belt of agricultural land that had protected Essex from the Greater London Council (GLC) urban sprawl. I went before an inspector appointed by the Environmental Secretary to argue the case and we won. It was a famous victory for which I might have gained more credit had not the clouds already been gathering around my personal life.

In Wickford, I was instrumental in naming a road on an industrial estate after a wartime New Zealand pilot who had crashed near the site. William Henry 'Ace' Hodgson survived but died later in another flying accident in March 1941. Group Captain Peter Townsend, who was Hodgson's commanding officer (and, incidentally, nearly married Princess Margaret), was the guest of honour, together with the New Zealand High Commissioner. The road was named Hodgson's

Way and Townsend and I took a helicopter flight from Battersea in central London to a marquee on the site. During the flight, I noticed how few green fields there were between London and Essex.

I also suggested to the Transport Secretary the name that was finally chosen for the new Thames Bridge at Dartford – the Queen Elizabeth II Bridge. It was opened in October 1991, but I was not invited to the opening.

Deep down, throughout the inevitable public attention I received as a local Member, I was still a shy person and regarded each speaking platform to be a challenge. On the train home after a meeting, a visit or a speech, I would re-run in my head everything that had happened, cringing at my errors and clocking anything that had gone well to use for the future. I was incessantly self-critical. I am bound to have made enemies; It is in the nature of politics that you disagree with others, but I hopefully made more friends. I always tried to answer political questions directly if I could. I admired precision in others and tried to be precise myself; I did not like others to beat about the bush and so nor did I.

Invitations to political social events in the constituency were enjoyable. They became the basis of my social life too. It is true that I had no social life with other of my parliamentary colleagues. I did not want to 'socialise' with most of them and it was very rare if I did. My dealings with most of them might be described as friendly and correct in the House. There were very few with whom I would take hospitality outside the House. My constituency social duties were never a chore to me as I know, from the moans of some of my colleagues, they were to many. I have always enjoyed meeting people, the more varied the better. The garden parties, the summer shows, the antiques markets, the charitable endeavours of others, all requesting my presence – these were all of interest.

Then, in the constituency, there were your party workers. You got to know them well and shared in their highs and lows. They became a constant feature in my life, almost 'family' in a way that other MPs could never be. Once one had done the rounds of speeches in the early years, local ward committees and the association wanted to invite other speakers and other MPs and ministers to address them. Similarly, I would visit other constituencies to speak.

Of course, Enoch came to speak in Billericay and he was generous in the warmth he showed towards me. We had a wonderful fundraising committee in an industrial group, chaired and organised by Tony Mudd and his wife, based in Little Burstead. The group also arranged dinners in the terrace dining rooms of the House, with myself acting as host. At the time, this did not appear irregular or break any rules. Indeed, whatever rules applied at the House, I abided by them.

Jeffrey Archer was a guest speaker in the Mudds' palatial house, which could seat sixty or seventy people for lunch. He was a passionate speaker in defence of the Prime Minister and the government and always attracted a large and enthusiastic gathering.

John Major also spoke to one of my industrial group dinners in the House. He was a late replacement for a minister who had an important ministerial engagement at the last minute. Within one hour, John had stepped into the breach – he was my whip at the time – and spoke fluently. These dinners at the House were fundraising, political and social events. They were an important part of a Conservative MP's activity and most had such a group. They allowed me to meet a wide cross-section of industrial and commercial interests and I enjoyed these engagements greatly.

I could not understand how my successor, Teresa Gorman, could have fallen out with Tony Mudd to such an extent that she sued him for libel and, against all the evidence and my personal knowledge of the facts of the case, won. I was a witness for Mudd. He was an accountant and tireless worker for the Conservatives and a good supporter of myself. He should not have gone to his grave so disparaged. I went to his funeral to pay homage to a friend, but also as a rebuke to Teresa.

Michael Heseltine also spoke to my association industrial group in the House when he was Secretary of State for Defence and visited the constituency to speak to my Women's Advisory Committee when he was on the back benches. He was the blue-eyed boy of such engagements. Inevitably, he spoke well and charmed the ladies. He very kindly offered me a lift back to the Commons in his car. I was a tad nervous; he was a so-called leader of the 'wets' by this time, but I had always admired his speaking ability greatly. I had already come under pressure with regard to my personal life at the time and his gesture of the lift was much appreciated. The conversation in the car was entirely political; he wanted to hear my views on immigration. We disagreed, but he understood I had points to make and, unlike so many, thought the debate should be heard. As Secretary of State for the Environment, he was responsible for the 'right to buy' policy. Many of my constituents had much to thank him for in helping them place their feet on the first rung of the property ladder.

There was another blue-eyed boy of the Women's Advisory Committee, and he was Alan Clark. He agreed to speak in Billericay one lunchtime and, as I was in London, I arranged to meet him at Liverpool Street station at 10.30 a.m. He did not appear on time and an aide in his ministerial office told me, when I called him from a public telephone box, that he'd been delayed but was on his way. He arrived dishevelled; he looked dreadful. His tie was awry; his shirt crumpled; his suit not quite sitting right. His normally precise hair was unkempt and untidy. I sensed he had had a rough night. I greeted him and said there was a train in five minutes. 'My dear boy,' he slurred, 'I couldn't possibly catch a train. Let's go to the Great Eastern Hotel for a drink.' I couldn't refuse, but thought it odd and concerning. I was downcast; we were going to be late. Upon reaching the bar, he ordered a large glass of Fernet-Branca, an Italian digestif, and I watched as he downed the bitter liquid in one. We caught the next train and, during the forty-minute journey, he underwent a miraculous transformation. A flick of the shirt here, a touch of the tie there, a finger comb of his hair: gradually he became the immaculate Alan Clark that the ladies knew and were expecting. I was astonished. I kept his secret and he wowed them as he always did, no trace of a slur to be found.

Sometimes I was asked to host outside organisational dinners at the Commons. Charles Manners, 10th Duke of Rutland, asked me if I would host a dinner of the Fire Mark Circle at the House. He couldn't do it at the last minute so I gladly took over, not exactly sure until I looked it up exactly what a 'Fire Mark' might be. In the eighteenth century, buildings that were insured had metal plaques affixed to them that carried the emblem of the insurance company. Fire brigades were at that time owned by the insurance companies, so these 'fire marks' would act as a guide to them, letting them know which building was insured by which company. These signs became very collectable, especially by Americans. The dinner and people attending it were fascinating. Little did I know how big a part the Duke's ancestral home of Belvoir Castle was to play in my later life, or how familiar I was to become with his Fire Mark collection. By way of thanks, I was given a book on Fire Marks by the Circle, which actually proved very useful, much more so than I had initially realised.

In addition to the meetings in the constituency, where I was always called upon to say something, if only to draw and announce the results of the raffle, I was frequently invited to speak in other parts of the country.

Early on, I accepted an invitation from a Conservative Association treasurer in Hackney to speak at one of the oldest clubs in London, the City of London Trades Club, formed in 1714. It originated in one of the eighteenth-century coffeehouses and it was a great honour to be invited to speak to its annual dinner, which was held in the splendour of the Savoy Hotel in London among lots of white napery, twinkling lights and everyone dressed to the nines. I was seated between the president and my partner for the evening, a friend called Annette. The president had taken time early in the proceedings to show me the wonderful and valuable silver loving cups the club possessed and which came out of the bank vaults for show on special occasions. He knew every hallmark, located usually on the base of the cup, and took understandable pride in turning the cups over so I could see the historic marks. The evening progressed with great ceremony under candlelight, including the scarlet-uniformed Royal Boatmen carrying in the traditional roast beef. I was so engrossed in the spectacle I had not realised the Savoy waiters had filled up the loving cups with port. I picked a cup up to show Annette its hallmark, turned it over quickly and accidently tipped the equivalent of at least two bottles of port over the white table cloth. The staff quickly mopped up and covered the ensuing red stain, which steadily engulfed the top table, but I still felt stupid.

I did my best to encourage young people into politics. I felt, at the time, it was an honourable profession. As well as my secretary, Lyn, I employed research assistants. Some came through the Monday Club. As far as I was aware, they were all 'straight', and if they were aware of my homosexuality they were far too polite to mention it. I think it's fair to say that I encouraged one eighteen-year-old on to the right track to become a parliamentarian, the present Speaker of the House of Commons, John Bercow. John and his mother had a meeting with me in the Members' cafeteria. Of all the eating establishments in the House, that was my favourite. It was the least pompous and the staff were solicitous and, in a way, 'motherly'. I know he may now decry his role in the Monday Club, but at the time John was an enthusiastic supporter. During the meeting, he wanted to know how he should progress a political career, whether he should go out to work or try to go to university. I strongly advised that he should, as I did, go to a university. It would be a financial sacrifice, but that was the route I thought he should take as a first step to gaining a political career. He was bright, earnest and articulate, if at times a little strident in the expression of his opinions. He thought everything through before he said or did anything. He was very supportive to me, especially on my views on immigration and race relations at the time, though I understand he now describes this period of his life as 'utter madness'. If so, there was not an ounce of 'madness' in him at the time that was detectable. I bear him no animosity for his apparent volte-face and am only pleased I had some small role to play in his political career.

From my university days at York, I knew how difficult it was for university and college Tories to get MPs to speak. Therefore, I never refused a speaking engagement invitation from them if I could possibly avoid it. It meant I have been to most towns and cities in the UK at least once – if they had a university or a college – and I enjoyed the travel. I debated many times at Oxford and Cambridge. At the former, in 1979, I was heckled at a party meeting by Keith Vaz, who was himself elected to the House in 1987. I gave as good as I got; it is all part of being a Member of Parliament under scrutiny.

Actually, I spoke infrequently on the subject of immigration and race relations, but that was the subject for which I became known. Most MPs preferred to ignore the issue. I usually spoke at universities on economic matters or on free speech, but if asked a question on immigration I would not shy away from giving my opinion. Many of my parliamentary colleagues fell foul of left-wing students and anarchists, who denied them free speech in the very institutions that historically protected the right to free expression. When such democratic abuse took place, the politician was rightly praised in the media for standing up to be counted. They were lauded, and rightly so, in the House by other of their colleagues as they described their 'trials' in the Members' tea room and were praised even by political friends and opponents alike for their determination.

This support did not often appear either in the House or in the media when I was the subject of such an attack. Other politicians may have thought that, as I had the temerity to speak on race-relations matters, I was somehow 'fair game' in bringing this abuse upon myself. The media thought the better story was to keep attacking me. I believe free speech is all about allowing your opponents to say things with which you profoundly disagree and it matters not whether the opposition comes from without or within your political party.

So often were my clothes in need of dry cleaning from liquids and other items, including beer, paint and eggs, that were thrown at me, that I had a favourite old green Barbour waxed jacket that I was fond of wearing on these occasions. It became caked in the stuff, but it saved my suits. I kept it for many years afterwards, each stain a battle trophy from this or that university. It certainly brought back memories.

I tried to take it all with good humour. This did wear a bit thin when, at the University of Bristol, phials of acid were thrown at me, burning the science bench in front of me with whiffs of toxic smoke enveloping the meeting. So concerned was the Vice-Chancellor that he gave me tea and a book on the university. It was kind of him and he had no need to be so defensive. The vast majority of students just wanted to get on with their work; it was just a tiny minority who wished to stir things up, and how better than to confront, in their eyes, an 'incendiary' Tory.

On Friday 13 March 1987, I visited the University of Hull Conservatives. Met at the station, I was warned about a crowd of demonstrators, not all students, apparently barring my entry to the lecture hall where I was to speak. When I was unable to gain entry at the front doors, my car drove to a back door, but as I made my way from car to hall door, I was surrounded by the mob and physically prevented from entering. I was punched, jostled, kicked and spat upon. I was advised by my hosts to make my way back to the car, but that was not easy as I was surrounded and it took a while. As I got back into the car, people pulled the rear passenger door against its hinges so, when I sought to close it, I physically could not. I had to hold the door as near closed as possible as we drove away, to avoid the door hitting those around the car who were bashing the windows, roof and bonnet. I was in physical danger, and the car manoeuvred to get me to safety. I was subsequently driven away to a police station, where I was surprised to be asked to make a statement about the incident. When I reached London, Peggy told me that the press had contacted her. They had said, 'Your MP has just run over students at Hull University in his car.' No mention of the near-riot or the physical attack on me. 'What have you to say now?' Peggy replied: 'Harvey doesn't drive.' It was not my car and I certainly was not at the wheel; I was being driven by security guards employed by the university. They had been in danger too. Indeed, the repercussions of this event went on for months. The university authorities were sued by some of the students for damages and the university asked if I would be a witness. Of course, I said yes. At virtually the doors of the court, they caved in and settled the action in the demonstrators' favour. So much for the historic role of universities preserving free speech in our country.

The morning after the incident in Hull, I got up early, went to buy the newspapers to see how my visit to the university had been twisted – knowing there would be no mention of my talk on the subject of free speech as I had not given it, though a copy had been issued in advance to the press. As I was opening the front door of my apartment, I was arrested by the Metropolitan Police.

— PART 2 —

CHAPTER 7

TRAVELS

I did not travel out of Yorkshire much as a child. Very occasionally, in my late teens, I would visit London and stay with my brother. I would go to Blackpool for the odd Conservative Party conference and stay with my father's great-aunt and her husband. But Yorkshire was my remit. The wonderful visits from York to Leeds and to Scarborough by steam train and to Ripon by bus were memorable. The age of steam was almost at an end, but it was splendid to ride in carriages pulled by real locomotive engines; the smell, the sounds and the glimpse of fire, especially at night, in the grate heating the boiler. It was very atmospheric and almost romantic in a way that current train travel is mundane, matter of fact and routine. Before my boyhood wish to be a Member of Parliament became ingrained, I must have had a strong desire to be an engine driver.

How I managed to avoid leaving the UK until my twenties, I do not know – economic reasons might have predominated. Then, in the summer of 1970, Wilf Proudfoot, who was an MP, shocked that I had not travelled abroad, invited me to join him and his family on a visit to Spain. It was to take over five weeks. They took two cars and a caravan and with these we motored through France, up and over the Pyrenees into north-east Spain to Palafrugell. There we all camped for a few days and, while Wilf's wife and his younger children stayed, we and the eldest son took off in a car and drove around Spain, staying at *pensiones*. We took in Zaragoza, Madrid, Toledo, Córdoba, Seville, Granada, Cádiz and Algeciras. Outside Gibraltar, we stayed with Lord St Oswald, dining al fresco and sleeping on his lawn, the lights of Gibraltar twinkling beneath us, snakes curled up in lemon trees above us. In the morning, we looked across to North Africa.

We drove up the Mediterranean coast to Málaga, Nerja and Barcelona. It was a wonderful, eye-opening adventure; new geography, new climate, new food, new culture, new colours, new aromas – all of which I soaked up and decided I wanted more of. The trip gave me a love of overseas travel that has never left me, as well as a love of the journey, not only the time at the destination; I like the process, not just the objective. That New Year's Eve, I flew to Tenerife and stayed at Puerto de la Cruz. It was to become a tradition that I would normally take my holidays in the winter and it was Tenerife to which I initially became attracted. I did also visit Yugoslavia. My most memorable time there was walking round the walls of Dubrovnik as the sun was setting, with vivid red banners flapping all the way down the main street and the sound of the Dubrovnik Symphony Orchestra playing Beethoven's Ninth Symphony. It was all to commemorate President Tito's eightieth birthday in May 1972. I also recall the limited food supplies with which this Communist country had to wrestle. On the island of Korčula, which claims to be the birthplace of Marco Polo, I visited a restaurant that promised more than the standard chicken or pork that was the only fare available everywhere in the country at that time. This was different; it had a huge menu. I made my selection and the waiter took my order. He then returned, saying, sorry, but no, what I had ordered was not available. I chose again. The same process ensued. 'What have you got then?' I asked. 'Chicken or pork,' came the reply. But why then, I asked, have such an appetising and large menu with so much choice? 'Ah, when we have it, this is how much it would cost, but we don't have it'; impeccable logic. I returned to Croatia a number of times, later, when Communism was no more, and, among other things, the range of food had increased and that restaurant on the island of Korčula was able genuinely to offer its full menu at last.

While in war-damaged Dubrovnik, with its many white, UN peace-keeping Land Rovers very much in evidence, I hired a car and drove south to Herceg Novi in Montenegro. I was foolish to do so, as war was still taking place and the Serbian Army was all over the place. I stopped at a large hotel on a bay. I had been told it was full and that it had been taken over by the paramilitary police in Montenegro but when I went up to the reception desk, I saw lots of room keys hanging behind it. The polite lady behind the desk said, in broken English, 'Full? Full? We have not been full for years.' I got a room and learnt about the political difficulties posed by the police, who were using part of the hotel as a base. They disliked the Serbs, who were like an occupying force in their eyes. On our return to Croatia, had I run into a Serbian Army patrol, I would have been arrested.

I travelled extensively in the 1970s. I enjoyed travelling with friends as I believe travel, and the experiences travel generates, need to be shared. I started visiting India in 1978. India was to be my great travel destination. In my life so far I have visited the western states of India, from Mumbai to Trivandrum, more than twenty times. For a period of six years, up until 2010, I would have a pattern of life where I would work 24/7 for nine months of the year and I took three months of the year out – December, January and February and rented a beach-side house in northern Kerala, one of the most Muslim areas of that country, and dropped out of the UK. I employed a driver and a cleaner/cook, both of whom, and their families, became friends. I visited Cochin (Kochi), Calicut (Kozhikode), Kannur and, inland, Mysore. There I visited the summer palace of Tipu Sultan, who was defeated and killed by the Duke of Wellington, Arthur Wellesley as he was then called, in 1799. I was to come across Wellington's history at Belvoir. Tipu was a great general and dubbed the 'Tiger of Mysore'. He claimed it was better to live one day as a tiger than 1,000 days as a sheep – a man after my own heart.

The last time I visited Kerala, on the first day I walked on the usually deserted beach to find a crowd looking in the sand. Police were everywhere and I approached to find out their concern. It was a pile of bombs made from coconuts. They had been collected from a local village before they could be used in another episode of frequent communal strife. Together with the locals, I stood over them. The police moved us away and then exploded the bombs – lots of noise, and sand flying everywhere. A local television film crew approached us and asked for comment. I was the only European there and explained that I had come across bombs in the UK before, so it was not just a 'Kerala thing'. No, I told them, it would not stop me from enjoying my stay. The interview was played non-stop on television for the rest of the day.

I also started flying into Sri Lanka as our gateway to southern India and I got to know that island too. I had first visited Sri Lanka on a parliamentary visit on behalf of the Commonwealth Parliamentary

Association, when I was privileged to meet President Jayawardene. He was a tall, white-haired, slender man in his eighties, dressed in a white gown – impressive in both appearance and manner. After the formal week of visits throughout the island and many meetings, I took a further week of holiday, at my private expense, relaxing on a beach in the south – so far as you can relax with an armed guard all the time in attendance because of the authority's fear of a terrorist attack. I often had to ask the guard if he could move his position slightly as his sub-machine gun was casting a shadow over my tan.

During that visit, I was walking near to shops outside my hotel when I was approached by a Muslim in flowing white robes who asked me to enter his boss's shop. I did, and at that moment the monsoon rains opened up. Trapped by the deluge, I was brought a Coca-Cola and the two of them showed me their gemstones. I have never been a constant or comfortable wearer of jewellery. I was wearing no rings, so they knew I was not a likely customer, but they were still generous with their time and knowledgeable and friendly. I left them with a business card, a copy of my manifesto, which I had on me, and posed for a photograph. I sent them a letter of thanks from the House of Commons upon my return.

Many years later, in the same area of Sri Lanka, a friend and I bumped into another friend we had first met in Zanzibar; he was English and had married a local Sri Lankan girl. While my friends reminisced, I walked down to the beach to find the same shop. Just as twelve years or so earlier, I was approached by a Muslim in flowing, white robes and offered a drink. In the shop was the same guy I had been approached by before. He had married the boss's daughter and was now a partner in the jewellery business. As we talked, I noticed behind him on a shelf there was the photograph of me taken in the shop from all those years earlier. He said I had brought him much business and he was grateful. He still had my manifesto and letter from the House of Commons. He had collected press cuttings, knew all about my life through the media – and he still wanted to know me! I returned to my friends and said, 'You are not going to believe this.' They didn't, so we all went to the shop in a tuk-tuk.

The shop owners and I have remained good friends over the years. One of them visited and stayed with me at Belvoir and later gained the Duchess of Rutland as a customer. Alas, in 2014, their shop was devastated by communal violence and the business wrecked, their stock stolen. On their behalf, I wrote to the High Commissioner in Colombo and to the International Aid Minister here in the UK, but failed to get a reply.

I say these things not only in mitigation of my so-called appalling stance and false image on race issues often portrayed of me in the media, but because they are true. One should not have to mention such friendships or bonds of brotherly love, but I am sure no one else will set the record straight in this regard, so I feel I must. I do not think those political opponents who accused me of racialist behaviour could possibly know the personal hurt they caused me by their ill-informed and erroneous suggestions. I am from an age when discrimination was a good word, where to discriminate on every conceivable ground you could detect in a person was a good thing, not a bad thing. Like so many English words, that one has been hijacked by the politically correct.

I was honoured to go on quite a few parliamentary visits abroad. The first one was to the USA, in the summer of 1979. An all-party group made up of newly elected MPs paid visits to the Oval Office in the White House and then on to Denver, Colorado, Minneapolis–St Paul, Connecticut and New York. At the outset, we were asked what we would like to do in New York. Labour Members wanted to study urban deprivation in the Bronx; I asked if I could do a night patrol with the police. I was ridiculed by them, but by the day of my visit others tried unsuccessfully to join me, and wanted armbands and badges for their children. It was an amazing evening.

On arrival at the NYPD 6th Precinct Police Station, I was told to sit in the back of the patrol car, which I did. Our patrol area was Greenwich Village. We attended a road accident almost immediately. No one was hurt, but paperwork seemed as burdensome there as here. We then parked outside the apartment complex of an NBC television presenter who had been burgled. His television set had been stolen. As the police officers entered his complex, they noticed I had not moved. They came back to get me, saying I would be far safer with them than sitting in their car. We were then called to a shop where there had been a robbery and, during their visit to the store, we hurried next door to a Chinese restaurant. An argument had broken out between diners, staff and three blind people and a lot of shouting and disturbance was taking place. The blind people had guide dogs with them and the Chinese restaurant manager had refused them entry on the grounds that dogs were barred from restaurants by New York City statute. Oh, said the blind people, a newer New York City statute says you cannot discriminate against blind people with guide dogs. If there is a table free, the dogs can also enter. My police officers did not know who was right, so they radioed for assistance and, as the argument was getting out of control, I was pushed forward to try to hold the peace. The manager had been in London and so I talked about his visit and discussed disability rights in the UK for blind people. As I was holding forth, a police sergeant arrived with the reinforcements, thought I was the source of the problem and promptly started to arrest me! One of my police officers explained to him that they did not think that was such a good idea. He let me go.

At the end of the busy shift, I was given badges and I thanked my police officers profusely. They said they had been ok as they were wearing bulletproof vests! Mind you, as New York City was bankrupt at the time, they had to buy the vests themselves. It was a great experience and I was the envy of my colleagues on the trip when I told them of the adventure. I went on patrol with police forces thereafter in Basildon, North Carolina, Sri Lanka and South Africa. I could compare their role and their response (Basildon police came out best) and I was grateful to all the forces for the opportunity.

An invitation was extended to me in January 1985 to attend President Reagan's second inauguration ceremony. It took place on Monday 21 January, which was also one of the coldest days ever in Washington; snow and ice were everywhere. The outside parade and festivities were unfortunately cancelled and my host organised a stretch limo to take me across town to a hotel where the Republican Eagles had hastily arranged a party. No one was on the streets and there were no cars on the roads, it was so cold. As we approached Pennsylvania Avenue, the car was surrounded by police and security men. We had to get out and brave the freezing temperatures. Why? Well, just at that point, Nancy and Ronald were making their way down the avenue in their cavalcade to the Capitol for the swearing-in ceremony. I can honestly say I was the only person to wave to them on their way to that ceremony, and they both waved back to me.

After an excellent party, where I met the Canadian equivalent of the Red Arrow pilots, I spent the night attending many of the opulent balls in Reagan's honour. He had been an excellent Governor of California and he made the best President in my lifetime. Without that strange but powerful combination of Mrs Thatcher and him, I believe the Cold War may never have ended.

In London, I had become very friendly with a red-haired New York Jewess, Wylma Wayne. She had an art gallery on Old Bond Street and, through Terry and her, I met David, the Marquis of Granby. She wanted me to hand-deliver a painting of Mrs Thatcher to the White House for the President, which I did after many transatlantic telephone calls, eventually gaining security clearance.

On other visits, I went as far west as San Francisco, once with Emma, Duchess of Rutland, as part of a speaking tour, and once with a colleague of mine at Belvoir Castle, Sarah, to promote a range of castle botanical drinks.

Sarah and I also visited Dallas to represent the castle at an exhibition. I do not think I have been travelling with anyone where we have laughed so much. On arriving at a central Dallas hotel and while still unpacking, the fire alarms rang and we were told by loud audio recording to make our way down to the exit immediately, not using the lifts. We met in the corridor on the seventeenth floor of the skyscraper and did so. Exhausted, we reached reception but found we were the only guests who had moved. Everyone else just ignored what proved to be a false alarm.

In 1981, I visited North Carolina and met the owner of Biltmore House at Asheville. William Cecil Sr very kindly showed me round the house, which is located in the Blue Ridge Mountains. It gave me a taste for stately homes, which came in very handy later in life. He later went on to establish a vineyard on the estate. On the same trip in 1981, an American friend and I caught an Amtrak train from Charleston to New Orleans. It was a long journey, made longer by the incredibly slow speed of the train. All that land and yet progress was slow. We arrived even later than scheduled and when we turned up at our hotel we were told our room had been resold. My friend used his skills to complain, but to no avail. A big

American football convention was taking place; our rooms had gone. He pushed me forward to see if I could make a difference, hoping my English accent would help matters. The further south and the further west in the USA I travelled, the more I found an English accent carried weight. I asked to see the manager and he said there was only one room left in the hotel: the rooftop presidential suite. I said that would do nicely. For the same price and, on the edge of the jazz quarter, we lived in style, hoping the President would not come to town.

I visited Gabon on a parliamentary visit in 1982. It was only when the group of ten or so MPs arrived that we discovered there were to be celebrations of its President's one-party rule. The President was Omar Bongo. We met him in his opulent palace, surrounded by urban squalor. He kept us waiting for two hours, which was apparently a huge compliment; he normally kept people waiting for two weeks. Despite his diminutive height, he was an imposing figure – reputed to eat the vital organs of his political opponents. Just before we arrived, such human organs had been found in the fridge of one of his supporters. Together with the British ambassador, we were lectured for an hour, President Bongo explaining that he would like a Land Rover for each of his eighty or so Members of Parliament. He also wanted them to learn English and therefore wanted language laboratories for them all. He had admired the Queen and her royal train; he would like a similar train to journey into the jungle (Gabon is in equatorial West Africa). He also wanted a new building to house his Foreign Office. On leaving, the Labour MPs in the group were full of beans – they chortled at the export orders they had just acquired. Our ambassador quickly disillusioned them and sided with the Conservatives: 'No, he doesn't want to buy them from us – he wants you to give them to him.' Bongo was accustomed to the French government doing this for his every whim; the Labour MPs' rose-tinted view of the commercial world collapsed.

We attended a buffet reception in our honour and ate bear, monkey, crocodile, snake and other delicacies in his gold-plated palace. We were invited to attend a military parade – it lasted for four hours, and we were seated in direct sunlight on the seafront at Elizabethville looking at the Atlantic; only Bongo and the French ambassador sat in shade. After about forty-five minutes, we realised his forces were just marching around the block in an attempt to keep the parade going. Many of his civilians were marching round too, dressed in brightly coloured material adorned with his own face printed upon it. Every half-hour, his three war planes would fly overhead and his three or four naval vessels would sail by, turn round and sail by again. By 1 p.m. we were exhausted and returned to the British embassy. There, the ambassador told us of his secret. He always took with him a novel to read and hid it behind the large programme – I thought he might have shared his little secret before the parade. My visit to Gabon ended in disaster: I caught malaria, likely bitten by a swarm of flying ants in the jungle. I perspired madly at night and had a bad headache, but I was determined to catch the flight back with the other MPs, which I did.

A trip to Norway to witness the winter training exercises of the Royal Marine commandos was an experience at the other end of the temperature scale. I was a last-minute replacement for one of my colleagues with more defence interests than I, who had dropped out unexpectedly. It was a week's visit and I found it fascinating. Part of the trip involved sleeping out in a tent with a sergeant and six marines in -36 degrees; a domestic freezer operates at -26 degrees, so care had to be taken not to end up like a frozen fish finger. The sergeant, who had obviously been tasked to not cause a by-election, asked me to let him know if I felt cold. I can feel cold in the middle of summer in England, so how was I to know when to complain? The technique to survival was the layering approach, wearing just the right amount. You must not sweat, or the moisture might turn to ice. The remedy if a marine became too cold was to place another marine in his sleeping bag to increase his body temperature – I am sure that sergeant stayed up all night checking my breathing.

It was in the Arctic Circle with the Royal Marines that I spent an afternoon skiing, the only time I have attempted it, and driving a Ski-Doo. I have a photograph of myself accelerating away by pushing too hard on the pedal with a marine hanging on for dear life. I was also shown a very large JCB machine that moved snow. The driver asked me if I wanted to have a go; he said, despite its enormous size, it was as easy as driving a car. I said I couldn't drive a car. He thought for a moment and diplomatically replied, 'Sir, it's easier than driving a car.' So I took the controls, drove it about and found it very exhilarating. We watched night-time exercises through special binoculars, used night sights on guns and saw a marine dressed in black, carrying a flaming torch, who skied up to a female civil servant, also part of our group, with a box of Cadbury's chocolates – Milk Tray – very James Bond and theatrical.

Fortunately, part of the exercise we were not asked to emulate was when the marines, including officers, had to ski into the icy water through a hole chipped away in the ice in the middle of a lake. The first thing they rescued was their rifle. If they got out without it, they couldn't fight so were as good as dead. Then they had to pull off their heavy rucksack and place that out of the water; it contained clean dry clothes and without it they would die of hypothermia. Only at that point could they try to haul themselves out of the water. The deprivations of these exercises were mitigated by the excellent food in the mess, which made a change from the powdered food rations mixed with melted snow available in the tents.

Such close encounters with our armed forces made me respect the work they do on our behalf. I invited some of the marines to the House of Commons for drinks later as a thank-you for looking after me so well – and preventing that by-election.

I once travelled to Taiwan with the redoubtable Jill Knight, then the MP for Birmingham, Edgbaston. We flew first class with British Airways from Heathrow to Amsterdam and then direct to Taipei. We were to be there for seven days, and Jill had prepared everything. Her speeches were organised, as were her clothes and matching jewellery. On board the plane, she advised me that the only way to fly long haul was to have caviar and champagne in continuous and copious amounts. Sound advice if you were a drinker, which I was not. Still, I found keeping the glass full and untouched did the trick. It was an enjoyable flight. However, on landing, we discovered to our mutual consternation that our luggage had not made it onto the China Airways flight at Schiphol. We arrived in this hot and humid country with only what we were wearing. This was a problem for me but a calamity for Jill. We were immediately taken shopping and a 24-hour shirt and suit service kitted me out for the trip. Our luggage was delayed most of the week. On our return, Jill wrote the most magisterial rebuke to Lord King, then chairman of British Airways, and covered me in her remarks. I received very good compensation from BA as a result.

Jill and I got on very well and enjoyed the trip, on which I spoke to 1,000 schoolgirls, all dressed in white and navy, on the subject of the British Parliament. I liked Jill's company and her feisty but polite and courteous manner, and have very fond memories of our time together on the other side of the world.

I have not been to mainland China, but I did once visit Hong Kong. Only afterwards did I realise my trip there was a dummy run for the Prime Minister's visit three months later. I had a helicopter flight over Hong Kong, a visit up to the border, eyeing the Communist guards, eyeing us eyeing them. I visited a new housing development and community developments. I was given afternoon tea by the Governor, Sir Edward Youde, who was very pleasant and generous. He was as diplomatic as his calling insisted, but not stuffy, and he had a large, black Rolls-Royce, complete with Union flag flying and a chauffeur in white uniform and peaked hat. He asked how I was to return to my hotel, the Hilton. I had no idea, so he sent me back in his car. The looks on the faces of the American guests at the hotel as I stepped out were matched only by their disappointment on not recognising whoever it was. Nevertheless, it was one of the best entrances I have ever made anywhere. Sadly, Sir Edward died in office four years later in Beijing. Deservedly, he was honoured with a state funeral on his death in Hong Kong, and I was honoured to have met him.

I was abroad on three historical events of note. Returning to our apartment hotel in Tel Aviv after breakfast on the morning of Sunday 31 August 1997, the porter said he was sorry for our loss. We had no idea what he was talking about and I wondered whether he was talking about one of our relatives. We soon found out about the incident in the Pont de l'Alma in Paris. It was Princess Diana, and we watched the television coverage for the morning.

On 15 August 1998, in Omagh, Northern Ireland, the biggest single loss of civilian life to a terrorist bomb took place, and I was in Gdańsk in Poland. I watched the horror on the hotel television.

On 11 September 2001, I was flying from Kuwait to Colombo. On arrival, people surrounded us to inform us of the tragedy unfolding in New York. We watched the news footage with other tourists in morbid fascination over and over again until we could take it no more. Our hosts were very supportive in the hotel; they had their own domestic terrorist activity. I had seen it on earlier visits to Sri Lanka – burned-out buildings, army on the streets and the continuous looking under cars and tuk-tuks. We moved quickly to the Galle Face Hotel, much safer in the centre of Colombo, with a military establishment next door and the navy patrolling just off-shore. But, even there, an air of unease pervaded. We drove south and toured the areas that were to be so devastated only three years later by the Boxing Day tsunami in 2004. We decided to return home a week early rather than risk the airways being closed in the event of the USA launching a revenge attack in the Middle East that would leave us stranded.

Travel in recent years has always appeared more fraught. In the 1970s, it was set to grow with no limitation in sight. Television travel programmes showcased the whole world and rightly encouraged foreign visits and holidays. More and more people could afford to go abroad. However, the West's political and military interference everywhere in the world keeps coming back to haunt us. Continued mass immigration is an obvious and ongoing example, but travel will also regrettably be a casualty. Future generations will be restricted in their travel plans as governments, and public perception, make large parts of the world essentially off-limits to Europeans, where they cannot travel safely and certainly not with insurance cover.

Cleopatra's wedding present, Syria, was always somewhere I would have wished to have visited but now, and for the foreseeable, long-term future, that will be impossible. This is to be regretted and a legacy from today's meddling politicians in other people's and other nations' affairs. That concern is not weighed sufficiently when foreign policy decisions are taken. I feel I have lived at the best of times for travel. On my trips abroad I have enjoyed being introduced to new concepts, challenges, outlooks and meeting many interesting and fascinating people, and I am sorry such opportunities may be lost to those in the future. They will have to rely on the internet, which is no substitute for the reality, or for life itself.

CHAPTER 8

THE FIRST SCANDAL

Most political scandals, whether sexual or financial, seem to follow a predictable path these days. The politician is exposed in a Sunday newspaper, the Prime Minister or Leader of the Opposition pledges support on the Monday and the luckless person resigns on the Tuesday, if they have anything to resign from, which is not always the case. In any event, it is a sudden fall from grace. The scandal that enveloped me in 1986 lasted a year or more. I mention this because the personal shock that affects the politician and his family and friends is immense, even if they are in the eye of the storm for less than a week. The minute-by-minute media scrutiny and analysis can have devastating consequences. When I was hit by scandal in 1986, the whips gave me only one instruction, and it was underlined by my constituency party hierarchy. That instruction was: whatever happens, do not resign. Even with a majority of over 14,000 votes, the Billericay seat was not thought to be impregnable in the run-up to a general election, which could be about a year away. The one move used successfully to deflect the media onslaught which was to come had been ruled out of bounds; it was not available to me. I had nothing else to give up, no sinecure or position, as a sacrifice that would satisfy or appease the news pack. I was given no further advice from my party. I determined the best bet was to continue, however difficult it would be, to do my constituency work as well as I could and to say nothing (or as little as I could) about my predicament to the media. It had to be business as usual; silence was the name of the game. With hindsight, I wish I had taken a different course.

The climate of political life in 1986 was completely different to that prevailing now. I believe one Labour MP, Chris Smith, had 'outed' himself as being 'gay' in 1984 – however this was an option available only to Labour MPs. He went on to become a Cabinet minister. If I, as a Conservative, had admitted to being a homosexual, I would have forfeited the position I had long aspired to hold and which I thought I had trained myself to be rather good at, namely, being a back-bench Member of Parliament. I realise that just saying that is to risk today's political classes' incredulity. For the politically ambitious, being an MP is not an end in itself, it is a stepping stone to greater and better things and, for many, a rather small and inconvenient one. It is that motivational force of wishing to advance up the greasy pole that gives power to the whips, a power of preferment which, in my case, was redundant. Not that I ever used such a position – what might be perceived as lack of ambition – to further my ends. I had no 'ends'.

I had thought one could be a homosexual discreetly and in private as long as I did not frighten the horses by revealing in a moment of madness in some 'liberal' colour supplement or red top Sunday paper that I actually was one. I did not 'know', but I guessed that a number of my colleagues in all parties were, what might be called in the theatrical world, 'gay'. But it was something about which we never talked. Furthermore, I do not think I gave off vibes of 'homosexuality' to others. I may be wrong on this, but I believe and certainly hope I do not emit the stereotypical signs of homosexuality, as might be portrayed in most film or media depictions of homosexuality, even to this day. None of this should be taken by the liberal elite that I was ashamed of being homosexual or that I conducted my life in an hypocritical manner; I was not and I did not. My closest friends knew my sexual proclivities and it did not matter a damn to them. It never occurred to me that others would try to 'out' me or that I was even in a vulnerable position. I had forgotten about my very public 'split' with Terry years earlier. The 'attack' on me by the *Sunday People* in the summer and autumn of 1986 came as a profound shock. I was not prepared for the possibility of people selling their stories, and certainly not homosexual ones.

I believe the 'attack' was sanctioned at the highest level in the Mirror Group, by its criminal publisher Robert Maxwell. The same Robert Maxwell who was friends with Eric Moonman, not that he had anything to do with this, and who, after his death in 1991 (under mysterious circumstances on his motor yacht), it was found had fiddled his employees' pension fund and effectively stole the House of Commons wine cellar. He cannot have been pleased that his Mirror Group had to give me a grovelling apology in the high court when I sued them for libel. In any event, the extent to which he used his paper's resources in my pursuit was remarkable.

I hope my reader will forgive me if I do not go into the details of what I am supposed to have done or not done or what I do or do not do in my bedroom. Throughout my life, I have tried to keep such matters private. Not, as I shall explain, because I thought they were illegal and wished to keep such 'criminality' quiet; on the contrary, I perceived everything to be legal. I think such matters should not be for public consumption, whether a person is in the public arena or not; they are too personal. What I was not prepared to discuss with the media at that time was the fact that I was a homosexual; it was none of their business. I was sensitive about my private life being discussed in public – I still am.

With hindsight, the press's interest in me might have been even greater, if that were possible, had they known that a homosexual police detective constable, who I had met in 1985, had introduced me to a top-flight professional footballer in his twenties. Neither of them were 'out' in the parlance of the day. Oh – and with no racial intentions whatsoever, but for the avoidance of doubt – the footballer was white.

In my case, in 1986 the 'criminality' revolved around not what happened or did not happen in my bedroom, but around the age of consent. For homosexual activity, it was then twenty-one years of age, and had been since 1967, before which homosexuality was illegal. What a travesty that was. Furthermore, there was a difference between the heterosexual age of consent, set at sixteen years of age, and the homosexual. In order to maintain my privacy, I was not part of any homosexual community (to the extent that any existed), but I do have an opinion on what was going on at that time. Though I can produce no evidence for it, the view at the time was that, in practice, the police would not prosecute 'offenders' where activities were consensual, taking place in private and where the people involved were over the age of eighteen. It was concluded that the police had better things to do with their time.

Initially, I perceived the tabloid press 'attack' upon me was largely to portray me as a homosexual, knowing that such a description would be deadly to my parliamentary career. It was the *Sunday People* and

one of its freelance reporters that seemed to be the main protago-
nists. Their lurid descriptions of what I am supposed to have done in
my bedroom filled their newspapers for a period of six weeks in the
autumn of 1986. It was meant to embarrass and it did; it was meant
to intimidate and it did. Perhaps they offered the most money for
stories, I do not know. What I do know was that I was determined
to stay quiet and not respond. At the time, hardly an article would
be printed without there being at least one, if not many errors contained within it. The press seemed to think it was my 'duty' to alert
them to their colleagues' errors; I disagreed and refused to fall into
what I considered to be a trap. I wanted nothing to do with them or
their increasingly wild stories; I kept my distance.

It is natural, I believe, for a person caught in the headlights of
the press in such an onslaught that a certain fascination exists in
the victim's psyche about exactly what is being, or about to be, said
about them. The evidence is gathered by the newspaper and, if it
is a Sunday paper, on the Saturday, as late as possible, the victim is
'door-stepped'. This is an attempt both to comply with apparent
fair play of giving the person the right to reply and yet put the fear
of God into them at the same time. I think I was in my constituency when the *Sunday People* first asked for a comment. I cannot
recall my exact words, but I would have been brief, a variation on
'no comment'. I returned to my London flat in a state of concern;
what would they write?

In the age of the internet, all it takes is a few clicks on one's
home computer and up comes the story, wherever you may be in
the world. In 1986, the equivalent was catching the last Tube to and
from Earl's Court, where the first newspaper editions were always on
sale at a stall outside the station just before midnight. I went there
with fear and trepidation. The first time I read that a person called

'Max', aged nineteen years of age, had been equipped with a tape recorder for sound without my knowledge by the *Sunday People*, I recognised that there were likely to be problems. On the Sunday, I decided to ring Scotland Yard and volunteer to be interviewed; the Metropolitan Police refused to take me up on my offer. They would not interview me for six months.

My understanding of the situation was that the *People* had trawled the gay clubs of London with my photo asking if anyone had seen me in an intimate and sexual manner. One such person was found and was subsequently paid to visit my flat to act as an agent provocateur. The newspaper placed bugging equipment on his person, asked him to lead me in a sexual conversation and to confirm my sexual preferences; it was entrapment. The person had met me on one occasion previously when he had confirmed he was over the age of consent – that is, over twenty-one years of age. He certainly looked over twenty-one years of age. He confirmed again in conversation with me, documented on the paper's own tape-recording device, that he was over the age of consent. He also confirmed that anything that had taken place between us had been consensual. He made no complaint to the police and spoke to the newspaper in return for money, which they offered him in return for a story. Following the newspaper's published story, he again made no complaint to the police. When the police interviewed him later in 1986, he still did not wish to give evidence against me, and there was doubt that he would testify against me. He understood at the time that he was threatened by the police if he did not agree to be a witness, so, reluctantly he made a statement. He was under duress by the police, certainly not by me.

Maxwell hypocritically attacked the *News of the World* for the manner in which it was investigating Jeffrey Archer, when his own newspapers, egged on by the publisher, did far worse against me.

On that basis, a hue and cry was brought down upon my head. Once one newspaper prints such a story, the rest of the media piles in, wants to embroider the initial scoop, seeks 'your side of it' by way of balance and, before long, dealing with the press becomes a full-time occupation. How does this play out? Well, on the Sunday, every other national newspaper and media outlet, including radio and television, want your take on the story. In my constituency, I had a local evening newspaper and local radio and television stations in Essex, all of which approached me for comment. As the week began, more national papers made contact after seeing what others had printed on the Monday and Tuesday mornings. By Wednesday and Thursday, the various weekly papers in the constituency were asking for comment. You were soon back to Friday and Saturday, when the Sundays were asking further questions and raking up further intrusive issues. As a Member of Parliament, I had to deal with the media on political issues, policy and comments, but this paled into insignificance compared with what took place on stories concerning my private life. It was not uncommon to return home and find twenty or thirty messages on my answer phone asking me to return the call to this or that journalist. And all this after a day at the Commons, answering the queries of the press from my office there. I tried as best I could to return calls. Whatever else, I did not want to be accused of being rude or impolite, and no journalist ever alleged that I was; I just did not wish to talk about my personal or private life. Reporters were removed from my Commons office when I was absent.

I was on the front page of Sunday newspapers, or page two or three, for six consecutive weeks. I believe at the time only Princess Diana was subject to such press intrusion. I coped with great difficulty. I had a permanent headache. I felt sick and weak. Apart from all else, it was a great and unwelcome distraction from the job I was doing, or trying to do, for my constituents. However hard I tried to concentrate on this work, every minute of every day was taken up with thinking of what was to be said next, how I should react to the latest inference of alleged impropriety in my life. Again, rightly or wrongly, I decided to keep quiet and try to hold my head up high – easier said than done in the light of what was being said. I am not going to disinter here what was truth, half-truth or pure fiction from all those column inches at the time. I have recently re-read some of them and still feel, on balance, that I was right not to comment in detail about them. I think, though, I should have considered more carefully what I did say, and probably should have said more than I did. At the time, I felt betrayed; outside of my immediate family and close friends, I did not know who to trust. I did not know if I could trust anyone ever again, and these feelings of betrayal and lack of trust have left their legacy even to this day.

With that being said, I will consider just one of the allegations in some depth. In February 1987, the *Daily Mirror* published a story that was then taken up by other newspapers and is still widely publicised now on the internet and used against me. It concerned a short holiday visit I had made to Morocco and, in particular, to Agadir, where I met an art dealer I had previously become acquainted with in London. It was and is alleged that an Arab youth, aged fifteen years of age, was 'found' under my hotel bed on this holiday. The legal age for consent in Morocco was apparently fifteen, although I was unaware that it was as low as that at the time. The *Mirror* journalists visited the Hotel Ali Baba (which subsequently changed its name), spoke to a receptionist and took photographs, which were annotated in the paper to display the room in which I stayed.

The *Mirror*, in that at least, had it right; it is true to say that I stayed at the hotel. I arrived into Agadir mid-evening and went for a drink later on in one of the café/bars around the edge of the main square, on Avenue du Prince Sidi Mohammed, close to my hotel. While there having a soft drink – I drink alcohol infrequently – a group of young men started talking to me, some in French and some in broken English. One of them who spoke good English stayed behind when his friends left. We continued chatting for a couple of hours. He was twenty-five years of age and a footballer. He wanted to come back to my room to have another drink, to get to know a Westerner and improve his English. I agreed, but he warned me that hotels did not like 'locals' going past reception and into guests' rooms. I knew some hotels had such rules, and, to get round them, he said he would enter through the garden. As requested, I opened the sliding doors of my room, ushered him inside and closed the curtains. We were alone for about five minutes, talking about London, when there was a knock at the door; it was the night receptionist, who was complaining that I had someone in the room. I told him to come back in ten minutes and we agreed to go back to the bar via the garden. On opening the curtains, however, I saw a large, hooded, brown-gowned Arab carrying a baseball bat and looking very threatening. I closed the curtains. My new friend was worried; he said if he was caught by the hotel authorities they would beat him up and/or hand him over to the police. I believed him and was concerned for his safety. It was difficult to conceal a person in such a basic room, though. The wardrobe, behind the shower curtain or the room curtain offered no shelter. We eyed one of the two twin beds. He went underneath it but, alas, his muscular build meant the bed ended up resting upon his torso and not on the floor. Enter the receptionist, who let in the man with the baseball bat through the sliding doors. They looked disappointed that my friend was nowhere to be seen and were about to leave when suddenly they noticed that one of the beds was moving up and down – the curse of having to breathe. The young man was dragged to reception, with me in hot pursuit, where they confiscated his identity papers. Afterwards, we went back to the bar, where he explained they would blackmail him for his papers, inform the police or both. I was certainly not prepared to accept that, so I returned to the hotel and paid something like the equivalent of £30 for the return of his papers. No doubt the hotel night receptionist and the blackmailer were amply rewarded by the *Daily Mirror* for the story. Lastly, and again to disappoint the web fantasists, despite what has been written on the internet, I have never been removed from Morocco, or any country for that matter, and have since visited Agadir a number of times.

If I had not wanted to keep my sexuality private, maybe I should have revealed the full story in 1987. However, I was in 'silent' mode at that time. With hindsight, it might have prevented those now attempting to use a twisted version of this story to support the false paedophilia allegations that have wrongly surrounded me in 2015, despite the fact that the 'boy' in this story was twenty-five years of age.

The press went to extraordinary lengths to get so-called stories. While I was on a parliamentary visit to Finland with, among others, the delightful Clement Freud, during the night my hotel room telephone rang. There was no one at the end of the line. I thought it might be an urgent call from London, so I went down to reception and asked if they could identify the number. They agreed and found that the call was made from a room in the hotel, for which they gave me the number. I was leaving for the Arctic Circle very early the next morning and called the number before I departed. The 'guest' turned out to be an investigative journalist from the *News of the World* and he was trying to find out if anyone but me would answer the phone in my room in the middle of the night.

I will say just one thing more about the spate of stories (some accurate; some wildly inaccurate) that appeared about my private life over that year of horror. If the minutiae of anyone's sexual activities were to be set down on the front page of every local, national and international newspaper, as mine were, in the same detail and to the same extent as the allegations made against me, they would be regarded as absurd and ridiculous. However puritanical and so-called moralistic a person might be, I do not believe he or she could withstand the exposure of their sexual activities in the public arena, whether they be a Channel 4 newscaster or a newspaper publisher. To make my case, I cry in aid that true example of such a publisher who would employ a young man to dress up in a Roman Legionnaire's uniform and made him crack half a dozen eggs over his helmet at the end of his bed while he made love to his wife. When a few years later I mentioned this accurate anecdote on the *Richard and Judy Show*, they both started laughing and found it so difficult to continue with the programme that they went to a commercial break. During the break, Richard tried to persuade me to reveal the publisher's name; I refused, but then as the break was ending he winked at me and said, 'Don't worry, I have sussed who it is!' The programme re-started with both of them still smiling.

A great deal of tosh is talked about the morals of sexual activity. Once the idea that sexual activity is the sole preserve of procreation is disbanded, a position I respect but which, obviously, I do not hold, then it follows that what one does in the bedroom, I believe, should be a matter of private agreement, as long as it is consensual and legal by way of the age of participants. Sex should be enjoyable for both participants and the 'nanny' state and its busy-body representatives should keep their noses out of the equation. Of course, those who investigate us in the media, government or the police force are not asked to declare their own sexual proclivities, and nor should they be.

I was often besieged at my London flat by reporters. I once arrived from the House of Commons in the early hours of the morning and within minutes, the doorbell rang and I was asked by a reporter, with photographer present, 'Mr Proctor, who will you be sleeping with tonight?'; at 6 a.m. the same two rang the bell again and asked, 'Mr Proctor, who have you been sleeping with tonight?'

On another occasion, reporters, including a tall, young man from the *London Evening Standard*, kept vigil during the day at the block entrance to my flat. He was Shekhar Bhatia. I thought it unfair on other residents that they had to run the gauntlet as they entered their homes, so I put on a tracksuit and pretended to go for a run, thinking that would dislodge them from the entrance. Once I had entered Bishops Park and was out of sight and had lost them, I could return to my home and rest. Just my luck, however, Bhatia turned out to be a very good athlete and, while I 'lost' everyone else, he kept up with me with consummate ease, meaning I had to run round the park being interviewed – not my intention. I arrived back in a state of exhaustion; the reporter had not broken sweat. Well, at least the entrance was clear.

Throughout the period of endless comment – the aim being either to cause a by-election or simply to sell newspapers – whatever else I thought I had done, I did not think I had committed a criminal act. Following the instructions I had received not to resign, I had to maintain my position not just as an MP, but also as the parliamentary candidate for the general election that everyone knew would be coming in 1987. A very small number of people in my constituency voiced opposition to my running, but I managed to win all the association votes on motions against me by large majorities. On one occasion, before a key vote of the Executive Committee meeting of my Conservative Association, the *Sunday People* sent more than a dozen reporters to the constituency who showed tapes and photo-graphs of me to forty of my committee members on the door steps of their homes late at night. The *Sunday People* was not reporting the news; it was seeking to *make* the news for its proprietor. Robert Max-well was using his paper's journalists to try to trigger a by-election, and doing it mob-handed. Their nefarious endeavours failed, but I received call after call from committee members who revealed how they had been cold-called late at night by reporters trying to per-suade them to alter their support for me. In the main, they refused.

At one meeting to discuss my position in the light of the press allegations against me, the wife of one of my constituency chair-men, who also disagreed with my views on immigration, was determined to resign as my agent; I gained wind of it in advance. I decided to buy her the most enormous bouquet of flowers and, at the start of the meeting, presented it to her. She spent the rest of the meeting very red-faced, not knowing what to do with the flow-ers. Her position was not helped when she revealed later that she had thrown the flowers away – people thought that she could have sent them to a local hospital or retirement home.

It was in the early autumn of 1986 that I first went to a solicitor and sought his advice. He was in practice on the Fulham Road. The advice I required was not so much about what had been appearing in newspapers, which I thought was unpleasant but not necessar-ily a legal matter. What was a legal matter, however, was that I had recently returned home from the House one evening to find a mes-sage on my answer phone from someone I had known, apparently in court before a judge, who was threatening to sell his story and go to the police if I did not 'have a word' with the magistrate and try to get him acquitted. It was a classic blackmail sting. For the record, in those days, MPs did not have 'words' or contact of any kind with judges. I assume that continues today, but I am not convinced, as they now seem to contact the Director of Public Prosecutions all the time. I took the tape to the solicitor, told him the context – it turned out I had no need, he had read about and knew of me – and asked for his advice. There was no way I was going to allow myself to be blackmailed. The solicitor obviously agreed; he said he would represent me. He said I should keep the tape in a file with my legal papers. Obviously, he added, I should have no dealings with the person in question. I did not. If the police contacted me, which they subsequently did, I should let the solicitor know.

It was the morning of Saturday 14 March 1987 and Terry was about to go on a round-the-world trip. He was separated from his wife and was staying with me before his departure. I had returned from Hull University literally battered and bruised from the encounter with the mob of rioters and had decided at 8 a.m. to go downstairs to the news agents to see how the media had covered my visit. I arrived at the block entry door just as a woman carrying a parcel was about to press the doorbell, coincidentally, to my flat. In granting her access, I had inadvertently foiled the police's ham-fisted efforts to gain entry to my first floor apartment by deception – they were not expecting me to actually let them in! Their amateur subterfuge failed and I was shortly after introduced to Detective Chief Superintendent Drummond Marvin and his Detective Inspector. Marvin, of the Metropolitan Police Force's Serious Crimes Squad, was a thick-set man in his late fifties; he seemed avuncular and almost jolly. We went upstairs to my flat and, to give Terry a little notice, as I opened the door, I said something like, 'I am not used to having the police in my apartment so early in the morning,' in an exaggerated, loud voice.

Marvin was at pains to ensure I said absolutely nothing. He said they had a warrant to search the flat but told me not to say a word.

In total there were five or six police present. I was told I would be taken to Cannon Row Police Station to be arrested. It was, they said, a formality. While still in my flat, I was asked if I had a solicitor. I rang him even though it was a Saturday morning. When I explained that the police were proposing to search my flat, the solicitor said he and his firm could not represent me and suggested I find another solicitor. There was a strong feeling of abandonment. I felt very alone.

Among the items the police took that day was the 'blackmail' tape from a filing cabinet that contained all my legal papers. Much later, Marvin wrote an article for the *Sun* newspaper. He had retired and was evidently adding to his retirement funds, also writing articles on Lord Lucan and Russell Harty. About myself, he said that he thought he was right to have taken action against me for two reasons. One, that I could have been susceptible to being blackmailed and, he claimed to have found a blackmail message on my answer phone. (He did not, as I have already described – it was in my solicitor's file of papers.) Indeed, he was prepared to use the potential blackmailer as one of his star witnesses against me; blackmail was a far more serious offence then than gross indecency, and still is, but it would not have served Marvin's position to have admitted it and acted upon it. His article in *The Sun* contained a number of inaccuracies. He also wrote and gave oxygen to the fallacious concept that there was in existence a 'Westminster rent-boy ring', of which I was a part. It was a lie; I was not part of a 'ring'. My sexuality was private and discreet and certainly not shared with any of my parliamentary colleagues. Unbeknown to me then, it was a lie that was to wreak havoc yet again in my life some twenty-eight years later.

When I left my flat with the police, I was not surprised to find the *Sunday People* reporters and photographers at the door. How did they know of the exact time and date of the search? I wondered. I soon found out that it was because they had been working hand-in-glove on the case with the police and had long ago passed them all the papers they had on me, including tapes, statements and photographs. The police – maybe for money or for publicity – had tipped off the press. The police 'organisation' was the leakiest of bodies and still is. They were working together, not on behalf of complainants – there were none, other than journalists – but to do Maxwell's bidding.

I had been tipped off that the police themselves had been entering gay bars and clubs all over London, emulating the press, asking if anyone had been 'with' me. A publican telephoned me at the House of Commons to say they had been in his south London pub and he felt I should be alerted to the lengths to which they were going. They were showing my photograph to everyone, he said, and sometimes in a threatening manner.

During the search of my flat, I went with the police to be 'bailed' at a central London police station. I was not interviewed or questioned in any way. That night I attended a wine and cheese party in the constituency, and I told those present what had happened. I felt at a very low ebb but at least, I thought, I could start to explain matters to the police. However, I needed a solicitor first, and one that was not going to let me down the moment I needed him most. At this point, I still felt I was innocent of any charges that might be levelled against me.

After months of relentless pressure, I was physically and mentally very tired. Having to respond to this constant battering from the press was exhausting. I tried to keep my head up in public, but in private I was in despair. I had fought long and hard – far harder than I had ever had to fight to defend my political views. I now felt an air of destructive inevitability crossing my every move with regard to my private life. I found it easier to take abuse and hostility than support and affection. I still do.

At the House of Commons the next week I sought advice as to who to engage as my solicitor. I talked to colleagues, particularly those with a legal background and, after consideration, I contacted the firm of Kingsley Napley. I knew Sir David Napley had defended Jeremy Thorpe, the former Leader of the Liberal Party, on a charge of murder, but it was explained to me he was also good at dealing with the press and with what was explained to me were 'famous' cases. I certainly thought I fitted into the first of these two headings.

I had not met him before I went to his Covent Garden offices to discuss my predicament. He was a short, dapper and smartly dressed man, seventy-two at the time, with a very short haircut. He hid his dislike of me well. I got the impression that he thought a lot of himself, with good reason if one considered his track record of legal cases. I believe he was, coincidentally, friendly with a solicitor and leading light in my Conservative Association, which should have alerted me to the possibility that other matters might colour his judgement other than purely legal ones. I believe from the moment we met he determined his role was not to 'get me off', but rather to mitigate any punishment I might receive if prosecuted. His junior was Michael Caplan, who was reassuring, friendly and had a firm grasp of detail. I thought he was, understandably, in awe of Sir David. I myself was rather terrified of him, but the die was cast.

It was agreed that Sir David would henceforth deal with the press and speak to Marvin of the Metropolitan Police. I was to say nothing to anyone. To that extent having Sir David was a relief. When I returned to the House after our meeting, I bumped into Alan Clark, dressed as ever in one of his navy-blue suits. He collared me in the car park entrance under Big Ben and said he thought I was 'sailing very close to the wind'. I am not a nautical man by any stretch, but I got his drift. He was concerned about me, but supportive; he told me to keep my head down. I do not think we spoke again. I really liked the man and had known him all the time I was in London. He was certainly a chip off the old block.

Shortly afterwards, on the same day, I met Geoffrey Dickens in one of the House dining rooms. He had been friendly during my time in the Commons and was particularly supportive of my views on immigration. He said he was very sorry for my problems – he appeared utterly genuine – but just wanted to ask me one thing: 'Do these police matters involve children?' I said no, but that my solicitor had told me not to speak about anything. I know a little more today about the two so-called Dickens Dossiers of 1983 and 1984 than I did at the time and so can understand his question better now than then. But if I had been mentioned in those papers, if he thought I was a paedophile, I do not see how Geoffrey could have had that conversation with me in March 1987. Nor could I see how he could have had such friendly conversations with me during our years in the House if he felt in any way, I might be a paedophile.

The next month, in April 1987, I was working late at the House of Commons waiting for a vote. It was pointed out to me that the next morning's edition of *The Sun* was carrying a story that I was to be arrested by the Metropolitan Police and charged. I considered my position and decided, whatever happened, I did not want to be on my own, and my brother kindly invited me round to his flat in Brook Green for a late supper, after which he asked me to stay overnight as it was very late. While watching breakfast television with him the next morning, I was alarmed to see police, journalists and television cameras at my apartment block in Fulham. Detective Superintendent Marvin had turned up to arrest me and had the press for company. His ploy having failed, he said I was 'on the run'. I telephoned Sir David Napley, who was very angry with

the police. He had apparently agreed that 'when', not 'if' they were
to arrest me, they would contact him first and make an appointment.
It was just Sir David's style, but he had not mentioned it to me and,
of course, such politeness would have prevented Marvin getting his
publicised arrest. Sir David issued a statement that said I was not
fleeing the police but rather avoiding the press. With that, the arrest
by appointment was back on track, and he agreed with Marvin that
I would be interviewed at Bow Street Police Station that afternoon.

Before the interview, I met Sir David, who explained procedures
He said I should answer 'no comment' to all the questions the police
asked of me, which I did. Sir David did all the talking. I was shown
photographs of 'Max', the person who had been paid by the *Sunday
People* to entrap me, who they said was nineteen, and another person
called 'Jason', who they said was seventeen. I was charged with four
counts of gross indecency under Section 13 of the Sexual Offences
Act 1956. It was often used for the sort of thing that might occur in
a public place, lavatory or common. But, in my case, if it happened
at all, it happened in the privacy of my own home – discreetly and
consensually. In any case, the evidence was clear: no one had made
a complaint, certainly not 'Max' or 'Jason'.

On returning to Sir David's offices, we discussed the situation.
I explained that, with regard to 'Max', it was true that I had met him
twice. I thought he was over twenty-one at the time; he looked over
twenty-one and he had told me he was, indeed, he had claimed so on
the newspaper's own concealed tape recording. With regard to 'Jason', I
said I could neither recognise nor recall him; I believed we had not met.

I said I presumed I had a defence in that, although I might inadvertently have had sex with a male person under the age of twenty-one,
I did not believe him to be so. Sir David said that unfortunately there
was a lacuna in the law in the homosexual case compared with the

heterosexual. If a man had sexual relations with a girl under sixteen (the legal age of consent for heterosexual couples), he would have a defence if the jury believed him when he said he thought she was over sixteen. I, as a homosexual, had no such defence; whether I knew it or not, if 'Max' (or anyone else I had been involved with) was under twenty-one, I had committed an offence. This was the first point at which I became aware that I had committed an offence, and I immediately told Sir David I would plead guilty. He said that the birth certificates of the two men would need to be checked, but he had no doubt that the police would have got those details correct.

There was still the matter of the second man, however, 'Jason', who I told Sir David I was not sure I had ever met. He said if I pleaded 'not guilty' to offences concerning 'Jason', there would be a full trial. The police would continue to seek out more people who would say, for whatever reason, that they had been with me. He said the police had possible ways of getting people to say things whether they were true or not. In any event, I would not be able to continue as an MP if I pleaded guilty, as was my intention, to the charge relating to 'Max'. I felt devastated. My mother and brother had been through enough, I thought; there was no virtue in having a trial that dragged on for weeks and in which more and more salacious information would be fed by the police to their bedfellows and 'sources' in the press.

Rightly or wrongly, I followed his advice to plead guilty to all four charges of gross indecency. The rest of the meeting was focused on mitigation. Sir David immediately asked me to see a psychiatrist at the Royal Free Hospital in Hampstead, and when I asked why, – 'I am not mad,' I said – it was at this point that he stated his belief that homosexuality was a disease – an illness. I was shocked at his admission and realised then that I may have made a mistake in my choice of solicitor. It was, however, too late. When he realised I was reacting adversely to his suggestion of psychiatric treatment, he took a new tack. He said that, by way of mitigation, he would wish to inform the stipendiary magistrate at Bow Street that I was not a paedophile, but if he did this in open court the press would report it in such a way that I was. If he had a medical report, however, he could just hand that to the stipendiary magistrate and it would not have to be read in open court. I knew I was not a paedophile and, without any better ideas or options, I gave in to Sir David's remorseless pressure on the subject; an appointment at the Royal Free Hospital was duly made.

I felt utterly defeated as I left Covent Garden. All my life's work – my ambition to continue to be a good constituency MP, the dedication – was for naught; my life as I knew it was at an end. I was desolate. I returned to the House of Commons where news of my arrest and charges were rife. I knew now my political enemies were to be victorious and I sat in my usual place in the Chamber, aware that it would be for the last time. Proceedings continued, but I was not following them; my mind was elsewhere. After a time, I felt I had had enough; I stood up to leave, walking down the few steps to the floor of the House to turn right to the Bar and my final exit from the political world. As I reached the floor, however, I was grabbed by several government whips and physically made to sit on the government front bench between them as business continued around us. We made small talk, they asked how I was feeling – I said hardly anything – but I very much appreciated the gesture as well as the friendship and the support that it signified. I knew the eyes of the House were on me; it was like saying goodbye to an old friend. Ironically, it was to be the only time I ever sat on the government front bench. On my way out of the Chamber, I stopped at the Bar of the House, turned and slowly bowed to the authority of the Speaker's chair and left for the final time.

The Chief Whip at the time was John Wakeham, who invited me shortly after to a meeting at 12 Downing Street. I think they sent a car for me. He wanted to know what I was going to do. I told him I had conducted my affairs in the last twelve months in such a manner as to avoid a by-election, and, as the general election was almost upon us, I had succeeded in that aim. Further, I was not going to resign as an MP, but would explain to my association officers that I was not seeking re-election and was therefore only standing down as their parliamentary candidate. We then discussed the date of the general election. It had not been announced, but I needed to coordinate the timings with my solicitor for my court hearing date. I said I would write a letter to the Prime Minister explaining why I would not be seeking re-election, which would be copied to my association officers when I met them shortly before what otherwise would have been my selection meeting on the Saturday. It was a very friendly and sympathetic meeting with John.

Next I told my secretary Lyn. She asked me if there was any other way; I said there was not. I then met my agent, Jill Schneider, at the Orsett Hall Hotel on the Friday night for dinner. She wished me to continue to fight, but I said I could not. I had fought for twelve months or more and the fight was gone from me. I was to plead guilty the next week and I could not stand for reselection unable to tell my association what I was to do in just a few days' time. Survival was now the name of the game. She was understandably upset; we had fought through very difficult months together, during which she had been incredibly supportive and helpful. I thanked her and apologised. The next day, I handed in my resignation as a candidate to my officers. It was a subdued and emotional meeting. I got through it, though, and returned to London, leaving the association to choose another candidate. Whatever they may have thought – and I know feelings were mixed – I saved them from having to fight what would have been a difficult by-election. Had the general election and my court appearance not virtually coincided, who knows what might have happened.

Days before my court appearance, I went to the Royal Free Hospital and met the psychiatrist. I am not a great fan of the profession, although recognise the work they do for those suffering mental health problems. He was elderly, tall, had white hair and wore spectacles and I think a white medical coat. It was late in the afternoon, there was no one else about, and we spoke for nearly two hours; it was not a perfunctory interview. He asked some very detailed and personal questions and, at the end of the session, he said, 'You are certainly no paedophile.' He also said he did not think homosexuality was a disease; very reassuring, I thought. He then asked me a question I have thought about long and hard in the years since: 'Are you sleeping OK?' Well, as a matter of fact, and somewhat surprisingly, I told him, I was. I think due to a combination of physical and mental exhaustion after the year or more I'd spent under constant pressure from the media. 'Well,' he said, 'you might find the coming days difficult. I will prescribe you some sleeping tablets. Mind you, I am of the old school, and the tablets I prescribe are barbiturates. Do not exceed the stated dose or you will die.' I took the prescription and folded it into my pocket. I had not ever contemplated taking my own life, but now, thanks to the kind doctor, I had the wherewithal to do it. I think he thought he was being helpful. He invited me for a drink at a local Hampstead pub immediately after our discussion; he was friendly and we chatted over my position. I never saw him again. He wrote a report after our appointment which Sir David was pleased with and used in the court proceedings.

The day before my appearance at Bow Street Magistrates Court was traumatic. I had a bath in the afternoon, during which time

I thought all about what had happened to me. It was as if running in my mind was a continuous tape-recording of everything that had transpired, and now I was placed in this impossible position. I re-played it in my head over and over again, trying to see how a different outcome could have been forthcoming. In Sir David's opinion, I could have had treatment for my 'illness', but for most other sane and sensible people, including myself, I could think of no way out of my predicament. As I got out of the bath, I realised there was a way out – a coward's way out, maybe, but a way out none the less; the barbiturates in the bathroom cabinet. I dressed and took the bottle into my sitting room, where I placed it on the table before fetching a glass of water. I think there were between twelve and fifteen tablets in the small, plastic, medical bottle with, I think, a white, child-proof lid. I pressed down and turned the lid, letting the contents spill and roll across the table. I determined not to write a letter; I would not have known what to write. My silence, or virtual silence, of the last year could continue.

The telephone rang. I didn't immediately answer it. When I did, it was Matthew Parris, with whom I had served in the House of Commons until he took up a media career. He asked me to his south London house for supper, an invitation I politely declined; I had another thing to do. He insisted; he knew I was in court the next day. At this, my mind removed itself from self-destruct mode and allowed other thoughts to dominate: my mother and brother, who had been so loving in such trying circumstances; my friends, who had been so supportive; the letters of backing I had received urging me to fight on, including friends from my Young Conservative days – they all suddenly flashed through my mind. I gave in to Matthew's persuasive tongue – and he can be very persuasive – and accepted. I placed the tablets back in the bottle and returned them to the small, built-in cabinet in the bathroom. I do not recall too much about the kitchen supper I had that night. Matthew has mentioned how a number of his friends were there, including a barrister friend of his. The barrister said he doubted I would go to prison – I could have been imprisoned for five years on each of four charges – but he thought I would receive a fine. Matthew's act of kindness certainly saved my life that night, although he did not know it until 2015. After the supper I returned home, sorted out what I was to wear the next morning, and went to bed.

Matthew had demonstrated that, no matter what, I still had friends, and that politics and a political career were not everything in life. For me, it certainly loomed large but, although I did not know what form it would take, life could and would continue. My thoughts of suicide were not prompted by the fear of going to court the next day and all that would entail, including public humiliation and, as Sir David put it, 'shame and despair', but rather that it was to be the final chapter of my political life. I could not think of life after politics, which had held my attention for twenty-six of my forty years.

On 20 May 1987, I dressed and took a mini cab to my solicitors' offices, from which it was a short walk to Bow Street Magistrates Court. Both solicitors had been formal and correct; I do not recall either of them putting me at ease. Michael Caplan was certainly the more friendly of the two; Sir David, who wore a bowler hat and puffed on his pipe, seemed ambivalent. I chose a suitably sombre dark suit. The streets were incredibly busy, both for traffic and pedestrians, and on the walk to court, the reporters and photographers, who had congregated outside Kingsley Napley offices in Covent Garden, seemed to grow in number as we approached Bow Street. I recall a white-van driver leaning out of his vehicle and shouting at the media snapping at my heels, 'Leave him alone!' (Well, I have left out some of his more choice words…), which was especially reassuring as other pedestrians had shouted abuse at me. As I approached the doors of the court, I had to push my way through the crowds of people, some of whom were there demonstrating against my political views. On entering the building, a peace prevailed. My solicitors went to find which court was to be used. On their return, Sir David said to me that if I was sentenced to a term of imprisonment he would immediately appeal. I might be incarcerated for a few hours at a police station, he said, but no more. Chief Superintendent Marvin was very solicitous as to my well-being; I think he recognised that, for me, the sentence of the court was immaterial. I had already lost everything – or so I thought.

The appearance in court is still rather a blur, though I do remember feeling incredibly alone in the dock. The courtroom seemed empty, but I have vague recollections of some heckling from the public gallery. I remember pleading guilty to four charges of gross indecency; I did not recall the detail at the time, nor what the prosecutor, Sir David or the stipendiary magistrate said. I know that the speech of the prosecutor contained inaccuracies, par for the course with anything to do with me on this matter. I was unaware, however, that the prosecutor would go into so much alleged detail as he did, and thought that I had pleaded guilty to stop such falsehoods being articulated. At the time, these details rather passed over my head and I think I had to ask my solicitors what the fine amounted to later. I do recall Sir David passing over the medical report on my mental health. To me, though, it all appeared a rather bureaucratic exercise in wrapping up my parliamentary career.

In his lengthy mitigation statement to the Court, Sir David said:

> This case came before the court because it was initiated by a journalist … The way it was done was little short of disgraceful.

Money was offered to these people to give evidence about what went on in private ... Additionally, there was a technical break-in to his premises, when they took property out without his permission, and wired someone for sound and sent him in. This was done in return for money. Ten years ago, Parliament was thinking of making this sort of conduct an offence. The Lord Chancellor at that time said he was not going to do it because he could trust in the future the responsibility of the press not to do it again. This shows the Lord Chancellor was wrong, and it should now become a criminal offence.

In a similar vein, I wrote in the *Evening Standard* in December 1987:

I'm certainly not suggesting that this change in the law should only apply to MPs. What happened to me can happen to anyone, whether they are in public life or not. There are all sorts of people who have had difficulties in their private life which some journalists chose to exploit and their lives have been ruined as a result. The journalist goes on to his next story; the victim lives with the pain. To me, that's quite wrong. The time has come for something to be done about it. Our legislators should bite the press before the press bites them ... You realise that while the public's memory may not be that long, the press, like the elephant, never forgets. In ten or twenty years' time, journalists will still be able to look me up in their cuttings and stir it all up again, embellishing as they go.

Fortunately, and in the light of events twenty-eight years later, my mind was not on the future; I had concluded I hadn't one. As I left the court and entered the waiting area outside, Marvin approached me with my solicitors and asked me to leave the building by the back door, as there was a large crowd outside demonstrating against my political views at the front entrance. I thought for a moment, then told Marvin, 'No, you have brought me here – I entered by the front door and I will leave the same way.' He said he could not guarantee my safety and that I would have to wait until they summoned up reinforcements of police to protect me; so be it, I thought. It was, after all, not a complainant, but the police and the press that had brought me to court in the first place. The phrase used by Terry weeks before crossed my mind: 'You are being hung out to Dreyfus' – a reference to the infamously unjust trial of Captain Alfred Dreyfus, in which the press played a huge role, that went on in France between 1894 and 1906. After fifteen minutes or so, police reinforcements in place, I walked back to my solicitors' offices through the throng as the political taunts and shouts raged, then gradually diminished. There was a little small talk with Sir David and Michael in their offices, mainly over paying their bill, but during which the former told me that the Earl of Longford had been concerned about me. I sensed that the solicitors thought it had gone as well as they could have expected. I thanked them and bid farewell.

When the coast was clear of demonstrators and the media, I made my way to a friend's car parked nearby and he drove me to his mother's home in Hastings, where I spent three nights away from London and from the press besieging my flat and phone, the column inches of the newspapers and the television and radio reports. I have only just read some of those reports recently and find I do not recognise myself from the descriptions of me that they contain.

What might have been the alternative? I wonder now. I might have decided to plead 'not guilty' to all four charges. The basic facts were these: the 'evidence' was derived from a 'sting' operation by a Sunday newspaper, who paid people to give them a story. There must be grave doubt as to whether this tainted evidence would have been accepted in a court of law. There were no complainants. If the hidden tape recording had been deemed inadmissible and the two males decided not to succumb to police threats, i.e., not willing to be witnesses and refused to give evidence, the prosecution case would be threadbare. Everything was consensual. It is conceivable that, had the case gone to a jury trial, with a barrister who believed in my case, a jury would not have convicted me notwithstanding the letter of the law.

However, the alternative of a full-blown trial, and the accompanying headlines that would appear every day for weeks, when my mother was still alive, seemed intolerable. The relentless pressure upon me had so worn me down by this point, the idea of a quick end seemed a relief. Sir David, perhaps influenced by others in the establishment, did nothing to suggest any other course of action. It so happened that the general election and the trial overlapped. There were those in the establishment that wanted me gone as they hated my political views, especially on immigration. Had I stood for re-election, I feel sure my association would have continued to re-select me; a trial immediately after the 1987 general election would have allowed four or five years for me to maintain and, if necessary, regain the trust of my electors, especially after a not-guilty verdict.

There must have been, based upon what I know now, at least fifty or so MPs who were homosexual at that time. So why was it I who was selected to be the victim of press harassment concerning my sexuality? It is my belief that it was a combination of Robert Maxwell's links with the Labour MP whom I had defeated, Eric Moonman, and the fact that I was perceived to be right-wing, especially on immigration.

On returning to my flat days later, I found handwritten messages had been stuffed through my letter box from the press, my answer phone was full of invitations to discuss what had happened, to go on this or that 'show', as though I was some kind of freak. I replied to none of these requests; I was no longer 'in' politics, so I didn't have to.

Life remained difficult in the immediate aftermath of the trial. The general election was three weeks away and during that time I remained the MP for Billericay, trying to clear up constituency cases as well as deal with new ones. I continued to do my best for my constituents. I noticed my conviction was not used by opposition political parties in the election campaign. I think that is very significant. Teresa Gorman, my successor as Conservative parliamentary candidate, wanted as little to do with me as possible, turning down any advice my experience might have to offer. So, apart from constituency work, I spent my time stripping my Common's office, boxing up papers and files and filling the spare room of my flat with packing cases. The officials and police at the Commons were very diplomatic and supportive, as was Lyn, my secretary. At home, I started the laborious work of shredding the confidential papers of my constituents. It was to protect their 'secrets' and confidences, not mine. It took many weeks and covered my flat in a thick, white dust.

The press continued to write about me. Journalists, and their reports, were mixed: some ventured articles about how good a constituency MP I was regarded to have been; some would approach me in the streets and on the Underground expressing their personal sorrow at my departure. On election night, *Spitting Image* depicted me as a schoolboy with cap in their polling evening special, a remarkably inept and inappropriate choice, I thought, coming from such a usually prescient programme.

In the streets, I was abused, shouted at, spat upon and at times I had to run fast to avoid physical confrontation. Certain investigative journalists followed me whenever I left my flat. On one occasion, I rang a pursuing reporter's news desk and asked if they could stop him from following me. When I refused to comply with requests for stories, journalists made up their own – I had become a recluse, was ill and dying of Aids, for example. I went to Harrods to delete the 'MP' description from my account card – I thought that would be exactly the kind of thing the press might look for and report to my discredit if I did not. Terry went with me. A newspaper report the next week said I had been seen shopping in Harrods with a teenager, obviously flying in the face of the court decision and taking no notice of the magistrate's strictures. Terry, who was at this time in his thirties, was actually very flattered by the description.

I had no savings, no income, lived in a rented flat and I had to sign on to receive unemployment benefit. I did not know how I was to survive. I had worked all my life; now I was not just unemployed, but unemployable. What boss would take me on knowing the press would be round the corner, waiting and watching? I survived through the help of family and friends, but even so it was a quiet and haunting time. I was depressed and very lonely.

I thought I had lost everything – my career, my vocation, my salary, my reputation, my self-respect and my future. It was not true; I had one thing left to lose. A few months after the trial, an attempt was made on my life. I was subject to a violent attack in which I was held captive, plied with the sleeping tablets I had been prescribed but not used, and made to listen to how I was to be murdered. A number of close friends know the truth of what happened, but I have not been prepared to discuss the circumstances until now.

I was lonely and withdrawn and two men, one of which I knew and was the son of a policeman, wanted overnight accommodation.

They asked to stay overnight in my flat and I obliged. Nothing untoward occurred that Thursday night. The same request was made on
the Friday evening and, after considerable persuasion, I agreed. In
the early hours of the Saturday morning, I was set upon and a large,
glass ashtray was smashed over my head. I was hit with a hammer
and a carving knife was held at my throat. Blood spattered the wall
and I was knocked out. When I awoke, I was bound. I could hear
the two men as they discussed how they were going to steal my
belongings and my cash card and keep me prisoner until the Sunday
night, when I was to be killed. At 7 a.m. they left to get breakfast and
'milk' my account. I was left tied to my bed, falling asleep under the
influence of the drugs. After about an hour of attempts to release
myself, I was able to free one hand and telephone one of my friends,
who came over and saved me from a certain death. He took me to
hospital. On my return, they tried to break in, my friend having had
the sense to change the lock while I was being treated.

It was in this way that I discovered even when you think you have
lost everything, there is always one more thing you have left to lose
– your life itself.

I kept the attack secret until the 1990s, when I revealed it to a
police Superintendent, who was coincidentally sitting next to me at
a business lunch, and he said I had done the right thing in not making it public. I had no wish to become 'public enemy number one'
again, by going to the police and reporting these serious crimes.
As a 'victim' I thought I would not be believed. If I was believed the
press would regard me as in some way having 'caused' the attack.
I kept all the hard evidence for a couple of years and then ditched
it. To overcome and recover from this dreadful experience, I took
a short holiday abroad with the friend who had rescued me. In the
late afternoon on my first day in the main street of the city where

we were staying, I was mugged at (rather large) knife-point and my brand new bright-blue boat shoes were stolen by a bicyclist. My French is not good, but my assailant pointed at the shoes and said, 'Ou tu es mort.' I got his drift and handed them over, returning to my hotel barefoot.

It took me a long time to concentrate on what I was to do in the future. I lacked self-confidence and all avenues appeared barred to me. I am pleased to say that I was contacted by a number of former Conservative MPs, my colleagues with whom I had served in the House and, much to my surprise, they were solicitous. Teddy Taylor, the then MP for Southend East, very kindly invited me to lunch at St Ermin's Hotel. I thought he might, for religious reasons, be rather anti-me, but at the time he was supportive and solicitous. It was not until 2015 that he fell for the fantasists' paedophile smear and attacked me in his local press. Neil Hamilton and Gerald Howarth and others remained very friendly. In times like this, I found, you get to know who your friends are. I did not solicit support; I did not wish to place anyone I had known in an invidious position. I kept my distance and responded only when contacted. I was not, as some would have people believe, calling in favours; I had no favours to call in. I had no knowledge of the personal lives of my colleagues and the little I knew about my friends did them no discredit. The idea that there was a Westminster 'rent-boy ring' as later suggested by Marvin in *The Sun*, or that a Westminster paedophile ring existed, were absurd suggestions. The notion that I could therefore extract sums of money from other members of these alleged 'rings' by blackmail or them bribing me to stay quiet was and is preposterous. It is also untrue.

I once attended a drinks party with a number of MPs and executives, possibly British Rail. Harold Wilson was in full flow speaking to the group in which I was standing when he was asked if he had ever thought of accepting a bribe. He thought for a moment and said, to everyone's great amusement, that he did not know whether he would be bribed as he had never been offered enough money. I guess I consider myself almost in Wilson's situation; only in my case, no one has offered me a penny. I have never been bribed.

What did happen, entirely unsolicited by me, was that a number of Conservatives decided to raise funds which would allow me to finance my own business. It was clear no one would employ me, but working for myself meant I had expectations. With capital, I could employ myself. Tristan Garel-Jones very kindly organised a group of investors who, in conjunction with a small sum from myself, put up the money to buy an off-the-shelf company called Cottonrose Limited, an appropriate name, I thought, as the business comprised a retail shop selling cotton shirts, silk ties and waistcoats. This was in 1988, and I felt I finally had something to look forward to, something to plan for; I had prospects I was very grateful to those sixteen or so investors who provided me a lifeline, a future.

A number of other people invested as a direct result of watching me on a television programme called *After Dark*, a talk-show broadcasted live on Channel 4 on which a group of people discussed the controversial topics of the age. It was back in the days when channels did not broadcast throughout the night, which meant it had no pre-arranged end time and the guests could talk into the early hours. The programme continued for as long as the directors felt it was effective or as soon as they thought discussion of issues had been exhausted. In my case I think it went on for nearly three hours. It was the antithesis of today's sound bite culture; today's politicians would be singularly inept at participating in such a programme. It took the format of an after-dinner conversation among friends, around a table with drinks, only we were no friends. This particular programme was about press intrusion into private lives, and I was asked to be a guest. I had not participated in programmes on radio or television for a long time but, after some persuasion and the knowledge that my business venture was to open in the summer of 1988 and that this would help promote it, I agreed. The subject of press intrusion bonded me and the other guests, who included Peter Hillmore, Lester Middlehurst, Laurie Manifold, Christine Keeler, Nina Myskow and Annette Witheridge. It was chaired by a Professor of Law, Ian Kennedy. Boy George had been invited to attend but did not show up, so it was imbalanced, but this worked to my advantage. Channel 4 did not initially want to tell me the names of the other guests, but I insisted. I think they did not want me to research them. I bet the journalists knew I was participating so they could prepare. I had heard of some of the guests, but not others. I couldn't think why I had heard of the name Witheridge when her name was mentioned until I was about to leave for the studio. Then I remembered she had written about me, so I found her press cutting in my files and placed it in the top pocket of my camel jacket and set forth. I thought it might come in useful; it turned out that I was right. I recall I was so concerned that it was likely to be a 'set-up' that I took my own bottled water and glass in case the drinks available were tampered with by the production staff or other guests.

The programme entered their list as one of the most watched and most video requested; apparently one such request came from Buckingham Palace. It was generally regarded that I had put up a good performance, including a demolition job on Witheridge with her black lipstick and black varnished fingernails and sweating (or is it 'glowing'?) profusely; with no defence, she physically melted. She admitted she had written a piece suggesting I had contracted

Aids after my court appearance, had left it to others to check the truth of the story with me, which they had failed to do, and when, a month or so later, she had discovered there was no truth in the allegation, she had done nothing to correct it and nor had her newspaper. There were other knock-out blows and as a result of the programme I managed to get further investors. Bereft of editing, the programme allowed me to speak my mind, at length and allow my personality to be seen by the viewer. Such opportunities were rare when I was a Member of Parliament. It annoyed my enemies, but my friends – and, oddly, certain newspaper journalists and TV critics – rather liked my contribution to the programme. I am glad I did it. After the show, I had a drink with Christine Keeler. I really could not understand how she could have nearly brought a government to its knees. She was charming with me, but vulnerable, and did not seem strong enough to wield that power. She had been caught up in the Stephen Ward and John Profumo scandal almost by accident. Afterwards, the show's producers used to invite me to their end-of-series parties, which I enjoyed attending.

I put all my endeavours into organising the business – finding a small but characterful shop on the pedestrianised Brewers Lane in Richmond upon Thames, just off Richmond Green. Historically, it had been one of the first streets to service Richmond Palace. I used my contacts in the rag trade to establish the shop, including getting my friend Michael Fish to help me, the man who invented the kipper tie in the sixties (not the meteorologist). His new design for ties had a very wide blade and, when asked by Turnbull & Asser bosses what they should call it, he suggested his nickname, 'kipper'. He worked in my shop for the first week to show me the ropes. I bought a pen-and-ink cartoon that had appeared in the *Spectator* magazine with a shop window bearing a sign 'Shirt lifters will not be prosecuted'.

I got the joke and placed it on display in the shop. I decided to call the shop Proctor's Shirts and Ties. I did not want the press, customers or anyone else visiting the shop, not knowing it was me running it. I did not wish to pass myself off as anyone else, or persuade anyone to buy things in ignorance. I was still lacking in confidence, but wished there to be no doubt that it was me – warts and all.

It was 1 August 1988 when the shop opened. The first person on the doorstep among the press, photographers, the curious and the odd customer, was a solicitor. He acted for a journalist who claimed I had libelled him in an article I had written in the *London Evening Standard* magazine under a series title of 'Answer Back'. I had written nothing about my case until that point but had been persuaded by the paper's deputy editor at a dinner party thrown by my friend, an owner of a deli and a restaurant. My friend had tried to encourage me out into the social world I was loath to inhabit in my attempt to shy away from controversy. She was very reassuring and persuaded me to write 'my story' or, rather, a small part of it, with the help of one of her paper's reporters.

As a result of this article, which, as I say, I had not volunteered to write, here was a journalist suing me for libel. I had no money to defend myself; it had all been invested in the business. The courts were not sitting, yet I had to go before a judge in chambers. I sat on my own on one side of a mini courtroom; the journalist with a phalanx of lawyers and hacks on the other. I had to give a solemn undertaking that I would never repeat the anecdote about him again. The judge eyed me severely and said, 'And if you do, you will be in contempt of court and I shall imprison you.' So much for the alleged freedom of the press in certain segments of the media. I had not named the journalist in the offending anecdote, nor, directly, his newspaper, and I have long since forgotten his name. Maybe now, twenty-eight years later – during the majority of those years where, as a result of this injunction, I have not spoken to the press about my personal life for exactly that reason, daring not even to mention the reason for my reticence – I can be permitted to take the risk and declare it now.

CHAPTER 9

RICHMOND YEARS

In a strange way, having your own shop, serving in it most days and attending to customers, is akin to having a constituency. You meet lots of people, you have conversations with your customers, hear their moans and proffer, if they ask for it, rudimentary advice to solve this or that problem; that is how it seemed to me. It was not dissimilar to attending an MP's advice surgery.

Surprisingly, the thing I missed most about not being an MP was not the House of Commons. Of course, the building, the Palace of Westminster, was a splendid place in which to work. But I did not miss the late nights, the divisions, the hanging around for seemingly endless debates. Those few former colleagues still in the House tell me I would not recognise the place, so drastic have been the changes these last thirty years, PMQs being a pale shadow of its former self. In addition, the reduction in the length of back-bench speeches, the curtailment of what little influence MPs had on the government of the day, although partly balanced perhaps by the increase in influence of certain select committees, has been noticeable. Overall, the hold over the executive by Parliament and its Members has diminished. Reform has had the effect of increasing the power of ministers and the whips and diminishing the power and ability of MPs representing their constituents, articulating their opinions and doing the job I cherished. No, it was the constituency and my constituents that I missed the most.

The shop in Brewers Lane, Richmond, was small and so the mood was intimate and conducive to conversation, or maybe it was that many customers knew my background and wanted to chat; I certainly did. Such conversations allowed my confidence gradually to grow and patch the huge holes the scandal had punched in my personality.

An old kilim-bench-type stool provided the visitor with a modicum of comfort while they sipped the mug of tea or coffee and we put the world to rights. I was fortunate in having a remarkable mix of customers and callers. Professor Edward Goldsmith ('Call me Teddy') became a frequent caller when he was in the country. He was the founder of *The Ecologist*, an area of politics I was largely ignorant of, and he put me right on many 'green' issues. He certainly carried the prevention of waste into his personal life, once bringing to me a dozen or more of his brother James's shirts when he thought they had reached their life's end. Teddy had me remake them, cutting out his brother's initials on the chest, so for every three or four shirts I managed to make two perfect ones. The shirts were originally made in Hong Kong of reasonable quality, beautiful, cream silk. The make was inferior in cut to the ones I made for Teddy. It took a while to produce them, but he was very happy with the end results when eventually they were ready. Recycling can be an expensive and long business.

Most Saturdays, the managing director of Claremont Fabrics, Richard Jeffries, would call to choose a shirt or tie and at Christmas buy presents. His business was fabrics, including wonderful silks and heavy velvets. He knew about material and rated my two-fold cotton poplin shirts and heavy woven silk ties very highly. He was very interested in Richmond society and what the council was up to and I gradually shared his interests. I looked forward to conversing with a cultured and impeccable man and was very sorry when he died, suddenly, in the late 1990s.

A great character of Richmond, who owned a famous antiquarian bookshop on Richmond Hill – Baldur Bookshop – was Eric Barton, and he and I became great friends. He would visit me twice a week, never take a coffee as he was on his way to the pub for a tipple, but would often 'borrow' (never to pay back) the odd fiver for his drink. He said that his wife kept him on a tight rein as he had an eye for the barmaid, so often left his house penniless. He was a very wealthy man and very particular about who he wanted in his shop; he didn't like the 'riff raff', as he would say. He was also a skilled practitioner in the noble art of customer intimidation. When it rained and those not so interested in his specialist books attempted to seek refuge from the wet, he would shout at them that he was just closing, dashing out on urgent business and rush to place the 'closed' sign on his door. For a time, one of my neighbours was also an antiquarian bookshop. Trade was usually slow for them, but one morning I was told that they had made a good sale. Meeting Eric on the way to the bank in Brewers Lane, I mentioned this information, saying they had good news to impart. 'Oh,' he said, 'I cannot be doing with good news today,' turned on his heels and fled on a different route to his favourite pub. Yet, he was the most polite and well-mannered of men. He always wanted to know how I was, whether I was in good health and how the sale of shirts was going. He had a great brain and he used it in support of Dylan Thomas and Oscar Wilde by raising funds and supporting their memorials.

Eric loved cricket and was a member of the MCC, often sitting in the front of Lords' Pavilion during Test matches. He was an expert on the game and we would often talk about England's team selections and was impressed that I was old enough to have watched Gentlemen versus Players matches when I was in Scarborough, and we discussed the players of the '50s and '60s. Eric was also an expert on all things Jack the Ripper, the many books written about him and the investigations as to who he might be. He had the driest sense of humour, often pretended ignorance through dementia of the simplest of points, yet could handle the most complex of issues. Eric was a white haired bespectacled brilliant man who 'flapped' his way around Richmond and I always enjoyed meeting him. He was well loved and very much missed when he died in 1997.

Peter Sallis, the great character actor in *Last of the Summer Wine* for thirty-seven years and the voice of Wallace in the film cartoons *Wallace and Gromit*, lived locally and was a generous customer, enjoying both the merchandise and the chat before and after the purchase. He also had a dry sense of humour and was very supportive. Initially, he visited the shop with his delightful wife, then on his own. There were several actors and actresses who dropped in as customers. Keith Barron, a very talented character actor, was a very friendly and expansive customer who always wanted conversation as well as a brightly coloured striped shirt or two. I enjoyed his amusing repartee. Lionel Blair was very courteous and often called in to chat and be his amusing self. There was much laughter and jollity over many years in the shop, a marked contrast to what had gone before. I am indebted to everyone, customers and visitors alike, who contributed to so much amusement, so many bon mots and such good humour at that time.

The RFU Twickenham stadium was not far away, so I had several England rugby players who often called for the odd evening shirt they had forgotten to pack and soon I realised I had to stock in large collar sizes. Many customers wanted black silk bow ties and I only sold ones that had to be tied, so I gave customers lessons on easy ways to do so. One night, just before closing, I had a telephone call from a regular customer. He couldn't get to Richmond but was desperate to have his bow tied as he was rushing out to an important dinner party with his wife. I subsequently met him in a Kingston upon Thames car park to tie his bow for him so he was correctly dressed.

The local newspaper was owned by the Dimbleby family and I often chatted to David as he walked through the lane to his offices. Ronnie Wood lived round The Green and was a frequent buyer of waistcoats, often made to measure by my brother.

Many customers visited my shop because it was me running it; others just liked the merchandise. My name was over the door and on the shop sign and on the labels on most of the stock.

My neighbours and I were a happy retail community and, in the first year, I joined in their self-help efforts to promote shopping, especially Christmas shopping, in the lane. It was such co-operation that led me to join the Richmond Borough Chamber of Commerce. I became vice-president, then president for two years, and ultimately chief executive. I was privileged to be president in the year we celebrated the chamber's centenary, receiving a letter from Her Majesty the Queen by way of congratulations.

In my work for the chamber I gradually got back into the routine of meetings, events and social activity, using my former political knowledge to the chamber's advantage. On behalf of the chamber, I held many meetings with local Richmond borough councillors and council officials, helping to increase the role and influence of the chamber while I was connected to Richmond. I enjoyed the work. It was of a non-party political nature but for much of the time I was dealing with Liberal Democrat politicians. Initially, the local MPs were Conservatives (Sir Jeremy Hanley for Richmond and Toby Jessel for Twickenham) but then, from 1997, I dealt with the Liberal Democrat MPs Jenny Tonge and Vince Cable. I established a good working relationship with each of them and all were helpful to the chamber and business interests in the borough.

Similarly, on behalf of the chamber, I forged links with the local Richmond Police, which was useful to both the police and the chamber. One of the police inspectors who worked in the borough almost throughout my time there was often in communication on business matters. He was also very helpful when we needed police help in organising our charity Victorian evening every December. Charities were always making a beeline for help from local businesses and the chamber was often the conduit.

In the summer, we organised charity cricket matches and I played. My previous political connections came in handy in obtaining ministers to speak or help the chamber. For example, John Redwood came to attend a town centre exhibition, town centre management being an important issue in the 1990s.

Christine and Neil visited my shop in Brewers Lane, Richmond, when Neil was a minister at the Department of Industry. They were on their way back from a ministerial engagement in West London and very kindly dropped in to say hello en route to the office. Extraordinarily, within minutes of their entry, two young men entered the shop and started shouting homophobic abuse. Neil and Christine took it in their stride. I was not embarrassed. It had happened before a number of times. I waited for the shouting to die down. I thought they had fired all their oratorical barbs and, as one of them took a step backwards, thinking he was retreating to the entry door, I took a step forward to find my chin connecting with his fist. I collapsed in a heap 'seeing stars'. When I came round, I heard two things: a banging and a shouting. The banging was Neil's head hitting against a door, as he was being punched by one of the attackers. The shouting was Christine, who had gone outside into the lane, crying out for help. Christine's shout is very loud indeed. I tried to intercede between Neil and his attacker and sustained the odd blow. The attackers fled into the town centre with the cries of Christine growing to a crescendo. So alerted, the tenant in the flat above the shop and a visiting plumber from the Isle of Wight pursued the men and saw them get on a bus outside Waitrose. They telephoned the police on mobile phones and surprisingly the attackers were caught. Neil and Christine, and eventually me too, went to Richmond Police Station and made statements. Subsequently it was discovered Neil had a broken nose and I had a broken finger. The men were sentenced to six months in prison for their alcohol-fuelled rant and attack.

Had it not been for Christine's gutsy behaviour in alerting everyone, they would have got away. As always, I am grateful to her for such action. I learnt that day, at first hand, how much of a battle-axe Christine is, although in private she is gentle, warm, inviting, giggly and fun. Neil and Christine have had their ups and downs politically and privately, their downs monstrously not of their own making, and they have bounced back magnificently. They give me support and their example encourages me to battle onwards.

That night, I went to hospital for an X-ray on my finger. As I sat there in Charing Cross Hospital A&E waiting room, a newspaper photographer entered and asked at reception if I was there. They rightly refused to say and he did not recognise me as I sat behind a newspaper. He would not take no for an answer, however, and went into each of the examining cubicles seeking me out for a picture.

Press intrusion and abuse, a recurring theme in my life, did not stop even at the doors of a hospital.

Of course, the unfortunate consequences of my past public difficulties were never far away. Neil Hamilton's broken nose and my cracked finger demonstrated the homophobia that was directed at me. Obnoxious graffiti decorated the shop from time to time, but could be washed away. Sometimes my neighbours would kindly clean it away if they saw it on a morning before I did. I had two hanging baskets full of blooms hung outside the shop, which helped to make the lane look even more beautiful in the summer months, and in one summer season these baskets were destroyed regularly. Eventually, I started reporting these incidents of criminal damage to the police – they asked me to do so. Every time I did, I received a pro forma letter from the Richmond victim support team asking if I needed any emotional help or support. Eventually I had on file eighteen such letters, one for each basket I 'lost'; at least the system worked. We never caught the culprit, however; I assume they just got fed up of bothering me.

My friend Bee was a frequent visitor to the shop. At many times in my political life she put her analytical mind to work on my behalf and came up with a lateral solution to whatever the problem might be. She was very distressed when my personal life dredged up problems for which there could be no solutions, lateral or otherwise. Notwithstanding that calamity, we remained friends. Later, I would meet her on rare trips to London from Leicestershire. She made wonderful, precise meals, served with bread and delicious wine, and the conversation was always top-notch. We would talk constantly on the phone about current political events. She continued to help me with life's problems and was always willing to translate a document or write a letter for me in French. We hardly ever looked backwards, always forwards. I spoke to her in hospital the day before she died; she was looking forward to leaving the doctors for home and her beloved dog. When she retired from work, she always had dogs from Battersea Dogs & Cats Home. Together they kept each other fit, with constant walks around her home. I was shocked when she died. I thought our friendship would be never-ending. I am fortunate to have met her and proud to have known her. She was a solid rock in a crisis, whether personal or political. I miss her analytical mind, her ability to think laterally, out of the box, her calming influence, too, and capacity of putting everything into proportion. I went to her funeral in the little Catholic church off Ham Common and as I write these inadequate words of tribute to my dear friend Bee, surrounded by my own dogs now, I am shedding tears for the memory of a great woman and a true friend. How I wish her intellect, wit and fortitude could be available to me at this, my darkest hour.

After I moved to work in Richmond upon Thames I met two wonderful ladies who were to play a large part in my life in the 1990s. Doris Miles had a shop called Shades of Richmond next door but one to mine in Brewers Lane, between George Street and Richmond Green. She was a great character and already in her eighties when we met. Her shop was a jewellery and curio shop. Originally it had been a millinery shop during the Second World War. It had changed over the decades but dear Doris had not told her insurers. An insurance claim in the 1990s after she had been burgled one Christmas was met by the insurers, even though they thought she sold hats not gold!

Doris was the doyen of Richmond's retailers and the Chamber of Commerce. She had known Dylan Thomas from visits to his watering hole of the Britannia, the pub next door. In the war she helped to raise funds for spitfires. After the war, she refused grants which were offered to her for war damage to repair the roof of her shop above which she lived. She thought married families with young children were more deserving of the grants; she never did get her roof fixed properly.

She was hospitalised from time to time throughout her old age and was placed in a hospital near Barnes Common. She hated it. She thought people were being bumped off in the night and, on one occasion, asked me to 'kidnap' her and take her to my home for lunch. Over that lunch, we talked and the next day I arranged for her to leave the hospital, getting social services to sort out special banisters to help her get up her stairs. Only by doing this could we get her released. I put up the rails myself. She survived another ten years. She worked in her shop every day and was very knowledge-able, a deep well of information about Richmond and its history and the people who lived and worked there. We would converse every day about business, or lack of it, what tomorrow might bring and how we might overcome some problem or other. As she got into her late eighties and nineties she remained incredibly active. She hated old people and loved to be with younger and active adults. She gave Terry a splendid portrait of herself and small pieces of silver. She would often drop into the shop to pass on messages or suggest ways of doing business better.

Every Christmas, the Chamber of Commerce organised a charity retail Victorian evening based on a mythical visit by Queen Victoria to Richmond. A horse-drawn carriage procession brought 'the Queen' through the streets to the town centre; Doris played the monarch, while I played the Duke of Wellington on horseback, leading the procession. Every year she insisted on wearing a new wig and my brother made her a wonderful dress for the part. It was arduous, but she was Victoria to a T, and she stayed up discussing the even-ing until late into the night. She walked round the town centre with the Lord Lieutenant – the real one – helping charities raise funds at the many stands. At the end of her life, just months before she died, aged ninety-six, she played Victoria again – the only occasion when someone had to be made to look younger to play the part.

Towards the end of her life she was robbed at the shop frequently, but she was determined and would often beat off a shoplifter here or a thief there. Doris bore these attacks with incredible good grace and shrugged and carried on with her work, which was her life. Doris would accommodate young ladies and young men in her humble Dickensian home. They would help Doris to live, looking after her and protecting her. One such young girl was Elizabeth, who was on a type of 'gap year'. She now runs a major German BMW dealership. Doris was very special. She would dress immaculately, colour coordinated in every respect and went to Ferragamo shoe shop in central London every year, liked only one style of classic shoe and bought several pairs a year. When she died, she had over 100 pairs in a wide range of colours – the Imelda Marcos of Richmond.

The Christmas before she died, she stayed with Terry and me at our Kemptown flat on Marine Parade in Brighton. We had drinks at the Grand Hotel before Christmas Day lunch at a French restaurant. She drank port and lemon and enjoyed her stay very much indeed. I drove her to and from Brighton and she was in her element socialising around the town, soon to be a city. It was to be her last big outing.

Within Richmond, Doris was very well-respected and her friendship and support meant much to me. I spoke at her funeral on 28 June 2000, which was very well attended and held in the Mary Magdalene parish church. It is a great pity she did not make it to her centenary. If anyone deserved her telegram from the Queen, she did.

For many years, Liz Carran had organised the Richmond May Fair to raise funds for the church. Liz and I met in my role as chief executive of the Chamber. She helped me to organise the Victorian evening. I tended to raise the money from the shops and businesses and Liz would organise the charities and help with council and police permissions, as the main street was pedestrianised for the night. Liz also helped me in the arduous task of raising money for Christmas lights. She was married to a successful architect and they lived around Richmond Green and were very hospitable to me and to the charitable endeavours they supported.

Organising these two major events was almost a full-time occupation and Liz managed skilfully to combine home life and her charity work. We held many meetings in my shop, in between serving customers, and many evenings saw us working together to bring a little bit of magic to Richmond each Christmas. During all of this, Liz was very charming and supportive and had that certain ability to attend to detail. There are so many people who speak airily and adopt broadbrush approaches to life, but it's those who can get their hands dirty and deal with the minutiae of events who appeal to me the most. Liz was just such a person. I found her to be strong, resolute and robust, with great personality and enjoyed her company.

Other business owners in Brewers Lane also became friends. The jeweller opposite was Lionel Jacobs. He had been caught out in the Lloyd's insurance problems but had kept his business going despite losing much money. He was a man of few but genuine words, quietly spoken, precise and warm. He could not do enough for me and as our shops faced each other, we watched over our mutual interests. He came to dinner many times. Other antique and jewellery shops frequented the lane and they were all friendly. A pub – the Britannia – a flower shop, Magnums Wine Bar and a chocolate shop completed the mix of retail, all of which complemented each other. Neighbour disputes were few and far between and co-operation was the name of the game. Generally we all supported one another and I am grateful for their assistance at that time.

While in Richmond, I also got to know Judith Stott. She was a child actress and the former wife of Dave Allen, the comedian. She had acted with John Gielgud, Edith Evans and Peggy Ashcroft and lived in a wonderful apartment at the top of Richmond Hill, with the Turner view of the River Thames. She liked to drink and would often get a driver to drop her off in Brewers Lane and pop into the shop for a coffee. She was extraordinarily theatrical, dropped names with every breath, including that of Albert Finney, something I found unappealing at first and slightly unbelievable. Judith won me over with her amusing tales culled from the theatre. One night she invited me to go with her to the theatre in the West End. We had an early supper and Finney was in the play. At its conclusion, she dragged me to the stage door shouting 'Finney! Finney!' Much to my surprise, when the stage door man told him about Judith, he appeared and welcomed her with open arms and invited us up to his dressing room for drinks with others. I did the rounds and came across a rather short gentleman whom I did not recognise. I thought he might be a jockey. He stuck out a hand and almost whispered, 'Al… Al Pacino.' I asked him: 'What do you do?' 'I'm an actor,' he replied. Well, Judith was perfectly correct in everything she had said; silly me for momentarily having doubts about her famous friends. When I went to her flat she showed me letters from the great and the good of the theatrical world. She came to stay with me for a fun weekend in a cottage I rented for a while near Odiham in Hampshire. We became good friends, though our relationship was anything but smooth.

Judith came to dinner at my flat to celebrate the engagement of Emma Watkins to David Granby; they were to become the Duke and Duchess of Rutland in January 1999. Eight of us dined on a menu that recreated the luncheon served on the *Titanic*'s launch from Belfast in May 1911. Terry cooked in our very small kitchen all fourteen or fifteen courses. He is an excellent cook and we prided ourselves on entertaining, wining and dining in civilised style, with delicious food, good wines and courteous and fine hospitality. Among the other guests was Matthew Parris. I had met Matthew in the House of Commons and he seemed perfect to balance up the company. He got on famously with Judith, or so I thought; too famously in fact. Unfortunately, she developed a crush on him. Well, more of a fantasy affection, but would henceforth ring him up at all hours of the night to pester him into a love match fuelled by a tipple or two. Politely he declined but she became ever more persistent until Matthew could stand it no more and rang me to complain about my guest and to see what I could do to put an end to the one-sided, theatrical romance. I was sympathetic and said I would have a word. I did have a word with Judith, several in fact, but to no avail. The 'stalking' continued. Eventually, when Matthew suggested the police, I countered by suggesting he have a word with Judith's brother, Richard Stott, who was at various times the editor of the *Mirror* and the *People* between 1984 and 1992; poetic justice, I thought, as those two newspapers had done me down in the same period. Whether he did or not, I do not know, but Matthew wrote about Judith and that dinner party in his column in *The Times*, which then found its way into one of his books. Thankfully, I managed to keep my friendship with both of them.

Emma Watkins is another strong woman who was to become part of my life at this time. A farmer's daughter from the Welsh borders, she was bold and strong when I first met her, the day after she had first met David on a blind date in London, organised by Christopher Cole, who made wallpapers. Emma amusingly says she thought David, on receiving his business card saying 'The Marquis of Granby', was a pub-owner. Christopher Cole would never have had a publican in his smart home, a landlord most certainly. Somewhere in her character there was a strength of purpose and a resilience that would be required in her future with David, and with Belvoir, his stately home and estate. At the engagement dinner party she was bubbly, but subdued in comparison to Judith. Emma, who had trained as an opera singer, was soon to gain the theatrical attributes that had stood Judith in good stead.

David was Terry's close friend. They had met through Sarah Churchill in the mid-1980s and both worked at Wylma Wayne's Fine Art Gallery in Old Bond Street. Shortly thereafter we were introduced. His title was then the Marquis of Granby and he arrived at my flat with a suitcase early one morning. Despite lifts, he had managed to talk the porter of my block into carrying his luggage to my flat door; the porter did that every time he visited. Later, and often during the 1990s, the four of us met for lunches and dinners and I warmed to both of them. They would bring their first three children – all daughters – to our home, Emma often in a state of complete exhaustion.

I reached Richmond from Fulham by commuting by bus and train. I often shared my morning bus journey to Putney station with an elderly, tall, erect lady with grey hair. We often chatted at the bus stop. She also lived in my block of flats, so we had many common complaints and we used our morning conversations to voice mutual moans. She was an intelligent lady and we got on well. I was chairman of the residents' association and one morning, as I was leaving, the porter told me sad news of the death of one of the residents. I did not recognise her name so the porter described her, the tall erect lady with grey hair, and told me that the funeral was the following week. The porter also said, knowing I had always wanted a larger, top-floor flat overlooking Bishops Park, that her nephew was coming down from Scotland and wanted to sell her flat immediately. He asked if I wanted him to mention my interest to the nephew, and if I wanted to look over her flat. I said I didn't want to do anything inappropriate on the day of the funeral but he assured me all would be well. I went to the funeral service at All Saints' Church, Putney Bridge, as did many others. After the service, I accepted the invitation to look over the flat. It was wonderful, and though it needed a lot of work, I was happy to take it on. I agreed a price and within six weeks we had moved from the first to the top floor of my block. A week later, I went to the bus stop as usual and thought I saw a ghost. There was the tall, old lady with grey hair, very much alive. I did not tell her that I had been to her 'funeral'; I thought that was a tad too insensitive. I felt I had somehow bought the property through false pretences, but it was a very good flat and I welcomed the opportunity to live there.

I could look out across the park to the River Thames where, earlier, in the great London storm of 1987, huge old London plane trees crashed down through the embankment railings. It was a park through which I often walked on Sunday afternoons to find tranquillity, where I listened to the brass band concerts and where I played lots of tennis. I could see, in the winter months, the Star and Garter pub above which Mrs Kennedy from York University days had lived and described the view looking back the other way. I could just see All Saints' Church on the northern approach to Putney Bridge. In the 1970s, the vicar there was Richard Harries, who later became the Bishop of Oxford and is now Lord Harries of Pentregarth.

One curate of the church, Peter, lived in the block in the 1970s. He had a magnificent laugh; once heard never forgotten. We had given hospitality to what I thought was this impoverished young man many times. He kindly invited Terry and I and others to lunch. He said the eight of us would be eating in the French style, just a fork and knife each on the table. Our Saturday lunch appeared to comprise a platter of cold meats and bread and we had no wish to offend him. So we all spun it out as long as we could, cutting our ham into ever-decreasing squares. After over an hour, our host said, 'Thank goodness you've finished' and then served the most wonderful chicken casserole. He said he had to leave us to eat it alone; he was officiating at a wedding and had to dash to the church as he was late.

Joanna Lane (née Ball) was initially a friend of Terry's. She had worked at the BBC Television Centre in graphic design and had won a BAFTA for her work on *The Singing Detective*. She also gained fame in 1985 for designing the original logo and mascot for BBC's Children in Need, a teddy bear. When finished, she suggested naming it Pudsey Bear after the town in which she was born. I didn't meet her until 1987 – internet fantasists please take note – after she had left the BBC and was no longer involved with Children in Need. They should also be aware that although, coincidentally, she lived very close to the street in which the Elm Guest House in Barnes was located, she only resided there from 1988, many years after it had been closed down. Terry and I also visited her there in complete ignorance of the Guest House's alleged notoriety or even of its former existence, which none of us knew anything about until reading articles in the press more than thirty years later. It was in the 1990s that Joanna asked me to be the company secretary of Jo and Co, her freelance graphic design and film company. She had long since left the BBC. I was then chief executive of the Richmond Chamber of Commerce, was happy to help a friend and said yes on condition it was in name only. She agreed and her accountant did all the paperwork. To confirm, I have never had any connection with Children in

Need whatsoever, by and large my connections with the BBC have been critical and difficult ones, especially after *Panorama*'s 'Maggie's Militant Tendency', and certainly not social nor anything to do with allegations currently levelled against me.

Joanna is a very determined woman. Her physically small build betrays the strength of will and purpose. She is very analytical and, through her profession, a whizz on computers. We enjoy each other's company and I know her American second husband and her daughter, whom I first met when she was living in Barnes and who I taught to play chess. I regret Joanna being dragged into the sensationalism of 2015 and I find those web-based fantasists and trolls who did so very disagreeable, doing a great disservice to both the truth and to the internet, which can be such a force for good. They never let the facts get in the way of a good fantasy, however inaccurate they are and however damaging they can be. Joanna was rightly very upset to be contacted by the mainstream media as a result of such 'nutters' trawling the internet. Our friendship is as strong as ever and I am grateful to her and her family for their continued support and confidence in me.

Also in the 1990s, a very good friend of ours, Stanley, took his own life. He had helped a lot in the inspiration for our shop. He was Scottish, from Aberdeen, and had had terrible childhood problems, but to his credit overcame them and built a wonderful life in Jermyn Street selling shirts. He too worked for Turnbull & Asser and then Kent & Curwen and was full of sensible advice on the retail business. He had style and a great eye for colour and had known Terry and me for many years. He was a sensitive soul. Upon his death, I was called to identify his body. We arranged his memorial service in St James's Church in Piccadilly and held a party afterwards in Knights Arcade to celebrate his life. Ken Williams, the managing director of Turnbull & Asser, attended the service and the party and kindly contributed towards the costs. I gave a panegyric and, at dead of night, we threw his ashes into the River Thames from Putney Bridge, the casket hitting one of the bridge supports with a resounding crack. He would have been proud and amused that he went out with such a bang. We miss him.

We all knew Shirley Bennett, wife of the late Cyril Bennett of London Weekend Television, and their three children, Joseph, Rachel and Sophie. Sophie died tragically at age twenty-three in August 1989 in the Marchioness disaster on the River Thames. I went to her funeral and met Michael Grade. Later, I helped Shirley with the ongoing problems concerning the dreadful incident, including preparation for meetings she attended. Stanley lived with the family in Wimbledon and Sophie's death had a profound impact on him. Afterwards he questioned life itself.

It was Valentine's Day 1995 when my mother died. Of all the women in a man's life, his mother must stand pre-eminent. It does in mine; she provided complete and unconditional love. My feelings on her death were intense. She had been short in stature but tall in character. It was natural that when my father left home, I sided with her. That bond of affection mixed with sadness for her plight proved everlasting. In adversity, she was doughty. We had managed to live through a very difficult period. Mother and I had started a small bed-and-breakfast business in our house. In summer months in Scarborough, people toured the streets in cars looking for a vacancy sign. They might be a family supporting their tennis-playing daughter in a match, a semi-professional wrestler looking for a bed for the night after his one night of stardom, a couple just wanting a weekend away from the industrial blackness of an urban part of the West Riding of Yorkshire, or people from Scotland on their week's holiday. It was a great mix and though not many nights were involved in a season, it had helped us financially and had been part of my growing up, expanding my confidence at meeting people and being able to hold a conversation at a young age with virtually anyone.

Mother had always been hard-working and hospitable. She could economise too. She had been used to wartime conditions. We could not afford meat that often but she made wonderful 'meatless' stews and we could walk on the promenade at Scarborough, taking in the sea air and the richness of the sea views. She would often introduce me to her friends, just friends she had met while out and about, and talked proudly about the achievements of my brother and myself. She was always beautifully dressed, by my brother. Everything, including the hats she always wore, matched to perfection. But she had been living on her own with a Yorkshire Terrier to keep her company when I had left for university. Later, in the 1970s, my trips home from London were not as frequent as I would have wished.

After my parliamentary career had ended, mother lived with Granville in Brook Green, Hammersmith. She became well known in the area, which was fortunate when Alzheimer's disease hit her and she sometimes forgot where she lived. There always seemed to be a kind person around to point the way home. Those who have a parent or relative suffering from this illness will know how devastating it can be. At times she would forget me and my name and wonder who was sitting having tea with her. Initially, stupidly, I would get irritated at her loss of memory, not knowing how the disease manifested itself. She had always drummed into Granville and me that she never wanted to end her days in a nursing home or geriatric home sitting in those awful, plastic-covered chairs round the edge of the room contemplating among the many, one's solitary end. I knew what she meant, having canvassed such homes when I had been a parliamentary candidate. We made her a promise that she would never face that end. She didn't. Hilda died peacefully and safe at my brother's home; she was eighty-three years of age. Her funeral was held at Richmond Crematorium on 20 February. My great friend and concert violinist Marius Bedeschi performed beautifully. He played 'Meditation' by Massenet from the opera *Thaïs*. We also heard 'Greensleeves', dating from 1580. It is a very traditional folk song and tune and was perfect for a traditional English lady.

I recall, when I was an MP, mother had loved living in Billericay in the 1980s, where she easily made friends and acquaintances. We had fun times together and she enjoyed the socialising part of my role, and contributed to it by her presence and her fond memories, which she shared with any and all who would listen. She was pugnacious in her support of me, especially when she felt I had been wrongly pilloried in the press. We never talked about my private life; she was as discreet and as diplomatic as all my constituents were on that account. She had shrugged her shoulders when someone had tried to burn the house down and took it in her stride. She had seen the toll eighteen months of press intrusion into my private life had taken upon me, and she never added to that stress by questioning me.

However, one Friday night, at the height of the 'scandal' I was returning from the House of Commons to my Billericay home to change and go out for an evening engagement. I was late and the train delayed me still further. My mother answered the door to find a newspaper reporter and photographer, both large of build and much, much taller than my mother. Hilda explained I was still travelling home. They didn't believe her. They thought I was hiding in the house. They forced their way past my frail mother and searched the house. It was a small house but they had hunted me downstairs and upstairs, looked in the wardrobes and under the beds.

They only said they wanted to interview me. On my return, my mother was understandably upset. She could not understand why anyone would so violate her, and my home, in such a way. We sat down, I made a pot of tea and tried to calm and reassure her. What would Lord Justice Leveson have made of that I wonder?

After the first eighteen months of Richmond retail, I had inadvisably opened a second shop in Knights Arcade, Knightsbridge – but on the wrong side of Knightsbridge. The arcade had been featured in *Dance with a Stranger* and it was a great film location, but not good for retail. It was too soon in the history of the business and in the wrong location. It was a beautiful-looking shop and we equipped it well. The opening party went famously. There were well over 100 people present, including MPs, ministers and Cynthia Payne and Screaming Lord Sutch and his bulldog. Cynthia Payne and I had met initially in a TV studio. She was always impeccably dressed and a lovely lady. As I write, and by strange coincidence, I find she died today. She is described by a friend in a newspaper obituary as an eccentric. I did not find her to be so; rather a woman of generous and kind heart, intelligent and full of English common sense. Her use of luncheon vouchers was a very sensible business decision. She used her voice to good effect to demolish the snobbery surrounding prostitution so prominent in our legislative and media societal classes. We got on very well. She was down to earth and full of fun. Cynthia later came to a garden party Terry and I threw in Petersham. Westminster city council filled in a large, long-existing hole at the entry to the arcade on the afternoon of the opening party for the shop when they realised that ministers were attending. That is the type and level of political leverage that could be applied in those days – nothing higher or more sinister to my knowledge. We had two Brazilian musicians at the party who were playing bongos and sitar. Newspapers reported on our Frascati party and wrote about the complaints of the residents living above: 'There was so much noise, it sounded like the London Symphony Orchestra and there was only two of them!' The launch party over, I needed staff as I couldn't be in two places at once. So, among others, I enlisted the help of David Manners, at this time still the Marquis of Granby, who was rather good at selling shirts.

This shop cost a lot of money to set up and lost a lot of money very quickly, even after we negotiated a rent reduction. Other shops in the arcade closed soon after we opened, business got worse and after only eighteen months we cut our losses and closed. The debts of Knights Arcade unfairly saddled the successful little shop in Richmond, which stayed open for another twelve years, but, eventually, I had to give in to the inevitable and that closed too.

While living in Petersham, Terry and I threw a party. It was held in our home which had been a gatehouse to Ham House, or rather on scrub land just behind it. Terry and I temporarily lived there between selling the Putney Bridge flat and before moving to a James Sterling 'brutalist' flat off Ham Common, which Terry renovated to perfection. When we decided to host the summer garden party, we had no garden and no lawn. We planted grass seed and made a lawn during the six weeks from conception to party. On the day, the Mayor of Richmond arrived in a large chauffeur-driven limousine that parked ostentatiously outside the small house, which was near to the site of a famous hole, the Petersham Hole, which didn't get filled in for more than a year. That hole was just outside Tommy Steele's house, but no one knew whose responsibility it was to fill it in, so it remained. Our party attracted the great and the good of Richmond, including councillors, charity representatives, MPs, business colleagues, family and many friends. It established my rehabilitation in, shall we say, 'polite society'. Mandy Smith, a flower seller in Richmond town centre, very kindly gave us huge quantities of flowers on the Sunday morning of the event. I no longer felt an outcast. It had taken ten years but, at last, a day in my life could go by without me thinking about the disaster of 1987, so profound had been the effect upon me. It was in Petersham that I learnt to drive in three months. At the party's end, I drove Cynthia Payne home, the car full of amusement and giggles.

Bryony Brind visited Terry and I with her first husband to be when we lived in Petersham. We had an excellent lunch and toasted them both for their forthcoming wedding. It was held in St Paul's Church, Knightsbridge, and the reception at the Royal Yacht Club. I recall queuing on the steps for a long time as everyone was being photographed by *Hello!* magazine. We were also invited to her second wedding ceremony, but Dame Barbara Cartland, her future mother in law, died shortly before the event, which was postponed. I am sorry that Bryony died in December 2015 at the young age of fifty-five. She was a charming, urbane, bubbly and very talented woman, and just fun to be with in social settings. It was good to have known her and be her friend, even for a short time.

Terry and I went on to live in Brighton, Battle, Hastings and Newhaven. I used to commute by train or car. It was while we were in Brighton that a reporter entered the Richmond shop wanting 'dirt' on David's personal life; he had become the Duke of Rutland. They wanted to know if I was still in contact with Terry, as he also knew David. I dismissed the reporter, telling her that she could not expect me, of all people and after what had happened to me, to talk to reporters about the private life of my friends. I put up a smoke screen of ignorance about Terry, without actually lying. I rang David to warn him that he might be 'door-stopped' at any moment (he was, the next day) and to be careful, but I didn't mention the incident to Terry. I did not want him to get upset on David's behalf and thought he might try to talk to the reporter, which would only have made it worse. Knowing what had gone before, we were very protective of our personal space and our private life and, of course, our friends. We were in the process of selling the Brighton flat and, a couple of days later, Terry was expecting an estate agent to call at lunchtime. Sure enough, the doorbell rang, Terry assumed it was the agent and let them up the stairs. It was about five minutes and lots of small talk later before he realised it was a reporter he was showing around our apartment and not the estate agent. Terry rang me at the shop once he had discovered her true identity and I groaned and, over the phone, politely asked her to leave. The best laid plans… Terry inferred that he was not in touch with David to avoid comment. In fact, he was coming the next day to stay for a long weekend. Thank goodness she didn't come a day later.

Late in 2001, we decided to take up David's invitation to go and live on his Belvoir estate. We had turned down his offer several times before but now decided, on this occasion, to accept. We decided to open yet another chapter of our life in the rural idyll of Hidden England. I thought I would never see London and the south again and that my working life was possibly at an end. Little did I know that I was about to enter the busiest period of my life.

CHAPTER 10

BELVOIR YEARS

Terry and I arrived at Belvoir Castle in December 2001 after a long car journey up the A1. I had visited before, but not often. Our estate house was not ready – it needed renovation and it was taking longer than expected – so we were very kindly invited to stay for a few days in one of the many bedrooms at the castle. David and Emma were also settling into their new abode. They had been Duke and Duchess of Rutland for nearly three years, since the death of David's father, Charles, in January 1999, but had only recently moved into the castle. For them it was like taking over the control of a small country and one where those running it were appointed by your predecessors. What we discovered in those first few days was that, although David was chairman of the trustees that ran the estate and the castle where they lived, he was only one of four trustees and he was certainly not in 'control' of it. Emma was not even one of the other trustees.

We were looked after at the castle by the butler, Paul Horton, and his wife, Linda, who was the housekeeper. He was known as 'Horton' but I always called him Paul. Not being a public schoolboy, I never understood the passion for referring to people just by their surname. He was a guards officer who had been the under butler to 'Petchey', the previous Duke and Duchess's butler. Petchey went with Frances, David's mother, hence Paul filled the vacancy, which he did with great distinction. Paul and Linda became our friends over all the years we spent at Belvoir.

We moved into our new home just before that first Christmas. Our house was called Engine Yard Cottage and, as the name implied, it was in the Engine Yard of the estate, where a big engine pumped water up to the castle. Indeed, we were on the pumping system before water reached the castle. Parts of our house dated from the early eighteenth century. It was located just under the castle hill among other buildings, where the team of sixteen or so workers who repaired the other 300 or so houses on the estate were based and where they stored their tools, including a carpenter's workshop. The house had a large garden and outhouses and views over the fields towards Bottesford. There was a large house next door, built in about the same period as the castle, the fourth to be built on the site in the early nineteenth century. The estate bookkeeper lived there. It was a very quiet location, especially at weekends when the Engine Yard team was not at work.

That first Christmas, David and Emma and their children had gone away, the castle was virtually empty and so there was no 'calling' for the spring water, no demand. If no water went to the castle, though, none came to us. We ran out of water on Christmas morning. Being new, we did not know why or what to do, so we rang David. He got the deputy agent, the late and much loved Tim Stansby, to leave his Christmas lunch and come out and manually arrange for the water to flow. We quickly got to realise, living in the countryside, that who you know, and how to contact them, is an important requisite to having a tranquil life. The estate functioned by having a few dedicated people who knew through experience what to do in all circumstances and were prepared to put things right. This knowledge had to be nurtured and loyalty earned.

I have always in my life tried to get on with people of all ranks, titles, positions as well as those with none. I have never seen the sense in going out of one's way to upset or annoy people. Sometimes, especially in the political world, it is inevitable that you will make enemies, but there is no need to make them gratuitously. I know, to my surprise, I have made many; to some I may be the devil incarnate, but I like to think none of these are people who have actually met me. I try to understand people, know how they 'tick' and operate. I used the experiences of my extraordinary and varied life to settle into my new, unaccustomed rural circumstances and if not exactly make friends, then send out signals that I was no threat. After all, I thought, I had come to Belvoir to recharge my batteries for six months, to have some thinking time as to what I was going to do with the rest of my life and possibly even semi-retire.

David and Emma would visit Terry and I frequently, David almost every day, usually for a coffee and a chat with Terry. It was during such soul-searching mornings that we discussed the thorny issue of insurance in some detail. In particular, we were told that the insurance of the castle and its contents, including a fabulous art collection, was a no-go area for David and Emma and could not even be discussed. The other trustees were sensitive to debate upon the matter. It was a high-cost item in the budget but, extraordinarily, it was 'off limits' to them. They had had other friends look at the matter for them, all of whom had made suggestions and forwarded ideas.

They all petered out, however, mainly, I think, because they were not present to deal with the detail and, on issues like insurance, the devil is in the detail. Terry and I had no experience of insurance matters but knew friends who did. David and Emma asked if I would take on the issue as a project, for which I would be paid. I agreed. Insurance renewal was in three months' time, so I set to work. Initially it was a reading exercise. The estate and castle was run by four trustees in a main trust, the 9th Duke's Will Trust. I am no lawyer and the legal documents took time to assemble, assimilate and comprehend. What was clear at an early stage was that the trust could not function without the unanimous agreement of all four trustees. It was not a case of 'three votes to one: sorry, David, you lose'. In fact, if David did not agree, nothing could be done. David, however, did not know this. As David was the chairman of the trust, he had a way of controlling the agenda of meetings, and he was also the main beneficiary of the trust. On pointing these matters out, suddenly his position strengthened, and he no longer feared going to meetings to be out-voted. With this, we had started the process of regaining power over his estate. I was happy to repay the compliment – he had worked for me; I was now in harness working for him. Almost every day, we planned the next move. It was like a poker game.

The main objective was to get quotations from a number of insurance brokers, not necessarily just reappoint the existing brokers. It was a long job but, using David's position as trustee chairman, several brokers were asked to compete for the business. It was not necessarily lucrative business in itself, but having the Belvoir estate and castle insurance in your portfolio was significant in attracting other accounts. Starting with the insurance of the castle, and with difficulty, we acquired four competing quotations, interviewing each of the brokers' representatives in the drawing room of the castle.

There were and are few insurance companies that can deal with this type and scale of business, so that created complications, and one did not wish to upset the rather small market. Eventually the figures – in secret bids – were to hand and were analysed and distributed to all the trustees. Although the incumbent subsequently lowered his figures, he was still more expensive. On the day before renewal, David and I met in his study. The three trustees had sent out papers purportedly renewing the incumbent broker; David invited the more 'economic' broker to take on the role. Who would blink first? With twenty-four hours to go, the castle had two insurance brokers and two sets of insurance firms covering it.

One of the specialist insurance firms in the incumbent's team rang to discuss insuring the art collection. The Duke asked me to answer the phone enquiry for him. I said the Duke had appointed another broker and if they placed the business it would be at their cost. They withdrew. Only the Duke's preferred broker and insurance team were in place. The other trustees had had to 'blink'. He had won this battle and, taking everything into account, I estimate that this one move concerning insurance saved the castle and estate cumulatively over half a million pounds while I worked at Belvoir. If I knew nothing about insurance at the start of the project, I certainly did by its completion. Insurance can be an extremely dull, though important, subject, so it was a great relief that I had the privilege to work with some very interesting and professional people, including Colin Payne and Sara Mitchell and others, over the years.

The trust I built up with David and Emma working on these matters and on a variety of legal and trust issues proved significant for the future. We were reaching the summer opening season for the castle, which in those days stretched from Easter to the end of September. There was a vacancy for someone to run the ticket office and I was asked if I wouldn't mind taking it on as another project. I think some people thought it was in some way beneath me to sell tickets and ice cream, even serve in a shop – but I had been doing that for years. I relished the opportunity of taking on a different challenge and a new way of operating the ticket office, running a kind of information centre for the castle and presenting the initial face of the castle to the general public. I was in my element.

I gradually got to know other members of staff, in particular those who ran the castle opening office, and the volunteer guides, who were a mine of information on the history and contents of the castle. Shortly before he died, I was very fortunate to be taken on a private guided tour by an elderly man who had worked as a volunteer guide for many years. He gave me a spectacular tour, but made it clear it was not only what you said factually about the place that mattered, but also how you put it across to the visitor; the manner of delivery and timing were all-important. Well, I had experience of delivery and timing from many years of public oratory, and so I could now use that experience in a new way, relating Belvoir's fascinating history. It was also a good idea to say something personal about the incumbent family, which I could obviously do very easily.

The opening of stately homes in Britain depends to a very large extent on a dedicated team of guides or wardens. Belvoir was no different, and a small but gifted group of people were available to lead visitors on marvellous tours, a team of which I soon became a member.

The history of Belvoir follows the history of the country. The first person to build a castle on the site was Robert de Todeni, who was William the Conqueror's standard-bearer. 'To the victor the spoils' after 1066 and all that, only Robert's spoils were extensive. He was granted land currently comprising the whole of what is now Leicestershire, Lincolnshire and Nottinghamshire, and part of Derbyshire too. Castles tended to be built in the middle of your land on a defensive site, so Robert came to the top of the hill, looked out over the admirable view and said, in impeccable Norman French, 'Bel voir', or 'beautiful view'. The English, then as now, could not pronounce the Norman French, so balderdised the name that sprang from this utterance, calling the place 'Beever', which they could pronounce.

Of course, the present castle is not that same one as built by Todeni. The first castle survived until the first civil war, the War of the Roses in the fifteenth century, when it was pulled down. Henry VIII came to the throne and up went the second castle, to be pulled down by Cromwell's parliamentary forces in the second civil war in the seventeenth century. They were frightened it would fall into royalist hands who would threaten Parliament's wagon trains through the vale. Charles II came to the throne and Belvoir was rebuilt, but this time as a manor house. Kings had got wise to nobles building fortified properties in their realm that could provide a base against the monarchy. Built of green timber, no one liked the third castle as it was a very cold house in which to live – gaps developing between windows and walls – and it was pulled down, altered and rebuilt and changed into the one that exists today by the fifth Duke and Duchess of Rutland, John and Elizabeth. During that rebuild in October 1816, there was a great fire. The cause was never established but the building was eventually finished in the late 1820s, after Elizabeth's death in 1825.

The Manners, the name of David's family, were Norman French too, but they were granted land in Northumberland and built Etal Castle in 1341. The Todeni and de Roos families ran out of male heirs and a Manners son, George, married into the family. So, as a result, the Manners family have been in control of Belvoir by inheritance since 1508/09. George's son Robert was created the Earl of Rutland by Henry VIII in 1525 and John Manners a Duke by Queen Anne in 1703.

I had great pleasure in being associated with the 300-year anniversary of the dukedom in 2003. A special exhibition was held and Terry and I were instrumental in persuading a local artist, Elizabeth Sharpe, to do line drawings of each of the eleven Dukes, which hang in the Collection Room at Belvoir. I am pleased I had a small hand, too, in the book written by the Duchess and Jane Pruden on the history of Belvoir. I was also asked to read the first draft of Catherine Bailey's book *The Secret Rooms*, about the lives of the families of the eighth and ninth Dukes of Rutland and to help with photographs for the book. It is a fascinating read, but not the book that Catherine originally thought she would write about Belvoir. The place, it turned out, has a mind of its own and it would make a very interesting period film – a real-life *Downton Abbey*.

The 'Secret Rooms' are the Muniment Rooms (archives) of the castle, where the ninth Duke worked long and hard and where he died, on a sofa which is still there. It is one of the innermost sanctums at Belvoir. David is writing his book on Captain Lord Robert Manners and he works in these rooms now together with Peter Foden, Belvoir's archivist, and Emma Ellis, the Duke's researcher. They make a formidable team. If David was in the castle he was usually to be found in his study or in these rooms, well away from the office bustle or the prying eyes of tourists. His reluctance to meet visitors was legendary, but when their paths did cross he was polite and charming and they would go away incredibly impressed by his knowledge of history and the military collection in the castle.

Opening the castle to day visitors effectively began after the Second World War, although in Victorian times, when the family were out and strangers drove their horse and carriage up to the Portico entrance, there was always a race between the butler and the housekeeper to see who could reach the door first and gain the financial reward for showing the curious around the building. In recent years, the numbers wishing to visit have diminished, and care has to be taken that the requirement to open – with its inevitable security and other costs – is not loss-making.

Working in the ticket office, situated below the castle on the rather steep hill, I was a bit removed from the 'action' at the castle at the top, seeing people only as they arrived and departed, but I was able to gain much feedback from visitors, which helped Emma and David in determining the future of this visitor attraction. The elevated view from the ticket office was wonderful, looking towards Nottingham across the Great and the West Wong. A 'wong' was a common termination for the name of fields in Leicestershire dialect. It was very pleasant to work there, meeting so many people, hearing their stories and their concerns, answering their questions, and was again similar in many respects to meeting one's constituents. I did six summer seasons operating the ticket office, which fitted well into our initial yearly plan. Working non-stop for nine months of the year, including weekends – there was work to be done in the months before and after the actual opening – then 'dropping out' for the three months from December to February. This was the time of my rewarding and refreshing visits to India and Sri Lanka. In the age of modern technology and mobile phones, however, I could never escape completely; there were still frequent calls from the castle, but they seemed easier to manage while basking on an Indian Ocean beach 4,500 miles away.

It was in 2002 that David asked me to become his private secretary. I could deal with his secretarial and diary work while I was waiting to sell visitors tickets. Meetings could take place at that time or we would meet at my house, which was just across the road. Dealing with his work meant I was privy to all matters affecting the estate.

It also meant I contributed to the decision-making process in most areas of the business, not that I ever abused that position. I had no real, hands-on knowledge of such issues as farming, shooting, fishing and forestry, but gradually I learnt, which helped me to help David. The longer I worked for David, the more I was trusted with the details. My previous careers obviously assisted my work for him; political contacts came in useful. A private secretary is a keeper of secrets. Those secrets are not 'private' just for a limited time but for life, so I hope I will be forgiven for not revealing them here. We would meet most days and work and socialising would often go in tandem.

Quite early on I was asked if I would also look after wedding events. This was not the role of an event planner as there were good people already in the office who organised advance arrangements for the castle opening, weddings and other events, but there was a need for me to provide a mix of hosting services on the day, including acting as a kind of toastmaster, making announcements, liaising between the bride and groom and the castle office, and ensuring all their expectations had been met (and hopefully exceeded) on their very special day. It was a role tailor-made for me in many respects. Most weddings took place inside the castle but the first venue at which I was asked to work was held in a marquee by the side of the upper of two lakes in the castle parkland. It is a very picturesque setting with beautiful views of the castle, especially at night when it is floodlit.

I was told that during a previous wedding within this same family, a number of men had arrived with guns and robbed the guests of jewels, wallets and watches. As a result, the castle said they had arranged for me to have security guards. I thought, innocently, that was a bit over the top, but went along with it. I said that if there were any problems I would just call the police, at which point the office told me 'Do not name the family or the police will not come!' A few days before the wedding day, I met the man organising my 'security'. I am 6 ft 4 in., and I had to look up at him. He said I should not worry – I was concerned about security – he would have three or four security guards, and he said the family itself would have their own security men coming up from London. They were 'big', he said, looking upwards. He was not lying about that and, on the day, they were all dressed in sinister black. As it turned out, the wedding went without a hitch and the bride and groom were dancing on the tables at 4 a.m. (I was due in the ticket office at 9 a.m.) They were the last to leave with me and all my worries were unfounded. They were excellent guests and, however anxious I might have been, I enjoyed hosting this, my first wedding.

In total, I hosted over 300 weddings while I was at Belvoir, usually on a Friday or a Saturday. The castle had its own small and beautiful chapel where Church of England weddings or blessings could be held as long as church rules were adhered to and the Duke's chaplain officiated. But the weddings were of every religion, type and creed. Civil weddings were held in the licensed guard room and the ballroom. The vast majority were magical and uplifting occasions. Every conceivable type of entertainment took place and added to the excitement of the event. With up to 200 or so guests attending each wedding, I was privileged to have been privy to such times and am very thankful to have had the opportunity.

Eventually I took a course to obtain a personal 'drinks' licence. It was the equivalent of becoming qualified to become the old pub licensee, but without having your name over the door. It was a long time since I had taken an 'exam' and I was nervous, but passed the written test and the police check. As a result I became the Designated Premises Supervisor (DPS) and the official holder of the wedding licence for the castle, on behalf of the Duke. The wedding registrars – those who officiated at the actual civil weddings – of Leicestershire County Council were efficient, charming and excellent people with whom to deal. Usually they operated in pairs, and I hope I made them feel welcome and attended to their needs. One of them had agreed to officiate at Terry's and my civil partnership ceremony. We kept putting it off and would have done it only for legal reasons, not because we felt we needed to emotionally, still less to have a 'marriage'. I may be a homosexual, but I am a traditionalist in these matters as far as I am concerned, but happy for others to do as they wish.

So popular did weddings become that a semi-permanent marquee was established by the lake. Although the civil ceremony itself could not be performed there, bigger wedding receptions could be held. The constraint was local neighbours and trying to ensure they were not disturbed by the inevitable music, firework and noise from the PA system. I did my best to placate the locals on this and on other issues, tried compromise, chaired meetings of residents to discuss estate matters, sat on local tourist committees, attended parish council meetings and dealt, together with consultants and lawyers, with planning matters, including government inspectors.

I enjoyed working with the staff of the castle, permanent and temporary, and the outside caterers, wedding planners, florists, cake makers, entertainers, bands, disc jockeys, lighting contractors and firework operators. There were so many different and varied aspects to the role. Robert, as cannon master and the chap in charge of black powder, would don his Scots Guards uniform – red tunic in summer, grey top coat in winter, with bearskin – and fire the seven French naval cannon captured off a French warship by Captain Lord Robert Manners in the eighteenth century. They are fired to celebrate a wedding and are the oldest regularly fired cannon in the country.

They produced a very loud report and flash which always had the guests impressed. Robert would do this work to raise funds for military and other charities. Fireworks would often be lit afterwards and one of my duties was to ensure no sparks drifted over the castle towers and roofs and, if they did, to make sure no fire ensued. We wanted no re-run of 1816.

Looking back on my years at Belvoir, being able to play a small part in so many people's very special day is one of my most endearing and enduring memories. I was privileged to be part of their weddings and I know that so many people enjoyed their day, often returning in years afterwards to remember it. I am in possession of many letters of thanks for the role I played and I cherish them all. Every wedding was a joy and a memory. Watching brides walk down the Earl's staircase in procession into the Guard Room, or enter the ballroom through the Picture Gallery, was a pleasure. Every wedding was unique and magical because it was the different individuals who made each occasion so special, set against the magnificence of the castle backdrop.

In my role as licensee I only had to suggest to a couple of people that they had had enough to drink and should consume no more. Technically, I had to be at the castle whenever any guests consumed alcohol, although I could depute my duties to another member of staff if they also had a personal licence.

My position as DPS necessitated me having close contacts with the fire brigade and the police. The castle was situated in Leicestershire but also on the borders of Nottinghamshire and Lincolnshire too; Leicestershire was the lead authority. Before I became involved, the castle was close to being closed down for falling foul of fire regulations. It was through no fault of the efficient and excellent Mary McKinlay, who had strove might and main to obtain the licence.

A new fire consultant who had just taken over, Jonathan Smith, and I developed links with the fire brigade and gradually I used my position with David and Emma to ensure fire safety improvements were made each year. I arranged for local firemen to have familiarisation trips to the castle and one year it was agreed that some firemen would camp on the estate and do exercises there, including using the steep North Terrace wall for abseiling. I was waiting in my office for them to arrive to do a recce when the receptionist phoned to say my guests had arrived. I greeted them at the back door, some in yellow fluorescent jackets, and walked them across to the wall of the North Terrace. I told them they were welcome to go over the side of the wall on ropes and drop down to the grass floor fifty feet or so below us. I started to get a sense of unease when most of them started to turn white; firemen should be used to this, I thought. I suddenly realised that perhaps they were not 'my' group. Indeed, they were not, rather visiting engineers and surveyors there to see one of my colleagues to discuss putting in a new biomass boiler. I am not quite sure why, but I turned not a hair, said something along the lines of 'but there is a much easier way of getting down to the dooms (tunnels under the castle) to get to the proposed site of the new boiler' and led them back through the castle, much to their relief and astonishment I am sure. My firemen arrived shortly afterwards.

There was a famous, weekend family shoot party which became infamous. After a black-tie dinner in the state dining room on the Saturday night for thirty people, there was a loud disco in one of the rooms that had been the Queen's Royal Lancers' Museum until converted into a shoot and corporate dining and sitting room. It was set up by Adam, who was a whizz at technology, speakers, disco lights and all types of music – from rhythm and blues to tunes from a guest's own country – and he changed the room into a London-style night club, acting as a DJ. As a special attraction, he had purchased a smoke machine which worked really well – in fact, too well. During the disco at about 1 a.m., unbeknown to everyone, a wisp of smoke escaped from the room and, acting like a cloud, engaged not one but three smoke detectors. The music was so loud that the party goers inside the disco room failed to hear the insistent blare of the castle fire alarm system, which was automatically passed to the fire brigades of three counties, each sending two appliances, with two more following on. The alarm system included a Second World War air-raid siren on the castle's roof, so the music from the Rolling Stones must have been very loud for no one to hear that. The immense thickness of the stone walls did not help. The first that guests knew anything may be wrong were the flashing blue lights of six fire engines parked outside on the North Terrace – disco lights of a kind that was not intended. I was called from my bed – as I dealt with all fire and burglar alarm call-outs – and arrived in time to placate three white-helmeted chief fire officers. All was well, but I had to wait another seven hours until the fire alarm engineer arrived to replace all three smoke detectors. In future, we had special alarms fitted with strobe lighting inside those disco rooms and the problem never occurred again.

I had also established good relations with the local police beat and community officers when I was working in the ticket office. They would drop in to discuss vehicle crime and rural thefts, take in the view and show a presence. I presumed they knew about my history, or that it would be passed around by word of mouth, but it was never raised with me. Their attitude to me was friendly and was one of mutual assistance. The ticket office was frequently the subject of attack at night and, living close, I could hear the audible alarm ring before being telephoned about the alarms going off, so I was usually the first to arrive. One night, a car drove directly at me and I had to jump out of its way, and on another night I saw the occupants of a car robbing the buildings. The police arrived and apprehended the culprits nearby. One night, the castle's main gates were broken in an attempt to steal them. A spate of four or five gamekeeper quad bike thefts and robberies of outbuildings and barns kept the police and myself busy.

Because of my day-to-day involvement with insurance matters, I handled security and burglar alarm issues. I built up a good rapport with the head of Leicestershire's Police Alarm Unit, Sarah Black. She had the power to refuse police attendance, so threatening insurance cover, if the number of false alarms rose too high in a year, so it was sensible to maintain good relations. Because of the large number of guns, historic Brown Bess muskets, shotguns and others, held within the building, a review concerning their safety was held over a period of six months. Eventually, a plan was agreed that included armed response officers should anything untoward occur. Out of the blue, on a Friday, the police informed me by email that the new plan would go live that night. Unfortunately, at the last minute, a senior officer who had not been involved in the laborious discussions altered the plan and I did not receive the email in time. The next morning, when we had a Tiger Moth plane event in the parkland, I returned from buying my morning paper to find about four or five police cars parked in the car park, a dog handler's van unit and a police helicopter landing. I had just received an alert that one of the temporary cleaners had triggered an alarm by entering a part of the castle into which she should not have gone – not one covered by the original armed response plan – but still. The officers asked me to show them up to the castle – all six of them, heavily armed. I took two of them to the back door and, as they did not know the layout, they pushed me forward – the phrase 'human shield' came to mind, had there really been intruders. They were not satisfied with seeing that the alarmed areas were intact, however, and wanted to see inside the two rooms. The Duke kept those keys, so before contacting him on the private side, I told my 'minders' I would just see if the Duke was in by seeing if his car was parked at the private entrance. On opening the private door, I was greeted by the other four officers pointing sub-machine guns at me. In any normal circumstances, faced with such a situation, one would raise one's hands in submission. Stupidly, I did not. I closed the door and said to the two officers what they must have already known: 'Your colleagues are pointing guns at me!' No bullets were fired, but on the Monday I received an apology from a senior police officer and the original plan was reinstated. Again, it was treated as an exercise.

I also had links with the firearms licensing department of the police as the Duke had a shotgun and firearms licence, as did other members of the family, and the Duchess became a firearms' dealer when she launched her own range of shotguns. I became, in law, her 'servant', which meant I could deal with guns on her behalf. I knew nothing about shooting, only ever attended one pheasant shoot while I was working at Belvoir, but had excellent relations with the police's John Toon, who was full of good advice.

In all, I had good relations over thirteen years with Leicestershire and Lincolnshire police forces. I was well-known to them. Anything I was asked to do to support the police I did to the best of my ability. The Belvoir estate and the local constabulary were on the best of terms, and I played an important part in establishing and maintaining that relationship. We relied on each other and those officers who met me and knew me professionally in that period, thanked me for my assistance and support to them. It was mutually advantageous.

I think they will be incredulous when they read the details of what occurred in 2015. Indeed, in October 2015, I was contacted by a department at Leicestershire Police, who were astonished to learn that I was not still working at the castle.

One thing tended to lead to another in my work at Belvoir. My role was forever changing and about six or seven years ago I was asked to work at the castle full time, giving up my wonderful ticket office location to move to an even more splendid office in the Speak-a-Word Room at the front of the castle, where I would become the private secretary to the Duchess as well as the Duke. This was to prove to be an exhilarating, if not always easy role to fulfil. Emma gradually took on the role of chief executive and David continued that of company chairman – not that running the estate and castle remotely reflected any other company or business entity I had worked for or known. Initially, the office was in the room where, historically, tenants on the estate could have a word with the Duke of the day to discuss farming and rent issues. Later, it moved to the rear of the castle, once the estate office was relocated in the castle itself and not in the Charles II buildings at the foot of the Castle Hill. My desk became 'a moveable feast', relocating many times depending on the mix of work with which I was dealing; the one constant position was that there was always more work to do than the hours in the day would allow. This is a given situation for all staff who might work at Belvoir in order to keep costs down and balance the books.

On occasions, I was asked to use whatever diplomatic talents I possess to smooth things over with difficult employment matters, family issues, disputes with neighbours, customers and suppliers. I would also be called in to aid or back up a business position or seek to persuade.

Because I dealt with day-to-day insurance matters, I was asked to oversee the negotiation of film contracts. Having a feature film on location at the castle could be very lucrative, but was always difficult to control and manage safely. *The Young Victoria* was filmed over three weeks in the Elizabeth Saloon, the Ballroom, the Tapestry Room, the King's Suite Bedroom and the Regent's Gallery. Sarah, Duchess of York, was involved with the film's production and because the Queen would not allow filming at Buckingham Palace or Windsor Castle, location managers did the next best thing and secured Belvoir Castle to represent the royal abodes. Emily Blunt, Rupert Friend, Miranda Richardson and Mark Strong acted at Belvoir. Strong played Conroy, adviser to the Duchess of Kent and Strathearn, Victoria's mother, in a scene in the Elizabeth Saloon, which was then above the Duke's television room. Conroy was getting drunk as Victoria's mother was losing influence over the young Queen. He had to kick a stool and throw a glass in a fireplace. Over the radio system came David's dulcet tones, 'They are destroying my furniture!' (expletives deleted). I dashed in to see the second take of Strong kicking a prop stool high in the air and turned up the radio to let them hear the Duke's concern peppered with even more expletives. I was able to use those famous film words – 'Cut, cut!' – in front of the French–Canadian director Jean-Marc Vallée. Strong knew the stool was fake but the rest of the gilt furniture was for real, Louis XVI style, so he kicked it less hard and not as far. The wooden floor where the stool was landing was padded and protected and calm was restored. The glass to be thrown was made of theatrical, sugar glass. As we had kicked up such a fuss, the crew gave me a set of these sugar glasses. They were beautiful in appearance even at close quarters. I thought they would come in handy so I placed them in my office. Three months later, as Emma and David were walking through my office with friends, I reached for one of these wine glasses and held it up, saying I had discovered the set in the castle – were they not a good find? Once the nods of approval came, I smashed it at their feet, and said I thought it was not good enough for Belvoir: collapse of stout party all round. The Duke and Duchess took a pair of them to try the same trick on others.

Emily Blunt and Rupert Friend acted out the honeymoon scene at Windsor Castle in the same bed that the real Queen Victoria had slept in on her visit to Belvoir in December 1843. She visited with Sir Robert Peel and the Duke of Wellington, who was a frequent visitor.

The parkland deputised for Windsor Great Park. Albert and Victoria were meant to ride on horseback in the rain but with no rain, rain-making machines were brought in to create the right effect. The director wanted just enough sheep in shot in the background, so I turned into a shepherd and, together with crew members, tried to achieve just the right number of sheep on the screen.

We all got on so well that they came to my house for the 'wrap' party. Terry made a splendid chicken biryani and vegetable curry, with naans and pickles for over seventy people to enjoy. When the film was screened I arranged an exhibition with about eight costumes from the film. Sandy Powell won an Oscar and a BAFTA for best costume design.

A Royal Night Out, starring Rupert Everett, Sarah Gadon, Bel Powley and Emily Watson, was also filmed at Belvoir, deputising again for Buckingham Palace. All the actors were charming but disaster struck when an arm of one of the English Hancock and Co. glass chandeliers in the Regent's Gallery was accidentally damaged by an electrician changing its light bulbs. The Duke was not impressed and a magisterial rebuke was delivered, similar to one that an outside catering company received after they ironed a tablecloth on the State Dining Room table, requiring it to be completely re-polished. The glass chandelier arm dropped to the floor, shattering into thousands of pieces, and had to be remade by the Queen's chandelier maker, Wilkinson. It is nigh-on impossible to tell which arm was damaged, but it formed a substantial insurance claim.

Kate Moss was photographed for the sixtieth anniversary edition of *Playboy* magazine. The shoot took a whole day for one photograph and was a 'closed set' because of the nudity. Every time a piece of furniture needed to be moved I had to enter to move it, with Kate suitably re-robed. For the life of me, I could not understand why there were rails and rails of clothes set out in the Guard Room (the makeshift changing room), as none appeared to be required. Kate Moss and I got on very well, as I did with all the models, actors and actresses to whom we played host.

Belvoir was often featured in television documentaries. Again, I was often given the role of looking after the crew and making sure the castle remained intact and was treated with respect. The one condition I personally set down was that I was never to be in front of the camera lens. My days in the public eye were long gone – or so I thought.

Terry did appear on a National Geographic television documentary with Eddie Izzard. Eddie knocked on our house door while trying to re-enact the Norman Inquisition, which led to the creation of the Domesday Book. The Normans were very inquisitive. Acting out the role of a Norman Lord, Eddie wanted Terry to itemise what we had. He kindly signed our Visitors' Book. Come to think of it, I did not ask the Metropolitan Police officers to do the same. Before we left Belvoir, the drive through the fields to our Barn Farm House was used as a scene from the First World War in a film documentary about Duff Cooper and Lady Diana Manners, daughter of the 8th Duke of Rutland, who married Duff, and their correspondence. It was part of a Channel 4 series to commemorate the First World

War, which was also filmed in the large library and the Regent's Gallery of the castle.

My work at Belvoir was incredibly varied. When I went to my desk I never knew what to expect or in what area of the business I would be working next. Eventually, I was asked to take over the castle opening business, the administration of the ticket office and activities in the parkland. My desk job kept me busy but in addition I had hosting duties in the castle in the evenings and at weekends. There was a wide range of events to be dealt with, some to organise and some to host, including triathlons, car and running races, a large annual fireworks championship, horse and carriage events. A big national caravan rally, Land Rover trials and the CLA game fairs brought thousands of visitors to the estate.

There were many associated activities at Belvoir. The Belvoir Cricket Trust was launched by the Duchess to raise funds so that children in local towns and cities could enjoy the mix of rural pursuits and cricket. The MCC played an annual match against a Duchess's XI at the picturesque Belvoir cricket ground. In the evening, usually on the evening of the Trent Bridge Test Match, a robust formal dinner was held in the state dining room of the castle. I would act as toastmaster and be pleased to show guests the picture gallery after dinner. The day brought back memories of my childhood attendances at the Scarborough cricket festival. Emma was president of the Rainbow Hospice Charity and I was delighted to help with their charitable endeavours and lots of other charitable work within the castle. I was, for a time, clerk to the Earl of Rutland and Dr Fleming's Hospital Trust. It was very interesting to work with such an important and historic, charitable trust.

To try to get on top of a pigeon problem at the castle, two Harris hawks and a barn owl, called Rodney, Scooby and Persil respectively, lived in two game larders in the inner courtyard. I always ensured their interests were cared for at the castle and dedicated band of volunteers looked after these wonderful birds every day of the year. The birds delighted visitors with their flights over the castle and gardens.

Laury Dizengremel is an artist in residence on the estate under Emma's patronage. Laury recently produced a peacock sculpture featured in a television documentary on Lancelot Capability Brown's gardening connection with Belvoir, made by Emma and Alan Titchmarsh. I had attended an inaugural conference to promote the tercentenary of Brown in 2016 and became inspired that Belvoir should be a part of the celebrations. The Muniments Rooms contain original plans by Brown for Belvoir's parkland. Because of the near bankruptcy of the 4th Duke, and the lack of money and the death of Brown, they were never put into effect. I was very keen that the 300-year celebration of Brown's birth in 1716 and his links to Belvoir should be commemorated and so was pleased that my suggestion long ago for a television series and book by the Duchess was achieved. Many of the plans have been enacted by Emma and Alan in this important project in conjunction with Love Your Garden and Channel 4 Television, which will prove a lasting and enduring contribution to our heritage.

Art, music and theatre have all played a part in entertainments at Belvoir and it was a pleasure to help organise these functions. Emma trained to be an opera singer so concerts often take place. So too have military activities taken place, with the Duke being a former air cadet. It was an honour dealing with the armed forces in the RAF survival training exercises and military triathlons held in the parkland. There was the noted evening when an army event was being held at the castle and the army chief attending did not quite make the horse-shoe bend in his car as he drove up to the castle and he ended up being suspended precariously halfway up a tree with a long drop to the valley floor. Fortunately for him there were soldiers able to extricate him from the car just minutes before the Secretary of State for Defence drove past. The bend is now known as Brigadier's Bend.

The year at Belvoir was definitely seasonal and there was an old-fashioned pattern to it. The period from September to February was the partridge, duck and pheasant shoot season, with four or five family shoots interspersed with the commercial and valuable let day shoots and overnight parties. The main focus of the estate was to entertain shoot groups at this time. The summer months were occupied by opening the castle to day visitors, which was legally only required for thirty days each year. Increasingly over the years the legal minimum was followed more or less to allow more time for weddings and corporate events. Harvest Festival was celebrated magnificently and Christmas was wonderful also, with a traditional carol concert hosted in the private chapel and decorations writ large throughout the castle. Many Christmas trees used to decorate the castle were grown on the estate. Increasingly important, New Year became a business attraction, with parts of the castle, including some of the formal private rooms, rented out.

The one thing I resolutely refused to have myself while I lived in London was a pet. I did not think it fair to have a dog in the capital, living as I did, inevitably, in apartments. I have an inner fairness and keeping a dog in a confined space with little chance to exercise I believed was just not right. I had largely forgotten the company a dog can be for a child.

It was not until about thirty years later that I acquired another pet. My trips to India came dramatically to an end when it was determined by two votes to one that we should acquire a dog. Terry and Adam outvoted me. But what type of dog to get? I didn't want anything

too big; I had a fear of Alsatians. Adam didn't want anything too
small. So when we heard there was a springer spaniel for sale, aged
only ten months, it seemed a perfect compromise. It was an outside
dog, so we prepared an outhouse for our new guest. He was called
Brandon. In Kerala Malayalam that means 'crazy', and he certainly
appeared to be a very nervous dog. We had had him for three weeks.
One Friday night I was working at the castle, it was a wedding and, to
celebrate, fireworks and a noisy cannon were fired. In panic I think,
the dog sprang up against the door and out of the shed, just as my
friends were at the front door to try to calm him down. He ran off.
We all searched the surrounding countryside for days, the footpaths,
woods, fields and ditches. The Belvoir Hunt and the Belvoir gamekeepers kindly looked for him, as did the Duchess of Rutland and
many friends. We put up hundreds of posters, but to no avail. We all
went to Switzerland for a working break with the Duke and Duchess and, while having supper in a restaurant one night, my phone
rang, it was a message to say an-off duty police woman walking her
own dog had found Brandon dead in a ditch very near to our house.
We had searched that ditch before, so we came to the conclusion
that he had fled scared and took some time to regain his bearings and
when he did weeks later, very close to the house, had been knocked
over by a vehicle. We were all saddened. While we were still away,
the estate workmen buried the dog in our garden within sight of
our kitchen sink and the carpenter kindly made a wooden cross for
Brandon's grave. I determined never to have another dog, the grief
was too intense and we had had the dog less than one month.

My friends disagreed and wanted another dog, although not
another springer, its memory would be too deep. A couple of weeks
later, I was inveigled into going to see a litter of boxer pups in a
village twenty minutes away from home. Seeing puppies can be

very undermining of one's resolve not to have a dog. I was nervous at the size of the mother, but one pup was red and had a completely black face. We agreed to have him and two weeks later we picked up Zeus. Zeus was very much king of the dogs. He was perfect. He lived in the house but was equally at home outside. I exercised him at weekends and Terry walked him during the week. He would be protective, could be fierce even, but was extremely good with children. He had the multiplicity of boxer facial expressions, using the folds of skin around his face to good effect. As a puppy, he had met thousands of people in the castle's ticket office, so was very used to human contact. He was a very intelligent dog.

After nearly three and a half years, we bought another puppy from the same kennels, the same mother but different father. Zeus's half-brother was to be his friend and playmate. He had wonderful white markings on his face, although some black too, on the back of his neck, a bit like an arrow, and his chest and the tip of his tail was also white to set against his red colour. He had white socks too. We called him Duke after John Wayne. They and we were very happy. However, within six months, Zeus died in June 2012. He had, unbeknown to us, a congenital heart disease apparently common in young boxer dogs. The cause of his cough and exercise intolerance was not immediately picked up by the vet. When it was, we took Zeus to a dog heart specialist in Leamington Spa, but it was already too late; he died five days later. We were all devastated by the loss of our dear friend. He had been the perfect, boisterous, but polite and civilised, creature. Had we not already had Duke, I would not wish to have had another dog or go through the same heartache again. I still shed a tear for dear Zeus and keep his ashes close, a reminder of a handsome and wonderful animal who was a big part of my life in those four years.

Having a dog, still less two dogs, put an end to long overseas trips.

The idea of working 24/7 for nine months of the year and then dropping out of work and of Belvoir for three months and going to India was a non-starter. We did not like the idea of placing our dogs in kennels. The odd few days with a friend was just about in order for us to have a short break. So, my life from 2008 was working at the castle 24/7 for twelve months of the year – not what I planned or anticipated in my sixties. But we would have it no other way in return for the support, loyalty and love of our dogs. Duke missed Zeus but gradually grew up into being the diplomatic, kind and intelligent dog that he is today.

In 2014, Adam and Charlotte, who by now were living together with us at Belvoir, rescued an Akita puppy in desperate need of a home. Fearful of our reaction to yet another dog, they secreted her into their bedroom, not knowing how to explain the new arrival. No need, but they had the dog for four days without mentioning her or without her being noticed, so private was their living accommodation. The little bundle of pure white fur, looking a bit like a polar bear cub, woke early one morning, headed down the stairs and introduced herself. We called her Sushi. Duke took to her well, helped in her training and we were a family of six. It was not long before Sushi was bigger than Duke – together they were a formidable and strong duo. Their environment of a large garden and big fields with no livestock in the area was perfect. It was sometimes difficult to take them for walks, especially in the shooting seasons when pheasants and partridge abounded. Game birds took priority between September and February – the shoot season – although some gamekeepers liked to keep dogs away from certain areas all year round. Our dogs only wanted to play with the birds not kill them, but the birds didn't see it that way. Finding an area to walk one's dogs was surprisingly not always that easy, even on the 16,000 acres of the estate.

During one such shoot season, I was walking my dogs in the spring gardens near the castle on a lovely, crisp, autumnal late afternoon. The shoot that day was at an end and the 'guns' (people who had been shooting on the estate) were preparing to leave in a convoy of 4x4 cars when, simultaneously, and on a converging path, Duke gave chase to a pheasant. The lead car hit Duke on the the exit road. I did not see the impact but I heard the thud of a collision drifting through the trees up to the footpath where I was standing. The car stopped; my heart sank. I was convinced that Duke had met his end. I waited a minute or two and to my joy saw Duke alive. He was limping back on three legs, the fourth bloodied and battered. I picked him up carried him back to my car and started to walk towards the vehicle that had accidently collided with him. To my shock the car and those cars behind it drove off – they must have known Duke's owner was in the area. No attempt was made to see how the dog was at the time, nor did they contact the castle on that Saturday or later to even mention it. We knew who it was. It does him and his driver no credit that they just drove off, seemingly unconcerned. I hope his conscience is sullied by the memory, but I doubt it will be. Fortunately, Duke bravely wore his bright red bandages with good grace and made a full recovery.

Belvoir might seem at first glance an out of the way place with nothing happening, but strangely life there became very busy. Many people seemed to pass through, visit or stay. The castle was a great magnate and work often involved visits by interesting people who I had the privilege to meet, some to escort round the tourist attraction and some to host: maharajas, princesses, scientists, sportsmen and women, pop groups, singers, businessmen, Cabinet ministers, actors, chefs and people from many other walks of life.

Party politics very rarely interrupted my life. David was an

enthusiastic member of the UK Independence Party (UKIP) and held
the odd function at Belvoir. Emma and the Duke's mother, Frances,
supported the local Conservatives. At election time, poster battles
played out on the gates of the castle adorned with UKIP posters
and those at Belvoir Lodge directly opposite, festooned with Alan
Duncan's face, the local Tory MP. Both hit the dust on election days
as the lodge's outbuildings were used as a polling station and elec-
toral law necessitated no political posters near to a voting booth.
David did entertain UKIP leader Nigel Farage to lunch, at which
I was present. Farage seemed polite but self-impressed. Labour and
Conservative ministers and MPs crossed Belvoir's doors frequently,
but throughout my period at Belvoir I was careful to keep my own
counsel. I let people think what they wanted and my political views
had to be prised from me. I was happy to praise Mrs Thatcher and
discuss my time in the House if pressed, but no more.

Terry and I lived a quiet life, but we enjoyed throwing supper
parties. Terry is an excellent cook and we enjoyed a little socialising. Terry's food became legendary, with considerable time spent on
the planning, hunting down the perfect ingredients and preparing
everything from scratch. We had moved on from the London party
lifestyle and more likely than not we would turn down the frequent
invitations kindly extended by David and Emma to wine and dine
at the castle. We enjoyed staying at home and gained a small group
of friends locally. We had met Sally Wood when she worked in our
London block of flats; her husband John and their daughter Louisa
had houses on the estate and were engaging. When John died we
were just off to India for a visit and we arranged a service in India
where we stayed, in St John's Church, to celebrate John's life. David's
sister Charlotte and her partner, Lol, were two special guests who
enjoyed Terry's charming eccentricities, or at least tolerated them

well, such as the occasion when they came to dinner but Terry forgot about the food. Charlotte, like us, loves dogs and she's an excellent gardener, often bringing her crops as presents, including sumptuous fresh vegetables and herbs.

When we were celebrating the birth of Adam and Charlotte's baby in the Chequers pub in November 2014 we met Mercedes and Paul, and they have become very supportive and loyal friends. They too have a very strong dog, Tara.

Over the years, I was fortunate to meet many special people who worked, and some who still work, at Belvoir – those who got used to the inevitable ups and downs of working at a stately home, who stayed and became part of the team. Over these years I got to know many of them as friends as well as colleagues. We helped each other, knowing we were a small-knit group. I could not have been as effective, as I hope I might have been regarded to be, without their help and the help of all those who did a work stint at the castle. We all fell in love with the magic of Belvoir.

The business of running an estate and a castle was and is not easy. When the Duke and Duchess first took over, they visited the then well-established but now late Duke and Duchess of Devonshire at Chatsworth for friendly advice. Devonshire told David that, in his experience, 'They [the Duchesses] tended to raise the money and we [the Dukes] tended to spend it.' That may not be entirely true at Belvoir, but it was good advice.

David and Emma have had great business problems with the estate but have overcome them with flair and good humour. As time went on, Emma's confidence grew and, with the help of consultants and advisers and that loyal band of staff, she has managed to move in the right direction. When she first became David's Marchioness, Emma was regarded to be the breath of fresh air Belvoir required.

As the difficulties of maintaining the financial viability of the estate loomed large, and major changes in directions had to be signposted, inevitably Emma's popularity with some locals waned. Costs in maintaining a large building with acres of slate roof and an estate of over 16,000 acres needed to be controlled. It was bound to happen that taking tough, important but essential manpower decisions was not easy. Man management is always difficult when cutting back on a workforce that had been loyal but inevitably expensive. The financial viability of the whole operation needed a tight hand. It also needed an articulate and charismatic figurehead. That is the paradox with the Duchess. She is often regarded either as a leader, full of bonhomie and someone who can do no wrong, or she is perceived to be a bully with few man-management attributes. These characteristics are incorrect and cartoon depictions.

Emma's role as chief executive is not an easy one, though it was one of her own making, and I was uncomfortable with some of the early advice she took from others. The role has developed for the good of the business and the good of her family, but above all to support David and to hand down the immaculate heritage of Belvoir to the next generation. Change is essential to keep any organisation vibrant, but alterations can be personally painful, and there is no reason to change for change's sake. Recognising the need for variation I did my best to try to ensure it was as painless as it possibly could be. Without Emma, much would not have happened that needed to happen, it needed to move with new circumstances. Change is not a criticism of a previous generation but rather a reaction to new priorities. The estate housing stock is in the process of modernisation and is no longer moribund and fading. The farming aspects of the estate are professionally managed and carefully controlled. Forestry is under control; the parkland a joy to behold.

Initial knee-jerk reactions made under pressure with limited knowledge and experience have given way to thoughtful deliberations with an advisory board, strategy committee and well-managed trustee meetings, with good financial and legal discipline. Before changes were made in the business as much information as possible was gleaned. Internal arguments could be intense, deep and hurtful at times, but that was because people 'cared' for the heritage and the survival of one of Britain's finest treasures. On balance, the Belvoir estate is in a much better position now than when Terry and I first went to live there and, without Emma, it would not have been possible. David fully recognises this.

Emma and I co-operated on her speeches and her lectures, especially ones made abroad, and on book tours. Her energy knows no bounds. We visited the USA several times taking in Dallas, San Francisco, Philadelphia, New York and Boston. I would operate the slide show that accompanied her talks and deal with travel and hotel matters. We visited the Kimbell Art Museum in Fort Worth, Texas, and saw Poussin's painting 'Ordination', which was sold to the Kimbell from the Duke's art collection. We were honoured to have dinner with Kay Fortson and her family as well as the curator and members of the Kimbell Foundation. Close ties have developed with the Kimbell. Emma is, in this, a very good standard-bearer, not just for Belvoir, but for Britain too.

When we had first arrived to live at Belvoir in 2001, David and Emma were by then the Duke and Duchess of Rutland, but they were not in control of their own estate. It took a number of years to help them gain that control, but, once gained, Emma herself took control both of the castle and the business of opening the castle to the public, and eventually of the estate itself. Running the Belvoir estate was like running a small country. You needed a variety of skills and no one person can possibly embody all of them, although Emma tried. If things in the business got too much, Emma had her family of five children. She was and is first and foremost a very good mother. In difficult circumstances, she put her children first. She adores them all.

Emma liked the press, the cameras and the media. I had grown wary of it by the time I was at Belvoir. It was my condition of me working there that I would never go before a camera or be quoted. For Emma, the media was glittering and refreshing and placed her in the centre of Belvoir life and the centre of attention. Emma speaks well in public and wows the visitors and guests with great civility. She is an impressive act. David was always more reluctant at working with the media but when he wanted to be, he was naturally rather good at it. With experience, Emma learnt it was sometimes best to turn down an unwise 'opportunity', even cancelling a television series after initial shooting had begun when she realised it wasn't the right thing to do.

The pressures upon David and Emma are immense. In particular, Emma has huge responsibilities for the wellbeing of HMS *Belvoir* and all who sail in her. Our working relationship was sometimes challenging. Emma liked a good argument and if I thought she was wrong I would oblige, but our friendship, our ability to talk way into the night after supper at our cottage, our mutual concern for each other in the many difficulties that life has brought to us, shone through. I have seen the real tears, the real heartache too, and I have tried my best on such occasions to help, advise, console and support her and the family as best I could. It was not always easy to please all of the family all of the time, but always having her heart in the right place, despite all else, Emma Rutland and I remain good friends.

Another great character in the Vale of Belvoir is Imogen Skirving. She owns the splendid boutique hotel, Langar Hall, just outside

Nottingham. You drive to it up an avenue of lime trees and it is an oasis of peace and tranquillity in what can be surprisingly a very busy world. The food and wines are excellent. Imogen often entertained me in her private library but the dining room and the conservatory are idyllic lunch and dinner venues. She is well known for providing accommodation and a base for cricket Test Match Special commentators when Test matches take place at Trent Bridge, and also for hosting a romantic wedding location. Ed Miliband's was one of these, and Paul Smith is a regular guest.

Imogen also has a love affair with India. It is our mutual interest and desire. She has visited India many times and we have visited the same locations and restaurants in northern Goa, though never at the same time. Terry and I once searched out Imogen's daughter Louise on a beach there, not knowing her or even what she looked like. It was in the days when Goa was not the mass-market destination it is now. When we saw this good-looking girl, every bit as good-looking as her mother, we just knew it had to be her.

Imogen is very bright and built up the hotel business in the family home, running her business with skill, verve, old fashioned elegance and an iron hand – a very rare combination of talents. Physically small, she towers over Langar and is responsible for its quality and charm. Her management of staff is exemplary and an example to all. She is a lady of intellect and, above all, fun. She lightens up a room with her personality and is a joy. I am fortunate in knowing her and in recent times she has been of great support. When mates are in short supply, Imogen weighs heavily in the balance of friendship.

Another friend who visited Belvoir was Wylma Wayne, Terry's art dealer friend. She had continually featured in my life as a friend. I have mentioned her red hair. She was an incredible character: sharp-eyed and sharp-brained, with a ton of gravel in her voice. Her art gallery specialised in dealing in Rembrandt etchings and Churchill paintings. She was a valued friend of Lady Sarah Churchill and we once spent a wonderful evening at the American embassy in Grosvenor Square on the night of Reagan's first presidential victory. She was an ardent Republican and we went to several fundraising events together. She lived at times in Arlington House near to one of the Rutland's historic houses, and the Ritz Hotel. At other times, Wylma lived in Catherine Place, Victoria, by the side of Buckingham Palace, in a large flat with a panelled sitting room in which, I believe, the documents concerning leaving the gold standard were discussed, if not signed. She liked the Arlington House flat as it had a wide staircase from her bedroom from which she would descend in one of her many sparkling gowns to impress her guests. After closing her gallery, she dealt from home in Victoria but, alas, she then became ill for many years, which restricted her movement. I visited her in that treasured sitting room surrounded by paintings by Winston Churchill.

When she died, all her belongings were taken swiftly to the United States by her family, but not her remains. A small group of us buried her ashes on Thanksgiving Day in 2013 under an American tree planted in the parkland, on the Belvoir estate overlooking the castle. The tree was a Liquidambar Styraciflua, commonly known as an American sweetgum tree. It is native to eastern North America and a kind lady at the garden centre said she could find the very thing when we described Wylma. She said it was American, had five-starred pointed-shaped leaves which turn red in the autumn, but the clincher was that it had 'balls' as fruits. It fitted Wylma perfectly. The Duke's Chaplain said a Jewish prayer, Psalm 23, and the Aaronic Blessing.

David, the groundsman, kindly prepared the site to receive her ashes which I sprinkled around the young tree's roots. The weather was perfect, affording magnificent views from the tree to the castle.

To celebrate her rich life we held a traditional American Thanksgiving dinner in her honour in the private dining room of the castle, with turkey and all the trimmings. A friend of ours, Joanna Lane, who lives just outside New York City, and Brooke, one of her American academic friends who was studying at Oxford, attended. Together with the Duke, Andrea, Terry, Adam, Terry's son Tom, Duke the dog and myself, we all paid homage to Wylma's life. It was a memorable and moving occasion. Later, we had supper at our house and the conversation about Wylma went on into the early hours. It was a very appropriate send-off to Wylma – a larger-than-life character I was so pleased to have met. I think she would have approved of our Anglo-American send off, and she will be forever remembered in that most English of settings.

David and I visited France twice on wine selection visits, which were enjoyable but surprisingly hard work. We also visited Bassano in northern Italy in connection with a loan of one of the Duke's paintings by Jacopo Bassano. Travelling with, or for, a Duke could open doors in a similar way that it did when I was a MP abroad; a dukedom was respected more than it currently is in the UK and I can understand why, though I do not take much notice of titles. David earned his respect.

The Duke was often asked if he would loan his paintings to foreign exhibitions and art galleries. He did not agree to all such requests, but when he did he set down three conditions for any loan. David and Emma were close friends with Susannah Constantine and Sten Bertelsen, her husband, and they are my friends too. So Constantine Fine Art always had to be used to transport and handle the paintings. Nail-to-nail insurance should be covered by the lending gallery, with foreign government indemnity where possible. I was always to be the courier both there and back to oversee security and the hanging and lighting of the paintings. Constantine's are very professional and all their staff are experienced and excellent in the skilled work they do. Usually, they would collect the relevant painting and me from Belvoir and transport us by air-conditioned truck via Eurostar to European destinations, or via air to New York. Over the years I became a bit of an expert on handling fine art and thought it was enthralling. I enjoyed meeting foreign curators. There was only one difficult moment, in January 2015, when our truck was surrounded by fifty or sixty would-be migrants at Calais as we waited to board the train. Three of them blatantly broke open the back doors of the lorry in front of us and hid themselves inside the truck. The value of our cargo was many millions of pounds, as we were also carrying paintings from the National Gallery and Windsor Castle. Fortunately, they did not gain entry into our vehicle and passed us by.

I took a David Teniers painting – 'The Proverbs'– to Karlsruhe, two Stubbs paintings to Munich, a Jan Stein 'Grace before Meat' to southern Netherlands and two Poussins to the Louvre, as well as the Bassano to Bassano.

The Duke was asked in 2007 if he would loan a painting of Roger Manners, the 5th Earl of Rutland, to Jamestown in Virginia for an exhibition commemorating the four-hundredth anniversary of permanent settlement in the USA. Some Russian and American professors feel that Roger might have been Shakespeare. There are many people in the frame for being the bard, and Roger was the English ambassador in Denmark and there are many Danish references in Shakespeare's works. Some feel Roger wrote some of the sonnets. The Duke is not convinced. All was revealed when I arrived and met the curator, who was Russian. She had studied under the Russian professor who wrote a book claiming Roger was definitely Shakespeare. She wanted her show to reflect what was happening in Europe in theatre, design, politics, fashion and trade at the time of this permanent settlement. Not surprisingly, the painting had pride of place in the exhibition.

I enjoyed this important part of my work, although it is not always obvious why it should be done. Not everyone valued its significance, not just to Belvoir, but to the country. Allowing paintings to be viewed abroad is good for Belvoir and for Britain. It increases the provenance and authenticity of paintings and so confirms and adds to their value. It is self-interest. It brings to foreign attention the wonders of Belvoir and is a significant contribution to art appreciation and spreading our heritage around the world.

It is a matter of public record that, in 2012, Emma and David's marriage split asunder and they separated. Terry and I had known them since before their marriage in 1992. We tried very hard to help where we could as friends although professionally I worked closely for both of them and knew the difficulties in their relationship. I often kept both their secrets simultaneously. I was privileged they should trust me and I have no intention of letting either of them down now by revealing any of them. It was not uncommon for both of them to call down to our home to have a heart-to-heart conversation separately but on the same evening. Never being married, I was really the last person to give advice on such things but, knowing them for over twenty years, I lent a sympathetic ear. The trials and tribulations have abated somewhat. Their division was emotional for them but also for all of us. I had known each of their children from their births and a great sadness pervaded Belvoir for many months. Emma has written extensively about these matters, David less so; their reaction reflected their personalities.

They have their own partners now. Terry and I have known both Phil and Andrea very well for a number of years. We get on famously and have enjoyed down-to-earth supper parties in our homes with civilised conversation and laughter – so much laughter and fun as well as tears. Personal relationships can be fraught with difficulty. It is best not to look too closely at these intensely private matters. Suffice to say I wish them all well in their futures.

My time at Belvoir was a delight. I achieved a way of life I never thought would be possible after 1987. I worked on after my retirement age and was in my element doing a great job, at full power and health and using all the experience I had gathered in such a varied career towards a worthwhile objective. I suppose I had become one of those people who knew what to do if things went wrong, even on a Christmas Day, and sought to put things right not because it was my job but because of dedication and loyalty. I enjoyed my work and my home, my family and my dogs. I did not realise how transitory it was all to be. It was to be a chimera.

In January 2015, I flew to the US, first to visit a shoot show in Dallas on behalf of the estate and then on to New York to collect a painting I had taken to the Metropolitan Museum of Art the previous October. Flying into New York, I had seen the Met building from the air as we took the scenic approach into JFK airport past Manhattan. The plane's captain pointed out the art gallery as I had the privilege of flying across the Atlantic in the cockpit of the huge cargo plane. The 'cargo' was 'The Last Supper' by Pieter Coecke van Aelst (1527) and, though a very large painting, it was to be an important part of an exhibition of his tapestries. As there was some doubt as to who painted the picture, the Met had sent specialists, including Maryan Ainsworth, to look at the painting in 2013 and a dendrochronology test was arranged. It proved the wood for the five panels on which it was painted was growing on trees in the Baltic in 1510 and, incredibly, that two panels, including the one containing the faces, were from wood from the same tree! It was clear it was painted by van Aelst; so the two trips to New York were definitely in the diary.

I stayed at a hotel on the Upper West Side; from there I could walk across Central Park to the Met. Unfortunately, while working on packing up the painting, a nor'easter winter storm, Juno, blew up and New York decided to close down, including theatres, cinemas, taxis, subways and trains. Traffic was banned from the city's roads, leaving them open for emergency units. It was difficult to move more than a block. My cargo flight back via Amsterdam was delayed for three extra days which upset Terry. I had already been away for more than a week but there was nothing I could do; I was snowbound.

On Tuesday 27 January, I tucked into my sunny-side-up eggs, bacon and porridge and copious amounts of coffee in the sidewalk café next to the hotel. I looked out at the non-stop progress of snow ploughs clearing the roads for emergency vehicles and thought how ill-equipped British cities were for dealing with snow by comparison. I wondered when I might be back in the States. Little did I know that, within a few weeks, everything I had strived for, everything I valued, everything that gave my life stability and vitality was to disintegrate into dust. Picking up the *New York Times*, I read with sadness an obituary of a former colleague; it was that of the late Leon Brittan.

CHAPTER 11

BABY

For the first time now I write about what had happened in mid-February of 2015, a couple of weeks before the Metropolitan Police raid on my home on Wednesday 4 March, and which, unbeknown to me at the time, really started the drama that was to overtake my life in 2015. I can reveal that my house had already been raided by police and social services from Leicestershire. On this Thursday afternoon, I was working, collecting the Duchess's Land Rover from Ilkeston in Derbyshire together with Vaclav. He worked as a butler but had many other duties besides. I enjoyed his company. Terry telephoned me to say that two officials were in our house and were threatening to take Adam and Charlotte's baby into care. They had only ever been perfect parents, so it came as a complete surprise to me. It was incomprehensible why these officials would wish to do that. I was to find out that it wasn't Adam and Charlotte, but maybe it was Terry who had apparently caused the visitation.

One night while I was away on business in New York in January, Terry had too much to drink and, being lonely, he had telephoned everyone he could. Friends know he can be very loquacious at such times, including the local police. At the time he made inappropriate comments on a call to the local police about his good friend Emma, I was in the Ralph Lauren children's department in New York with friends who had kindly taken me there to buy gifts for the baby. Charlotte arrived home during the course of the conversation and explained to the police operator that Terry was alright, just a little under the influence. There was no problem. The next morning, the local beat police officer turned up, concluded it was Terry just being Terry and reported all was well. But, in talking to Terry, he noticed there was a baby in the house. I presume he reported this up the line of command but this was not clear. So, on this Thursday, Detective Constable Julian Allen introduced himself to Charlotte and Adam and asked to enter. He said he was a child protection officer working in conjunction with Leicestershire social services and introduced Louise, who was eventually identified as a social services officer. Julian did most of the talking. They already knew the child's age as the small car in which they arrived was fitted with a baby chair already installed, one just the right size for a newborn baby. The car was not of a size to take the baby, Adam and Charlotte, and all of the baby's things. They had a prearranged plan to take the baby into care. Inadvertently, Adam asked whether they had come because of Terry and his drinking. They hesitated, then said yes. Adam says they were not definitive as to the reason for their visit. They made no mention of me, but asked who else lived in the house. They were told a male friend of Terry's.

They said that Adam and Charlotte had to move out of their home, to find another place for the baby, or if they did not do so immediately they would take the baby into care. By the time I arrived home, hoping to resolve the situation, the two officials told me that they feared Terry would fall over and hurt the child. The child could not stay in the house. Adam, Charlotte and Terry had not been inactive in the couple of hours it had taken me to return home. Rightly, they were more concerned with preventing their child being taken into care than to establish reasons. They were a young couple and nervous of this unwanted and undeserved intrusion. To prevent the baby being taken away, they had talked to Andrea, the Duke's partner, who was having lunch with David in the castle and who immediately and without hesitation invited all the family to move into a part of her house with her; for that gesture we will be eternally grateful. It was about a ten-minute drive away. We went to her house in a convoy of cars. I drove Adam, Charlotte and their baby in my car. The officers raised no objection. Terry stayed at home to look after the dogs.

The accommodation, not surprisingly, passed muster although the police officer had questioned Adam as to whether, as the property was 'rented' it could be considered 'stable'. I spoke to Andrea in the kitchen while the parents were quizzed in their new rooms. They were asked how they knew Andrea, obviously astonished by the swift turn of events, and how they knew me. They asked if they knew my 'history'; the officers obviously did. How did Adam come to live with Terry and me? What was the set-up of their home at Barn Farm? Who lived where? The police officer said allegations had been made against me but did not elaborate. Adam and Charlotte, understandably concerned for their baby, only remembered this comment much later and did not mention it to me until months later.

As Julian and Louise were leaving, I happened to mention to Adam and Charlotte that Terry and I would call round later to check all was well. 'Oh no,' said the social worker, Terry could not see the baby ever again ... and nor could I! 'What?!' I exploded. 'Why me?' 'Because,' said Louise and Julian, almost in unison, 'because of what happened to you in 1987.' I was shocked and momentarily rendered speechless. That had nothing to do with children. It was twenty-eight years ago and the convictions then were no longer convictions. 'Yes,' said Julian, the police officer, 'the police are suffering from paranoia, but those are our orders.' Both seemed to be operating outside their normal comfort zone. Why was no mention made of this when I was at my home? I asked them. Why was it that they lied to me about the reason for moving the child when I was at my home, *our* home? They both shrugged nervously and sheepishly. I believe it was to get us all out of the house under subterfuge. I was so taken aback, I let them leave without even arguing. Seeing how distraught I was, Louise said she would talk to her bosses to see if they would change their mind with regard to access and talk to me in the morning.

I felt sick, as if I had been kicked in the stomach. Before the birth, I had been horrified at the thought of sharing my home with a baby. We had arranged for Adam and Charlotte to move to a flat in the nearby village of Bottesford in the spring of 2014, but it was full of damp and no place for a new baby. So they had moved back to Barn Farm. The baby was born in November and, in the three months the baby had been in our house, I had become used to the idea. These were very happy days. I had not even cuddled the baby for fear I might do it wrong or drop her. Yet, to be told by social services, who did not know me and were apparently going on what they thought I had done twenty-eight years earlier at the bidding of the police – Leicestershire or Metropolitan – that I might be a threat was false, distasteful and extraordinary. We were all bewildered, but Adam and Charlotte were convinced by their dealings with Julian and Louise that this had nothing to do with Terry and everything to do with me. They thought they had been deliberately forced from their home on my account and by false pretences. I believe they are right. No legal papers were shown to them by the two officials. The only paper given to them, showing a telephone number written on scrap paper, proved to be useless as the number was incorrect. I believe illegality took place that day. It was abhorrent. The authorities had attempted to effectively kidnap the baby.

Adam was asked whether he had had any dealings with the police and social services in the past and what he thought of them. He said when he was a child he had sought help from the police and social services and they had done nothing to help him. Now, when he and his family felt safe and secure, they had their future plans of a foreign abode for the first year of their baby's life and they were content at last, along came the police, who had torn his family from their home. It was devastating for them. He was very critical of them, yet stayed polite. Despite his mentioning his historic childhood abuse problems to DC Julian Allen that day and later to DS Matt Flynn, both of whom said they would assist during both incursions of our home, they have done nothing to help him. I find that extraordinary but, in the light of later developments still to unfold, not surprising.

The next day, we were told that social services had had a rethink. Louise said the baby could come back to Barn Farm, but only under the supervision of Charlotte and, as she could not stay awake 24/7, the baby, and effectively the parents, could not stay overnight. Additionally, Adam was not permitted to supervise his own child. Still, it meant we could all see each other and we were grateful to her. Louise said that social services would hold an inquiry concerning the baby and Terry and I, which could take two months. The next week, Louise and another social services officer arrived to interview Charlotte and suggested she and Adam should sign a document that would indicate that they had agreed to the arrangement. Adam and

Charlotte said they would consider the matter. No court papers concerning the movement of the baby out of the house were ever produced because the matter was never placed before a court. At no time was Terry or I interviewed by Leicestershire social services or the police about the issue and no report was concluded. They later told Adam and Charlotte that the report would not be finalised until 'the case' was concluded, by that we understand them to mean Operation Midland. However, this was only the half of it.

A few days later, the Duke rang to say he had been visited by Leicestershire Police and social services and asked whether he knew about me and my work at the castle. As I worked directly for him, he said yes. Did he know what had happened in 1986/87? Well, yes, he did – who didn't? Belvoir staff, estate residents and pretty much everyone, including the local police, knew. I had not kept it a secret, nor could I. It was a matter of public knowledge throughout the world, especially in the internet age. I was a well-known figure in the locality. Did he know about the baby and its movement? Well, yes, he did, as it was hardly likely I would not discuss it with him when his partner Andrea was giving shelter to my family. Being a private secretary meant 'secrets' worked both ways. Emma, on her return from abroad, also kindly offered to put the family up in the castle or on the estate. David said they had told him there would be a tribunal inquiry about the advisability of me continuing to work at the castle and I would be asked to attend. He was also told by them not to mention any of this to me. It had to be kept secret and confidential. He rang to tell me as soon as they left the castle.

A few days later, when challenged about the delays on their report, the Leicestershire social services worker said that they were waiting for information from the archives department of the Metropolitan Police to give them more detailed information on the court case involving me in 1987. It was being treated very carefully, she said, as I was a 'VIP'. When I had tried to ring Louise previously – she worked part-time – she said it was not surprising her office had refused to comment or had said they knew nothing about the movement of the baby. Nothing in writing was ever given to Adam, Charlotte, Terry or myself about anything connected with these matters. I felt as though I was being regarded as guilty. I felt as though I had to prove my innocence, of what, I was unsure. I had not a clue. I had no means or platform to even prove I was innocent even if I knew what I was supposed to have done. Such feelings of incredulity were to prove decisive in my later actions.

It was confusing and baffling. How could I be kept in the dark about these issues? Specifically, how could the police go to my employer in secret seeking my dismissal? In due course, representatives of the castle were asked to meetings at Leicestershire County Hall to discuss me and my future. Despite what they had told David that day, I was not told about these tribunals, I was not invited to attend any of these meetings, nor was I ever invited to comment in writing or orally on any of these affairs. First, I was suspended by the castle to give them time to work out my future role there. The pressure on the castle from Leicestershire Police and social services grew. Because the public toured the castle and I worked on weddings and other public events, they argued I could not be allowed to continue to work there under any circumstances. The castle and its advisers were given deadlines to get rid of me. The advice of their new employment lawyers at the estate, who did not know me but who were guiding the Duke and Duchess, must have been that third-party pressure from the police and social services was sufficient reason to dismiss me. Eventually, I was offered the choice of dismissal or resignation. I resigned on 24 March 2015.

So, there were two motive forces that caused me to lose my job and my home: the raid on the house by the Metropolitan Police and the horrible paedophile insinuations Operation Midland unleashed around me, and also the earlier incursion by Leicestershire Police, whether at the behest of the Met or not, concerning the baby of the family.

Did the Met pressurise Leicestershire Police to break our family apart? Was it their aim to get Adam, Charlotte and the baby moved out of our house before the raid on 4 March? The Met policeman's comments to Adam and Charlotte rather suggested that they were aware that they had at one time had lived there, and that they were not allowed in on the day of the search, using a ban they had set up and thought through earlier. On what legal basis did Julian and Louise try to kidnap Adam and Charlotte's baby? What was the real reason for their actions? If it was on the basis of Terry being unsteady on his feet, not a baby in a household with an elderly relative in the land would be safe. Why did they leave no official paperwork for their actions – not even a legitimate business card or an effective telephone number? Did they use the baby issue to undermine me with the Duke and Duchess and their advisers and my professional position at the castle? Did the Metropolitan Police inform Leicestershire Police and social services about the detail of 'Nick's' allegations about me, or at least some of them, in February or March but made known only to me in late June? I do not know for sure, but think I should be told the answers to these questions in due course. I feel aggrieved, bitter and angry and, at a minimum, I think I am owed an apology, as are Adam and Charlotte.

My use of the word 'Kafkaesque' on the *Today* programme on 5 March was, in part, due to my background knowledge of these events and what I was not privy to say at the time about these matters.

I write about them now only with the kind and express permission of Adam and Charlotte.

Prior to these traumatic developments, Adam had been working up a business project on the sale of e-cigarettes over the internet, including a website which he could develop and operate overseas. However, he needed a UK distribution mechanism, and this was something I was going to help him with once I had cut back to a three-day week at the castle. This inevitably disintegrated under the pressure of unfolding events.

Adam and I had also travelled abroad the previous October (2014) to successfully find suitable accommodation for himself, Charlotte and the baby. This trip was interrupted when he received a call informing him that Charlotte had been taken to hospital with a problem concerning the pregnancy. Adam flew home immediately by a circuitous route. Charlotte remained in hospital until their child was born, prematurely, but fortunately in perfectly good health in Nottingham. A suitable house had also been located abroad.

The trauma of all these events surrounding the Leicestershire Police and social services for all of us was intense. It completely destabilised Adam and Charlotte and their long-established plans to take their baby abroad to live for the first year of its life, which should have been a joyous moment. Their move went ahead, but with much greater difficulty. For Terry and I, the aggravation and dislocation of normal life was like revisiting the old days of the earlier scandal, except now we had the extended family of Adam, Charlotte and the baby, not forgetting our beloved dogs. We had responsibilities for all and had become part of the rural community where we lived and I worked. However hard to believe, I felt it would be an even worse upheaval than in 1987, with a very bleak future, if there was a future at all. As I write, I am not sure I can be responsible even for myself.

CHAPTER 1 2

THE RAID

Flynn walked in and although he seemed to know who I was went through a perfunctory identification procedure. All this was before the days when we locked the doors. He gave me a copy of the search warrant. I wondered what the magistrate had been told to obtain his signature upon it, if anything. Whatever it was, it was not disclosed to me. Flynn wanted to know who else was in the house. He explained other officers would be coming in and, over the next few minutes, they did. I didn't count them, but there must have been at least fifteen of them, maybe more, many in pale-blue, forensic overalls. I had seen this scenario on TV drama serials. I had seen men like this on television when Sir Cliff Richard's house had been raided in the presence of BBC cameras. I mean, I had in fact seen the very same police officers in those uniforms – it was the same search team apparently. I had never expected them to pay a visit to my house. It was, and was intended to be, an intimidation tactic. The early moments are still blurred, but I think they said something about photographing rooms. In any event, cameras began to flash.

Terry smoked grass (cannabis) for medical reasons, having being introduced to it in India many years before in Goa. He had some in a bag in an upstairs room and in two smaller bags, one in each pocket of his dressing gown. He suddenly remembered the bag and stupidly went upstairs to conceal it. I was not a cigarette smoker, nor did I smoke cannabis. I used to call them 'funny' cigarettes. As a libertarian, I was content for others to smoke cigarettes and to smoke cannabis. I used to represent a cigarette-making company called Carreras Rothman based in my constituency of Basildon in Essex as a Member of Parliament. I thought trying to control by illegality the smoking of cannabis to be futile, costly and socially counter-productive by driving its manufacture and retail underground. A sharp-eyed policeman in the search team noticed the 'bag' had been moved since the room in which it was originally located was photographed. As I had been followed by Flynn for the whole time, he knew it wasn't me who had moved it. They knew it was Terry. He admitted it and told them where he had relocated it. They thanked him. They said they would deal with the matter later. Within fifteen minutes of their entry, the police's 'fishing' expedition had scored a direct hit; round one to them.

Attention then turned to me. A woman police officer asked me about my welfare, solicitous about my health. I think age played a part; they didn't want me to collapse on them. That certainly would be bad public relations. I think I filled in a form or two, or she did so on my behalf. They had covered their backs. Flynn was with me throughout. He was the 'diplomatic' police officer of the team, the 'good cop' of the day. It seemed to run against his nature. I sought answers to questions: What was I supposed to have done? Why was there a search? They were not forthcoming. It was, he said (as did the warrant), to do with historical child sexual abuse. Well, I knew

I had done none of that. This would not take long I surmised wrongly; some hope. Flynn promised me early on that at the end of the search I would be given a list of the items that were to be taken. I would be asked to sign for them. In the event, no such list was produced, nor my signature acquired for any detailed list.

In an outhouse, once a stable, were three cardboard boxes. They contained papers from 1986/87 concerning the earlier scandal in which I was involved. They, together with legal, parliamentary and constituency papers also in those boxes, were to form the basis of a book that I intended to write when I had the time. The boxes had moved with me over the last twenty-eight years awaiting an opportunity to see the light of day. I was unsure exactly what they contained, such was the passage of time since I had last flicked through them. Indeed, one box of papers might have been ruined by an unexpected flood from a water tank some months before, but I had not even had time to investigate. So I told the police the relevant papers relating to the period of their inquiries, not that I was told exactly what that period was, might be in these three boxes outside and I asked if I could be present when they opened them. I thought it not a big favour to ask and they agreed to my request, but it was one eventually denied. I was soon to learn that they agreed to anything but just did their own thing regardless. They put the boxes in their van without even looking at them. Had I not mentioned them they might have ignored them. Their choice of things to take appeared arbitrary and quixotic. How much easier it would be to write this book if I had them with me now. I told them that, apart from my diaries, some photographs and odd papers from the 1970s and 1980s, there was little in the house of the period. Of course, they were not going to take my word for it and the search continued. Maybe it would have been wise to have contacted a solicitor at that stage, but I knew

I had nothing to do with these inquiries so decided against contacting professionals.

Time dragged on. Terry decided to leave the house and go to a friend's house. He got a lift with Adam, whose home it also was. Terry had seen enough of the police. I made small talk with Flynn, not an easy job, while seemingly endless items and personal possessions were bagged, tagged, photographed and piled up for removal.

Comings and goings were few. Leicestershire Police officers, maybe Lincolnshire too, assisting the Met, had cordoned off the track from the road to the house. They were there to turn back the nosey caller and keep the press at bay. On the surface they had learnt their lessons from the BBC's blow-by-blow account on the raid of the home of Sir Cliff Richard. The Met officers had apparently stayed overnight locally in hotel accommodation. But they had numerous vehicles, including a mini bus.

Adam, Charlotte and the baby had been staying with a friend, so they weren't there when the police came barging in. Earlier, Adam had sought entry into what was still his home. He needed lactose-free milk powder and fresh, clean clothes for his baby. The police refused his request. Adam frequently returned but the answer remained the same. He was turned away at lunch time on the grounds that the policemen were having lunch and there were insufficient officers available to let him into his own home. Eventually, Adam's persistence met with success. Later in the afternoon, Adam and Charlotte returned to get clothes for their baby. Again the police denied their request. Adam asked them whether they were investigating alleged child offences and the police said yes. Adam reminded the police that it was child abuse they themselves were committing by refusing his modest request for his baby's food and clothes. With a bit of help from me, Charlotte was allowed entry. It was her home too. She was questioned about where she lived and said, 'Here, this is my home.' They said it couldn't be her home now. Maybe they realised they had released too much information about their part in the conspiracy that had darkened our world only days before their raid. They quickly changed the question to enquire where she was staying now. She said with a friend. But through persistence and not through police forethought she gained the baby clothes. This had been appalling and insensitive behaviour by the police. Round two to us.

The operation seemed to be being controlled by a undistinguished-looking Detective Inspector wearing a flat cap, who sat in his parked car at the gates of the house. Rudely, I thought, he never introduced himself or said a word. I think he was the 'communications' hub, keeping in touch with superior officers at Scotland Yard on the progress of their search. Flynn referred to him frequently through the search but was desperate at the end of it that I did not introduce myself to him. I think he knew I would be wanting to register my complaint at his discourtesy in refusing to introduce himself, to his face. He did not want his superior officer to face my growing concern.

At one point during the search, in the late morning, I think it was, I left the house. I needed to go to the castle concerning, I think, alarms. It might also have been because the police were also searching my office within Belvoir Castle where I worked. There were so many of them in the room I could hardly get into it. I was surprised that I was allowed out of my home – and with my mobile phone. I thought of leaving it with a friend but as I had nothing to hide I did not. It was collected from me – almost as an afterthought – just before the police left at the end of the search.

The search was now in its eighth hour when Terry returned home, tired and emotional – and completely drunk. He slumped on the white, leather sofa horizontally and commented on the progress of the search. His language had become quite spicy. He suggested that if the police were intent on searching for the bodies of three alleged victims, could they please dig in three specific places in the garden where he wished to establish flower beds later in the spring. It was Terry's way of trying to release the tension. The matter was so serious but also so ludicrous at the same time. Terry knew I was no murderer or child sexual abuser, historic or otherwise. He was with me in the 1970s and chunks of the 1980s. The police were not there, well, not on a daily basis. For a moment Flynn flicked a smile at Terry's suggestion and then regained his composure. His 'diplomatic' facade was beginning to wear thin under Terry's remorseless logic and common sense fuelled by drink. Flynn urged me to see if we could get Terry out of the way. I said the police had come into my home uninvited and this was an inevitable consequence of their stressful visit. I said Terry needed to go to sleep. In the bedroom was his supply of prescription sleeping tablets. He might benefit from taking one. Flynn agreed I should get him a tablet and I moved through to the bedroom where they were kept. A tall police detective constable dressed in the pale-blue uniform, whom I got to know as DC Danny Chatfield, a former reporter, stopped me and, when I asked where the tablets were, he said he had 'bagged them up'. He refused to let me have them even though I argued that the tablets could not possibly have anything to do with alleged events that occurred thirty years earlier. He was adamant. I had kept my temper until that point but when I returned to the sitting room I said to Flynn that if I did not get a tablet for Terry I would withdraw my co-operation with the search. He couldn't believe they had been 'bagged' either and under my pressure he called Scotland Yard. After about fifteen minutes talking to his superiors, the police capitulated. Terry got his tablet and his much-needed sleep. Round three to us.

The search, however, went on. They rearranged the possessions in the stables/outhouses, leaving them much tidier than before they had arrived, though I am not sure the spring clean could justify the cost of the search. The quantity of items marked to be taken by the police mounted, but no justification was given as to their choices. Why take two metal shoe horns given to me as Christmas presents by the Duke and Duchess of Rutland a few years ago? Why take a rolled-up window blind that Terry had used at our previous home at Engine Yard Cottage as a giant address and telephone book – his eyesight was not good – when it could have had nothing to do with life thirty years ago? Many of the items taken were not even mine. Other members of the household's belongings and work items were removed, including a large number of computers and hard drives. They even took one of the baby's socks, which was decorated with Winnie the Pooh's image and had a rattle connected to it. The attitude of many in the police search team was brusque and bordering on rude. DC Chatfield, playing 'bad cop', was impolite and aggressive. During the 'wash-up' meeting at the end – at which point it was nearing 11 p.m., and we had endured fifteen hours of their presence – he was anxious to leave. I was anxious they should leave too. The promised list of everything they had taken was not forthcoming. It would take too long. Maybe overtime, or lack of it, got in the way of procedure. Chatfield, in particular, had become further agitated when the Duke rang me during the meeting to ask how I was and what had been happening. I refused to rush the call; it was my boss calling, after all, and I was in no mood to make it quick – as Flynn realised. But Chatfield continued moaning on throughout my conversation with David. In his mind's eye, I was guilty. Exactly of what, I had no idea at the time.

As Flynn was leaving, he advised me that I would not be identified by the press. It had been my concern throughout the day that

I would face a barrage from the media in the morning. I said I would not make a statement unless I was named. I picked up my strategy of dealing with the press over twenty-eight years earlier; say nothing or as few words as possible. Little did I know at the time that, two hours earlier, a journalist from a news website (Exaro), Mark Conrad, had already rung my office and left an email in my inbox asking me to contact him to confirm that the police were in the process of searching my home.

Exaro, according to Wikipedia, is 'an investigative news website. Launched in October 2011, it specialises in carrying out in-depth investigations. Its journalistic creed is "holding power to account". It sets out to produce "evidence-based, open-access journalism – not spin, not churnalism, not hacking – just journalism about what should be transparent but isn't."' It was originally established to look at financial matters but has become preoccupied with historical child sexual abuse in the last two years. I have discovered it may be far from transparent about its own dealings. It has acted as a clearing house for internet fantasists and together with elements of the Metropolitan Police Service is in an unhealthy union. It has not held itself to account.

So, the police had lied to me. Scotland Yard had issued a statement, not revealing my name of course, but that a man in his sixties had his house raided at an address near Grantham. In addition, they had already informed 'Nick' – the traducer – of the raid on my home. Perhaps he passed on the information to Exaro. Or did the police give information to the BBC or Exaro directly or indirectly, for love or for money? Whichever way, it was the Metropolitan Police that revealed the information that they must have known would result in my identification. Any one of them could have sold the story to the press. They knew what would happen; I did not. Sure, it had happened in 1986/87, and deep down I doubted things would be different now, but I actually believed Flynn's words. I would say nothing.

I cleared up the house from the invasion, made myself tea and had a snack. How could I be in such a situation? I wondered. I had no idea. I had done nothing wrong, yet here we go again, I thought. I did not know what my alleged involvement was, and they had said at the outset that they only wished to get at the truth. I made it clear that I wished to be interviewed at the earliest opportunity. I was asked to contact them to arrange an interview which would be early and, if I got a solicitor, I should ask him to make contact. I was exhausted. Terry was asleep. My dogs gathered round me, full of loyalty and support. They licked me, and I was thankful for their affection. I turned on the television (by now it was after 1 a.m.) and fell asleep.

I awoke on the dot at 7 a.m. As my eyes opened there was an old picture of me staring back at me from the television screen, a BBC news story related the previous day's raid and allegations of child murder. It mentioned historical child sexual abuse, Cabinet ministers, MPs, Dolphin Square, a Westminster rent-boy ring and military establishments. Terry, now awake and equally astonished, switched over to BBC Radio 4's *Today* programme – part of our usual waking-up ritual. Their news bulletin, however, had just reached the discussion of the police raid on my home too, as well as allegations of murder and other abuse. Radio and television news reports seemed to be coordinated. It was obvious I had been lied to by the police. Everything I had feared had come to pass. The police raid had legitimised internet myths, but what to do about it? I had for eighteen months refused politely all media requests for comment. I had said nothing. Should I continue my stance?

In 1986 and 1987, I had tried to say as little as possible to the media about my scandal. As a result, the press often made things up – including my comments. Should I continue to adopt the same position? I had no time to consult friends; I knew that if I was going to say anything it had to be done quickly.

Terry and I talked it over. He was very insistent I should speak out this time. I had to fight this injustice, he thought. I said I wasn't sure. To placate him, I said I would try to contact the BBC's *Today* programme. I was not hopeful, though if I was to talk, I felt it best to do so here. It had been one of Mrs Thatcher's favourite programmes and it was one widely listened to by the movers and shakers of the political world. Surprisingly, I got through to a researcher on the programme with only a little insistence at the switch board. Something I think along the lines of 'it's being alleged I am a child murderer, could I set the record straight?' The researcher talked about what they knew already. They would have heard the news bulletins too. They commented on who else might be involved – not names so much as categories of people – MPs, ministers, Cabinet ministers, generals. I think the bit about the military and generals – something that later became an issue as to how I knew they were involved – had also been mentioned by DS Flynn earlier. I said I was prepared to be questioned on anything but had little to say other than I found myself in a Kafkaesque situation. I had been raided by the police but without explanation of what it was I had supposedly done. I insisted on a live (not pre-recorded) interview. I had often been caught out before by being edited badly, especially by the BBC. I was told that I would be interviewed live by James Naughtie after the 8 a.m. news. I had heard him many times on this programme and respected his journalistic abilities. While I waited, I spoke to staff at the castle and Emma, the Duchess, rang me on my mobile. She wanted to know if we were OK. I explained what had happened the previous day and that I was about to give my point of view on Radio 4. She decided to listen to me on her car radio as she was driving back from her parents' home in Wales. I had no time to prepare; it was going to be an 'off the cuff' interview over the telephone, while Terry listened to the radio in the kitchen. The interview was broadcast as follows:

James Naughtie (JN): Police, as we have heard on the news, searched the home of the former Conservative MP, Mr Harvey Proctor. The Metropolitan Police say it is part of Operation Midland, that is, an investigation into allegations made by a man now in his forties who says he was, with other young people, abused at various addresses in London and in the south of England at parties attended by prominent people. The police have said publicly that they believe his allegations are credible. Well, Harvey Proctor, former MP, joins us now. Good morning, Mr Proctor.

Harvey Proctor (HP): Good morning.

JN: Can you just tell us what the police have said to you?

HP: The police have said basically what you have just said, that they are investigating historical sex abuse allegations going back to the 1970s and the 1980s.

JN: Were you aware before police arrived at your home of this operation, which is known as Operation Midland?

HP: I may not have known of the detail of it but anyone would be blind if they hadn't seen the press relating these matters over the last year and I find myself in a very Kafkaesque, sensitive situation.

JN: In what sense?

HP: Well, I think you and your listeners are intelligent enough to know what I mean.

JN: Well look, well look, let's go back into history. It was known that you left Parliament, very largely as a result of your conviction, which was public knowledge in 1987, in which you vigorously defended yourself.

HP: I'm sorry? I pleaded guilty to four charges of gross indecency in 1987. Those offences related entirely to the age of consent for homosexuality.

JN: Absolutely.

HP: That age has been reduced first to eighteen and now to sixteen. The offences I committed in 1987 are no longer offences and there is legislation on the Statute Book which would allow me to wipe them clean if I wished to do so.

JN: Indeed, well, it is very good to have made this clear. Your story is well-known. In your biography there was an incident when you ran two shops in the 1990s when you were attacked, and that incident is there in the public domain. I do not think you have ever spoken publicly about what you think lay behind that attack. Why do you think you were attacked?

HP: Do you mean physically attacked in my shop or—

JN: Yes.

HP: —or why I was attacked by the press for eighteen months? The latter is because of my political views at the time, which I have kept quiet about subsequently. The attack in my shop, I believe, was a homophobic attack.

JN: Did you know the men who committed it?

HP: No.

JN: No.

HP: They were prosecuted and imprisoned.

JN: Let's go back to the Kafkaesque situation in which you find yourself. Do you mean by that that you have no idea really how you have come to be in this position?

HP: Correct. I have never attended sex parties at Dolphin Square or anywhere else. I have not been part of any rent-boy ring with Cabinet ministers, other MPs, or generals or the military. I conducted my private life in a discreet manner. It wasn't I who 'outed' myself, it was the press who did an assortment of things to 'out' me. They wanted to say I was a homosexual. Of course, there were offences committed. I did not know at the time that I was committing those offences because the people concerned who were actually under twenty-one said to me they were over twenty-one. That is confirmed on one of their tapes, one of the papers at the time sent in a person to my private apartment and tape-recorded a conversation with me. On that tape that person who was carrying the hidden tape recorder admitted that he was over twenty-one. It turned out he was nineteen.

JN: And that was the reason for the conviction. Let me just take you back a few years from that point. We were talking there about 1987, I think. You've said, in very clear terms, just a moment ago, you have never attended the sort of party that has been publicised, at which prominent people were alleged to be involved in the sexual abuse of young people.

HP: I was a discreet person. I was regarded in the House of Commons as a very independent MP and a 'loner'. The last thing I would dream of doing is talking to other MPs or ministers or anyone else about my personal life. It wasn't that I was ashamed of being a homosexual, it was I did not think it mattered a damn [to] the work that I did on behalf of my constituents.

JN: The question I was going to ask you – the one people will be interested in – you are obviously aware of the rumours and allegations that are flying around in great quantity at the moment. Looking back at that period after you first came into the Commons, which is the period we are talking about, the very late '70s into the '80s, again, you have been very clear. You say you have never attended such a party. Were you ever aware yourself that there was, not just, you know, a link between people who were conducting homosexual relationships in private, perfectly legally, but paedophilia or the sexual abuse of young people? Did you ever have reason to believe that that was going on in an organised way even if you were not part of it?

HP: Absolutely not. No. And if I had known about it at the time I would have contacted the police.

JN: What do you make of the allegations that are being made and in such profusion?

HP: I believe that the number of victims grows by the day, the number of alleged perpetrators, through death, diminishes. That is a problem. It is certainly a problem for me. I suppose my problem is that I am still very much alive. I am sure that some of the allegations are true. But I am also sure that a lot of the allegations are pure and utter fantasy. I noted in your report earlier on me that you tagged along the fact that this operation is supposedly investigating the alleged murders of three young gentlemen.

JN: That is what the police have said.

HP: I know nothing about that either.

JN: I think to be absolutely clear what Tom Simmons, our reporter, said was earlier wasn't – was simply saying that Operation Midland covered those allegations which the police had said but many other allegations as well.

HP: I do not think I have been over sensitive in thinking that there is an element of guilt by association in your report but I will let that pass.

JN: Just let me ask one final thing.

HP: Of course.

JN: We are presumably correct in assuming that you will assist the police to the best of your ability in this matter?

HP: The police wish to interview me. They talked in terms of that interview taking place in a matter of weeks. I asked for that interview to take place at the earliest opportunity.

JN: In other words you want to tell them precisely what you know or don't know and what you think as soon as you can?

HP: Exactly.

JN: Harvey Proctor, thank you very much for talking to us.

HP: Thank you.

After the interview was concluded, Emma rang to say how magnificent she thought I had been on the radio. Others quickly telephoned with their support too. People who hate broadcasts or think you shouldn't have done it stay silent. Of course, I had no knowledge of what was being alleged against me but I thought, despite my inevitable lack of preparation, it hadn't gone too badly. I thought I could have done better, but I was very rusty at being interviewed on or by the media. I still didn't realise by how much I would need to sharpen up my dormant oratorical talents and polish up my writing abilities. My life had been delineated by the good use of the written and spoken word, and though in the battle against injustice I could count on very little of my own strengths, the use of English was certainly one.

I felt aggrieved and frightened. I felt concern for my brother who had put up with so much twenty-eight years before and who, by coincidence, was coming to live on the estate in another house on the following day, making the long move from Devon. I felt concern for my friends. I knew what many of my new friends did not and old friends may have forgotten: that the pressures that would mount on me and on our relationships would be intense. I felt much foreboding.

Having decided on a different strategy this time – to respond to the media – I had to consider how to deal with the storm of interest I knew would be unleashed. A combination of the Metropolitan Police, notwithstanding their puny and self-serving denials, the BBC and certain sections of the media had placed my name in the public arena in connection with the foulest allegations. It was not my choice. My choice had been to respond or not. I chose the former.

That morning went quickly as I busied myself with the task of fielding telephone calls on the landline and my mobile. It soon became apparent that the media scrum had started to gather, not at my home, but at the gates of the castle and at those of my previous residence. The press could often get it wrong, and they had on this occasion. I rang the castle and suggested I make a short statement and visual appearance to satisfy the pack and get them on their way. My suggestion was dismissed. Three hours later, with PR advisers now on board and the press pack growing to more than thirty across the estate, I was being begged by the castle to do so. I was prepared to make a short statement, but where? The staff at the castle suggested my home initially. I was not too keen on that location, however, since I'd successfully kept them away up until now. Wherever I made the statement, they insisted that the castle was not to be in shot. I pointed out that my house had great views of the castle which could not be obscured wherever I posed. I suggested a barn that was regularly used for 'shoot' lunches and afternoon teas. Belvoir is one of the pre-eminent estates in the country, shooting partridge, pheasant and duck. In non-shoot season, February to September, the barn was deserted. Indeed, it was so remote that it had been burgled and broken into twice in the last twelve months – I had been with Leicestershire Police on both occasions to examine the crime scene. I had, until the beginning of 2015, a very good relationship with the local police and it seemed ironic that I should select this barn as the backdrop to my statement. It stood in beautiful country scenery, unsullied by a castle. Because of its use by shooting parties and because of my past, all we had to do was not to mention its name – 'the Happy Beater'.

I worked on a very short statement referring the media to my interview on the *Today* programme that morning. I decided I wanted the radio interview to be reported with no further statement. I did it to satisfy the visual media, the camera crews and the photographers, who wanted up-to-date footage and images rather than adding verbally to what I had already made clear. I read the statement to the castle PR representative. The media was given the venue and the time – mid-afternoon – and set up their cameras. I donned an infrequently worn navy-blue suit, navy and white spot tie. It was one from my old shirt-and-tie shop. To the extent that one can look smart in a stiff breeze, I think I did.

The Duchess, anxious that my home should not become identified, placed at my disposal a father-and-son team who worked on the estate as, among other things, security. I was driven from my home and back by Nick and his son. (For the avoidance of doubt, this Nick had nothing to do with 'Nick' the traducer who looms large in this book.) They used a roundabout route to throw the press off the scent and were very supportive as we drove over to the barn. I stepped out of the back of the car and I strode to the awaiting microphones, made my statement, returned to the car and drove off. Nick said the whole thing took fifty-eight seconds; he seemed impressed by my brevity. The media would soon disperse, but I understood later that the press corps were astonished by the concise nature of the statement and that I had taken no questions. I suppose they thought it had been a long wait for less than a minute of 'action'. I thanked Nick and his son for their support and they returned me to my home.

Terry and I had known Nick's mother, Kate Pacey, very well for over thirty years. She had worked as David's excellent housekeeper before he married. We were all very close and she would have been astonished at the turn of events. Her comments would have been very supportive. She sadly died on 27 December 2012.

So the job was done, but only for the day. I watched the evening news bulletins and answered the phones, rejecting requests from the BBC and others for more in-depth interviews. Friends and people I did not know emailed their support. They phoned and wrote letters. Staff and former colleagues at the castle, especially those I had worked with for many years, were incredibly supportive. In the weeks that followed, when I was alone in the house – Terry was abroad often – they seemed to keep a special watch over me. I think they sensed my mental position was stressful and so visited me at home regularly. Some of them may have thought I might have been contemplating suicide. They would have been right – I was. It crossed my mind, as it had in 1987, although no method came to mind. What did obliterate the notion was their encouragement and the deep-seated sense of injustice that pervaded everything. They believed I couldn't possibly have done what my traducer had alleged, although there were no exact details to hand at that time. I *knew* I had not done what my traducer had told the police, on which, based solely on that, my home and my life had been turned upside down. I was not guilty of any of this, but if I commit suicide, I thought, the snide comments would be passed around. 'No smoke without fire,' people would say. 'He was up to something with kids.' I would be remembered as a very evil man so I was determined, however difficult it might become, that I would fight this injustice to my dying day.

'How could this happen to me?' I wondered. Yes, in my deepest and darkest thoughts I admit I had a certain amount of self-pity at the time. But also, throughout my life, I have had, deep down, an inherent sense of fairness. This wasn't fair. It wasn't fair on me, and it wasn't fair on others, some now dead by all accounts, who also served their country and whose reputation was now also being trashed – not that anyone had told me their names by this point. 'This is just not right,' I thought, 'I must see it through whatever the cost.' I did not realise just how high a price I was to pay.

CHAPTER 13

REACTIONS

The search of my home, or it could be better described as a 'fishing' trip, on Wednesday 4 March 2015 by the Metropolitan Police Murder Unit was not done in isolation. On the same day, the Metropolitan Police Service also raided the home of Field Marshall Edwin Noel Westby Bramall, Baron Bramall, KG, GCB, OBE, MC, JP, DL, the head of the army at the time of the Falklands, and later chief of the Defence Staff, and the two homes of the late Lord (Leon) Brittan in London and in Richmond, Yorkshire. Unlike in my case, they did not release a statement with this information to the press, Exaro, 'Nick', the BBC, or anyone else for two days, until it was made public on Saturday 7 March 2015. Why? I believe that the police determined to continue using the media to seek out further 'victims' and 'evidence' to back up what 'Nick' had told them about me the previous November. It was revealed in the media that my castle office had also been searched on the Wednesday and again on the Thursday. They had dragged out their three 'searches', releasing information drop by drop, knowing it would be covered over the weekend in the press, and it was. The Metropolitan Police Service was continuing to use the press to appeal for 'victims' to come forward.

Meanwhile, I was considering what to do following my initial media interview of rebuttal. The police had lied to me on the day of the search when they said I would not be identified. They lie now when they say they do not release names until people are charged with offences. It was true that their statement did not mention me by name, but it certainly did by gender, by age and by my approximate address. Do the police think that journalists are idiots? The police know full well what they are doing; they have admitted they told 'Nick' my traducer. They must have known of his history of internet fantasy, his wish to spread the 'survivor' story via Twitter and allegations on his blog, which was for a long time publicly accessible, and his links with Exaro. After all, and by their own admission, an Exaro journalist escorted 'Nick' to the Metropolitan Police for his first interview, or should I say 'meeting', as Exaro are fussy on this pedantic issue of describing a meeting as an interview. 'Nick' revealed information and made allegations about me and others to the police in front of an Exaro journalist. I believe that is the truth. Did the police also tell Exaro and the BBC directly, either officially or unofficially, about the timing of my house search and the searches of the houses of Lords Bramall and Brittan? If not how did they discover the information? I know from 1987 and my dealings with them then that the police are the leakiest of 'organisations'.

In any event, my name and my connection with Operation Midland was in the media arena via Exaro and the BBC before I woke on the Thursday morning. Exaro knew the police were in my house at least two hours before they had left. Mark Conrad of Exaro had reported that the police, under Operation Midland, were in my house on their website the same day. In the spirit of 'holding power to account', I wonder whether Mr Conrad will ever indicate who it was that informed him – 'Nick' or the Metropolitan Police? They had associated me with paedophilia, child abuse and child murder in the media before I'd even spoke to the *Today* programme, or anyone else for that matter.

As well as fighting off the press, I now had to consider my legal position. Should I contact solicitors and, if so, which ones? London solicitors were suggested to me but I feared the cost and the travel that would be involved. My experience of Kingsley Napley, with hindsight, had not been a good one. Perhaps, I thought, local solicitors might be better. Terry had a London QC contact and, through him, a Leicester firm was suggested. Before I called I wondered whether I really needed a solicitor. I mulled it over for a bit as I was considering what, if anything, to say to the encircling press hordes. I was not convinced I should appoint anyone, but agreed to place a call.

I was feeling uncomfortable with myself when Raza Sakhi and Nabeel Gatrad of Sakhi solicitors in Leicester came to see me at my home the next morning. They immediately put me at ease. I had no need to explain what had happened; it was all over the media and they had briefed themselves well. What I did explain was what had occurred, in legal terms, in 1986 and 1987. Raza, whose legal practice it was, explained he was a solicitor but also a solicitor-advocate and could practise in all courts. They told me they had expertise in criminal law but made it clear they were not skilled at dealing with the media. I felt I was being scrutinised but I also felt I was among friends. They were very solicitous as to my health and well-being in the light of what had happened and was happening to me. I was impressed by their concern. I was in a state of shock, so maybe they detected my position. They exuded warmth and I felt protected.

My intention was to interview them and reflect. Instead, I reflected instantly and appointed them.

They both reassured Terry with regards to his questions concerning the police's discovery of his medical marijuana. It could be dealt with by a caution, they said, and I was immediately relaxed on Terry's behalf. He visited his doctor shortly afterwards and was prescribed three separate sets of pharmaceutical drugs to replace one 'joint'.

Sakhi solicitors agreed to represent me. They said they would contact the police on my behalf and seek a date when I could be interviewed at the earliest opportunity. The police had left with large amounts of my possessions along with those of Terry, Adam, Charlotte and the baby and of friends, without me being given a note of them. I wasn't ever (even to this day) asked which items were mine. My solicitors said they would seek to acquire a list of what had been taken and we agreed to meet again the next week. Terry and I felt confident with them both.

That afternoon, my brother Granville and his partner arrived after a long drive from Devon with their two dogs. They were all to relocate and live on the estate. Their furniture vans arrived late so I carried a lot of boxes by way of help and, tired, I got to bed after midnight. I felt the timing of my troubles was awful for Granville and for our determination to be together after all these years. On Saturday, I drove Terry to the airport and he flew abroad to be with Adam, who was preparing for his family to join him the next week. I was on my own and I felt an intense feeling of loneliness. On Sunday, two of my very good work colleagues from the castle, Fay and Danny, came for supper. I think they were surprised that I cooked. I had to be busy and, although no way near as good at cooking as Terry, I do try. I could not remain still and I talked a lot. I started to think about my predicament and was in reflective mood.

Our early Monday morning staff meeting at the castle took place in the Steward's Room and Emma referred to my performance on the *Today* programme in glowing terms, after which I received a round of applause. I was grateful, but found it difficult to cope emotionally with support – I always have. On Tuesday, I drove to Heathrow to pick up David, who was landing from abroad, and returned him to Belvoir. He asked about my predicament, but I had no news other than that I was meeting my solicitors again in the afternoon. He offered to attend but I preferred to talk to them privately.

In the afternoon, I saw Emma briefly at my home. She mentioned that the police and social services were wanting representatives of the castle to attend a meeting about me and my position the next day. Again, I was not to be invited to this discussion, nor was I supposed to be told about it. Raza and Nabeel arrived and briefly met Emma just as she was leaving. In the house, the three of us discussed my situation and they told me they had spoken to Detective Sergeant Flynn. They had made contact and were working on my behalf. Again, they were very solicitous about my welfare. None of us knew what I was supposed to have done, but we were dealing with the Metropolitan Police's murder squad, so that was in all our minds.

I had read a little on the internet about historical child sex abuse in the months before the search. I had been approached by the press and by internet fantasists in 2014 to answer questions and had refused, preferring silence. I thought it had nothing to do with me. In that summer, when I was in London with Adam and Charlotte for a fitting of her wedding dress with my brother, I had left Terry alone with the dogs. The dogs had got out, so Terry had left the gate open to facilitate their return. He had then fallen asleep on the bed and was subsequently woken by a *Daily Mirror* reporter, who had let himself in the house and was at the bottom of the bed asking questions about me. Terry finds it difficult to deal with the press, he should have asked him to leave but he did not. I was telephoned by the reporter while Terry listened – he used our house phone – and I asked him to leave. I thought, had the dogs been at home, the reporter would not have got near the house, still less inside it. I said I was not prepared to talk about the events of 1987.

As I say, I and my solicitors were in ignorance of any detail concerning what I was supposed to have done or what had been alleged. In the weeks ahead, I had to piece together what it might have been about myself; for this meeting, apart from considering which barrister or QC to use if, God forbid, anything did come to court, there was not much else to consider. They cautioned me on my personal security, after which I started keeping all the doors locked to the house. We agreed to stay in touch. After they had gone, David dropped by to get a briefing, but there was not much to add to what I had told him in the morning.

Very early on the Wednesday morning, I drove Charlotte and the baby to a ferry port so they could link up with Adam abroad. On leaving them, I felt very upset, but tried not to show it. This was not how it was all meant to be. I felt guilty, but not of anything the police might accuse me of; even without knowing the details I knew I had not done anything wrong. Rather, I felt that my whole life, where I had only tried to do good and to help people, had had the reverse effect. I was unsure if I would ever see Charlotte, Adam and the baby again. On my way home, I took a call from the castle, setting up an early morning meeting at my home the next day.

At 8 a.m. on Thursday, I was told by a castle solicitor and another official that, because of pressure by the police and social services at the meeting the previous afternoon, I was to be suspended from my position. During the period of my suspension, my role at the castle would be reconsidered. I felt numb, betrayed and isolated, that my loyalty was of no value. The authorities had sabotaged my professional duties without having any recourse or redress to them or their secret cabals.

When I picked Terry up at the airport at midday, he said immediately on seeing me that I looked white, gaunt and ill. I looked defeated; I felt defeated. On the way home, I drove round a roundabout three times, so difficult I was finding it to focus on anything other than my current situation. The phone was constantly ringing. I had nothing to say to the press but I was polite, if reserved. To my friends, I disclosed what I could but, with the exception of my professional position, I was learning information from the newspapers and the internet. I appreciated my friends' support and advice.

On 16 March, I had a further meeting with my solicitors. They told me the police had assured them I was not a 'suspect'. This made no sense. Why raid my home with so many officers? Why let so much publicity surround me and the search if I was not even a 'suspect'? My solicitors could not explain this position. All would no doubt be revealed on 23 March, when the Metropolitan Police Service had agreed to meet me. How strange and how coincidental it was that this date was to be cancelled by the Metropolitan Police Service.

Notwithstanding my 'suspension', David wanted me to undertake a duty for him that was already in my diary, namely, to go to Paris to bring back the Poussin paintings on loan to the Louvre. Obviously I was perceived not to be a threat to the French. At least, I thought, my mind would be taken off my immediate problems. Who should I bump into on my travels, however, but a former colleague and current Police Commissioner? He greeted me in a friendly fashion and in our brief conversation he advised me to 'keep my head down and say nothing'.

On my return to Belvoir, Terry and I threw a party to celebrate my brother's arrival and birthday, not that I was in party mood. One of the friends I invited to the party, whom I had not seen in years but who had telephoned me to express support, was Derek Laud. I had known him for over thirty years and it was good to see him again. We were able to talk through my various options, including how to deal with the media. Derek knew everyone and became, and is still, very helpful with his generous advice and amusing repartee. He has kept me sane through these troubles and I am very grateful for his valuable assistance.

Granville had not been well and developed a dreadful cough. He could not sleep, so on Sunday 22 March I took him to the accident and emergency department of Grantham Hospital. He wanted advice on what cough medicine to take. They conducted tests and he was kept in overnight and for a further six weeks. On 23 April, he had open heart surgery at Leicester. I visited him there and in Grantham and Lincoln Hospitals virtually every day in this period. I was very concerned that what was happening to me had adverse medical effects on him. A friend of his had accused me of causing his problems and apparently sought from his partner information which the friend could have sold to a newspaper. The so-called friend was rebuffed. I was upset that these events might have exacerbated his condition. I am relieved Granville made a full recovery. Helping to look after him in that difficult period also took my mind off my own problems. However, these intensified on Monday 23 March, the date when the Metropolitan Police Service were scheduled to interview me but which they then cancelled.

At a meeting at my home, I was told by a castle official that the Leicestershire Police and social services were meeting the castle representatives again on Wednesday 25 March and further, greater pressure was being applied to the castle administration that I should not work at the castle at all in the future as 'children visited the venue'. Again, I was not invited to attend this meeting, neither asked to submit any views or opinions, nor was I supposed to even know it was taking place. I asked the castle representative three times about what the Leicestershire Police and social services would do if my employer refused to co-operate, but I was not given a reply. I was told that the estate's employment solicitors had indicated third-party pressure (from the Leicestershire Police and the social services) was sufficient to justify my dismissal. It was, in effect, resign or be sacked.

My solicitors were shocked at the castle's position. I had no wish to place David and Emma in a difficult situation; they were my friends. I decided to resign. I drafted both my own resignation letter to the Duke and Duchess and their reply to me. I was still the private secretary after all. The announcement of my resignation was to be 5 p.m. on Tuesday 24 March. I did not wish Leicestershire Police and social services to tell the press about my leaving; I wanted to pre-empt any announcement the police might make or leak.

There was much sadness; my position at Belvoir was at an end. Emma kindly proposed to throw a drinks party and dinner in my honour. I politely declined; it was not appropriate. My brother's heart condition was thankfully on the mend; I knew mine could never be.

During parts of April, Terry was away, but before he went, he and others persuaded me that I should not rely on my *Today* programme interview. Things had moved on since then: the police had arranged and cancelled two interviews; there had been little in the newspapers apart from the Metropolitan Police Service appealing for 'victims' to come forward. What had appeared in the newspapers with regard to these matters were character assassinations of the dead; Lord Brittan, Sir Keith Joseph, Dr Rhodes Boyson and Enoch Powell had

all been defamed. It had become a never-ending, two-fingered gesture to the political generation I had the privilege to serve with in
the House of Commons.

One false tale related to an alleged homosexual party at a Tory
Party conference in the swimming pool of the Imperial Hotel in
Blackpool, where politicians allegedly cavorted with naked young
boys. As if this could possibly happen with journalists, broadcasters,
security men, police, detectives and hotel staff working overtime and
wishing or watching for anything untoward to occur. It was fanci-
ful even before I met a lady, who had a shop in Grantham, who had
worked in the hotel at the time and who told me that, during that
period, the swimming pool was not operational. Nor could I believe
the absurd allegations that Enoch was involved in satanic black masses
and ritual murder just because someone had mentioned it to a bishop
who had mentioned it to another bishop who had mentioned it to
the police, cruelly, after Enoch had died.

Conveniently for some and inconveniently for others, I was very
much alive. I was not going to pass by on the other side of the road.
It might be my last campaign, but I was up for the fight, however
arduous or difficult. No, I was not going to keep my head down and
keep silent; not this time.

I agreed with Terry's counsel and other friends that I should collect my thoughts together and try to disseminate them. Various
possibilities were discussed and explored. The BBC had been trying
to interview me, as had most television news departments, but a live
interview appeared out of the question and through long experience
I did not wish to be edited, a process I had always found to be unfair.
After great debate, I decided to give my first interview in many years
to a quality newspaper. It was suggested to me by a friend that I
should allow James Hanning, the deputy editor of the *Independent*

on Sunday and a journalist of repute, to visit me. James had been try-ing to ask me questions, by phone and by email, concerning my past and about the alleged historical child sexual-abuse ring at Westmin-ster for many months. In addition, I had been working on an article that I wished to place in a newspaper. The two possibilities seemed to fit together. It was agreed. A photographer arrived early to take photographs and I was surrounded by my dogs in protective mode. Sushi the Akita behaved impeccably; Duke the boxer took against the photographer and barked continuously as he was dressed all in black, a fashion feature which fails to impress Duke. Consequently, the former got in the photograph; the latter did not.

I answered James's questions as best I could; we were discussing events that had occurred over thirty years earlier after all. It was a difficult interview in the sense that I had to re-live painful moments in my past concerning 1986 and 1987.

It took me several days to write and redraft my article. It reflected my annoyance with the police, with the media and with the politi-cians – although I felt I could not mention the horrible situation with regard to Adam, Charlotte and their baby. I wanted to speak to the police; they had twice arranged interviews and then cancelled, elon-gating the process. My article of Sunday 3 May 2015 in the *Independent on Sunday* made no mention of 'Nick'. My rebuttal of things I was supposed to have done or with which I was supposed to have been involved was a rebuttal of matters, some internet gossip, that had been flying about in the media for weeks after the search and with which I had been linked directly or indirectly. Had I known the full details of what 'Nick' had alleged, my article would have been differ-ent, but I wrote my article on the basis of what I knew at the time.

The text of my article, which appeared in the comment section of the *Independent on Sunday* on Sunday 3 May 2015, read:

I, Harvey Proctor, am innocent of the allegations against me and I will maintain this stance until my dying breath. I served as a Member of Parliament for Basildon and for Billericay between 1979 and 1987.

I would like to say, on Wednesday 4 March 2015 the Metropolitan Police's Operation Midland team raided my home and, under a warrant investigating historical child sexual abuse, searched my house for fifteen hours. I was told at 11 p.m. that no statement would be issued to the press and my identity would not be revealed. That was a lie.

If not before, then within eight hours of the police leaving my home, details of the raid were leaked to the national media. Exaro News – an odd internet news agency – was tipped off before the police left my home. Mark Conrad, a journalist for the agency, was phoning and emailing my office at 9.34 p.m. – at least ninety minutes before the police left my house.

During and immediately after the search, I volunteered to be interviewed by the Metropolitan Police concerning Operation Midland's investigations relating to the allegations from the 1970s and 1980s.

My solicitors – Messrs Sakhi and Gatrad of Sakhi Solicitors, Leicester – arranged for me to be interviewed on Monday 23 March 2015. The police initially confirmed that it was convenient and then cancelled the interview at short notice, due to 'circumstances beyond (the officer's) control'. The appointment was rearranged until Tuesday 14 April 2015. It was through no fault of my own that, on Thursday 9 April 2015, the police again cancelled the interview, scheduled for 14 April 2015.

They have not contacted my solicitors since then.

In an email to my solicitors, they referred to themselves as the 'organisation'.

So the 'organisation' – strange term for the Metropolitan Police's Murder Squad – has raided my house, searched it for fifteen hours, removed my communications and computer equipment and many boxes of historic documents and other irrelevant material from the 1970s and 1980s, prompted me to retire from my job of thirteen years and to leave my home. They have ruined twenty-eight years of my life's rehabilitation after 1987 and they are not prepared to meet me and interview me.

They have said to my solicitors, but not to the media, that I am not a suspect and they merely wish for me to assist the police with their inquiries.

In 1987, Chief Superintendent Drummond Marvin of Scotland Yard's Serious Crime Squad was the officer in charge of my prosecution. I pleaded guilty to four charges of gross indecency. Offences which, because of the changes in the law regarding the homosexual age of consent, are no longer offences.

Chief Superintendent Marvin subsequently wrote a book and sold his story to the *Sun* newspaper. He wrote about three of his cases – Lord Lucan, Russell Harty and myself. In the article about me he stated for the first time, as far as I am aware, the felonious notion that there was a rent-boy ring at Westminster. If there was one, I was not aware of it, it was news to me and I was not part of it. Marvin's article was wrong on this and on other matters.

I have always tried to protect my privacy – not because I thought I was breaking the law but because I consider my sexual matters to be private. Not just for me but for everyone. I refuse to comment on these matters now safe to say anything and everything I have done has been consensual. But with alarming frequency, when I was visited by the police in 1987, journalists from the *Sunday People* were outside my flat.

I have not flouted my sexuality. It is the press and the police who have time and time again invaded my privacy. In 1987, the press wired a witness for sound and was sent into my apartment. The police trawled the gay bars of London showing my photograph to all and sundry asking, 'Have you slept with this man?' Today the modern-day equivalent is for senior police officers to go on the airways enticing so-called victims to come out of the woodwork, telling them, without even speaking to them, that they would be believed.

Now the guide to misinformation and the oracle of disinformation is the internet. It is a totally impossible media with which to engage as hundreds and thousands of comments appear daily with no chance of rebuttal.

At the behest of a weird assortment of alleged victims, ex-police officers, bishops, social workers, attention seekers and 'nutters', former, respected politicians have had their reputations trashed without a shred of evidence – Sir Leon Brittan, Sir Keith Joseph, Dr Rhodes Boyson and Enoch Powell, to name but a few. They are dead; they cannot defend themselves. I am alive; I can and I will.

Enough is enough. Someone has to stand up and say the emperor is wearing no clothes.

So let me be straight with you, the media, and through you, the police.

I have not murdered anyone.

I have not been involved with the sexual or other abuse of children or anyone else.

I have not visited the Elm Guest House in Rocks Lane, Barnes, London. I was not aware of its existence.

I have not attended sex parties at Dolphin Square, London.

I have not attended sex parties with other MPs or ministers.

I have not visited a so-called dungeon in Pimlico.

I have not abused anyone.

I have not attended sex parties during Conservative Party conferences at Brighton or Blackpool and I am sure none took place.

I was not part of a Westminster rent-boy ring in the 1970s and 1980s. I cannot believe such a ring existed.

I have witnessed the growing paranoia among various police 'organisations' with disbelief and disgust.

I wish to place on record my admiration for the work the uniformed bobby does and has done and which I have seen at first hand in my old constituencies of Basildon and Billericay, in the London Borough of Richmond upon Thames during my work with the Chamber of Commerce and at Belvoir.

The higher up the police command chain, however, the less I see to admire. For example, I find it incredible that a senior police officer has said on the media that a 'victim's' evidence is 'credible' before an investigation has been completed or a prosecution launched. It would not be acceptable on any other police investigation and is outright prejudicial from the very outset to any impending investigation.

So I know now the risk I am about to take. The risk of the 'organisation' seeking out trivia and revenge to undermine me in response to what I am about to say to you; but here goes.

It's time – with the spending on these inquiries approaching £100 million – to say to the police and the Director of Public Prosecutions:

Put up or shut up.

Arrest me, charge me, try me.

If you have evidence against me, bring it on!

To the Metropolitan Police Commissioner and other chief police officers, I say, get a grip. Direct your 'organisation's' scarce resources to conquering current crime and address current law and order issues. Redirect some of these scarce resources, for example, to the Missing Persons Agency in Sheen if you really care for missing people.

To the media, I say use your investigative powers to analyse what you are told about historical sexual child abuse fairly and properly.

Finally, to the politicians, who are currently culling favour with the electorate – what are they doing to redress the balance between the alleged victims who can keep their anonymity and the alleged abusers who cannot? When will innocent before being found guilty be more than just a totem of a supposedly liberal society? Who are the guardians of our liberty now?

And in the end why is all this happening?

Well, the only people deemed more unpopular than the media, journalists, police and politicians with the general public are paedophiles. So they are all pursuing this issue to try to get on the good side of the people of this country and rehabilitate themselves from their past lapses.

I do not wish anyone to think I am just saying these things now. I made my position clear – and with prescience – in an article I wrote for the *London Evening Standard* in December 1987.

In conclusion, I would like to thank my family, friends, colleagues and people I do not know and who I have not met who have supported me in these difficult days.

To reiterate, I am innocent and deny any wrongdoing and I am a law-abiding citizen.

In addition to my article, the *Independent on Sunday* carried a news report written by James Hanning. He telephoned me the next day to tell me that his interview with me had provided so much material that he would be writing a further article on me, which he did on general election day on 7 May in *The Independent*. He concluded that article with these words:

> There is an incongruence between the cavorting, almost beast-like Proctor of popular 1980s myths and the low-key, dignified but quietly angry figure who, for now, lives quietly with his partner on the Belvoir estate. Too easily has the media bought the caricature and too easily have the rest of us, police included, gone along with it.

Not bad on a general election day, I thought.

The Press Association and newspapers picked up my Sunday article and turned it into a news story. Matthew Parris penned a diary piece in *The Times*. He wrote:

> I know Harvey. We talked on Monday. I'm convinced he had nothing to do with any MPs' paedophile ring and doubt it existed. My guess is the police have realised this too but won't climb down and admit that by turning a routine search into a nationally publicised raid they have shattered a life and impugned a reputation. So they leave an innocent man to rot, until the interest they have stirred up has faded.

The reason why Matthew and I had spoken on the Monday was that I wanted to tell him what I had failed to tell him before, but which I knew James Hanning was about to reveal in his article, namely, that Matthew had saved me from suicide all those years ago.

I thought I had judged what I had written in my article about right. I noticed the police response answered none of the points I had made, but rather used the latest press interest I had generated to further their own ends with a statement. *The Times* reported that a spokesman for Scotland Yard had said, 'It is important that all allegations we receive, and evidence we gather, is fully tested and inquiries carried out to seek to corroborate, or otherwise, this information. It is vitally important that witnesses and possible victims feel confident to come forward.'

The police had been seeking 'victims' to come forward since 'Nick' went to them in early November 2014. Now, some six months later, with no 'victims' having presented themselves in the intervening period by all accounts, here were the police inferring yet again that there were 'victims' who had not come forward merely because they were not 'confident'. My position was that I wanted to give evidence to the police by way of an interview, which they had repeatedly postponed over the last two months. A few days later, on 6 May, DS Flynn contacted my solicitors to arrange a date to interview me. The purpose of my article, to spur the police into interviewing me, had been achieved. Could there have been some connection?

PART 3

CHAPTER 14

THE INTERVIEW

While waiting to be interviewed by the Metropolitan Police Service, I learnt that Leicestershire Police had not been inactive. They had sought to interview the teenage sons of my friends. In one case, the parents agreed and sat in on the interview conducted by, I understand, a social worker. Absolutely nothing came of their inquiries. Another parent, who I knew, was telephoned in Rome towards the end of May to gain permission for her sixteen-year-old son to be interviewed. The request came from DC Julian Allen, the same police officer who came to try to take Adam and Charlotte's baby into care. He was told by the parent that they would not permit the son to go through the ordeal of an interview with a social worker concerning me as they were sure I would not have done anything to her son or to any other children. The police officer was asked who he was trying to protect. He apparently went quiet and refused to answer. He asked the parent to reconsider and that his superior, a female police woman, would call again, which she did not. This is interesting as Charlotte and Adam had been told by social services in April that their inquiry about me would not proceed because they and the baby were no longer in the county. So was Leicestershire Police working for Leicestershire social services, as the police officer insisted, or was he working for the Metropolitan Police and their inquiries?

In the early hours of the last day of May, I started my sad drive abroad. I was taking Sushi and Duke, my dogs, away from their home at Belvoir to live with Adam and Charlotte. As I drove over the potholes of our farm track, I thought about how they would no longer be able to chase the pheasants and hares. At least the tenant farmer would be pleased that they would no longer potentially disrupt his shoot, though how two dogs could do so when the pack of hounds that came round every year could not, I never understood. It was a horrendous stage of leaving my home in Leicestershire and leaving the country I love too. We had to leave our house we loved so much. Terry and I had come to the decision that we would now have to do full time what we were going to do from time to time, namely live abroad and see our family there. It would be a gradual move. However, Barn Farm House would never be the same without the dogs. It felt as though my life was disintegrating, slowly but surely.

Space was limited in the car as I was taking luggage with me that David and Terry had helped to load up the previous evening so I had dropped Terry off at an airport to give us more room. I stopped every two hours to give the dogs a pit stop in the long drive, though I think they thought they would never see the inside of a room again. At last, we stopped at a pet-friendly hotel by the side of the motorway in France. The dogs were excited they could finally rest on a bed. We left early the next morning and after a long, tiring drive we reached our destination.

Duke and Sushi had continued to live at Belvoir until after the Metropolitan Police raided my house on 4 March 2015. It was always our intention to take them abroad with us for breaks in semi-retirement and I had initiated their passport applications before the raid but gained the documents a few days later on 16 March. It was never my intention to move abroad permanently, only to have my dogs with me while writing this book, but I lost my house. I mention this because internet fantasists have even used my dogs as part of their conspiracy theories about me, aided I think by a BBC journalist, who knew I had a third dog. I told him in a conversation a few days after my press conference, when I had just arrived abroad – something very few other people in the UK knew. The fantasists assumed wrongly that I had taken three dogs abroad in some carefully planned move connected with the raid. They also revealed in which country I was abroad in a matter of days of my arrival, also something I had told to the BBC journalist in confidence. How else could they have known if not from his tweeting or from conversing with him? My naivety, a result of obviously not having dealt with journalists on a personal basis for many years, resulted in me forgetting temporarily how the media had behaved so many years ago.

The third dog was a mini Chihuahua which we acquired later. It was bought by a friend abroad as a puppy for Adam and Charlotte's baby. It never lived at Belvoir. It was tiny, the smallest breed of dog, has black hair and it eats constantly. It also bites a lot, and as it's only several weeks old, allowances have to be made, but it's more of a puppy than Duke or Sushi ever were at a similar age. The other big dogs get on with Bobby, named after Bob Marley, surprisingly well. He has visited the vet many times, usually for vaccinations and injections, but for other things too. He is affectionate but no lap dog and was not easy to house train. He is a delightful addition to the household. We know him as our big, fat Mexican amigo.

Surprisingly, despite her thick white fur, Sushi settled into her new abode much better than Duke, who had a rough first week. It was hot for him and he panted a great deal. On the first Saturday Duke walked on a swimming pool cover, fell into the water he had not expected to be there, tangled himself up in the plastic material of the cover and nearly drowned. I managed to drag him out of the water just in time. Sushi is a much better swimmer. The next day, walking the dogs on a beach, Duke stumbled and, unbeknown to us, swallowed a mouthful of sand. He fell ill that night and in the morning, as he was still ill, we took him to the vet, who very kindly opened up on a Sunday. After two examinations and an X-ray, it was clear. In the afternoon, Duke had to have an urgent operation as the sand in his tummy had solidified and turned to cement, causing a blockage. Without the operation that day, he would have died. Thank goodness he survived. I am very grateful to Fran the vet and to his surgeon colleague for their skill. Duke survived, but I felt guilty having to put him and Sushi through such a move and a change in their lives when they too might have lived the rest of their lives in the rural tranquillity of Belvoir. This awful situation in which I find myself has even affected my dogs. But, of course, they maintain their loyalty and affection to me as I do to them. I love my dogs. It is completely unconditional. Without their presence and support it would be even more difficult to get through these personal difficulties. They well deserve these words, though some may find it difficult to comprehend the weight I attach to my four-legged friends.

Leaving the dogs with Adam and Charlotte, Terry and I returned from abroad on 14 June to prepare for our interviews. Our solicitors

told us what the Metropolitan Police had told them: Terry's interview and caution with reference to the cannabis matter would be
brief; mine rather longer, expected to be up to two or three days.
It actually took six and a half hours. On 16 June, we went to the Sakhi
solicitors for pre meetings, in their offices just behind the Leicester
Cathedral, where Richard III is laid to rest. My solicitors, Raza Sakhi
and Nabeel Gatrad, had not forwarded the disclosure document provided that same day by the Metropolitan Police Service to them by
email. I am sure they thought that its contents would be too distress-
ing for me to read alone and wanted to be with me when I perused
it. Before they gave me the document, they asked me to sit down.
It was only three pages long, but its contents were far worse than
anything I could have imagined. It was explosive.

The document started calmly, indicating the interview was to
be conducted by DC Danny Chatfield and DS Matt Flynn, the
bad cop/good cop team from the day of the search of my home.
It was to take place at Keyham Lane Police Station, Leicester. The
police had told me it could be anywhere I liked, so we chose a convenient location suggested by Raza. It was to be conducted under
caution, and it was to be video recorded. The document made it clear
I was not under arrest and that I was free to leave at any time and I
was entitled to have legal representation. The document then took
leave of its senses.

It said that I was to be interviewed in relation to three allegations
of murder and also several allegations of historical sexual abuse of
children. There followed details of the accounts of murder and several of sexual abuse. I now quote from this disclosure document:

'Circumstances
The victim in this investigation is identified under the

pseudonym 'Nick'. He made allegations to the Metropolitan Police Service in late 2014. Due to the nature of the offences alleged, 'Nick' is entitled to have his identity withheld.

'Nick' stated he was the victim of systematic and serious sexual abuse by a group of adult males over a period between 1975 and 1984. The abuse was often carried out whilst in company with other boys whom were also abused by the group.

'Nick' provided names of several individuals involved in these acts including Mr HARVEY PROCTOR. He states MR PROCTOR abused him on a number of occasions which included sexual assault, buggery and torturous assault. He also states MR PROCTOR was present when he was assaulted by other adult males. Furthermore, 'Nick' states he witnessed the murder of three young boys on separate occasions. He states MR PROCTOR was directly responsible for two of the allegations and implicated in the third.

The dates and locations relevant to MR PROCTOR are as follows:

Homicides

1980 – at a residential house in central London. 'Nick' was driven by car to an address in the Pimlico/Belgravia area where a second boy (the victim) was also collected in the same vehicle. Both boys, aged approximately twelve years old, were driven to another similar central London address. MR PROCTOR was present with another male. Both boys were led to the back of the house. MR PROCTOR then stripped the victim, and tied him to a table. He then produced a large kitchen knife and stabbed the child through the arm and other parts of the body

over a period of forty minutes. A short time later MR PROC-
TOR untied the victim and anally raped him on the table. The
other male stripped 'Nick' and anally raped him over the table.
MR PROCTOR then strangled the victim with his hands until
the boy's body went limp. Both males then left the room. Later,
MR PROCTOR returned and led 'Nick' out of the house and
into a waiting car.

1981–82 – at a residential address in central London. 'Nick'
was collected from Kingston train station and taken to a 'party'
at a residential address. The witness was among four young
boys. Several men were present including MR PROCTOR. One
of the men told the boys one of them would die that night and
they had to choose who. When the boys wouldn't decide, the
men selected one of the boys (the victim). Each of the four boys
including 'Nick' were taken to separate rooms for 'private time'.
When they all returned to the same room, Nick was anally raped
by MR PROCTOR and another male as 'punishment'. The other
males also anally raped the remaining boys. MR PROCTOR and
two other males then began beating the chosen victim by punching and kicking. The attack continued until the boy collapsed
on the floor and stopped moving. All of the men left the room.
The remaining boys attempted to revive the victim but he was
not breathing. They were left for some time before being taken
out of the house and returned to their homes.

Between May and July 1979 – in a street in Coombe Hill,
Kingston. Nick was walking in this area with another boy (the
victim) when he heard the sound of a car engine revving. A dark-
coloured car drove into the victim knocking him down. 'Nick'
could see the boy covered in blood and his leg bent backwards. A
car pulled up and 'Nick' was grabbed and placed in the car. He felt

a sharp pain in his arm and next remembered being dropped off at home. He was warned not to have friends in future. 'Nick' never saw the other boy again. 'Nick' does not identify MR PROCTOR as being directly involved in this allegation. However, he states MR PROCTOR was part of the group responsible for the systematic sexual abuse he suffered. Furthermore, he believes the group were responsible for the homicide.

Sexual Abuse

1978–84 – Dolphin Square, Pimlico. 'Nick' was at the venue and with at least one other young boy. MR PROCTOR was present with other males. MR PROCTOR told 'Nick' to pick up a wooden baton and hit the other boy. When 'Nick' refused he was punished by MR PROCTOR and the other males. He was held down and felt pain in his feet. He fell unconscious. When he awoke he was raped by several males including MR PROCTOR.

1978–81 – Carlton Club, central London, 'Nick' was driven to the Carlton Club and dropped off outside. MR PROCTOR opened the door. Inside the premises were several other males. 'Nick' was sexually assaulted by another male (not by MR PROC-TOR on this occasion).

1978–81 – swimming pool in central London. 'Nick' was taken to numerous 'pool parties' where he and other boys were made to undress, and perform sexual acts on one another. He and other boys were then anally raped and sexually abused by several men including MR PROCTOR.

1981–82 – large town house in London. 'Nick' was taken to the venue on numerous occasions where MR PROCTOR and one other male were present. He was forced to perform oral sex on MR PROCTOR who also put his hands around 'Nick's' throat to prevent him breathing. On another occasion at the same location, MR PROCTOR sexually assaulted 'Nick' before producing a pen knife and threatening to cut 'Nick's' genitals. MR PROCTOR was prevented from doing so by the other male present.

1979–84 – residential address in central London. 'Nick' was taken to the venue. MR PROCTOR was present with one other male. MR PROCTOR forced 'Nick' to perform oral sex on him before beating him with punches.

1978–84 – numerous locations including Carlton Club, Dolphin Square and a central London townhouse. 'Nick' described attending several 'Christmas parties' where other boys were present together with numerous males including MR PROCTOR. 'Nick' was given whiskey to drink before being forced to perform oral sex on several men including MR PROCTOR.

MR PROCTOR will be interviewed about the matters described above and given the opportunity to provide an account.'

It took me some time to read the whole document. I was silent for a while and just handed it to Terry, who had already read his much shorter paper. We discussed Terry's position first and then mine.

My first thought was how right I was to use the word 'Kafkaesque' on the *Today* programme interview. How could I start to defend myself against the claims of someone whose name I was not allowed to know? At least now I knew what it was I was supposed to have done. It was a horrific catalogue of unimaginable, grotesque crime. I was indeed shocked and I could well understand why Raza and Nabeel were anxious that they were with me when I read it; they did not know how I would react. My mind went numb for a while. Then I thought, how could anyone think I am capable of any of this. My brain turned to defence.

The document said I was supposed to have committed these crimes within a period of time, not on a specific date or dates. The period of the alleged crimes ranged from three months to six years. My mind, now warming up, flashed as to how was I supposed to defend myself by way of, say, alibi evidence over such long periods of time. The police had taken my diaries (and still have them), together with every-thing else – they would have a better idea than me what I was doing in these periods. The entire range of the allegations was between 1975 and 1984, although references to me were between 1978 and 1984. I was briefed by Raza and we agreed the mechanics of Thursday's interview. I was to answer all the police's questions. I was pleased the solicitors had confidence in me. I would try to help the police understand why they had got it so wrong. Terry and I went home.

There was, I think, a sense of relief. I now knew what I was supposed to have done. I also knew I had done none of this. The allegations con-tained not one scintilla of truth. The interview would be a series of my negative replies to their police questions – have you done this? My rebuttal would be interspersed with me questioning the police as to how they could be taking these things seriously. These allegations were, in the 18 December 2014 words of the Head of Operation Midland, Detective Superintendent Kenny McDonald, neither 'credible' nor 'true'!

On Thursday 18 June, over three months after my home was raided, Terry and I drove to Leicester together. Terry was taken to his interview with the police by another solicitor from Sakhi's, Dim-ple Patel, who, according to Terry was like a tigress on his behalf. I could believe it. She had told Terry to answer 'no comment' to most questions. He found this very difficult; he likes to talk. The police officers that interviewed him were different to those that conducted mine, but at the end of his interview and caution, they tried to ask Terry questions about me. Advised by Dimple, he declined. One of the officers told Dimple he would not have answered such questions himself. The whole Metropolitan Police team seemed to consist of at least five officers staying two nights in a central Leicester hotel. They had been to dinner the night before at an expensive Italian restaurant that was very difficult to get a booking at. This information was gleaned before Terry joined Andrea, the Duke's partner, who collected him from the police station and drove him home.

While Terry was being interviewed, Raza drove me to the police station, where we met Nabeel. I had taken the precaution of taking with me my own bottled water and glasses. It was a throwback to the precautions I took during the *After Dark* programme in 1988. I wished to keep a clear head. I had done quite a bit of homework by way of briefing on 'Nick' and on Operation Midland on the internet. I had been told I might not be able to receive a copy of the tape recording of my interview so I had bought a small sound-recording machine to take with me.

The two police officers were polite on first meeting but then took Raza away for a talk. He returned to say that they had confirmed I would not receive a copy of the taped interview. More astonishingly, they said I could only be accompanied by one, not two solicitors. Reluctantly, I gave in with regard to the tape, but I was not going to allow the police to determine how I could and should be legally represented. Raza said there was nothing in law that determined this issue. I was prepared to terminate the interview before it had even started. I think they knew if I had two solicitors we could take better and more copious notes, which, for some reason, the police officers did not want. I can think of no other reason for their reticence; I cannot think they were nervous about being outnumbered. Eventually, they caved in and accepted that I would be accompanied by both Raza and Nabeel.

The interview room was tiny and they appeared to have difficulty handling the videotape technology. The interview started badly – for the police. DS Flynn did not know my full name, or, rather, the order of my Christian names. It may seem a small, insignificant point, but I thought that since they had waited over three months to interview me, cancelled two arranged interview dates, collated all these monstrous allegations against me, the least they could do was know my exact name. We had a ding dong about this for some time before I eventually put them out of their misery and told them. They were very embarrassed. They also did not know my date of birth. We also put on the record our objections to not being given a tape. I started to record the interview on my tape machine and the police objected to that too. Raza and I left the interview room to discuss what to do separately, in another room and in private. The interview had been going for less than ten minutes. When we returned, we said we had decided not to walk out, as I had a right to do. I had waited such a long time for this interview, I felt it had to proceed. We switched off our tape machine. The following account relies on an aide-memoire of the interview which was produced by my solicitors and me at the time, based on handwritten notes and gives a flavour of the exchanges. It will not be word-perfect.

The preliminaries were lengthy but eventually DC Chatfield, who asked most of the questions, asked me about my professional and personal life in the 1970s and 1980s. They were not specific questions but related to colleagues, friends, business interests, where I had lived and when. They were anodyne. Soon, after just over one hour, the police wanted a break. (In fact, they wanted a break every hour or so; I would have preferred to just keep going.) Twenty minutes or so later we resumed. They now wanted to talk about the Monday Club. It soon became clear that they didn't understand the differences between certain types of clubs — political pressure groups like the Monday Club as opposed to gentleman's clubs like the Carlton – and other clubs. I suspect they were thinking of a 'gay' club. I tried to explain the nuances but I am not totally sure they understood my succinct explanation.

They then moved on to my private life and asked when I began practising my homosexuality. Chatfield asked me to tell him about my partners and my relationships. I said no. They asked me about my relationship with Terry. I declined his kind invitation to comment and described Terry as my friend. I was asked how many sexual partners I had had, at which Raza jumped in and said he objected and that the question was not relevant. I was asked about the age of my partners, sexual preferences, sexual toys and props and the like. I told them that I was not prepared to discuss my private and personal life.

Chatfield moved on to ask questions about regular contact I may have had with children between 1975 and 1985. I replied: 'None.' Chatfield asked: 'This boy "Nick" then?' I said:

> Which boy?! He's forty-seven! You haven't spoken to a boy, you have spoken to a man. Have you spoken to 'Nick'? ... Have you met 'Nick'? Does he exist? I have seen his blacked-out figure on television. I have seen his quotes on Exaro. You won't tell me his name, you won't give me a photograph of him, and does he even exist?

I did not get any answers, just a comment from DS Flynn: '"Boy" is used as a generic term.' DS Flynn asked if I regularly met with adults and children. I said no.

I was getting exasperated at the apparent incomprehension

flowing from the other side of the table, so I made my position clear:

> When are you going to prosecute 'Nick'? You've been taken for a ride. This has been a very slow investigation. You have waited for three and a half months to make the most serious allegations of murder, torture and child abuse against me. You don't believe these allegations, do you? I am exasperated with the police. I did not expect this from the police. Your standards have slipped. What you have done to me is monstrous. If you believed I did this, you would have arrested me. This is a game, a political and press game. These allegations are false.

Shortly afterwards the police called for yet another break. They were tiring; I was just warming up.

After the break, the police assured me 'Nick' existed and had been interviewed. I asked, 'Was "Nick" interviewed by police officers alone? Was there a journalist present?' Flynn said, 'I am not prepared to answer that.' Chatfield also responded, 'I am not prepared to say, point noted.'

I was then asked to comment on the allegations in the disclosure document on homicides.

(The actual allegations can be read earlier in this book, where I have set them out in full. Once again, I have to alert you that the exchanges that follow are not necessarily exact as they represent a distillation of notes made at the time by my solicitors and myself.)

> Harvey Proctor: Completely and utterly false. The police have interviewed 'Nick' and these allegations have been made. What duty of care do you have to your witness? Is he of

sound mind? Do you have a Detective Superintendent Kenny
McDonald on Operation Midland?

DC Danny Chatfield: Yes.

HP: I have a quote from him: 'They and I [police detectives]
believe that what 'Nick' is saying to be credible and true,
hence we are investigating the allegations.' Has he pre-judged
this investigation? His remarks are extremely prejudicial to
me and extremely upsetting to me. He has pre-judged the
matter before hearing what I have to say.

Answer or comment from either of the police officers there was
none, but their sense of embarrassment filled the room with an
overpowering aroma.

DC: Is any of the detail based on anything?

HP: No.

DC: Can you give us an address in Pimlico/Belgravia? [This was
a reference to the alleged murder of a boy in 1980.]

HP: There are thousands of houses there; of course I went to
houses. It is extremely unlikely that I didn't go to a house
in Pimlico or Belgravia. It is unhelpful that you have taken
all my diaries. These allegations are rubbish and not true.
You know it's not true.

DC: Were you a regular visitor?

HP: Can't remember.

DC: Nick is very specific about the number of boys present.

HP: Who is the other male regarding the alleged 'homicide' in
1980? Has 'Nick' told you?

DC: I am not prepared to say.

HP: I have never stabbed anyone in my life. I have not abused

children in the UK or anywhere else. I have never ever strangled anyone, placed my hands around someone's neck and
squeezed until they died. This allegation is completely
untrue. I have done none of this and you know that.

DC: Tying someone to the table, hands around the neck – is that
something you have ever done?

HP: No.

DC: [Reads from disclosure concerning alleged murder in Kingston.]

HP: The allegations are untrue.

DC: Did you go to Kingston?

HP: As an MP I went all over the UK, including Kingston.

DC: Did you attend any parties that you can recall with adults
and boys?

HP: No.

DC: Do you recognise the dialogue (concerning an allegation)?

HP: No.

DC: What about 'private time'?

HP: No.

DC: Is this something you witnessed? [Ref. 1981–82 alleged
'homicide']

HP: No, I have never punched or kicked anyone. The allegations
are completely untrue in every respect.

DC: [Reads from disclosure document re. alleged murder at
Coombe Hill, Kingston, May and July 1979.]

HP: I can't say anything about that incident; I was not part of
any group and have never been part of any group. It is
against my inclination to be part of a group. If the three
murders have taken place that is awful but I have no knowledge of this. You don't think I did this either. It is false in
all respects.

Raza interjected at this point and asked, 'Do you have any bodies?' There was a silence while Chatfield mulled over this dramatic intervention. It was clear from the silence they did not have names, let alone bodies.

DC: I can't answer that.

HP: I have been to Kingston Hill but not in relevance to this. I had two female friends in and around the area, their names are Joe and Shirley. I was not able to drive a car until I was fifty years old in 1997. I did not drive a car and did not pass my test until I was fifty. I only learnt to drive three months prior to that. I have only driven once before that and that was at the Ford Dunton Research and Development plant in my constituency. I didn't have a chauffeur and I used to hitch a lift with people or use taxis.

DC: [Reads from disclosure re. sexual abuse 1974–84.]

HP: The allegation is false and untrue.

DC: Have you been to Dolphin Square?

HP: I visited there on a number of occasions. General or Brigadier Chapman [subsequently I confirmed he was a Brigadier] – he wrote a book on tanks – invited me in 1970 or 1971 and the [typist] secretary of the Monday Club, Suzie F——, to Dolphin Square. I have no idea what the number was, but it was just the three of us on two occasions. Another time I went there to the home of Professor Hugh Ford, his wife and daughters. Another time I had lunch in the restaurant there with the singer called Biddy. He pulled a pair of white stuffed ferrets on wheels around London. He was an eccentric. The climate then was very different to how it is now.

DC: How many times have you been to Dolphin Square?

HP: About six times, no regular visits.

DC: No? Nick says they were doing things to his feet and he was screaming.

HP: No, this is wrong and untrue in every detail.

DC: We move on to the Carlton Club, 1978–81. I have not been to the Carlton Club.

HP: Have you been to any gentlemen's clubs?

I asked this question many times without reply. Chatfield had mentioned he had not been to the Carlton Club. He volunteered that information – it was not in response initially to anything I had said; I wanted to know if he had experience of any London gentlemen's clubs to know how much information to give him in my answer. (The interview between Jeremy Paxman and Michael Howard comes to mind.) I repeated my question many times; Chatfield just glared back at me. The police were not being helpful. This was a voluntary interview and they were not helping me to help them. I felt they were treating me as if I was guilty. This was not what I was expecting.

DC: Did you open the door at the Carlton Club?

HP: 'Nick' alleges that he was dropped off and 'Mr Proctor' opened the door. Thirty years ago no member or guests would open the door; they have a doorman or hall porter. I am not and was not a member. All new Conservative MPs are invited to be members, but I declined. I have been there on a number of occasions for lunches, dinners and meetings.

DC: Were there any children there?

HP: There might have been a child of a member of the club.

DC: Would they have to be a guest?

HP: You can't just walk in; the employees know who the members are.

DC: How many times did you go?

HP: I can't say.

DC: [Moves on to 1978–81 'swimming pool allegations'.]

HP: This is untrue and false in every respect.

Raza Sakhi at this point interrupted and asked the officers: 'Did the activities take place in the water of the pool or in the building?'

Flynn and Chatfield slowly checked 'Nick's' statement and replied, 'In the water.'

DC: Do you have knowledge of swimming pools in central London?

HP: I can't swim. I hate swimming pools; I hate the smell of chlorine.

DC: Have you ever been in a pool in central London?

HP: In the water, no. I remember going to the RAC club to see the pool. I was interested in the tiles and its beauty.

DC: Who with?

HP: I can't remember.

Subsequently, while writing this book, I recalled it was Terry who showed me the pool when we attended the wedding reception of a very good friend in the RAC club. Within the same year, I also attended the funeral of her husband and the christening of her daughter.

DC: Have you ever used the term 'pool party'?

HP: That is a contradiction in terms as far as I am concerned.

DC: [Reads out the 1981–82 allegation 'large town house'.]

HP: The allegation is untrue and false in every aspect. It is ridiculous to assume that I can help with the location of a town house in London. The allegation is untrue. I have never owned a pen knife. I am not interested in knives.

DC: [Moves on to 1979–84 allegations.]

HP: This is false and untrue and I have never punched anyone ever.

DC: [Moves on 1978–84 allegations.]

HP: This is false and untrue. I have been to Christmas parties in social and family circles but I have never attended a Christmas party at Dolphin Square or the Carlton Club. I have never witnessed a child being given whiskey at a Christmas party. You need to ensure that 'Nick' is of sound mind. If he is, you have to consider prosecuting him for wasting police time.

[The police then called a halt as they wanted a break. The interview resumed:]

DC: Nick has made allegations saying that he knew you, for a specific period of time, 1978–84. Did you know a boy during that time of those ages?

HP: Not that I know of. It is very difficult for me to say and answer that question. Has 'Nick' said what happened to him after 1984? Why did he stop seeing me (allegedly)?

DC: I can't answer that.

HP: He says that the last allegation was in 1984 when he was under sixteen. It seems interesting that the last allegation he makes is when he was under the current age of consent. He makes no allegation when he is sixteen – when he is over the current age of consent.

DC: Why is he saying this?

HP: That is a difficult question to answer. I know somebody who
has met him. He is a professional person, a distinguished
person, and he says 'Nick' is barking mad. What steps have
been taken to ensure that 'Nick' is of sound mind? Has he
been seen by a psychiatrist? Detective Superintendent
McDonald said 'Nick' was 'credible and true'. If he really
believes that, can I suggest you book a double appointment
for the psychiatrist? Because he needs his head examining
too. All of this has had a huge impact on my personal life.
I hit the rocks in 1987 and I have been trying to rebuild my
life. I regret that this has happened. These are the most vile
allegations, all of which are wrong.

DC: Do you know 'Nick's' identity?

[At this time I did not know 'Nick's' name.]

HP: If I did he will be quite safe.

DC: What's his name?

HP: I am not answering that. If you thought I had done any of
this then you would have arrested me.

MF: The purpose of speaking to you is to prove or disprove your
involvement. If someone knows 'Nick' that could be bene-
ficial to you. We can speak to them.

I said nothing, not wishing to reveal my sources. Nor did I wish to
remind them yet again that what Flynn was saying sat uncomfort-
ably with his bosses' conviction that 'Nick' was to be believed as
'credible and true'. They had earlier refused to comment on their
Superintendent's remarks, insisting I was the one to answer questions. I felt they could not differentiate between interviewing a
person who was as guilty as hell and someone being interviewed

voluntarily, someone genuinely trying to demonstrate they were completely innocent. The attitude of the police officers was determined by their senior officers. Even if they thought I was innocent, they were taking orders from their bosses, who had pre-judged the investigation. They appeared not to question whether what had been alleged had actually occurred. They just wanted to question my 'involvement'!

The police officers then started to ask questions that gave me the answer to the question I had asked them earlier – who were the other men allegedly involved in these crimes?

> DC: I am going to ask you whether you know the following
>   people in either a social, professional or political manner.
> [It was as if they were conducting a cheap television panel game.
> I was being asked to categorise these people. Chatfield read out
> names. I gave my answers.]
>   Leon Brittan?
> HP: I know him through politics and professionally, there is
>   no social connection, there is no connection with 'Nick's'
>   allegations, and I have never been to his house.
> DC: Edward Heath?

I gulped at the mention of Heath's name. I was astonished anyone could think I had done anything in concert with him. It was the first time he had been brought into the equation to my knowledge with Operation Midland and these matters. I knew now 'Nick' was either mentally ill or malicious. I also thought 'Nick' could not be as 'clever' as the police obviously thought he was. His research on the period had failed to detect the animosity that existed between Heath and myself.

HP: I first met Heath when I was a student at the University of York. He was like a wet fish and had a very clammy, damp handshake. I have had no personal or social dealings with him. I first met him around 1966. I disliked him intensely and his politics and I have never been to his house. If I had been invited to go there I would have declined his invitation. He sacked me from the Conservative candidates list; Mrs Thatcher restored me to it.

DC: Have you ever heard of Wilton Street?

HP: Yes.

DC: Can you think of anyone else who lived there?

HP: No. [There was a pause] Oh, you mean Edward Heath lived there? If I knew that at the time I have forgotten.

DC: Lord Edwin Bramall?

HP: He was the head of the army, a political connection. I have never been to his house and I cannot recall him or having any meetings with him, but that is not to say we didn't meet.

DC: Were you at Dolphin Square with Bramall?

HP: The police searched his house at the same time they searched my house. I can't recall being at Dolphin Square with him, no.

DC: Hugh Beach?

HP: The name means nothing to me. [At the time it did not; I looked him up afterwards.]

DC: Michael Hanley?

HP: No, not to the best of my recollection. [I looked him up on the internet later.]

DC: Maurice Oldfield?

HP: Wasn't he in charge of MI5 or MI6? I don't recall meeting him socially or at his home.

DC: Ray Beech?

HP: I could have met him, but I don't know him. [I had not heard the name. Afterwards I looked him up but could not identify him.]

DC: Greville Janner?

HP: Yes, he was a Labour Member of Parliament when I was an MP. He was vicious in his criticism of me regarding my views on immigration. I wouldn't know where his house was and I wouldn't socialise with him.

DC: Who were your close political friends?

HP: People like Enoch Powell, Patrick Wall, Sir John Biggs-Davison, Roger Moate MP, Ulster Unionists – I went to Northern Ireland once a year – Jim Molyneaux, John Taylor. I regularly went to Enoch Powell's house; he had nothing to do with any of this.

DC: Nick says that from the group of men, Harvey Proctor disliked 'Nick'. No niceties, Harvey Proctor liked to hurt and see his victims in pain. He would regularly force oral sex and hold Nick's head to choke him. He was always forceful. Always smartly dressed, cocky and arrogant.

HP: Have the police shown 'Nick' a photo of me? Can I see the picture?

DC: No. Why would he make this up? He has given details.

HP: Actually he hasn't given much detail at all!

MF: You've never met 'Nick'?

HP: No.

'Nick's' depiction of me was so far off-beam I could only presume he had identified the wrong man, hence my request to see the photograph upon which the police were relying for my identification. They would not provide the photograph then or subsequently.

MF: The Monday Club – it consisted of professionals with like-minded views?

HP: At the most it had about 2,000–2,500 members. Anyone could join, it was a 'pressure group', not just Members of Parliament. Its central HQ was on Victoria Street.

MF: What do you remember about the number of entrances at the Carlton Club?

HP: There was a main door; I haven't been there for twenty to thirty years. I think there was a separate ladies' entrance as ladies could not be members. There must have been an entrance at the back of the club for deliveries. I never went in the ladies' entrance.

DC: Did you open any door?

HP: Main door or back door? No and I don't recall ever going there with a lady or to the ladies' entrance.

With such inane questions as to the number of doors the Carlton Club had thirty years ago and whether I opened any of them, the interview came to a less than dramatic end. I was physically exhausted from the mental energy I had expended over six hours. Raza and Nabeel thought I had acquitted myself reasonably well. They were in confident mood. I did not think for one moment that the police officers thought I had committed any of these offences. Their demeanour became ruder and more aggressive the longer the interview continued. In the reading from notes listing their questions, they seemed to be going through the motions.

As I drove home alone, I reflected that it was for this that I had lost my job, home, position and future. I recalled in my head the film *A Man for All Seasons* and the trial scene where Thomas More looks at Richard Rich, the Solicitor General, and his red dragon badge of office, and says, 'Why, Richard, it profits a man nothing to give his soul for the whole world ... but for Wales?' I wondered what metaphorical badge 'Nick' was wearing round his neck. I could not fathom why anyone would do this to another human being. I wanted to know why and I wanted to shout out loud: I am innocent!

The media questioned me about the interview, which was again leaked by the Metropolitan Police. It was the usual statement of 'a man in his sixties from Grantham was interviewed under caution after attending a local police station by appointment. He was not arrested. He was interviewed by Metropolitan Police Service officers working on Operation Midland.' Of course, I was not named in the statement. The police know they do not have to 'name' you to allow the press to 'identify' you. The police think they are being clever in this subterfuge. But then the Met will have told 'Nick' and/or Exaro and maybe others, so it leaks out again, triggering another round of bad publicity about me. Initially, I made a limited statement confirming that the police had eventually kept their third appointment and I had been interviewed but not arrested, charged or placed on bail.

After a few days, I was determined I could not stay silent any longer. My strategy for dealing with this was to be very different to the one I adopted in 1987. I had to share my thoughts with others and see if they took a similar view to the outrageous nonsense that beset me. I started to draft a statement, which I intended to deliver in front of Dolphin Square on 25 June, as so much of the 'action' was alleged to have been committed there, and then sent it to my solicitors. For legal reasons, I was advised not to proceed. My lawyers were and are brilliant; I listened to them and took their advice. I turned my attention to domesticity.

Terry and I walked in the garden and looked up to the castle. Of course, we would miss our home, but also the many people we had got to know well there. People such as our gardener for many years, Matt, his wife and child; Catherine, who helped with household chores and was a great painter of animals (including wonderful paintings of Sushi and Duke); Steve, her partner, and their dogs. There were so many people we were attached to and would miss dearly. At least we had our memories, Terry commented.

Channel 4 continued to request an exclusive interview with me; they had been trying for this for some time. I was tempted, as long as it could be a live interview.

The BBC's news team also kept in touch, but there was no interest there in a live interview. They just wanted to know what I was doing, and as such it felt more as if they were prying than reporting. Their arch-rivals from *Panorama* had earlier in the year sought an interview; they claimed they were aware of 'Nick' and his fantasy and were out to expose it. I reminded them of *Panorama*'s Militant Tendency programme and said they could not expect me to allow them to edit my remarks on such a sensitive subject. They said they would not be able to offer a 'live' interview. I told them to go away and think about it.

After the police interview, my solicitors chased the Metropolitan Police for the return of my belongings – I especially needed my laptop, which I had bought to undertake the writing of this book, the idea for which, yes, does pre-date the police raid in March – and on other matters. I became increasingly irritated that there was no response; it was, barring all else, discourteous. On 3 August, DS Flynn said the Metropolitan Police Service wanted to interview me again for clarification of previous questions and to ask about new issues. It was likely to be half a day and on the same voluntary basis as the previous interview. They offered dates between 24 August and 30 September. I selected the earliest date. Flynn said he would look to see what property could be returned, but nothing was.

We asked again for a copy of the photograph of me that the police had relied upon to get 'Nick' to identify me. I was told no photograph would be provided unless I was charged or if the photograph needed to be shown in interview. I was trying to ensure at an early stage that 'Nick' had identified me and not someone else. My helpful suggestion was spurned. I did not realise photographic identification was to be so sensitive for the police. Why were they so nervous of providing such information? We were assured 'the disclosure document will be provided before the interview', so I could consult with my solicitors as I had done for the first interview. We expected the second disclosure document on Friday 21 August 2015.

My view immediately after the first interview, that I should issue a statement, had grown. My name had been drawn into media coverage surrounding the trial of Ben Fellows for perverting the cause of justice, in the case involving Kenneth Clarke. Fellows was acquitted. Also, a Superintendent of Wiltshire Police had shamefully stood in front of Edward Heath's former home, a man I detested in life but, out of principle, have tried to defend after his death, and sought more alleged child abuse 'victims' to come forward and be 'believed'. I had been dragged into this story too. Why? Well, Metropolitan Police Commissioner Sir Bernard Hogan-Howe had confirmed Heath was being investigated by Operation Midland, leading a race of police authorities and services to jump on the bandwagon hoping to hide their own historical errors in connection with genuine abuse. Hogan-Howe, with consummate hypocrisy, criticised the IPCC (Independent Police Complaints Commission) for naming Heath. He wanted the Met to look good with the 'establishment'. It appeared to me he was trying to have it all ways.

I knew I was to be abroad for several months, writing this book, and I had come to the conclusion that the police were playing a political game with the press and so did not want to leave the UK before placing my opinions on record. It was unlike any other legal issue I could recollect. I knew what would happen on 24 August and the second interview: the Metropolitan Police would issue their weasel-worded statement that would not, of course, mention me by name, but reveal 'a man in his sixties etc....' They would then tell 'Nick' and/or Exaro, who would broadcast it widely, at which point there would be more appeals for 'victims', who would be believed whatever they said. I thought only by confronting this head on would their bluff be called.

My view was that, as I was the only man alive who could meaningfully be prosecuted (in the gang of nine), I wanted the police, the media and the public to know that I was geared up to fight this to the end. I was not prepared to continue to be the Aunt Sally in this falsehood. If it meant firing bullets in my defence now, which a QC might prefer to use in the future, so be it. If I were to be arrested and charged, I doubted I should be able to afford a QC for lengthy trial proceedings; it would be my intention to defend myself in court, if it came to that.

When it comes to the media and politics, I believe I have the knowledge to choose the best course of action. It was a gut instinct which over twenty-eight years I might have lost, but it was all I had. My opinion was that I was not prepared to spend any more of the months of my life that were left waiting for the Metropolitan Police Service to come to a conclusion. That could take years. I needed to mobilise the media, who had been remarkably but understandably placid in the face of the onslaught from the police, Exaro and 'Nick', my traducer. They had a monopoly on the information and carefully placed it in the public arena when they so decreed. The media had no way to challenge them. The police, Exaro and 'Nick' all had an agenda, which did not amount to, in a word or two, justice or truth, but a constant manipulation of the press and the media to achieve quite the opposite. I started revising my previous, draft statement and arranged a date for a press conference.

CHAPTER 15

STATEMENT

July had been a month of many goodbyes, drinks and supper parties around the Vale of Belvoir. It had been sad to say so many farewells. On 9 August, I drove a van with some of our belongings abroad. It was another long drive with overnight stops. Other items from our home had already been placed in auction. I was away for a week and returned to organise myself for the second Metropolitan Police Service interview and the press conference which I had now decided to hold.

The interview with the police was to be held on Monday 24 August at 11 a.m. The previous Friday, I went to my solicitors' offices to go through the disclosure document. Although it had been promised, the Metropolitan Police Service rang to say that it had been written but had not been signed off by their senior officers. Was this caused by inefficiency or as a result of design? I wondered whether they got wind of my intention to speak out the following day and I worried that I had wasted a visit to Leicester.

On the Monday morning, I met Nabeel, who drove me to the police station. It was the same venue as the previous interview, but this time the car park was incredibly full. There was no apparent reason for it to be so; it was a very small police station. Raza, Nabeel and I walked into the empty reception just before 11 a.m., the appointed hour, and waited. Nabeel said he had not been sent the disclosure document we were to have discussed. It was still a voluntary interview, the police wanted my help, but I had no idea what they wanted to discuss. It would prove to be unhelpful to them; it appeared gamesmanship on their part. We did not receive this document until 11.20 a.m. – twenty minutes after the time the interview was due to start – which was also the first time we saw DS Flynn or DC Chatfield. It was to be the same two police officers, only this time we were to be treated to their bad cop/bad cop act. They appeared grumpy; maybe their overnight stay at a Leicester hotel had not gone as well as it had in June. I discussed the very thin disclosure document they provided with Raza and Nabeel. We contemplated just leaving but, again, gave the police the benefit of the doubt and decided to proceed with the interview.

The interview room was slightly larger this time, situated down a maze of corridors. I sat directly across the table from DC Chatfield, with the video tape recording machine between us. DS Flynn was at his side; Raza and Nabeel were by mine. The policemen seemed to have mastered the technique of operating the tape. They also remembered my name this time.

The interview went along the following lines although, again, I was not allowed a copy of their recording, nor was I allowed to tape the interview myself. As before, therefore, I rely on our contemporaneous notes to give a flavour of the interviews; it is not intended to be word-perfect.

DC Chatfield outlined that it was a voluntary interview. I was not under arrest, I could leave at any time. I was assisting with inquiries, was allowed legal representation, and was under caution, which was explained. He said there would be no fastball questions.

> DC: You have the opportunity to respond to the allegations. Is there anything you wish to add or say from last time?
>
> HP: I have not remembered anything else and I certainly know nothing about these allegations. I can identify all the people with whom I am supposed to have done these things now, but I still cannot identify one of them – Ray Beech. Who is he? What is he? Is he dead or alive?
>
> DC: Anything you want to say about those people?
>
> HP: No. In order to help you, can you disclose who Ray Beech is? If I were you, I would tell me. There is a reluctance from you to help.
>
> DC: No further disclosure from me. Based on your research, is there anything you can tell me about Ray Beech?
>
> HP: No. I am completely blank in relation to that individual; I have nothing else to add. I refer you to my previous answers with regard to the others I gave you in my first interview.

I now know who Ray Beech is but for legal reasons connected with Operation Midland I am not at liberty to disclose who he is. It took several weeks of work on the internet and with the help of friends.

> [Exhibits DJC/201 and Exhibit DJC/202 were shown to me – they were pictures of an unremarkable young boy which DC Chatfield said were photographs of 'Nick'.]
>
> DC: What can you tell me – anything – of this boy?
>
> HP: Absolutely nothing.

DC: Have you met this person?

HP: I've met tens of thousands of people. He could have been in an audience. I have never *met* that person.

DC: [Shows photos taken 1979–80.]

HP: He looks a happy boy considering he's been abused left, right and centre. He looks a very happy boy.

DC: This person says he knew you for a six-year period, ages eleven to sixteen. If what he says is true, you would remember him?

HP: Yes.

DC: So you don't remember him?

HP: No, absolutely not.

DC: In the last interview I mentioned a pen knife. The pen knife was handed to 'Nick' by you and he retained it. I have photos of the pen knife.

HP: You chose not to disclose this information in the last interview [by which I meant: 'Has this only recently been handed to the police?'].

DC: Several images are shown of the pen knife. Here is Exhibit DJC/203 – a photograph of the knife with blade closed; Exhibit DJC/204, with blade exposed.

HP: I have looked at the images.

DC: Do you recognise it? Have you owned a knife like that? Have you handled such a knife? Have you seen such a knife? Here is Exhibit DJC/205 – a photograph of a close-up of blade and engraving.

HP: [I responded no to all the above questions.] With regard to Exhibit DJC/205, what is the picture meant to show on the blade? No way can anyone identify what is written on there from the photograph. Three of the five people in here cannot identify the writing from the photograph. It is not my knife; I have never owned a knife ever.

DC: To the best of your recollection, you've never handled this knife?

HP: I am sixty-eight and never handled that knife.

Raza Sakhi: Are there any forensics?

DC: I am not prepared to answer. 'Nick' says the knife was handed to him.

HP: That was not mentioned last time, that I allegedly handed the knife to him. You didn't know about this knife two months ago. Is this the only new information from 'Nick' in the past two months? It is pretty pathetic.

DC: 'Nick' recalls the incident when you threatened to cut his genitals after 'he'd done what he wanted to do'. Edward Heath intervened and stopped you – he put the knife in 'Nick's' pocket.

HP: Of course, it is all false, as are all the other allegations. You've now revealed the name of Edward Heath [in relation] to an alleged incident. Was this alleged incident meant to have taken place at Edward Heath's house?

DC: Yes.

There was no hesitation in his reply. It was a loud, resolute reply. Then there was a pause and great confusion between DC Chatfield and DS Flynn. DC Chatfield rummaged in his case and consulted papers (lots of papers) very quickly. He then corrected himself:

DC: It was not at Edward Heath's address. Apologies for saying it was. It was in a large town house in London. My apologies.

RS: Did Edward Heath intervene?

DC: Yes.

HP: Are you prepared to tell me the location?

DC: No.

HP: This is another experience of the police not assisting to help their own inquiry. None of this is true. Any fake knives or named [famous] people don't help your case. I mean, it is just Edward Heath and me with 'Nick' in someone else's house? You are all saying it was Edward Heath, but not in his house?

DC: I have double-checked my information – you [are] saying this is absolute nonsense?

HP: Yes, absolutely. Your fantasy gets bigger by the minute.

DC: Another venue – Elm Guest House. Tell me about it.

HP: I know of it now, but not at the time this fantasy is supposed to have taken place. There is a fraudulent document with my name on it doing the rounds of the internet. I have never visited the Elm Guest House; I didn't know of its existence.

DC: What about this list?

HP: It's on the internet. It is a list which is fraudulent – names of guests alleged to have visited Elm Guest House. My name is on there; it implies I attended Elm Guest House. Let me be clear, all of this nonsense has had a tremendous impact on my life. I am furious. Two or three years ago, I wouldn't have known about Elm Guest House. There are too many fake allegations out there. I never attended Elm Guest House.

DC: How long have you known about Elm Guest House?

HP: I used to live in Fulham, on the other side of Putney Budge.

DC: Is it possible you've been, not knowing it was Elm Guest House? On Rocks Lane?

HP: No. I know Rocks Lane; I have not been to Elm Guest House. You've been taken for a ride.

DC: [Shows an image, DJC/206 – Elm Guest House, Rocks Lane, Barnes.]

DC: Are you able to assist? Been there?

HP: No.

DC: I refer to two allegations of murder.

HP: Last time you said there were three murders, but you said to me I am directly responsible for two of them.

DC: With regard to the 1980 murder, 'Nick' was asked to do an E-FIT (Exhibit DJC/207). It is a young boy, aged approximately twelve, thirteen, with brown hair and eyes.

HP: This could be anyone, I don't recognise him. What is his name?

DC: I can't answer. Here is another image concerning the murder in 1981–82, another E-FIT.

HP: How helpful!

DC: [Shows exhibit DJC/208.]

HP: How convenient, a blond person this time. Did 'Nick' suggest he do this E-FIT?

DC: Recognise the boy?

HP: No, again, it could be anyone. Have you got a name? Is there a body?

DC: Do you know Leslie Goddard?

HP: I don't recognise the name, no.

DC: Do you know any Goddards?

HP: Is he any relation to Lady Goddard?

There was a pause and a look of total incomprehension on DC Chatfield's face when I referred to Dame Lowell Patria Goddard, DNZM, QC, chairman of the Independent Inquiry into Child Sexual Abuse.

Leslie Goddard, I learnt later, was the father of a pop singer called Adam Ant, and had no relation to Lady Goddard.

> HP: You mean you do not know who Lady Goddard is?
>
> DC: My knowledge is not relevant.
>
> HP: The name doesn't ring a bell?
>
> DC: If allegations were true, you'd know the name.
>
> HP: Then I don't.
>
> DC: This is a name you will know well – Jimmy Savile. Do you know if this person had interaction with you?
>
> HP: Not that I can recall since I left Scarborough. I lived in Scarborough between the ages of eleven and nineteen. He was a frequent visitor to Scarborough and quite a character. Until 1966/67, when I went to university, homosexuality was illegal. At the time, I didn't know much about sex. I and other people thought there was something 'odd' about him, in relation to his sexuality. I am sure that on some occasions until 1966 I would have been at the same garden party, cocktail party or other event, but I had no personal dealings with him, absolutely not.
>
> DC: After 1966?
>
> HP: No.
>
> DC: Direct contact with him?
>
> HP: No.
>
> DC: Present at any events?
>
> HP: He might have been at a Buckingham Palace garden party, but not in connection with anything to do with your inquiry.
>
> DC: 'Nick' said that at one of the sex parties, Jimmy Savile was present.
>
> HP: Surprise, surprise, what a clever chap he is!

DC: Have you ever been in any circumstance such as a sex party where Jimmy Savile was present?

HP: No. If it came out last week that Dame Vera Lynn was under inquiry, 'Nick' would come out and say that she was invited to and [had] been present at these sex parties.

DC: Have you any knowledge of any GPs or doctors? Any knowledge of [any GPs] other than your own GPs? Were you familiar with any doctors?

HP: I am bound to have been, as an MP. I would have known many doctors in my constituency. I wouldn't recall now the name of my own GP at that time. No, a GP in Basildon?

DC: Someone you would have known personally if the allegations are correct.

HP: What's the name of this GP? This is ridiculous; how can I answer these questions?

DC: Thank you.

HP: My critical remarks are not directed at you.

DC Chatfield frequently stopped, during the interview, exasperated, and looked up to his left to one of the cameras in mock disgust at my answers. He did this, in an exaggerated, sarcastic manner, on several occasions during this part of the interview, in what I regarded to be a rude way.

DC: It is alleged by 'Nick' that this doctor was present at parties to 'patch up' any injuries to boys.

HP: You could go into the street and ask anyone these questions. I wasn't there, this is rubbish. Had you put this information in the disclosure document, I would have had time to consider the points and I would have thought more about this. These are ridiculous questions! No mention was made of Jimmy Savile, doctors or Elm Guest House at all in your second disclosure document, which was handed to me after this interview was supposed to start. You said at the start there would be no fastball questions. What do you call these? How much longer are we going to go on for?

DC: On a previous occasion, I provided some information but not names of people or venues.

HP: You are lying. I did ask for disclosure of locations and you refused some but you did give Dolphin Square and the Carlton Club as venues in the first interview.

DC: At the beginning of this interview I asked if there was anything you remembered after last time.

HP: This interview is in the process of disintegrating. You told my solicitors that disclosure was ready last Friday but needed to be signed off by senior officers. Your questions are extraordinary.

RS: Mr Proctor already signed that he knows nothing.

DC: Do you know anything about George Tremlett?

HP: I have heard of him – was he a councillor and leader of a council, Kensington and Chelsea, I think? I think I would have met him in the House of Commons. He was not a friend; I have not had sex with him or been to parties with him present.

I got George Tremlett's local government positions completely wrong from memory. It was thirty-odd years ago! I was thinking of a different Conservative council leader. Tremlett was on the Greater London Council. But I still had no social or sexual dealings with him. I subsequently discovered Tremlett was not mentioned because of anything to do with 'Nick' or his allegations.

DC: How many times have you been in his presence?

HP: I don't know. I was not present at any of these things 'Nick' has suggested. He was a Conservative, so political events maybe.

DC: Have you spent time socially with him?

HP: I've already answered your question; you're not listening.

DC: Do you know George Tremlett socially?

HP: I have already answered this question.

RS: Yes, Mr Proctor has answered those questions before.

DC: Did you share a car journey with George Tremlett?

HP: I doubt it. In London I travelled by Underground, but sometimes taxi, I cannot recall. I recall the name more than any interactions.

DC: Peter Hayman?

HP: I have never met him. I know of him through internet research. I do not know him socially nor in connection with this inquiry.

DC: No familiarity of knowing him from the photo online.

HP: This is the trouble with this interview. What part of 'no' do you not understand? You started this interview not being helpful, by not giving disclosure documents last week or with sufficient notice today.

DC: Terry Dwyer/Allen?

HP: I knew him in the mid-1980s. He came to my flat in Fulham. He tried to sell a story to newspapers about me. He attempted to blackmail me.

DC: How did you first know him?

HP: I don't recall. I met him – he was in his late twenties, early thirties – in the middle of the 1980s. It must have been socially but I can't remember.

DC: How long did you know him?

HP: Couple of years.

DC: Type of relationship?

HP: Sexual.

DC: Lost contact? 1986?

HP: Blackmail? I pleaded guilty to four charges of gross indecency in 1987. It was with regard to the age of consent. It was then twenty-one. A newspaper wired a young gentlemen for sound and got me to talk on tape. He was wired for sound by the *Sunday People*. I rang Scotland Yard and offered to give a statement in October 1986. They refused to meet me. In March/April 1987, I went home to find an attempt by this person to blackmail me on a telephone answer tape machine. He said that if I intervened in a court case in which he was being prosecuted and had a word with the judge, he would not disclose our relationship. I took the tape and sought advice from my then lawyers. They told me to keep the tape in my legal papers and do nothing more. I placed the tape in a filing cabinet at my home. When Chief Superintendent Marvin raided my flat he took the tape. Marvin retired and wrote an article for *The Sun*. In it he said two of the reasons he wanted to take action against me was that there was a Westminster rent-boy ring and that he had found a blackmail tape. He took the tape from my legal papers. The police didn't investigate the blackmailer but decided to use Mr Dwyer, the blackmailer, as a witness in their investigation against me.

On reflection, and with hindsight, the blackmail attempt might have been in the latter part of 1986 or early 1987. It is such a long time ago and I cannot refresh my memory with my diaries or archive box material. The police still have them.

DC: Sexual relationship between the two of you?

HP: Yes.

DC: Did you know his occupation?

HP: No idea.

DC: Do you know Barry Haddon?

HP: No.

DC: He was an associate of Terry [Dwyer]. Does that assist?

HP: I don't recall the name from that time. I recall it now as you are not the first person in recent weeks to make that inquiry – it was asked of me by a journalist.

DC: Line of inquiry relating to Operation Midland.

[I do not know what he meant by that comment.]

MF: To clarify, Elm Guest House – you've never been?

HP: No.

MF: You lived in Fulham. Been to any other areas in Rocks Lane?

HP: Not that road, no. I think there is a road called Rectory Road near to Rocks Lane.

DC: [Produces a map.]

HP: Between 1988 and 2000 I had a retail shop in Richmond. The route from Putney Bridge to Richmond crossed Rocks Lane. I got to know the area from 1988 onwards. I took that route quite often. In the late '80s/'90s I got to know a lady. I got friendly with her through Terry Woods. She sold her house and moved to Rectory Road.

MF: In Rocks Lane, did you attend any other premises?

HP: Not to my knowledge.

DC: Have a break, check we have gone through everything.

HP: I have no need to take a break. No, I have nothing else to say. I have helped the best I can.

The interview had lasted about two hours. Reading these notes back for the purpose of this book, I am struck by how unhelpful this interview must sound. It was certainly unhelpful to me not having a note of the areas the police wished me to help them with in advance. I certainly would not have made the mistake with regards to George Tremlett and his correct local government position. I confused him with another councillor who was a council leader. I recall meeting Horace Cutler, the leader of the GLC – Tremlett was deputy leader – but cannot recall Tremlett at all. If I met him, I had forgotten. Cutler was a member of the Monday Club; Tremlett was not I believe. The chairman of the GLC at the time was Bernard Brook-Partridge. He was a member of the Monday Club, a former employee of MI5 and I certainly had an odd drink with him together with others, usually at a watering hole near the Commons that was called St Stephen's Tavern. In any event, none of 'Nick's' allegations are correct. They are fantasy.

After this second police interview, I thanked my solicitors for their support and I drove home. My feelings were that the police and I were approaching these matters from different angles. I felt I was trying to help the police in determining that 'Nick's' allegations were wrong and to give them a feeling for the time. I was giving a voluntary interview to assist the police but also trying to clear my name. Whereas I felt the police were forgetting it was a voluntary interview and were seeking to validate and corroborate 'Nick's' allegations, believing I was guilty. They appeared to be seeking to defend 'Nick' in some way to defend themselves. All the questions would have been scripted by their superior officers. It was not a meeting of minds.

Alone, in my empty house, I worked on the statement I was to make the next day in London. In it I wanted to reflect on some, if not all, of the second interview that had just taken place. The statement was already very lengthy. When completed, I rehearsed the statement and timed it. In doing so, I found it difficult to get to the end of it without becoming emotional. It was now very long and not easy to deliver. I did not want to 'break down' in front of the press the next day. I knew I had to project my voice and that I had to hold my emotions in check to get my points across clearly. I did not know how the press, used to sound bites, would cope with its length and detail.

The previous week, my solicitors had agreed I should go ahead with my plan to speak my mind. A friend had booked the Marlborough Suite of the St Ermin's Hotel in Victoria, London; I remembered it as a hotel of faded elegance; it has since been renovated and, though no longer faded, it has lost its elegance. I suggested this hotel as it was one I often used when I was in London. It was next to Caxton Hall, which, though not that many people seem to have heard of it now, in the 1970s and 1980s was often used for political meetings and celebrity weddings. It was also where Sir Edward 'Teddy' Taylor had very kindly given me lunch after the events of 1987. He had commiserated with my position then, but in 2015 he was fiercely critical of me in his local press. He too has, I am afraid, fallen for the fantasists' claptrap. He has swallowed the line of the Metropolitan Police Service and those delusionists on the internet and likes of Exaro. As an honourable man, I am sure he will apologise in the fullness of time.

The morning of Tuesday 25 August was busy; the phone did not stop ringing. I was up at 5 a.m. One reporter rang to ask me what I was going to say. I declined to enlighten him, suggesting he come along. I said he would never hear a more extraordinary statement and to contact me afterwards if he thought I had exaggerated. He did the next day. He said I had undersold it. I talked to a representative of Channel 4 who had agreed to interview me live on their 7 p.m. news programme. They had got cold feet and only wanted to do a recorded interview. I was not happy about this. We compromised that I would be recorded but only for the length of time that they wished to allocate to the slot on their programme; they would only edit for legal reasons; and I would be shown the edit before transmission. This was agreed with their producer Tim Bouverie, whom I was to meet in the afternoon. LBC also wanted me to do a recorded radio interview immediately after the press conference and I agreed as long as it was transmitted after Channel 4's broadcast. I thought this was fair and it was agreed with all parties. I had spent the previous weekend inviting other television and newspaper representatives to attend, but I had no idea how much interest there might be. It was a very long time since I had invited the media to report about me at such length; I knew how fickle they could be.

I dashed out to print off the written copies of the final version of my statement, which later I could distribute to attendees, and then went on to Grantham railway station, where I met a friend who was travelling to the Royal Horticultural Society show. I had not seen him for a while and discussing his life over breakfast on the train took my mind off my own position. We had a drink at King's Cross station. These days I very rarely drink, but I had a gin and tonic. We made our goodbyes and I caught a taxi to St Ermin's. I went to inspect the room where the meeting was to take place; I hoped it would be large enough. While checking it out, realising that my intention of reading my statement from my laptop would not work because it would not fit under the light of the lectern, I eschewed technology and resorted to how I would have delivered a speech thirty years before, reading from paper. While I was deliberating if this was the right approach, a BBC camera technician came into the room to set up camera and lights. There was to be some coverage.

While waiting for Nabeel to arrive downstairs, I read my speech again and saw four or five more cameras coming into the hotel. Journalists, too, were drifting past. Nabeel arrived and was very reassuring. He said he would distribute my statement after it was delivered. I did not want the journalists to have a copy of my statement while I spoke as I wanted them to concentrate on what I was saying, and I certainly did not want them to be reading the script in advance. Tim Bouverie came down and said the press representatives were waiting, so Nabeel and I entered a very crowded room. Two journalists from the *Daily Express* squeezed onto the windowsill to my left. The room was packed. There were many lights for the cameras and a great deal of heat. Subsequently a few newspapers wrote that I was in tears at the end of my statement; I was not. I was mopping my brow with a handkerchief as I sweated under the hot lights; certain journalists have difficulties knowing the difference between tears and sweat.

A good friend of mine, Tony Vander Elst, very kindly videoed the entire press conference of 25 August 2015 and uploaded my full statement on 6 September 2015 to YouTube. This record was uploaded in the interest of truth and justice to provide the full report of my statement as balance against the selective and edited versions put out by Exaro and other press, police and political opponents in their respective reports and defensive responses.* Tony and I were friends in the 1970s and 1980s. He supported me after news of the search of my house and I met him in London during the summer of 2015. I am indebted to him for all his help.

---

* The video can be found here: https://www.youtube.com/watch?v=RLm7rdRBOF4 &feature=youtu.be

My statement can be read in full in the Appendix.

I was generally pleased with my delivery and I did not break down. Afterwards, I sat down – it was very hot in the crowded room under the lights and I had been on my feet for nearly an hour. My written statement was distributed, which took a few minutes. I think the feeling I received was one of disbelief by the journalists, both that I had said what I had said and at the length of it. I think many of them were stunned, not used to lengthy contributions from today's politicians, the sound bite being the order of the day. Well, they did think my last pronouncement outside the Happy Beater on 5 March was a tad short. It took them several minutes to settle down. I now got ready for questions.

One of these was about why I had not given the police a DNA sample. Nabeel, interrupted and told me not to answer the question but simply rely on the fact that I did not have to provide one unless I was arrested. During my first interview, I had asked the police why they wanted to do such a test and they said to eliminate my DNA from an item of clothing. As I knew that item of clothing was less than three years old and therefore could not possibly be relevant to anything that happened in the period 1978 to 1984 – the cotton for it would not have been growing at that time – I declined their request. My solicitors did not want my DNA to be in the same police laboratory as, say, a pen knife, for fear of cross-contamination. I could see their point.

Mark Watts, Exaro's editor-in-chief, standing in front of a bright television light, making him very difficult for me to see, asked a number of questions. At one stage, I apologised to him if I had missed his arm being raised, saying to him, 'Like "Nick", you are rather invisible.' He either did not hear my deliberately cynical and caustic remark or decided to ignore it. When later writing up 'as full a transcript as possible' of the question-and-answer session on Exaro's website, he conveniently, for Exaro, left my quip out of the transcript. One of his questions was why I had mentioned (and therefore must have known) that 'generals' were involved in the abuse when I was interviewed on the BBC's *Today* programme on 5 March.

Off the top of my head, I could not recall precisely where the word 'generals', as opposed to, say, 'brigadiers', had come from other than, for some months before the search of my house, I had not been idle. For a start, I had been monitoring some of the internet network of fantasists on these matters; I had numerous conversations with DS Flynn for the fifteen hours the police were in my house; I had spoken to a journalist that morning; I had also heard the BBC's 7 a.m. news on television, and seen my face upon it; and had heard a mention on Radio 4 of 'military establishments' being a location for the alleged abuse; not to mention I had spoken also to a BBC researcher immediately before doing the radio interview. Watts considered my reference to 'generals' incriminating. I am sorry to disappoint him. I actually said 'generals or the military' on the *Today* programme and, as I told the police in answer to their questions in my first interview with them, I have not knowingly met Bramall or Beach or, as far as I can recall, any general. If I did, I cannot recall the circumstances, but they certainly were not 'sexual'. Mark Watt's question and comments reveal more about Exaro than they do about me – that they think they can so control the output of 'Nick', the police and others that they can know everything that is in the media or internet arena. Wrong. He also seemed to me to want to break the integrity of 'my source'. As in all this, he was peeved I revealed something – that 'generals' and the military were involved – that Exaro knew but which they thought they could keep to themselves until they wished to drip feed it into the media at a time of Watt's choosing.

Mark Conrad of Exaro, the person who was trying to get a quote from me when the police were still searching my house, wanted to know what else apart from computers was taken away by the police. I am pleased that Nabeel asked me not to answer his question as it would have taken a very long time to answer as so much was taken. In fact, it amounted to a white van-load of possessions, including personal and family treasures, diaries, files, many photographs, virtually all my documents, including archive material from my parliamentary days, and communication equipment; everything that allows one to live one's life. At my age, the removal of my shoe horns was a considerable inconvenience. Eventually, I received a generalised list of items, but I am still not aware of everything that was taken. Much of it was stored in plastic boxes from previous house moves which were unsorted. No doubt in my mind Conrad could have got the answer from 'Nick' or the police if he was not already in possession of the information when he asked the question. He probably knows better than I do what the police have of mine. Indeed, I was not asked whether the things that were taken were mine. Many things belonged to Terry, Adam and Charlotte and friends who had left things behind or that we were storing for them. Many items belonged to the Belvoir estate. The search warrant was specific; the police action was indiscriminate – a 'fishing' operation.

There was an assortment of questions from a large gathering of reporters from the two wings of the BBC – the news team and *Panorama*. I answered their questions directly on various subjects: on 'Nick' being the sole complainant – yes; if the police said they were dropping any of his allegations – no; whether I contacted any of the others alleged to be abusers – no; the progress of the inquiry – slow; what happened in 1987 – read what my solicitor said at the time; and whether the police had named the three alleged murder victims – no.

Daniel Sandford of the BBC raised the question as to why I was angry with Superintendent Kenny McDonald. I said that the Superintendent had appeared on BBC television and said 'Nick' was 'credible and true' and that no other police officer would say that. Superintendent Kenny McDonald had prejudiced the investigation. I was asked what the police had said when I raised this matter. I said they told me that they were there to ask questions, not to answer them.

The questions appeared to be petering out and I thanked those who attended and walked out with Nabeel. It had taken the best part of two hours and I was a little tired.

I was driven to the studios of LBC, where I was interviewed by Iain Dale. I thought it was a reasonably tough interview and, at one point, I became a little emotional. I think I acquitted myself better than in my earlier question-and-answer session at St Ermin's. Maybe the quality of the questions was better; maybe I had had a pause and refreshed the brain cells in readiness. It was a quick interview, around fifteen minutes, and soon I was back in a car and on the way to the Channel 4 studios with Tim Bouverie.

After a little make-up, which I hate, I went straight into the studio with Krishnan Guru-Murthy, the interviewer. He seemed cheerful enough. However, it became apparent he had a fixation on what happened in my life in 1987 rather than what I was saying about Operation Midland now. I thought I was patient in answering his questions, which, halfway through the interview, veered off into a separate discussion of what I did or did not do in my bedroom in 1987 and the morality of my sexual behaviour. It was as if Channel 4 did not believe in the equality of the age of consent between men and women or in the reduction of the age of consent to eighteen and to sixteen, as it is now. Nor did the interviewer appear to understand the word 'consensual', seeking to infer he knew more about my relationships at the time than I did. Perhaps Guru-Murthy had his own agenda to try to undermine what I was saying now with regard to Operation Midland, or at least avoiding the main points of my statement. *Channel 4 News* had missed the opportunity of being on the campaigning side of a police scandal. I think my historic political views had blinded their natural liberalism. A supposedly 'liberal' broadcaster, Guru-Murthy had, in my opinion, just succeeded in reinforcing institutional homophobia. It was not something they would or could have done if the interview had been 'live'. The dynamics are altogether different. He was very friendly when I left the studio to allow them to get on with their hatchet job in the control room.

It was for just this kind of interviewing and editing that I initially insisted on a 'live' interview, which I was promised. The duration of the recorded interview was meant to be about the length of their allocated slot; it was not. It was quite a bit longer, to facilitate 'editing'. Nothing was taken out for 'legal' purposes as far as I was aware or told. Knowing I would be unhappy with this technique, to make the interviewer 'look good', I had insisted and been assured that the editing would be for legal reasons only and I would be shown the edit before transmission. I waited for the opportunity to view what I had been promised, along with Derek Laud, who had joined me in the green room after the recording to discuss the day's events. The clock ticked by until it was 7 p.m., when the item (it was to be the first on the programme) was broadcast. After the recording, up to air time, Tim Bouverie became unavailable, having been assiduous by his presence since 1 p.m. Channel 4 had 'ratted' on their promises. They were not going to show me what they had taken out 'just for legal purposes' because the purpose of the 'edit' was to attempt to make me look bad and unbalance what I had said in favour of the interviewer. It took them long enough. Well, in retrospect, I think they failed even with the power of their 'editorial' tool.

Before we left their studios, Derek had a blistering row with Tim over Channel 4's unprofessionalism in changing the deal of a live interview and then taking advantage of the recorded interview and reneging on their promises. I regret to say *Channel 4 News*, whom I thought were reputable, cannot be trusted.

BBC's *Newsnight* rang while I was at the Channel 4 studios and asked if I would be interviewed by Evan Davis. I agreed but I was nervous. Derek took me for dinner at Le Caprice. We relaxed and, after calves' liver, parted company, and I made my way to the BBC studios. In the green room was Brian May, the lead guitarist of the rock group Queen. He was friendly and wanted to chat. We spoke about Cecil, the lion that had been shot dead earlier in the year, and dogs. I did not have the opportunity to see his contribution to the programme, but he appeared interested in my position and I recall giving him a copy of the statement I had made earlier.

Evan Davis was polite and friendly, as had been Guru-Murthy – no guarantee of a fair interview. When I went into the studio I was surprised at the size of the backdrop, with huge pictures of me at the press conference earlier and surrounded by police in 1987. I was nervous but resorted to the tried and trusted remedies of deep breaths, sitting straight in the chair and keeping my hands still. Months later, I watched and tried to listen to Hilary Benn's wind-up speech in support of bombing Syria in the Commons' Chamber. I say 'tried' to listen because he waved his hands and arms about so distractedly that his bravura performance was diminished, and detracted from his words when viewed on television. In the Chamber itself, it would have been the most powerful and persuasive speech since the days of his father, Tony Benn, Michael Foot and Enoch Powell a generation previously. I was very privileged to have seen all three of them in parliamentary action, sitting across from them in rapt attention and in wondrous awe. There is nothing to match them in the House of Commons now.

Of course, I hoped my words came across well. *Newsnight* was an important platform and it was at the end of a long and exhausting day. Davis was a fair interviewer and I answered his questions directly. I managed to make my main point, that Superintendent McDonald's depiction and assurance on BBC television that 'Nick's' evidence was 'credible and true' was prejudicial. I also made the point that the police had a duty in law to investigate expeditiously and that I did not think they were expediting these matters. I criticised senior police officers for their lack of intelligence in thinking that Ted Heath and I would do anything together, including having a cup of tea. Davis saw the point immediately. I said it was cruel that I was being pushed to the brink of despair on the matter. I confirmed that all my options would be open in the future.

As I was on the last train home, I reflected that, up to that day, the police, Exaro and 'Nick' had been in control of the press agenda, appealing for 'victims' and 'survivors' to come forward, revealing sufficient information to keep the media on message, but not too much that they could question the investigation. They would be 'believed'. Everything was 'credible and true'. The media had been incapable of thinking it through for themselves, simply because they did not have the facts – the armoury with which to do it. My intention that day was to place on public record my innocence and to provide others with the facts and weaponry needed to establish my innocence, given the police were either reluctant, for political or careerist motives, or too slow and ineffective to do it themselves. I thought I had fulfilled a public duty. In placing all these facts in the open, in speaking out, where in the past I would have remained silent, I was taking a risk. I had, however, achieved my first objective. Things for Operation Midland would never be the same. I pondered on the need to do what I had done that day and the sadness that I felt in having to do it. I was so tired when I reached Grantham station, I caught a taxi home and went to bed, completely forgetting that I had earlier parked my car in the station car park.

CHAPTER 16

POLICE, POLITICIANS AND PRESS

A s I was waiting to get off the plane, having left the United Kingdom to write this book, a boy aged about eleven or twelve years of age, his face bathed in shy smiles, tugged his father's sleeve, whispered something in his ear and pointed at me. 'He thinks you're a famous football manager,' his father explained. I was not sure which one, though, and, despite being front-page news for several days, I was relieved, if a little surprised, that I had not been (correctly) recognised. It was two days after the press conference. There had been forty-eight hours of media interest in what I'd had to say. My last few hours in the United Kingdom had been busy. I had been interviewed by Andrew Pierce of the *Daily Mail* in the Angel and Royal Hotel, Grantham, shortly before my flight. If his article came across portraying me as being depressed, it was because I was; leaving the country I had loved all my life was a dispiriting experience. Attempts to get me to do radio and television since Tuesday had failed because I was not based in London, but I know programmes went on air without me. I was pleased that every paper had reported my statement. *The Guardian* carried the following editorial:

> There is probably no political issue on which *The Guardian* ever agreed with Harvey Proctor. In the 1980s, the former Conservative MP was one of the most right-wing men ever to represent his party. Though he was forced out of politics after involvement with young male prostitutes that would not be illegal today, he was no loss to the House of Commons when he left in 1987. But when Mr Proctor returned to the limelight this week, he spoke words that should be listened to with care and concern.
>
> Mr Proctor's house was very publicly searched by police in March as part of the Operation Midland investigation into allegations about a 1970s and 1980s Westminster paedophile ring. This high-profile search was part of a pattern. It included the police announcement, made outside Edward Heath's home this month, that the former Prime Minister was being investigated too. Swoops on the homes of the late Leon Brittan and the former army chief Lord Bramall, who is still alive, received similar publicity. Highly publicised police actions have also marked separate investigations into Sir Cliff Richard.
>
> Allegations against public figures, especially when they allege child abuse, must be fully investigated. Yet proper investigation must respect the presumption of innocence. That is especially true if the case involves the kind of allegations about which Mr Proctor spoke this week, which, if proved, would rightly ruin anyone's reputation. Yet police appear to be ignoring the presumption far too often. Mr Proctor is an unsympathetic figure; but if his denials are honest, which is for a court to decide, he would be a victim too.

It is hard to avoid the perception that the police are playing post-Jimmy Savile publicity catch-up. So is society more widely. For the many victims of child sex abuse who were ignored, or who felt in some way themselves to blame for their ordeals, there is a place for the big, symbolic gesture. It is important, in addition to the police investigations, that the Goddard public inquiry into allegations of an establishment cover-up will also allow survivors to give evidence of what happened and how it has affected their lives.

But it is also important that the process of establishing the truth is not swayed by the need to meet victims' and survivors' understandable desire for justice or by any attempt by police, journalists or MPs to surf the wave of public outrage against child abuse. Any justice that involves destroying the lives of other innocent people is no kind of justice at all. Naming a person against whom allegations have been made may be justified in some circumstances if it encourages other witnesses. But it is another thing to helicopter in on a dawn raid, having tipped off a TV crew in advance.

Due process ought to apply in all cases. But it is not due process when police issue a statement that untested allegations – which include immensely serious claims about which many outside observers remain sceptical – are 'credible and true'. Truth is for a court to decide, not the police – and not the media either. Responsible MPs would not abuse their privileges on such matters either.

The allegations may prove to be credible and true. But they may prove to be neither. There may be no charges. The claims may be shown to be false. In that event, police, media and MPs who should have known better and acted with more respect for the law would have much to answer for.

I would hope that, politically, to *The Guardian*, I am 'an unsympathetic figure', although I think my views on mental health reform and my work in the Commons on that subject might be shared. In many respects, I am like an old-fashioned, classical liberal before social democracy polluted its ideology. *The Guardian* was not alone in wanting me out of the House of Commons. It should not be forgotten that my views were incredibly popular, much to *Guardian* readers' annoyance and frustration. I am, however, indebted to *The Guardian* for grasping my arguments now so quickly, and bravely supporting them in such a forthright and rapid manner. It is just a surprise that, as Detective Superintendent Kenny McDonald made his statement, including the words 'credible and true' in his BBC interview on 18 December 2014, it took *The Guardian*, and so many other newspapers and media outlets, over eight months, and my words on 25 August 2015, to express their indignation at the police's position.

Remarkably, the *Financial Times* devoted a full-page article to this subject on 27 August 2015. I read it while waiting to catch my plane:

> The sight of a distraught former Conservative MP publicly confronting allegations of murder and sexual abuse of children has brought disquiet at Westminster over the way police are handling such cases.
>
> After years when claims of paedophilia by the rich and powerful were brushed aside – most infamously in the case of Jimmy Savile – some politicians believe that the police are overcompensating by pursuing inquiries based on incomplete evidence and in the full glare of the media.
>
> 'They have gone from one extreme to another,' said one former Labour Home Secretary, who declined to be named.

[...] Politicians at Westminster are reluctant to criticise the police publicly on such a sensitive issue. But some are concerned that Mr Proctor and other figures – Edward Heath, the former Prime Minister, Leon Brittan, the former Home Secretary, including past heads of the security services MI5 and MI6 – have been linked to the alleged paedophile ring and seen their reputations sullied unfairly.

No charges have been brought. The strict laws on contempt of court that apply to criminal investigations after any arrest are not yet in play in Mr Proctor's case, and most of the others named by 'Nick' are dead.

Steve McCabe, Labour's spokesman on children, said: 'What most folk would like to see is some decent police work to bring about some substantial charges and fewer newspaper headlines.'

Politicians are particularly concerned at comments by Detective Superintendent Kenny McDonald, head of the Operation Midland inquiry into the alleged Westminster ring, that he believed that what 'Nick' was saying was 'credible and true'.

One former Conservative Home Office minister said: 'How can the police know that before the evidence has been tested? The police sometimes appear to look like they are persecuting people because they are rich and powerful.'

'There are many in the higher echelons of the police who were scarred in the Tony Blair era by suggestions they were doing what the politicians wanted. There is a whole generation of coppers who don't want to be seen as too close to the establishment.'

Police have been under intense scrutiny in their investigations of allegations of sex abuse following the revelation that several forces, including Scotland Yard, received complaints about Savile that were never taken forward during his lifetime.

Peter Neyroud, former Chief Constable of Thames Valley Police and now an independent adviser on policing matters, said it was increasingly difficult for forces to handle a growing case-load of sexual offence allegations at a time when their funding was being cut.

He was particularly concerned that new guidelines on crime recording from Her Majesty's Inspector of Constabulary had made it harder to test the veracity of allegations before launch-ing a formal investigation.

'I think the requirement for everything to be recorded immedi-ately has led to forces jumping straight from receiving allegations to carrying out a full inquiry,' said Mr Neyroud.

'They are then under a lot of pressure from the press to be open and transparent about the nature of the crime they have recorded and to name suspects.'

[...] The police were also strongly criticised for agreeing to let the BBC film a raid on the house of Sir Cliff Richard over an alleged sex assault dating back to 1985: the pop star has not been charged.

Mr Proctor's emotional press conference, where he set out in detail the allegations against him, has also been criticised by some lawyers.

Peter Garsden, senior partner at the law firm Abney Gars-den, said: 'My view is that we should not be judging guilt or innocence at this stage, nor should Mr Proctor be attempting to manipulate the press and public into believing he is innocent in advance of any criminal charges. The venue for the trial of guilt or innocence is the criminal court, not the media.'

Sam Stein QC, a specialist criminal defence advocate at Mansfield Chambers, also raised concerns that in such cases, the extensive publicity might mean people would feel more reluctant to come forward with information in such cases, lest it be aired in public.

Theresa May, the Home Secretary, announced new time limits this year for police bail in an attempt to limit the duration of the 'legal limbo' facing those under investigation but not charged for an offence.

The former Labour Home Secretary told the *Financial Times* that this was vital, especially now that suspects' names were often circulated on social media. 'The problem is that there does not seem to be much urgency with which these lines of inquiries are being pursued,' the former minister said.

The two lawyers quoted, as far as I am aware, did not make their voices heard clearly eight months earlier when Detective Superintendent McDonald made his pronouncement that 'Nick' was 'credible and true'. When the Metropolitan Police Service in Operation Midland were appealing for 'victims' to come forward, indicating that they would be believed, these lawyers did not question whether police media pronouncements would have the effect on proceedings they attributed more recently to me. Peter Garsden might have declared a professional interest in that, since 1994, he has been head of a child abuse department in his practice and deals in child abuse compensation. Sam Stein QC might have been introduced as 'Counsel for SOIA' (Survivors of Organised and Institutional Abuse). It may be the *FT* who should have declared their interests for them.

When the search of my house was conducted and publicly connected by the police to Operation Midland, I felt deeply that I had been identified, tried and found guilty in the court of public opinion. I strongly felt I needed to respond. These lawyers did not say I had done anything illegal by voicing my opinion. I comprehend my strategy was unusual, not one that lawyers, even unsympathetic ones, would normally recommend, but I doubt very few had represented anyone in my position. I know it was not what was expected of me. I acted as I did for my own peace of mind.

The *Financial Times* article also mentioned the Home Secretary Theresa May's changes on bail time limits in the light of Paul Gambaccini's intolerable experiences. In my case, I find myself in 'legal limbo', and 'social limbo' too, since, unlike Paul, I have not been arrested, let alone charged. I am not even supposed to be a 'suspect'! It is interesting how the police appear to have changed their tactics with regard to bail in these so-called high-profile cases. They had no need to charge me or place me on bail to have the same effect as the arrest had on Paul. These proposed changes in bail limits will not affect me or people in my position, or anyone in similar circumstances, who are identified but not even held to be a 'suspect' by the police.

Like Paul, Sir Cliff Richard's treatment by South Yorkshire Police has been a disgrace. The length of time he has been their target must be intolerable for him, disproportionate and, though I am not a lawyer, I would say it is 'criminal'.

The former Conservative Home Office Minister, quoted in this article, should be aware that I am neither 'rich' nor 'powerful' – nor have I ever been. What astonished me the most, as my flight started to board, was that two former ministers from the Home Office – one Conservative and one Labour – whose comments I actually support, spoke to the *Financial Times* under condition of anonymity, but why? 'Nick's' disease of anonymity appeared to be catching. What are these two former senior government ministers afraid of?

As I watched from abroad, the next three months saw two extraordinary parallel trends. First, the press started to investigate, question and give their opinions on Operation Midland and 'Nick', which they had failed to do before for lack of argument and evidence. Second, the Metropolitan Police Service and Exaro went into reverse on their desire, up to 25 August 2015, for the mainstream media to report their comments. Up to that date, Exaro wanted them to report on these issues and criticised them for not reporting the case, especially the search of my house. But afterwards, a surprising change came about in their attitude. Indeed, the Metropolitan Police Service and Exaro's increasingly garrulous attempts to cover their tracks and slow down the media reached its crescendo in the publication of media advice from the Solicitor General. They wanted the press to keep quiet for fear of upsetting their carefully laid media plans, which were unravelling. It is not easy, but I will try to trace these two interesting and parallel developments briefly. At some future date, I'm sure it will amply reward longer and more detailed research by university academics.

The activities of the Metropolitan Police Service in trying to suppress the media investigating the scandal that is Operation Midland is one of the biggest challenges to press freedom this country has seen for decades. A liberal society must not turn a blind eye because the individuals concerned in the police operation are establishment or Conservative figures. The creation of a quasi-police state by the police itself by refusing to answer questions by journalists or under freedom of information requests is invidious and should be of concern to everyone who loves freedom.

Several reporters have made it clear to me that they could not investigate the workings of Operation Midland because they had no information on exactly what 'Nick' had been alleging or who he was alleging had been involved. If they had some information, quite understandable, legal reasons prevented their speculation about what or who was involved, apart from the leaks or 'drips' of information from Scotland Yard or Exaro, such as on the day of the search of my house. Generally, information was suppressed; that is, until my statement on 25 August, when I laid it all out for them as best as I could. It was, as Rajeev Syal of *The Guardian* wrote on 26 August, 'the first detailed response from anyone investigated by Operation Midland in connection with claims of years of child sexual abuse by a paedophile ring made up of men from politics, the military and law enforcement agencies'.

The descriptions of the press conference and of my remarks by the press and media indicate how 'different' and 'new' they thought it all was. The *Daily Telegraph* said it was 'dramatic'; *The Times* commented on my 'vehement' denials; *The Sun* said it was 'astonishing'; the *Daily Mail* used the word 'sensational'; and *The Independent* described my words as 'extraordinary allegations', a 'blistering attack' and 'sensational'. The column inches the papers devoted to my statement were also significant. The question was, as I relaxed in the sun recharging my batteries, would the press pick up the issues I had raised and run with them? Thankfully, they did.

Giles Whittel said in *The Times* on 27 August that, as Raza, my solicitor, alluded to in the first police interview, 'There are no bodies. There is only one accuser. There is no other evidence. The allegations should never have been made public.' General Beach and Field Marshall Bramall, both in their nineties and the only others alive, apart from myself, were interviewed by the police and reported as saying they were not in the 'Proctor sex gang'. That was a relief, because nor was I. I was not in their 'sex gang' either. There was no 'sex gang' or 'ring' or any loose relationship that drew us together.

I believe none of this existed. It must be a figment of vivid imagination, which has damaged the investigation of genuine child sexual abuse claims by genuine complainants.

John Mann MP enquired, after my statement, 'How does Harvey Proctor know' that these things didn't go on? I know because when he was the Leader of Labour Students, I was in the House of Commons. I know it's fabrication, and wishful thinking on his part, because I was there.

Newspapers became fascinated with the child abuse subject. The *Sunday Times* carried a report on 30 August 2015 by the former police officer who exposed Jimmy Savile as a serial child sex offender, Mark Williams-Thomas. He warned that many of the current allegations against political figures were unsubstantiated and amounted to 'paedophile madness' that could undermine efforts to tackle child abuse. He said behaviour by some in the police, media and on the internet posed 'a very real danger of undoing all the good that has been done' since he uncovered Savile's serial offending. Williams-Thomas also said 'the police in Harvey Proctor's case' were wrong to describe a witness as 'credible and true', since 'determining guilt is ultimately for the courts to decide'.

The *Sunday Times* went on:

> Williams-Thomas's comments will add to pressure on police after their naming of Heath as a possible offender, and the furious reaction of Proctor, a former Tory MP, to the allegations made against him of being involved in the murder of children. Proctor revealed this weekend that the unsubstantiated allegations had forced him to move abroad ... Williams-Thomas said: 'It is clear that a small number of journalists [and] well-placed individuals, including a few politicians, have been determined to

be at the forefront of trying to set out that a significant number of well-organised paedophile rings existed involving politicians both past and present.'

'Sadly, these individuals are not evidence-focused, preferring to pass off rumour as fact and, very worryingly, in a few cases putting pressure on victims of child abuse, which has led them to name high-profile people as offenders. Unfortunately, for some, media headlines and sensational headlines are more important ... Yet three years on, the actions of a few to distort and blow totally out of proportion or to treat unsupported rumour as fact ... has the very real danger of derailing the huge strides that have been made since Savile's exposure.'

In the same newspaper edition, Dominic Lawson, who wrote several lucid articles about these issues, said:

> Proctor's statement also attacked the investigative news agency Exaro. Its business model is partly based on selling stories about 'establishment child abuse' to Labour-supporting tabloids such as the *Sunday People*, and it seems to have 'Nick' at its disposal for such purposes. Most unusually, 'Nick' made his initial statement to the police with an Exaro representative present throughout. The consequent raid on Proctor's home was leaked to the press, even while the police were still on the premises.
>
> The barrister blogger Matthew Scott raised a number of interesting questions about all this: 'Has 'Nick' been paid for his story? Exaro has not let on. Why did he wait until 2014 before contacting the police? Why, for example, did he not do so in 1987 when Proctor was publicly implicated in what was then regarded as a 'gay sex' scandal?'

Whenever Exaro is challenged on this, it defends its conduct by quoting the police officer leading the investigation, Kenny McDonald, who some time ago announced to the BBC that he believed 'Nick's' allegations to be 'credible and true'. As this barrister pointed out, it is 'mind-boggling' that a senior police officer announced on national television that he believed a suspect to be guilty of multiple rape and murder before a single body had been found, and even before speaking to Proctor, the supposed killer.

Exaro does not take kindly to those who would give Proctor the platform that it gives 'Nick'. After the *Independent on Sunday* carried an interview with the former MP last month – in which he said these accusations had cost him his job and his home – Mark Watts, Exaro's editor-in-chief, tweeted that the newspaper had 'become "The Pindie"'. As in the paedophile *Indie*? Charming.

Let me correct one point. Exaro claim they were present only at the first meeting with 'Nick' and the police. They criticised me for using the word 'interview' when I should have said 'meeting' to characterise Exaro's handover of 'Nick' to the police for his debriefing. After all, the police surely must have wanted to know what Exaro had said to 'Nick' as much as what 'Nick' had told Exaro before seeing the police. I am sure in due course this will come out under investigation.

I have not spoken to Dominic Lawson, Mark Williams-Thomas or Giles Whittel, but they contributed magnificently to the 'debunking' of the police's and Exaro's position. Another journalist who should be commended for seeking out the truth on this scandal is Stephen Wright, the associate editor of the *Daily Mail*. He deals with crime issues, and has done so for many years, and he has written many searching articles on 'Nick', Exaro and the Metropolitan

Police Service, shining light on the fantasy others would have preferred to keep dark. Wright summed it up succinctly in an article
he wrote on 18 September 2015 when he said: 'It was possibly the
first time anyone could recall a murder investigation being opened
without any bodies and without anyone knowing who it was that
had actually been murdered.'

Nor were the *Sunday Times* and the *Daily Mail* alone in their attack
on the Metropolitan Police Service and Exaro after my statement. The
Daily Telegraph, *The Times*, *The Sun*, the *Daily Express*, *The Guardian*,
The Independent, the *Independent on Sunday*, the *Mail on Sunday*, the *Sunday Telegraph*, *The Spectator* and many others maintained an onslaught.

It soon became apparent that although 'Nick's' anonymity was
protected in law, the media were intent on finding out as much as
they legally could about him and his background, short of naming
him. By 18 September, the *Daily Mail* was setting out the connections
between 'Nick', Exaro, Peter McKelvie, the whistle-blower to the
Labour Party, and a politician called Tom Watson MP, now deputy
leader of the Labour Party.

Stephen Wright and Paul Bracchi of the *Daily Mail* wrote:

In October 2012, Tom Watson made an extraordinary speech in
the Commons asking David Cameron about claims of a 'powerful paedophile network linked to Parliament and No. 10'.

It was the beginning of another, high-profile personal cru-
sade for Watson.

Like his campaign against phone-hacking in the Murdoch
press, his war on paedophiles not only propelled him back into
the limelight, it also helped his party.

One of the people who supplied Watson with intelligence and
information was a former child protection officer called Peter

McKelvie. In the aftermath of Mr Watson's barnstorming performance in the House, Mr McKelvie spotted a tweet from a
possible victim which read: 'I was abused by the gang.'

The tweet, we have learned, was from 'Nick'. Nick and Watson eventually met.

In an interview with *The Guardian*, Watson spoke about the
meeting. 'It was a very traumatic and difficult conversation, as
you would imagine,' he said.

'He only told me about one murder. He spoke very slowly,
very intermittently, and I didn't need to hear any more.'

'What I am certain is, that he is not delusional. He is either
telling the truth, or he's made up a meticulous and elaborate
story. It's not for me to judge.'

'What I was hoping to do was build a relationship with him
and get him back into the system, so he could make his allegations
to the police. And to make sure he had a degree of protection.'

In the event, Nick did not go to the police – not initially, anyway. 'Nick'
had been a prolific internet fantasist for a number of years, since 2010,
if his Twitter profile is to be believed. During the course of 2015,
he continued to claim anonymity from the police while commenting via the internet on the twists and turns of alleged child abuse
revelations and, in the *Daily Mirror*, on Operation Midland. The Metropolitan Police Service must have put in place a strategic action plan
for monitoring activity on social media, using highly sophisticated
software to analyse the data, and reporting intelligence regularly to
senior police officers. I am sure they will have been watching me,
comments about me, 'Nick' and all his internet fantasists with whom
he interacts. The police have been seeking out new 'victims' – and
where better to find them than among the supportive chatter on

social media, blogs and forums? The 'stakeholders' of Operation Midland will also have contributed to this data. These will be lines of inquiry not in the public arena to which the police often refer. In the light of the Metropolitan Police Service's extensive technological resources and the knowledge they have that nothing has ever been presented on social media to corroborate any of the allegations made against me by 'Nick' and other internet fantasists, and over an extensive period of time, it is hard to come to any other conclusion than this is a 'set-up'.

So in summary, a fantasist – whether mad, mendacious or malicious remains to be seen – makes contact over the internet with a child protection expert (or the expert makes contact with 'Nick'), who introduces him to a Labour politician seeking advancement, who speaks to *The Guardian*, who has a former journalist of theirs who works for a bizarre little news agency called Exaro, which persuades 'Nick' to go to the police rather than to go to the Child Abuse Inquiry, which he had originally planned to do, because its chairman had chopped and changed so many times he gets bored and tired of waiting for his 'five minutes of fame'. You cannot make it up.

Exaro should face serious investigation as to their part in persuading 'Nick' to go to the police and the origin of his stories. Had 'Nick' been to the police before he went to Exaro? And if so, what did he say to the police the first time around? There needs to be clarity as to what 'Nick' said to Exaro and, after meeting representatives of Exaro, what he said to the Metropolitan Police Service – and what accounts for the differences. The manner in which Exaro treated another vulnerable witness, 'Darren', which 'Darren' has admitted, and whether 'Nick' was similarly treated, needs to be considered carefully too. The press have responsibilities in these matters. The Metropolitan Police Service attacked the BBC for showing photographs to 'Nick' of his potential abusers. Exaro did the same but received no such criticism. The Metropolitan Police Service should be asked why they discriminated between the BBC and Exaro in their treatment of identifying people. What links existed between the Metropolitan Police Service and Exaro?

Every day, for weeks, I was contacted by journalists from a variety of newspapers seeking clarification of points contained in my statement. It paved the way for their investigative articles. Very early on, Tom Symonds, the home affairs correspondent who had interviewed 'Nick', who asked me questions at my press conference and is in the News Department 'camp' of the BBC, rang me.

He quoted a newspaper article in the *Daily Telegraph* that inferred I had fled the country; I explained I had not. If the Metropolitan Police Service wished to arrest me and charge me, I said I would be on the next flight back to the United Kingdom. However, in the light of the uselessness of the second interview session with the police, I would not return voluntarily for a third interview unless I saw a full disclosure document setting out exactly what it was the police wished to discuss with me. I thought I was being interviewed for the BBC when Symonds spoke to me but while none of my words were used by the BBC, within hours this information was on Exaro's website. I was not best pleased; I might as well have telephoned Exaro directly.

In his defence, Symonds sent me this email:

> I needed a bit more space to explain than on a text message.
> Just to reiterate: I do not work with Exaro in any way. Frankly
> their editorial standards regarding what constitutes evidence
> and corroboration don't come close to ours. Mark Watts is an
> unlikeable character, he has criticised my work on Twitter and
> accuses the BBC of 'covering up' the matters you made public

last week. We have not run the stories Exaro has because we can't corroborate them.

Your message gave me the impression you felt I had somehow fed your comments to Exaro / Watts – this is absolutely not the case. We are rival news organisations with differing views of how to cover this difficult story.

After we spoke earlier I felt that your comments would help our audience understand your position better than the newspaper reports. If I'm honest, I probably overestimated the newsworthiness of what you said, but part of my job is to make the case for the BBC covering stories I am involved with reporting.

I filed the following copy to the BBC's internal wire service (seen by editors across radio, TV and online) at 11.51:

The former Conservative MP Harvey Proctor has denied he has fled abroad following the press conference last week during which he argued he is innocent of allegations of child abuse and murder.

Mr Proctor told the BBC he may return to the UK next year, but would be 'on the first plane home' if police wanted to charge or arrest him before that.

However, he said, having given eight hours of interviews to the police, he would not be making himself available for further questioning.

Speaking by mobile phone he said he was currently living in a European country with friends, working on his memoirs, and had returned briefly to the UK to hold last week's incendiary press conference.

Harvey Proctor said he began planning to move abroad part-time in October last year, after making a decision to go part-time at his job as an events manager at Belvoir Castle in Leicestershire.

However he left that job and had to give up the tenancy of a house in the grounds of the castle following a police raid in March by Metropolitan Police officers working on Operation Midland.

The investigation is examining a claim of child abuse and pos-
sible homicides involving a group of influential men in the late '70s
and early '80s. Mr Proctor's accuser is a man in his forties known by
the pseudonym 'Nick'.

Mr Proctor said he would not be prepared to undertake 'another
charade' by agreeing to a third round of questioning. But he said he
would answer questions posed by police via his solicitor.

He has claimed that before his first interview police told him he
was not a suspect.

Last week he strongly criticised the Met for pursuing what he called
a 'homosexual witch-hunt' based on the allegations of a 'fantasist'.
He was particularly angry that early in the inquiry a senior officer said
he believed the claims were 'credible and true'.

At the same time, I also told Symonds, in confidence, in which country
I was living abroad at that time. Within a day or two that confidential
information was being discussed on the internet, with one person
threatening to 'do me in', or words to that effect. I will return to the
BBC News Department in due course, but I think they should have
made more inquiries to substantiate the accuracy of both 'Nick's'
and Superintendent McDonald's remarks before they so freely gave
airtime to both of their felonious notions. What steps did the BBC
News Department take to corroborate 'Nick's' allegations before
they broadcast them? Or was the corroboration the words of the
Superintendent? I think I should be told. Both the Metropolitan Police
Service and the broadcasting authorities should learn the lessons of
the errors of their past incestuous relationship. It would be in the
public interest if the BBC, while protecting their actual sources, gave
an indication of the general nature of their source – police or journalist or anonymous 'victim' would be quite sufficient.

Meanwhile, the other 'wing' of the BBC on this issue, *Panorama*, was also keeping in touch with me, still wanting to interview me for their programme entitled 'The VIP Paedophile Ring: What's the Truth?' They had wanted me to be interviewed on this subject for months. I declined because the interview, inevitably, would not be live, and not because I was afraid to be interviewed, unlike Mark Watts of Exaro who was, obviously, scared stiff of being cross-examined.

In the weeks of this constant interest, however, one thing was crystal clear – the words 'credible and true' had entered the lexicon as a euphemism for 'unsubstantiated and false'. The impact on me was profound. I wrestled every day with an acute feeling of sadness. I was fearful it might pervade the writings in this book. While having no links with generals, I also felt a profound sorrow for Lord Bramall in experiencing the loss of his wife while in the middle of these matters. I felt sorry for Beach, too; neither should have to face these appalling allegations for so long, especially at their ages. I also felt sorrow for Lord Brittan's wife, struggling to come to terms with her husband's death amidst these allegations. I felt sadness in my own predicament, though I remained convinced that my speaking out, lancing the secretive boil, had been the right decision. Had I withheld the names of others, I would have been viewed with suspicion by the media. Virtually the whole of the democratic press in the UK, journalists and columnists, had spoken. I now wanted proof that I was right to have revealed all. It turned out I had not long to wait.

The proof started to come on 21 September 2015, in the form of a 1,200-word statement in which the Metropolitan Police Service effectively said that 'Nick' was 'credible' but not 'true'. Of course, they did not exactly say that clearly, but that is what they meant. It was a very confusing diatribe they placed into the media arena, written, I believe, by many different hands. Among other things, they said:

Our starting point with allegations of child sexual abuse or serious sexual assault is to believe the victim until we identify reasonable cause to believe otherwise. That is why, at the point at which we launched our initial appeal on Midland, after the witness had been interviewed for several days by detectives specialising in homicide and child abuse investigations, our senior investigating officer stated that he believed our key witness and felt him to be 'credible'. Had he not made that considered, professional judgment, we would not have investigated in the way we have … We must add that while we start from a position of believing the witness, our stance then is to investigate without fear or favour, in a thorough, professional and impartial fashion, and to go where the evidence takes us without pre-judging the truth of the allegations. That is exactly what has happened in this case … [We] acknowledge that describing the allegations as 'credible and true' suggested we were pre-empting the outcome of the investigation. We were not. We always retain an open mind as we have demonstrated by conducting a thorough investigation.

The Metropolitan Police Service said 'Nick' was 'credible and true' in December 2014. He was not only their 'key' complainant; he was their only complainant. Their Detective Superintendent was not 'impartial' or 'professional', and his view from the top, supported by his superiors, permeated the entire Operation Midland investigation, as can be seen from the excerpts from the two interviews his officers had with me, and in other ways. But 'truth' was now dropped from the vocabulary of Operation Midland. In fact, it had been lacking from the start of the inquiry. There was an acknowledgement but no apology. Interestingly, Exaro had stopped using 'credible and true' and replaced it with 'credible' a week or so before this police

statement was issued. Did they know which way the wind was turning before the Met's formal statement? Was there more collusion,
even at that stage?

The rest of the police statement was a rambling attack on the
media for their reporting of 'Nick' and his allegations. There were
warnings and threats concerning the risk that media interference
would affect or even compromise their investigations: 'There are
particular challenges where details of the allegations and those facing accusations are in the public domain. This can create potential
conflicts between media and criminal investigations, and have an
impact on vulnerable witnesses and those accused. This has been
especially true in Operation Midland,' they said.

The police now admitted that allegations were in 'the public
domain' (they placed them there themselves in December 2014) and
that they have an effect not just on 'vulnerable witnesses' but also
on 'those accused'. It is the Metropolitan Police Service who were
responsible for the names of some, if not all, those 'facing accusations' coming into the public domain. But it is interesting that they
use the minimum of language to discuss the position of the 'accused'
compared with that of 'victims' in a totally unbalanced statement.
Indeed, it is interesting that they use the word 'accused' at all.

Their statement continued:

> We would also like to make it clear that the Metropolitan Police
> Service does not name or confirm names of those arrested or
> interviewed. That is our clear policy. We will be as open as we
> can be about policing activity – for example confirming arrest
> activity – but not confirming the names of individuals. If a police
> employee revealed the name that would be a clear breach of
> policy and dealt with in the appropriate manner. Moreover,

the Commissioner told the Home Affairs Select Committee in March that he supports the proposal for granting accused people anonymity until charged.

Of course, quintessentially, this is nonsense, as the Metropolitan Police Service released sufficient information officially – who knows what unofficially – to identify me before the police left my house on 4 March 2015. Lords Brittan and Bramall were in the media two days later. In addition, the police have admitted they told 'Nick' about the search of my home. It was almost stated that they had to under the code of practice for victims, although I can see no mention of disclosure of searches to 'victims' in the code. At the very least the police must recognise the connection. Or are they saying that they do not mind the leaking of names, just that they will not confirm whether they have done so or not?! The Commissioner is talking here of anonymity of 'suspects'. The police have said I am not a 'suspect'. If they changed their mind, I was not informed. Suddenly, their statement talks about 'the accused'!

It continued:

> In recent weeks, one journalist reporting on Operation Midland has shown the purported real identity of someone making an allegation of sexual assault to a person who has disclosed that they have been questioned by police concerning those allegations. This action has a number of potential impacts. First, for those who have made allegations of sexual abuse, it is extremely distressing to discover that their identity might have been given to anyone else, particularly if that is to someone who may be involved in the case. Secondly, possible victims or witnesses reading the article may believe their identities could be revealed as well, which could

deter them from coming forward. Ultimately, that could make it harder for allegations to be proved or disproved. This might not just deter those who could provide information for this investigation but also concern anyone thinking of coming forward with sexual abuse allegations. Finally, the potential disclosure by a journalist of a name may possibly hamper an investigation.

This warning was police sabre-rattling to the press. The police were fed up with the more than one-month-long, continuous press attack upon them. They were frightened; they wanted the press to shut up. The love affair with the media was at an end. The freedom of the press was to be preserved for police and Exaro appeals for 'victims' to come forward who would be 'believed' and 'supported' but any journalist criticising the manner of Operation Midland's investigation techniques was to be persecuted.

This was, for the Met, the first of two concerted press campaigns. The next one would be in February 2016 when Sir Bernard Hogan-Howe took to the airwaves to proclaim, unfortunately for him, that Operation Midland was a very good investigation, but for one word: 'true'. Nick Ferrari on LBC led him, unknowingly, into a trap. The Commissioner defended his Superintendent (McDonald) by saying twice that his officer used the words 'credible and true' 'in making a quick recourse' in an interview and then again, that his officer used the words 'credible and true' 'very quickly in the interview', that 'one interview and one word does not make a closed mind'. At this point of the radio interview, Sir Bernard looked decidedly shifty and uncomfortable. It was because he was not correct. McDonald's mind had closed to the truth.

McDonald said on his BBC News Department interview on 18 December 2014 that 'Nick' had been spoken to by murder detectives and specialist child abuse investigators.

They [the apparent police crème de la crème police experts] and I believe what 'Nick' is saying to be credible and true, hence why we are investigating the allegations he has made to us ... I appeal to men who were subjected to abuse thirty years ago to come forward. We are investigating the murder of three young boys – we are determined to find answers.

Let us look to see what Superintendent Kenny McDonald actually said and how he said it.

It was not a 'quick' comment. He made it slowly and deliberately direct to a BBC camera. He was not 'roughed up' by the interviewer; he was composed. It was not a throwaway line. After he used the phrase, he was asked a question by the BBC interviewer concerning these words. Was it a mantra with all 'victims' of child sexual abuse or specifically with 'Nick's' allegations? He repeated the same words that 'the team and I believe what "Nick" is saying is "credible and true"' for a second time – again, slowly and deliberately. Unfortunately for Sir Bernard, he also said something else.

Within the briefing I have just given, we know the abuse has taken place in London, the Home Counties and within certain, military establishments. But the focus of the appeal today is Dolphin Square ... I appeal to young men to come forward. 'Nick' has shown great courage by coming forward. We need others to come forward. You will be believed. You will be supported.

Sir Bernard wanted LBC listeners to believe his Superintendent had just 'misspoken' in a 'quick' moment of, let us not put too fine a point on it, stupidity in front of a television camera. He had not. He had just briefed all of the press on Operation Midland at Scotland Yard, before the BBC interview. I have spoken to two senior reporters who were present at the briefing of the press earlier. The Superintendent had also used exactly the same words, that 'Nick' was 'credible and true', quite deliberately there too. It was the party line. The use of these words was intended and purposeful. This was no slip of the tongue because McDonald, and other senior officers, including DAC Steve Rodhouse, did believe 'Nick' was 'credible' – in his appearance, in his profession, in his voice and in his demeanour – he would make a good witness – and because they thought his allegations were also 'credible and true'. Why was this? I can only imagine it was because they wanted them to be 'true'. 'We know the abuse has taken place...' said McDonald. It was a fact, there was no doubt about it. 'Nick' was 'believed'. Whether he was 'supported', how and at what cost, the Metropolitan Police Service refuse to say.

His purpose at the briefing and during the interview was to whet the appetite of the media, so his appeal for 'victims to come forward' was well covered. The culture of believing 'victims' was given practical effect. The theory had been born earlier, as I shall explain and analyse later. The police would undo all their past sins of ignoring child sexual abuse – disbelief, Savile and all that – they just needed to communicate the message.

The BBC believed the Superintendent. He was the corroboration for 'Nick's' allegations. That love affair with the media lasted until 25 August 2015.

Sir Bernard must know all this. Had this flawed strategy come from the top? Her Majesty's Inspector of Constabulary, Tom Winsor, in November 2014, coincidentally when the Met was interviewing 'Nick', had told all police, 'The presumption that a victim should always be believed should be institutionalised.' A complaint of sexual abuse henceforth had to be reported immediately as a 'crime'. But Hogan-Howe did not demur. After Hogan-Howe's second PR campaign in February 2016, the Commissioner and the HMIC fell out over exactly what the HMIC's report actually meant: was it all 'victims' should be believed; or all allegations of sexual abuse should be reported for statistical purposes, not *necessarily* be believed?

It took my statement on 25 August 2015, a sustained press campaign and much heartache before Sir Bernard owned up in an article in *The Guardian* on 11 February 2016 that it was wrong to blindly believe complainants. Even then, he blamed his investigating officers for following the 'advice' and asked a retired judge, Sir Richard Henriques, to give him supporting 'fire cover' for his acceptance of such common sense ideas for fear of taking any initiative himself, and the flack his action would create.

There is no doubt he and his senior acolytes should have resigned before now for what happened on 18 December 2014. If he pleads ignorance to the Scotland Yard press briefing, where the most sensational of statements were to be made during his tenure of office, he deserves the sack for not being in control of his organisation. If he knew about the briefing, he deserves the sack for lying on LBC. If he failed to watch his Superintendent's statement and interview on the BBC, he should be sacked for lack of command and insufficient intelligence.

If Sir Bernard thought that his misleading LBC interview and the Met's tawdry statement would have a calming effect on the disastrous media situation in which they found themselves, he was sadly mistaken. The press returned to the fight.

The Guardian asked me for a statement on the police's partial climb-down and I replied:

> I feel I have had to do my own fair share of dexification because
> of the toxic nature of the accusations of murder and child sexual

abuse levied against me. This has had a devastating impact on my life.

Yesterday's confused public relations statement by Scotland Yard marks the beginning of what I believe is their exit strategy from Operation Midland.

These people are like burglars. They raid your home without consent and without any regard for the consequences. It's not what they take. It's what they leave behind.

I can foresee within the next twelve months:

- No evidence to corroborate 'Nick's' fantasy allegations will be forthcoming;
- Sir Bernard Hogan-Howe, Pat Gallan, Steve Rodhouse and Kenny McDonald will fall like a pack of cards;
- Nick will be prosecuted or sectioned;
- Exaro will cease to exist;
- The use of 'credible and true' by people in positions of influence will mean 'unsubstantiated and false';
- This torture for me and others wrongly accused will finally be at an end and I will be able to sleep at night and quietly get on with what is left of my life.

Parts of my remarks were also carried by the *Daily Telegraph*. Both newspapers incorrectly replaced the word 'dexification', which means a mix of 'to defend, to justify and to explain', with 'detoxification'!

Back in 2015, domesticity intruded again and, on Wednesday 23 September, together with Adam, I went to my nearest big city to do shopping and, incredibly, I was subjected to an attempt to pick my wallet by two men at an underground car park. I wish I had had my dogs with me. I survived with my wallet intact.

On the same day, ITV regional news went to elaborate lengths (for not much effect) in covering my position on 'credible and true', while more articles appeared on Chief Inspector Paul Settle and his part in the investigation relating to the late Lord Brittan. *Panorama* was still appealing for me to be recorded for their programme when, on Friday 25 September 2015, the law officers of the government, obviously pushed by the Home Office and by the Metropolitan Police Service, got in on the act. The Solicitor General, Sir Robert Buckland QC, MP issued a media advice to editors, publishers and social media users urging them to 'avoid identifying complainants in sexual abuse cases'.

Issued through the Attorney General's office, Sir Robert said:

> An allegation of a sexual offence has been made, no matter relating to the complainant shall be included in a publication if it is likely to lead to members of the public identifying him. Publishing such material is a criminal offence and could be subject to prosecution.
>
> In addition, while the Solicitor General recognises the legitimate public interest in the press commenting on cases of this nature, he wishes to draw attention to the risk of publishing material that gives the impression of pre-judging the outcome of the investigation and any criminal proceedings that may follow, or which might prejudice any such proceedings.
>
> The Attorney General's office will be monitoring the ongoing coverage of Operation Midland and editors and publishers should take legal advice to ensure they are in a position to comply with their legal obligations.

This was a bit like a 'D' notice. It was hardly reported by the media itself. At least Sir Robert's statement used my suggested word of 'complainant' rather than 'victim' or 'survivor'. It castigated the media, and warned them against even publishing stories that 'gives the <u>impression</u> of pre-judging the outcome' of Operation Midland. Had not 'Nick', the key witness, and an Exaro reporter through the Mirror Group not identified alleged 'abusers' under investigation by Operation Midland on 18 April 2015? Had not the Metropolitan Police Service just tentatively apologised for doing even more than that by using the phrase 'credible and true' on 18 December 2014? That was pre-judgement; the police were the main culprits. Was Sir Robert going to take action against the police? Of course not; and all the time the looming edifice of the *Panorama* programme was frightening Exaro, the Metropolitan Police Service and others. Sir Robert did volunteer to watch the *Panorama* programme on Tuesday 6 October during the Conservative Party conference, although I can find no trace of his comments about it after the programme was broadcast.

Panorama's programme was the muck cart following on from the Lord Mayor's Show. It emphasised the lines of attack the media had deployed since 25 August 2015. It lambasted the police, certain politicians, including Tom Watson, internet fantasists and Exaro. It carefully said little about Operation Midland, with one important exception. It demonstrated how one of 'Nick's' allegations, the alleged murder of a young boy in Kingston upon Thames, did not take place in the time frame suggested. It was a very helpful summary. One wonders why the Metropolitan Police Service did not ascertain that one of their alleged three murders was an illusion before proceeding to publicise them. They were too lazy; they wanted the press to do the work for them. If Exaro could produce 'Nick' and others, maybe the mainstream media could produce so many more 'survivors' to corroborate the initial testimony. All the police had to do was to appear 'supportive', 'believing' and 'thankful' to those who came forward. The trouble was, unlike in the Savile case, where hundreds appeared as a result of police appeals, no one did. Well, Exaro produced a so-called ex-lover of mine who supposedly knew me for three months in 1979, who said he knew nothing of the 'Nick' allegations and who Terry and I did not know (we were living together at this time). We could not know Exaro's lothario because they also kept his identity anonymous. We both knew he must be a fake or a liar and an attention-seeker as there was no such person filling that role at that time in my life. Terry says he thinks he might have noticed!

The real question for me was, would the press be cowed by the warning statements of the Metropolitan Police Service and the media advice by the Solicitor General? (Including one from the former on the *Panorama* programme before it was even broadcast, the defensive position now being used by Exaro, who dropped 'true' from their website with regard to 'Nick's' allegations a short time before the Met threw in the towel on the word.) The answer was a clear 'no'. The media took no notice and raised a collective two fingers.

Every hour, there was a new twist and turn in news from London. David Aaronovitch, Dominic Lawson and Stephen Wright piled the pressure on 'Nick', the police and Hogan-Howe, who was renamed by Richard Littlejohn in the *Daily Mail* as 'Bernard Hyphen-Howe', in damning articles. These journalists' articulate words and those of many of their colleagues I believe will be instrumental in the collapse of Operation Midland.

The Times reported 'Darren', 'a vulnerable complainant', had claimed he was manipulated by Exaro and was now critical of them. On Sunday 4 October, Sir Max Hastings leapt to the defence of Lord Bramall in the *Sunday Times*, and that paper also had another article on Lord Brittan. Much of the rest of October's press reports concerned Lord Brittan and the House of Commons select committee meeting scheduled to take evidence on 21 October 2015. Tom Watson MP, for his awful comments about Lord Brittan, taken by Watson straight from the mouth of a 'complainant' with fantasist pretensions, and the Metropolitan Police Service Commissioner were to be in the main line of sight for the committee.

Every day, when I sat thinking the steam must drop out of the subject soon, at least for a few days, the media would find a new line of justifiable attack and inquiry. *The Guardian* placed Zac Goldsmith, the MP for Richmond Park & North Kensington, in the firing line. On the afternoon of 27 November 2014, within days of 'Nick' being taken to the police by Exaro, Goldsmith had made a speech in the Commons. It was a bid to court popularity. He had repeated at length highly damaging allegations from Chris Fay, of internet notoriety, which the *Panorama* programme and others subsequently debunked, accusing Fay of being an unreliable witness. Goldsmith's speech was only drawn to my attention in October 2015. Although he had not mentioned me by actual name (a disease no doubt caught from the Metropolitan Police Service), I thought I should give him the opportunity to withdraw remarks prejudicial to me and to the late Lord Brittan. As he did not, I issued a statement that was printed in *The Guardian*. I said on 14 October 2015:

> I used to own a shop in Richmond upon Thames and it would often be visited by Prof. Teddy Goldsmith. He will not have wished to have seen his nephew smearing me and a former Cabinet minister [Lord Brittan] in his own party. Zac Goldsmith is a disloyal Conservative. He should consider his position as [London] mayoral candidate.

Leon Brittan's brother Samuel also said, 'It would be helpful if Zac Goldsmith clarified his statement and cleared my brother of these claims.' He did not.

In summary, I was saying Zac Goldsmith should step down as Mayoral candidate. As I am sure he will have plenty of time on his hands after that contest in 2016, I hope when Operation Midland collapses, as it will, Goldsmith will admit, on the floor of the House of Commons, that he was wrong and, like so many others even more intelligent than himself, that he was taken in by fantasists and that the 'Westminster paedophile ring' was a mirage. Though his future bid for preferment might, however, get in the way.

On 18 October 2015, the Metropolitan Police Service issued another statement that stated they

> had brought together all the various strands of non-recent child abuse allegations under a newly formed investigation team led by Detective Superintendent Ang Scott. Det. Supt Scott will run Operation Midland and Operation Fairbank, which began in 2012 to look into claims of child abuse at the Elm Guest House in Barnes, south-west London, and at other locations.

What they had not the guts to admit, even at this stage, was that Kenny McDonald was no longer in charge of Operation Midland. He had been, in the words of my statement two months before, 'shifted sideways'; to what we do not know. I thought this move, however unannounced, was another promising step. When asked by the press to comment on McDonald's move, I said, 'It was the first of many,' echoing the comments of John Mann, the Labour MP who said the same about me when my house was searched. I was sorry to learn that the Superintendent had been on sick leave, suffering, it was reported, from stress. I thought he could have saved himself, and a great many others, including myself, 'stress' if he had not been so quick to accept the opinion of others and pre-judge these matters without making proper and prudent inquiries. By mixing the two inquiries, and without admitting it, the police were dumbing down on 'Nick' and Operation Midland.

The statements by the Metropolitan Police Service were not communicated to my solicitors. We had to read about them in the press. Despite regular requests for information and frequent questioning by my solicitors, the Met have been largely silent since August 2015, although just before Christmas 2015 they emailed to say 'we are working to complete this inquiry as quickly as possible, however, it is unlikely that it will be completed before Christmas'. The police have not spoken to me directly for six months.

The timing of the police statement was just before senior officers had to face the Home Affairs Select Committee. Two days before the 'dismissal' statement, on Friday 16 October, more admittance of unprofessionalism started to seep out, if one can call a 1,000-word statement from the Metropolitan Police Service, a force that doesn't usually use 100 words if one will do, a 'seep'; it was more of a 'gush'. Again, in my August statement, I had referred to the disgraceful treatment by the Metropolitan Police Service of Lord Brittan. I said the police knew six months before he died that he would not face prosecution for the alleged rape of a young woman named with the pseudonym 'Jane', but they did not tell him. They just hoped he would die without them having to. What I did not say in my statement, and where the Home Affairs Select Committee did not get it right in their report, is the reason they did not tell him.

The Metropolitan Police Service admitted I was right without acknowledging my criticism. They should have told Lord Brittan that they were to take no action. The Metropolitan Police Service's excuse in their evidence was that it 'feared media criticism and public cynicism'. The Met claimed that, if they did as Detective Chief Inspector Settle was proposing to do, and which the Commons' select committee thought was also appropriate, that is, take no further action, they would be pilloried. The committee rightly lambasts the Metropolitan Police Service for this excuse: 'it risks undermining the whole basis of its investigations and public confidence in the police'. But the select committee stopped short of ascertaining the real reason that the Metropolitan Police Service kept appealing the decision of the Crown Prosecution Service (CPS), keeping the Brittan inquiry 'live', which they did until 24 June 2015 – six days after the police first interviewed me. It is an even more devilish reason because the Metropolitan Police Service will not admit it. They were never questioned about it.

The chairman of the select committee, Keith Vaz MP, the young student who heckled me at university in 1979, rightly would not let the committee discuss 'live' investigations such as Operation Midland. That is also why, when David Winnick (the elder Labour statesman on the committee) requested that the committee invite me to give evidence, his suggestion was rejected. Vaz jumped in whenever one of his fellow MPs on the committee veered towards operational affairs. He was right, but, by doing so, he prevented the real truth from emerging. It was all to do with ongoing operational matters.

The police did not want to drop 'Jane's' allegations against Lord Brittan because another so-called victim had just walked into their offices through the door opened by Exaro and Tom Watson. At the beginning of November 2014, 'Nick' was making allegations concerning historical sexual abuse about a number of people, including Lord Brittan and the other eight, including myself. He had earlier made allegations to the police, but these had not mentioned VIPs or myself. This only occurred after 'Nick' had talked to Exaro. The police established Operation Midland on 14 November 2014, as a result of 'Nick'.

Two unconnected people – complainants – were now making allegations against Lord Brittan. The Met was not going to close the file on one, having just opened a file on another, so Deputy Assistant Commissioner Rodhouse appealed the decision of 22 November 2014, made by the CPS, so that they could keep the matter of 'Jane's' allegations against Lord Brittan open while they simultaneously dealt with 'Nick's' allegations. In addition, though we do not know the details as yet, certain disgruntled former police officers had submitted complaints to the IPCC concerning alleged termination of investigations into VIPs. These were on Deputy Assistant Commissioner Rodhouse's desk and there had been speculation as to who might be involved in these matters.

This is the same DAC Steve Rodhouse, in gold command of Operation Midland, who was interviewed on the BBC *Today* programme on 21 March 2015 and who appealed for victims to come forward. He was desperate as none had. He was closely questioned on Operation Midland and was happy to answer all questions about it other than when he was asked, repeatedly, if there was any corroboration of 'Nick's' allegations, either by evidence or other 'victims'. He prevaricated and repeatedly said, 'It would not be right to comment on operational matters.' He said even to say if they had any other 'witnesses' would 'compromise the investigation'. He was hiding behind the cloak of operational matters to avoid having to tell the truth: there were no other 'victims', and that is why he was appealing for them to come forward, 'with confidence' that they would be believed. He was asked about the search of Bramall's and my homes but refused to comment. He knew he did not have to – the association had already been made. Our homes – and those of Lord Brittan – had been searched on the sole strength of 'Nick's' remarks. It was a fishing operation. He said he had every confidence in 'Nick', he was 'credible' but that the police were 'challenged' as no others had come forward. Rodhouse referred to 'Nick' as 'this young man' frequently, even though he is actually forty-seven! Rodhouse also said he believed they 'were getting somewhere with these wider inquiries' but failed to elaborate. He again appealed for more 'victims' to come forward. This was the same Rodhouse who had been criticised for not investigating Savile thoroughly. In the Brittan case, and in Operation Midland, he was evidently seeking to make amends.

The select committee failed to mention the outstanding involvement of Lord Brittan in Operation Midland and, as a result, certain journalists have fallen into the trap of assuming that the Metropolitan Police Service's wishy-washy 'apology' to Lord Brittan's widow concerning 'Jane' acquits him of all sexual-abuse allegations. It does not and will not until the Metropolitan Police Service pulls down the shutters on Operation Midland. I am sorry if in writing this I cause any further pain or distress to Lady Brittan, but I feel this catalogue of horror will only finally come to an end when the real position is plainly seen. However, if the Metropolitan Police Service follows the same procedure with Operation Midland as it did with Lord Brittan's inquiry in Operation Vincente, when there was only one 'victim' of 'Jane' and the one incident, how much longer can the Met spin out their investigations into the many incidents that 'Nick' alleges took place, at many locations on many dates over six years, including three murders?

As I near the end of writing this book, Operation Midland has been ongoing for well over one year. Nine months after Rodhouse refused to answer questions concerning corroboration, no bodies have been found, no names of the alleged murder victims have been announced and no corroborating 'victims' have come forward. Perhaps Rodhouse is waiting to make his annual appeal for 'victims' to be brave so he can support and believe them. To give one example of how the police have failed to investigate these matters expeditiously, two Operation Midland police officers drove all the way to Cumbria from London on 17 September 2015 to interview, without notice, a friend of mine who was at the University of York with me for one overlapping year. It was Jonathan Denby. He was not at home. The officers insensitively handed his wife a card upon which was written Metropolitan Police Paedophile Unit, or words to that effect. She was understandably shocked and alarmed as one of her teenage daughters was in the house and staff were in the vicinity. (I think the police needs retraining in public relations and in sensitivity.) The police officers then drove south, stayed overnight at a hotel, and went to interview my friend the next morning; this time by arrangement, just outside London. My university days ended nine years before the first of 'Nick's' allegations about me are supposed to have occurred. Jonathan's statement amounted to 400 words. He told them the allegations against me were nonsense and, according to Jonathan, they 'sort of nodded in agreement'. It turned out that the police had been advised to interview my friend by a journalist! In the spirit of 'holding power to account', I wonder if the Metropolitan Police Service or that journalist will own up, admit the nature of the conversation with the police and say why and for what reason he suggested the police should interview my friend and so want to elongate these inquiries?

The select committee also overlooked a rather important statement in their deliberations that had been made by DCI Settle in his evidence on Tom Watson. While being questioned by MPs, Settle confirmed that Tom Watson MP was a 'stakeholder' in Operation Midland and that 'within the Strategic Overview and the Gold Group we had various other stakeholders ... who have been of great assistance to us'. He said of Tom Watson, 'I don't regret keeping him informed because I am a firm believer that, once you have a stakeholder in an investigation, it is key – you do more harm to ostracise him than it would have done good.' I also find it extraordinary that DCI Settle only found it a 'betrayal ... and a very low blow' when Watson went over his head and appealed in writing to the Director of Public Prosecutions (DPP) concerning his decision not to interview Lord Brittan.

Settle thought there was insufficient evidence to establish that any crime had been committed by Brittan. This view was supported by the Crown Prosecution Service. It never altered its position. Watson, pressurised by 'Jane', disagreed. The Metropolitan Police Service sided with Watson, removed Settle from his duties and continued to hassle Lord Brittan, including interviewing him about a non-crime. This interview under caution was regarded by Settle to be illegal but this was disputed by senior Met officers.

Settle was not in any way uncomfortable with his relationship with Watson – until things went wrong. He should never have allowed a situation to develop, sanctioned by his senior officers, where his personal feeling of 'betrayal' was allowed to be laid bare when the relationship with Watson went wrong. While Settle and Watson were on good terms, Settle thought that having close relations with an MP, holding frequent meetings with him and discussing cases with him, was in order. They thought it was better to have Watson inside the tent than outside it. I believe it was not. It is ridiculous that no one thought of the party political connotations of such a cosy bunk-up.

A Labour MP working as a 'stakeholder' with the police in its investigation of a former Conservative Cabinet minister? It should have been obviously preposterous. I am surprised the select committee did not criticise this relationship in the first place. This and any other similar relationships are bound to sabotage police operations. It would have been better if the select committee had warned the Met off any such present and future intimate arrangements.

Subsequently, my solicitors have asked the Metropolitan Police Service several times if Tom Watson or Exaro or anyone else was or is a 'stakeholder' in Operation Midland. Both 'Jane' and 'Nick' were 'forwarded' to the police by Watson and Exaro. It was for this reason that Watson was allowed to keep an eye on 'Jane's' investigation as a 'stakeholder'. The police saw them in each other's incestuous company. Despite being promised a reply by the Metropolitan Police Service, deadlines for their answer passed and at the time of writing no reply has been obtained to our questions, a lack of expediency that intrigues me. Their very latest reply to my solicitors, just before Christmas 2015, did not answer the question. I am not asking them to provide a 'running commentary' on Operation Midland, so why are they so reticent? In the light of this reluctance to answer, I have come to my own conclusion on the matter, but I could not possibly comment here.

Among other noteworthy incidents during evidence-taking by the select committee on Lord Brittan was when Assistant Commissioner Patricia Gallan, standing in for Sir Bernard Hogan-Howe, who was on operational matters in the Gulf, referred to Paul Gambaccini's two complainants in his abandoned case as 'victims'. Scotland Yard's mindset is thoroughly fixated and despicable on these matters and they are badly in need of re-education. Suffolk Police abandoned their investigation of another case involving a person with a pseudonym of 'Darren' for lack of corroborative evidence, but still told him they believed him.

By the end of October, of the various matters I had raised in my statement on 25 August 2015, three had been addressed and admitted as correct by the Metropolitan Police Service. 'True' had been removed, albeit furtively, from the phrase 'credible and true'. The Metropolitan Police Service had apologised, although weakly, to Lady Brittan for not letting her husband know before he died that they were to take no further action against him with regard to 'Jane's' allegations. One of the officers in charge of Operation Midland, Superintendent McDonald, had been removed surreptitiously. All of this was done with the utmost possible ill grace by the Metropolitan Police Service. I doubt any of that would have occurred without me speaking on 25 August 2015.

The media reported and commented upon the select committee hearing with gusto, though not picking up connections with Operation Midland. Tom Watson's whistle-blower, Peter McKelvie, was reported to have fallen out with him, saying he had exaggerated his claims in the House of Commons in 2012. He also left the IICSA (Independent Inquiry into Child Sexual Abuse) as its expert adviser on child abuse when his expertise and professional judgement was called into question. The costs of Operation Midland were criticised, but the full truth of it was still not known. The Metropolitan Police Service refused to answer Freedom of Information requests about a whole range of issues concerning Operation Midland, too, which shows how sensitive they regarded their position to be.

Most days, the writing of this book was interrupted by telephone calls tracing the latest press reports, the up-to-the-minute state of play on Operation Midland, but nothing official was reported; it has all been conjecture. As I draw my remarks to a close, the general view is that it is only a matter of time until its collapse and how the upper ranks of Scotland Yard were going to explain it. The timing of the end of Operation Midland could have a connection with the timing of the re-appointment of Sir Bernard Hogan-Howe as Metropolitan Police Commissioner. The whole operation latterly appears to have been more closely connected with the career prospects of the Met's top brass than any actual evidence.

The government's public inquiry, initially launched by the Home Secretary Theresa May within a month of seven MPs – including Zac Goldsmith – writing to her in June 2014 demanding one, lost two chairmen, Lady Butler-Sloss and Fiona Woolf, and was re-formed as a Statutory Inquiry under the Inquiries Act 2005 on 4 February 2015. This public inquiry was a knee-jerk reaction by the government in response to the failure of police and institutions to the Savile revelations. Hogan-Howe has used its creation as justification for Operation Midland. Participants in this story feed off, and cry in aid of, one another. The inquiry was meant to examine how English and Welsh institutions handled their duty of care to child sexual abuse issues. Lady Goddard was appointed chairman in February 2015. The reformed Independent Inquiry into Child Sexual Abuse (the IICSA, known also since February as the 'Goddard Inquiry') had a bad start, losing senior staff and receiving complaints, until it announced on Friday 27 November 2015 details of the first twelve parts of their inquiry. One of these includes child abuse links to Westminster and, although they have refrained from using the word 'ring', Lady Goddard uses the words 'victims' and 'survivors' throughout its long opening statement. It is already a biased, unbalanced and flawed inquiry. There is nothing to convince me that the chairman is not assuming it's all true before a scrap of evidence has been uncovered, in exactly the same way as the police treated

'Nick's' allegations. The inquiry has also been given powers to compel sworn testimony.

My statement of 25 August suggested that the inquiry should investigate Operation Midland; I have since reconsidered my view. I thought about this rushed, depressing and extremely expensive policy mistake of establishing this inquiry and I have determined, even though it has powers to 'call' people under sanction, that, if asked, I will not respond to the call. I believe it will turn into a charade, a curiosity and the longest-running show in town. I will personally have no part of it. Where will Operation Midland end and Operation Goddard begin? Will 'Nick's' allegations be scrutinised yet again, this time by the inquiry? Will they enlist DAC Rodhouse to appeal for more 'victims' to come forward? I intend to comment further on this inquiry in my analysis.

The media continued their pressure on the police until terrorism in France and elsewhere quite rightly put a temporary stop to their investigations and interest. However, I woke up on Thursday 10 December 2015 to find it had started again. *The Times* revealed that they had spoken to 'Darren', a person who complained to the Suffolk Constabulary, and to the Metropolitan Police Service, about alleged VIP sex abuse, only for Suffolk to determine not to pursue his allegations. He informed the newspaper that 'Exaro' had tried to put pressure on him to make allegations against people by showing him photographs, including of myself. He said:

> I had to tell them that I never met Proctor – I feel rather sorry for him now. I want the authorities to realise that adult survivors should be allowed to tell their stories and walk away. They shouldn't be hounded. I've been through two and a half years of hell because of these people.

It is interesting that 'Darren', an extremely vulnerable man, criticises the very people – certain journalists, campaigners, politicians and the police – who have gone to such extraordinary lengths to get such testimony as his into the public domain. 'Darren' said 'he wished he had never spoken out about his allegations of child abuse and wanted no further contact with detectives who were still trying to investigate his claims'. His criticism is not of 'alleged abusers'; his fear is not that they have prevented him speaking out. It is interesting, too, that these people who supposedly profess to be so 'child friendly', having found him unable to deliver the goods, persuaded social services to look into 'Darren's' family.

It is my understanding that Exaro conducted a photographic test with 'Darren' on a commuter train during which he was shown photographs of myself and others and asked to identify me. This took place in December 2014, more than two months before my house was searched by the police. Exaro knew before November 2014 that 'Nick' had 'named' me to them, in circumstances which are still not altogether clear, but which are likely to have used a photographic test too. It is my understanding that the Metropolitan Police Service have discussed Exaro's methods in connection with these photographic testing procedures and, according to Exaro, are 'satisfied' with their procedures. Why is the Metropolitan Police Service discussing with any investigative internet news website, let alone Exaro, their procedures for testing witnesses in evidentiary matters? And why have they given Exaro their authority and badge of satisfaction? How can Exaro have followed correctly the complicated identification procedures contained in long codes of practice? Exaro's Mark Watts told *The Times*:

> We have carried out picture tests with witnesses in order to help
> identify people. When carrying out such tests, Exaro shows

a selection of photographs that includes pictures of 'persons not of interest'. The police, in relation to Operation Midland, have made clear to us that they are satisfied with how we undertake picture tests.

Which only confirms that the links of which I am complaining exist!

I am indebted to a commentator to *The Times* who summarised the position admirably:

> I find that very difficult to believe to be frank. It would almost certainly invalidate any subsequent police attempt at similar ID procedures and be open to challenge in court as to its credibility and admissibility. Police ID procedures are rigidly structured and strictly controlled, being conducted only by officers specifically trained in them and adhering to the Police and Criminal Evidence Act.

Despite this commentator's disbelief, Watts has confirmed 'Darren's' account concerning photograph tests. Did Exaro give the same tests to 'Nick' before he went to the Metropolitan Police Service? Is this the reason the Metropolitan Police Service are so reticent in showing me the photograph of myself they used with 'Nick' for identification purposes? Was it the same photograph shown to Nick and them by Exaro?

In light of these continuing and astonishing revelations, on Friday 11 December I asked, through *The Times*, for an independent inquiry to be conducted into the relationship between Exaro and the Metropolitan Police Service and, in particular, detectives on Operation Midland. I said:

> I want to uncover what links existed between Exaro and Scotland Yard officers in Operation Midland throughout the whole of

this inquiry. A police force, other than the Metropolitan Police, should establish exactly what Exaro was doing with vulnerable witnesses like 'Darren' and, now I come to think about it more closely, also 'Nick', and whether the law has been broken.

To be clear, I believe an independent inquiry should investigate the relationship between the Metropolitan Police Service and detectives concerning Operation Midland, other historical child abuse inquiries and Exaro and any impropriety there may have been between them on the handling of 'Nick', and other alleged 'victims', operational decisions and evidence. I am concerned that information has been leaked by police to Exaro and a criminal investigation should be undertaken. Exaro's role in these matters should also be investigated.

As a result of a curious occurrence, I believe the relationship between the IICSA and the Metropolitan Police Service should also be investigated independently. A man contacted my solicitors with information and, in keeping with the times and in light of what I am to write, quite understandably, he also wished to remain anonymous, so I shall call him 'Bob'.

'Bob' contacted my solicitors following my statement on 25 August 2015 and, as a result, I spoke to him and he emailed me. This is what he had to tell me. He served in the Royal Air Force from 1969 to 1976. In 1970, he was raped and abused for a period of twelve months. He was bullied, assaulted and threatened into not reporting the rapes. In 2011, he plucked up courage and reported it after suffering from post-traumatic stress disorder for forty years. Thames Valley Police (TVP) traced the perpetrator to an African country where he had risen to be the head of his country's air force. At that point, the TVP investigation ended and the Ministry of Defence's silence began. Bob also claims to have been assaulted by the police where he now lives for pursuing his case. 'Bob' reported his abuse to the IICSA and its secretariat, who have been unhelpful, albeit prior to Lady Goddard's appointment as chairman.

In January 2015, 'Bob' received a telephone call from a DC Benjamin J. Lamkin, who claimed he worked for Operation Midland. He had been passed 'Bob's' details by the IICSA's secretariat. Lamkin consistently refused to talk much about 'Bob's' military case of abuse, but repeatedly asked him about a number of names about which he said he was interested – preoccupied – including my own. Another name in which he expressed interest was that of Sir Peter Hayman. 'Bob' had worked as a housing and advice worker in Earl's Court, London from 1979 to 1984 and, among other things, had liaised with rent boys during his work. 'Bob' says he saw and met me very occasionally in Earl's Court. I have no recollection of him. He says there were never any allegations or rumours about me in Earl's Court to his knowledge, other than that I was a discreet homosexual. He says he relayed this to DC Lamkin and went on to tell him that this reputation was unlike that of the late Sir Peter Hayman, who reputedly sat with young lads on his knee in the Craven Club in Craven Street near Charing Cross station. I very rarely went to clubs, gay or otherwise, although it is possible I met 'Bob' at a homosexual or 'mixed' bar in Earl's Court in those six years that he worked in that area. I certainly did not meet 'Bob' at the Craven Club, of which I had no recollection or knowledge until my telephone conversation with him in late August 2015. 'Bob' confirms this.

'Bob' believes, as a result of his conversation with DC Lamkin, that the Metropolitan Police are looking for a 'scapegoat/patsy or three' as a diversion from having to investigate the military or police – 'and you [I] appear to be one'. 'Bob' concluded that 'homophobia in the police has not gone away'.

I have no idea if what he told me – outside my own knowledge – is correct or not, although, following the current police line on believing 'victims' and 'survivors', I found him to be 'credible'.

However, I also have in my possession copies of emails from a DC Lamkin to 'Bob', one of which has an 'Op. Midland' reference upon it and claims to be from DC Ben J. Lamkin, SC05(5), Paedophile Unit, Empress Building, and is dated 6 January 2015, two months before the search of my house. It states:

> I just wanted to check something. You mentioned the Carlton
> Club being somewhere you attended and witnessed young boys
> on the lap of an adult male. Can you confirm I have the name of
> this location correctly? I seem to have written Craven Club but
> feel it's probably an error on my part in writing it down at speed.

On the face of it, there was confusion in DC Lamkin's mind about which club they were talking about; DC Lamkin claims he thought 'Bob' mentioned the Carlton Club, or was he trying to get 'Bob' to confirm one of 'Nick's' locations where abuse took place as a gay club? There is a world of difference between the Conservative gentleman's club in St James, the Carlton Club, and a gay club called the Craven Club. It is interesting that the police do not seem seized of the difference, both here in this incident and in my interview, along with all the connotations that go with it. Or, had DC Lamkin mentioned, in his confused state, the Carlton Club within the office that day to other officers? Perhaps 'Nick' or one of his 'supporters' or journalist friends heard it mentioned and, hey presto, it's in 'evidence' as a fact. It is the most extraordinary of all coincidences and I think the Metropolitan Police Service have a duty to explain it and these peculiar, incriminating emails.

The whole episode reminds me of 1987, when the police trawled the gay bars of London showing my photograph to try to get 'victims' to give evidence against me. Now the police sit in their tower-block offices and telephone anyone whose details they have been passed by the IICSA to serve their own agenda as 'witnesses' in other cases – cases with which they are not and do not wish to be connected. In writing this important series of facts, I recognise I might be laying 'Bob' open to further abuse or assault. His evidence is protected under the terms of reference of the IICSA. Everyone should be aware, as a result of what I have disclosed, that not one hair on his head should be touched. If he is harmed or his identity is disclosed by anyone, a lawsuit for perverting the course of justice will be sought, however 'high up' the perpetrators.

Also reminiscent of the events of 1987 are the links between the press and the police. Nearly thirty years later, I would have thought they would have been regularised. They obviously have not. The police may have to pray in aid representatives of the media in the furthermost reaches of the internet now compared with mainstream media, but the connections still abound. The police thirty years ago were polite and considerate by nature; now they are slaves to bureaucracy, going through the motions at all costs, with no apparent care for those whose lives they trample upon and discard. Thirty years ago, I held my tongue; in 2015, I felt the need to speak and to write. I feel I have done my best to protect myself and those others who have been so appallingly transgressed. In the words of my political hero, in another context, 'All I know is to see, and not to speak, would be the great betrayal.'

I can do no more. So I now wait in suspended animation, far away from my cherished land, waiting for justice.

CHAPTER 17

ANALYSIS

People don't commit murder by accident, or, at any rate, if they do, they should still face the full weight of the law. I am not about to say that what the Metropolitan Police Service did in using the phrase 'credible and true' is remotely like murder, except, to me, I felt like it was an attempt to cast me as a murderer. I can never forgive that.

When the head of Operation Midland, Superintendent Kenny McDonald, took to the airwaves, casting himself in the role of Poirot, and repeatedly uttered the words 'credible and true', he knew, as a long-standing officer, exactly what effect this statement would have among the media, and more widely. As commentators on the internet have observed, these words persuaded even the most sceptical of people to believe all the allegations of 'Nick'; to believe all the fantastic claims 'Nick' had been churning out on the internet. The Superintendent's words validated all that 'Nick' had claimed on the internet, in his various guises, including on a television interview under the pseudonym 'Stephen' about his alleged abuse by Savile and his November 2014 interview with the BBC about me and, so-called, VIPs. It only remained for a real, live person to be fingered by the police. This occurred when my house was searched on 4 March 2015, along with Lord Bramall's and those of Lord Brittan. As an internet blog put it:

> The unmistakable inference was that Harvey Proctor had murdered boys and sadistically sexually assaulted others and that the investigating police believed that Harvey Proctor was guilty of these things ... Since then, the longer the police have failed to arrest Harvey Proctor the more unsustainable and untenable the situation has become.

I shall now try to analyse why this happened.

The Metropolitan Police Service will be forever associated with the phrase 'credible and true'. Sir Bernard Hogan-Howe, the Commissioner, has led us to believe it was a throwaway line, used by his Superintendent McDonald, head of Operation Midland, in the heat of the moment in a BBC television interview. I have already demonstrated the Commissioner was wrong. In an interview with John Humphrys on the BBC Radio 4 *Today* programme on 11 February, 2016 Sir Bernard again strayed away from the truth and said his Superintendent 'misspoke' and the mistake was rectified within a matter of days, certainly within six months, again a lie as it took the Met nine months to give its grudging apology and withdraw the offending phrase. Sir Bernard has a habit of shying away from the truth on radio. For ten months Operation Midland was conducted under this cloud and the truth only appeared a month after my statement pointed out the Met's error, and with no acknowledgement to me.

In addition, in appealing for 'victims' to come forward, it was constantly said that they would be 'believed' and 'supported'. What I think is important is to consider why the Metropolitan Police Service deliberately used that kind of language, and also why they clung to it for months after they surely would have realised they were on a losing wicket.

Following the Savile case, where the police, including DAC Rodhouse while with the Surrey Police, got it patently wrong, attempts were made deliberately to swing the pendulum back in favour of the 'victims' of child sexual abuse. The hierarchies of the Metropolitan Police Service and those of other constabularies may argue that they were working under the diktat of Tom Winsor, Her Majesty's Inspector of Constabulary – though he argues the interpretation of his report is incorrect – who said in November 2014, as 'Nick' appeared on the scene, 'all victims should be believed'. However, I believe the Met had pressure from another 'outside' source to 'believe victims'. The police were also easily susceptible to apparently intelligent argument from logical people, with an experienced track record and full of motivation – in this case political – but who were wrong, in the police's search as to how to re-establish their lost position of authority and restore their own authority. Their answer, in large part, appeared in the form of the ideas of a former DPP and current Labour MP, Sir Keir Starmer QC. His campaign to give 'victims' better treatment from the criminal justice system became political and culminated in his Victims of Crime Bill 2015. However, after he left his august position of being DPP in 2013, he made speech after speech in support of 'victims', which, clearly, were picked up by the police establishment, inwardly digested and used by them to bolster the central diktat.

There should be 'a radical review of how those who have suffered sexual abuse are treated', Sir Keir said to *The Guardian*. 'It takes real courage to come forward ... [and] many – if not most – still do not have sufficient confidence in our criminal justice system even to *report* what has happened to them.' There is 'a fear of not being believed' he says. 'The system makes judgements about people's credibility that are unwarranted' and there is 'a misplaced belief that fake accusations are rife'. Thus encouraged, the police left old-style policing behind them, thought they would become 'hip' and got it exactly wrong. Police training sessions, courses and seminars, no doubt, were awash with such arguments, advice and lines of 'with-it' notions, with the keener detective converts straining at the leash to put their new 'wisdom' into effect. A thrusting Superintendent or Assistant or Deputy Assistant Commissioner here or there would be delighted if a high-profile 'platform' presented itself, to put his or her newfound principles into operational practice.

Sir Keir and his political ideas would have a lot to answer for, even if 'Nick' had not appeared. The top echelons of the Metropolitan Police Service must now realise how illiberal and frighteningly dictatorial their mood swing in support of 'victims' became. They did this at the expense of the innocent accused – innocent until proven guilty – a protection gained over centuries and which has made our criminal justice system the envy of the world until the present operators of the mechanism trashed it. In the light of Operation Midland's failures, there can conceivably be a real danger of swinging the pendulum back the other way. The real supporters and guardians of genuine complainants are those calling for the historic balance between complainants and the accused to be restored.

Lord Janner, who was the only other alleged 'abuser' alive apart from the general and myself, died on 19 December 2015 when I was writing this book. His body was not cold before a furious solicitor, Liz Dux, went on television the next day to bemoan the fact that her six clients, who had separately made sexual-abuse complaints against Janner, and who, tellingly, were also seeking money from his estate, would not now have their day in court in a trial of the facts, which had been set down to start on 11 April 2016. However, none of these allegations related to the additional claims against him made by 'Nick' under Operation Midland.

Before he died, Janner was suffering from dementia. On 16 April 2015, the DPP had initially decided not to prosecute him over historic sexual child abuse concerning, among other matters, a Leicester children's home, but the decision was subsequently overturned. Janner and his family always denied these abuse claims. I do not know anything of their accuracy, but two days later, on 18 April, Mark Conrad, the Exaro journalist, wrote for the Mirror Group that 'Nick' was also claiming he had been abused by Janner. Conrad said 'Nick' had recognised his 'abuser' from a photograph he saw in a newspaper in June 2014. Conrad said 'Nick' claimed he was also abused at the same 'grand London town house' by Lord Brittan and another former Conservative MP. (My house had been searched one month earlier and Conrad knew about it before the police had left my home.) Obviously, Exaro and 'Nick' determined it was the right time to 'drip' this piece of information about Janner into the media – we should be told if there was a payment from the Mirror Group – ten months after 'Nick' claims he first identified his alleged 'abuser', six months after he, according to Exaro, named Janner to the Metropolitan Police Service and two days after the DPP had made Janner front-page news, by announcing there was to be no prosecution. It cannot be viewed in any other way than that 'Nick' was jumping on the Janner abuse bandwagon, ably assisted by Exaro. 'Nick', protected by his pseudonym, was commenting on Operation Midland's operational matters to a newspaper and criticising and identifying one of his alleged 'abusers', if not more. Exaro was facilitating the leaking of this information. I mention these issues at this juncture as the Metropolitan Police Service appear not to have criticised either 'Nick' or Exaro for these revelations! At that point, the police did not complain it was likely to compromise their investigations. Perhaps it was part of their media plan.

It is the sheer hypocrisy of Exaro journalists that was breathtaking. David Hencke described his colleague Conrad as being 'extremely assiduous' in an article on 'Jane', Brittan's alleged 'victim'. Hencke criticised the *Sunday Times* and the *Daily Mail* for writing articles on the Lantern Project and another alleged 'survivor', Esther Baker. He said: 'I am frankly surprised that both papers thought they could comment on the active investigation by casting doubt on the credibility of a survivor.' What does Hencke think Conrad and the Mirror Group did in identifying alleged 'abusers', other than commenting on and interfering in an 'active investigation'?

The Lantern Project is in itself interesting in their use of a technique called unstructured therapeutic disclosure (UTD). This is where 'victims' of alleged child sexual abuse are given details of the effects of sex abuse suffered by their counsellor and then urged to re-live their own abuse. It is fraught with danger. In late 2015, NHS Wirral decided to end its financial support of £187,000 a year of the Lantern Project for a number of reasons, one of which was its use of the therapeutic model. Others have inferred that UTD is reminiscent of a previous discredited technique called 'recovery memory therapy'. This therapy played its part in the historic false abuse scandal in Cleveland in 1987 and in the Orkney satanic ritual abuse scandal of 1991. They believed what was proved to be untrue by the contamination of their thoughts by unclean or tainted language which leads 'victims' down a path of association that can cause these false memories. False allegations, therefore, have been made by people without them actually (knowingly) lying. Professor Philip Jenkins, Professor of History at the Baylor University, North Carolina, wrote in the *American Conservative*:

> Central to that whole mindset is one simple statement that has achieved the status of a religious creed: victims never lie about child abuse. Children don't lie, nor do adults reporting their childhood sufferings. If you doubt this fact – if you use a word like 'alleged' victim – then you are an accomplice to that abuse. If you seek to challenge or discredit statements about abuse, then you are also striking at all future victims and survivors who would be discouraged from reporting their experiences. Doubt is of the devil.
>
> That approach helps us understand the extreme tolerance granted to purported victims who on the face of it sound deeply unconvincing: the ones with lengthy records of psychiatric treatment and commitment; with multiple convictions for petty crime and fraud; with decades-long involvement with substance abuse, involving the hardest and most destructive drugs; and the serial liars. What about the ones who utter not a word about the alleged crimes until twenty or thirty years after the event? Surely, these are not credible?
>
> Oh, ye of little faith. Listen to the experts, read the professional journals, and you shall know the truth. In fact, we are told, the degree of mental disorder and social malfunction in adult life is a *direct and inevitable consequence* of the childhood abuse, and the severity of that abuse is directly proportionate to the degree of adult dysfunction. In simple terms, the worse the acts of childhood molestation and rape, the more the lying and substance abuse. Of course they seem to be crazy people, drug

addicts, and persistent liars, and that proves the truth of their claims. Got that? Equally, the worse the abuse, the longer the time period before they might feel able to expose it to the world.

So all of this led me to believe not all people discussing these matters on the internet are fantasists. Some genuinely care; maybe they know the difficulties. There will be genuine people surrounding and counselling and supporting 'Nick'. I have not the professional or technical skill to determine these matters. I just have a feeling that they may have played a part in the predicament in which I find myself. I do not 'doubt', I 'know' what happened or, rather, I know what has *not* taken place. What I am at a loss to explain precisely is why 'Nick', not knowing him, has taken the course of action he has. He apparently shows no obvious signs of 'adult dysfunction'.

Language is very important in all these matters. I hope the police, lawyers, politicians and the media and the IICSA will take especial note. The use of the words 'victim' and 'survivor' should be banished before a trial verdict. They should be replaced with the neutral word 'complainant'. Where the word 'abuser' is bandied about before a trial verdict, the word 'alleged' should be attached. I know my words of advice will fall on stony ground with the fantasists on the internet. Professionals may also find it hard to believe that 'complainants' may or may not be 'victims' and 'survivors'. Or perhaps they know this perfectly well, though it does not suit their career path. The professional and the fantasist feed off one another. The general public will know exactly what I mean.

The language of the Met during this period must rely also on its director of media and communications, Martin Fewell. To a large extent, the Yard's rambling and slippery press statements and its deteriorating relations with the press must lie at his door. On appointment in 2013 he said, 'There has been a negative narrative in the media about the police. But to really turn this around, it is not just about releasing good news stories about the courage, bravery and quality of officers. Where there is justified criticism, you have to respond to it.' The Met's PR is at an all-time low. He has not responded to the daily press attack on the Met successfully. By refusing to answer the questions the press has legitimately asked of the Met, he has undermined his bosses. He is part of the problem and it is time for him to slip away quietly.

While on the subject of language, the Metropolitan Police Service should be renamed. I find it difficult to understand why detectives refer to it as 'the organisation' in such a corporate manner. I find it distasteful when Assistant Commissioner Pat Gallan goes before the Home Affairs Select Committee and talks about 'my business group' in relation to ongoing operations. The Metropolitan Police Service's official name was changed in 1989 from 'Metropolitan Police Force' to its present title following the presentation of a report entitled 'A Force for Change: Report on the Corporate Identity of the Metropolitan Police' by Wolff Olins corporate brand consultants in August 1988. It has since acted as a 'business', as 'the organisation', during which time its reputation has gradually evaporated and its effectiveness in dealing with the type of crime that most Londoners wish it to deal with – terrorism, violence (particularly on the street), burglary and gun and knife crime – has diminished. Its culture and ethos is demonstrably wrong. The extraordinary statements issued by the Metropolitan Police Service in 2015 necessitate a thorough overhaul of its press department. It will be forever tarnished by its connection with 'credible and true'. I can save the taxpayer tens of millions of pounds in this 'renaming' exercise – it should return to its old name: the Metropolitan Police Force. However, a change of title will be insufficient in regaining its worldwide reputation. In looking 'forward into the past', it should concentrate its personnel on the front line in its battle with crime, reducing the number of its senior officers, stripping back management and increasing the number of beat officers and patrol cars, and instead look at the present and the future. The Metropolitan Police Service and the CPS should stop treating the past with the social mores of today, as they obviously did in the Neil Fox case, adjudicated in December 2015 in his favour.

Although it will create problems – allegations of police state, secret arrests and the like – on balance, I believe it is a good idea to give anonymity to the accused in those cases where the 'victim' can currently maintain his or her anonymity. Sir Bernard has placed on record his wish that 'suspects' should also benefit from this better, balanced anonymity rule. The right of the complainant to identify themselves at any stage should also be vested in the accused, but one should have no rights to identify the other. The powers of identification should be vested in judges or the trial judge, not the police. However, as I have pointed out, that people named, as I have been, without being dignified with the tag 'suspect', let alone accused of anything, should also benefit from this change in the law; it must be all embracing. If the police pass information about an inquiry to a 'complainant', it should be a criminal offence for that 'complainant' to reveal the information to a third party or the media. The code of practice as to what information a 'complainant' is entitled to receive about an operation needs to be re-visited.

Sir Bernard's statement that the Metropolitan Police Service has not identified anyone in Operation Midland and that it is not their policy so to do in any inquiry is specious and should be closely investigated, especially in the light of Sir Bernard's calls for reform in this area. It has implications for the police information flow.

The Metropolitan Police Service, as with all UK police forces, should cease to issue any statements concerning the search of premises where they would negate the anonymity rules set out above, not only by omitting the actual name of the person, but any other information which would, to a reasonable person, allow identification. Such rules should also apply to those people who help the police with their inquiries or agree to a voluntary interview under caution. In all such cases, it should be for the person to identify themselves, not the police. These rules should be all-encompassing and include the internet and those who use it and the police themselves.

There is a degree of agreement on certain matters. These reforms must apply to all cases, not just to so-called high-profile ones. Indeed, it is in the cases where the power of the press is inevitably absent, that the potential for injustice is the greater. Arising out of the disgraceful police action in the Paul Gambaccini case, bail limits must be agreed and conditions fair to all parties must be upheld in practice, as well as being placed on the Statute Book.

On 13 March 2013, when he was DPP, Sir Keir said: 'False allegations can ruin reputations and devastate lives ... such cases will be dealt with robustly and those falsely accused should feel confident that the criminal justice system will prosecute those cases wherever there is sufficient evidence and it is in the public interest to do so.' Reputations of politicians, generals and others have already been ruined in this case. My reputation, carefully nurtured over twenty-eight years following my 'outing' by the press and aided by the police in 1987, has been left in tatters; my life has been 'devastated' in a manner where, through age, I have no time left to effectively restore it. I have lost my home and my job. I have lost my future, but I have lost my present too. In deciding whether to bring charges of seeking to pervert the course of justice, I can imagine the arguments now that it is 'not in the public interest' to take any action which will stop 'victims' from coming forward. The police's track record on such prosecutions is not great. Can anyone fail to understand my current lack of confidence in Sir Keir's arguments? The police's particular interest in me in Operation Midland – once 'Nick' and Exaro had confided – related solely to my convictions in 1987 and to my homosexuality and subsequent fantasist allegations, some fuelled by certain political opinions I hold, and based upon my sexual proclivities, which are legal but which I prefer not to discuss in the media or with the police. Whether a witch-hunt or McCarthyism, the end result for me has been character and practical assassination.

In writing this book, I have discovered an extraordinary revelation: the Westminster paedophile ring does indeed exist! It takes the form of an embryonic 'industry' that has been created to surround the subject of historical, child sexual abuse, to explore, track down, examine, investigate and inquire into it. The whole edifice consists of certain elements in the upper tiers of our police forces, civil servants in the Home Office, journalists and broadcasters, 'Nick' and other alleged 'survivors', news agencies, child support agencies, social services, lawyers and, naturally, politicians of all parties, most out for advancement at the expense of others, manufacturing a phantasmagoria which will be never-ending.

The IICSA has replaced the word 'historical' with 'non-recent' as a result of 'victim' pressure. It has, however, littered its terms of reference, and the same 'feel' pervades the whole of the opening inquiry statement by Lady Goddard, with the words 'victim' and 'survivor'. It claims it will report finally in 2020, but it is not sure. I am sure it will never end. It will become a standing inquiry, a bureaucratic abasement to fantasy. It will not come to one definitive conclusion, and any that it does make will call for yet more investigations.

As such, I believe we are witnessing the birth of an industry – sticky fingers in the honey pot of taxpayers' money (£180 million in 2016) – which will only spawn timeless vested interests. It will be a brave Home Secretary that finally knocks it on the head.

The IICSA has already established the first twelve initial inquiries – more to follow when they have exhausted these – one of which is named 'Allegations of Child Abuse Linked to Westminster'. The criteria for establishing investigations refers, interestingly, to where there are 'credible' allegations and 'credible' evidence. Even the language of Operation Midland continues; only the word 'true' has disappeared. Or has it? The IICSA is, now I mention it, setting up a 'Truth Project', where anyone can say what they want, unchecked, untested and unverified, both in person and in writing, for future posterity to gaze and reflect. Falsehoods will be written into history along with the bona fide and legitimate outpourings, diminishing the latter for fear of challenging the former. Nowhere in the terms of reference do the words 'genuine', 'real' and certain appear. Nowhere does it say in its ninety-odd-paragraph statement that fake victims or charlatans need not apply, nor any other words to that effect.

The IICSA's opening statement ends with an appeal, again echoing Operation Midland, for 'victims and survivors to come forward'. There is the same overwhelming belief, before a scrap of evidence is heard, that it is all true. Again, it seems more than likely that when Operation Midland closes, Operation Goddard will continue. And nor is it toothless: it has powers to name people it thinks may have committed abuse, and Lady Goddard is determined to do exactly that. So, even if there is no police charge, no prosecution, no court hearing, no verdict, the IICSA can continue the persecution of the pilloried on the same pretext, on the same set of squalid hunches, gossip and half-truths. And, you know what, I bet they will. They will do so because the internet fantasists, whom the IICSA will wish to appease, will never be satisfied until they see their targets nailed to the cross. Incestuously, the participants in this gaudy show will feed off one another. On the occasions when they think they have their 'prey' cornered, there will be a sickening concerted attack, where the bar for evidence for criminal prosecution is not reached, a one-sided campaign will be waged using the IICSA's many devices and channels. For the dead, the IICSA has powers not dissimilar to Parliament's 'Bill of Attainder'.

The late Lord Janner will now be an easy new target for the IICSA. I do not know the truth about the twenty-two allegations of child sexual abuse (not involving Operation Midland) that he faced. When Janner was alive, the police and the CPS did not prosecute him. When, through dementia, he joined the ranks of the living dead, they changed their mind and insisted on a 'trial of the facts'. Now he is dead, the IICSA will, I believe, launch a thirteenth investigation into the claims of at least six of his alleged 'survivors' to enable them to better launch civil action against his estate for 'compensation'. Having opened the door to 'compensation' claims for the six, the floodgates will be opened for many of the rest of what will become the IICSA's 'clients', especially against institutions, authorities and councils. Unlike the police, the IICSA will have no 'evidential' threshold to meet.

The IICSA has already tossed titbits one to another with its 'partners'; all the 'partners' in the gang will have a good time. Fact-finding trips to Australia to study 'tips' from that country's Royal Commission will be organised. Reciprocity will be the order of the day as foreign visitors will be shown the state-of-the-art inquiry into – nonsense. Multi-discipline conferences will be held; MPs will receive fat fees for claiming credit for establishing the 'business'; IICSA staff will be feted; professional 'cold calling' to 'discover' and 'tempt' the 'victims' and 'survivors' of institutions to put their trust in their tender mercies will gather pace; the real sufferers of child sexual abuse, usually to be found within family units, will be ignored. Truly, the Westminster paedophile ring is alive and well.

Am I being cynical? Only time will tell. Will Home Secretary Theresa May's comment, made on *The Andrew Marr Show*, concerning child sexual abuse by prominent figures, that 'what we have seen revealed is only the tip of the iceberg' be found to be 'credible and true', or will it be rather 'the tip of an ice cube'?

In conclusion, I have to say, while this subject is so incredibly serious and horrendous for the genuine victims of child sexual abuse – historical, non-recent or current – and for me, I could not have survived 2015 and all that has been thrown at me without keeping a sense of proportion. I must admit, with understatement, it has not been easy. In this regard, I have been aided by the writings of Prof. Philip Jenkins. He wrote in the *American Conservative*:

> To put it mildly, it was an awkward social situation. After murdering a small boy during a paedophile orgy, a senior Member of Parliament determined to castrate another victim with a knife. He was prevented from this act by a former British Prime Minister who was present at the event. That fellow-pervert suggested that this was going a little far, even for a group that had already murdered several other children. How far we have travelled from *Downton Abbey*.
>
> If I seem to be treating such a horrific story sarcastically, I honestly do not know how else to respond to such a monstrous and fantastic allegation…

To 'monstrous and fantastic', he might have added the word 'untrue'.

However, my real criticism of the Metropolitan Police Service is not that they regarded 'Nick's' allegations as 'true', but that they could believe they were 'credible'. Most reasonable people, not brainwashed by post-Savile dementia or under the spell of the dulcet tones of a former DPP, would immediately jump to the conclusion that the accusations were 'incredible'. They might have still been 'true', but on the surface they were, to varying extents, unbelievable, far-fetched, absurd and preposterous. Unless, of course, there was some corroborative evidence that backed the person up, whatever they looked like or sounded like. No such evidence has ever been handed to me or mentioned to me, with the exception of rather blurred photographs of a pen knife and E-FIT photographs that could have been likenesses of anyone. The pen knife was not in the possession of the police on 18 December 2014 or if it was it, or its image, was not shown to me on my first interview in June 2015. The police took the easy way out to make themselves look good, the one that fitted their bigger picture, in advance of the Goddard Inquiry, seeking out and placing in the frame many who were dead or dying, incapable of rebuttal, and some who were very elderly. That is the scandal.

They also sought me out as an easy target; they were wrong.

EPILOGUE

I had no intention of writing an epilogue. After I had completed the writing of this book, however, I read Paul Gambaccini's riveting book *Love, Paul Gambaccini* detailing his horrendous time at the hands of the Metropolitan Police Service's Operation Yewtree, including his arrest as a result of historical child sexual abuse allegations and constant re-bailing for over one year. He was innocent and was not charged. I was asleep when, on the eve of my birthday on 15 January 2016, my solicitor forwarded to me an email from Deputy Assistant Commissioner Steve Rodhouse, the Gold Commander of Operation Midland. Hitherto, my communication with the police had been at no higher level than Detective Sergeant rank. On the day of the search of my house, on 4 March 2015, I had received a stony glare from an embarrassed Detective Inspector. He deigned not to speak to me. It was quite a jump in rank to be dealing with a Deputy Assistant Commissioner and it was completely unexpected. It was such an extraordinary missive I have reproduced it in full.

It answers none of the questions my solicitors had been asking the police about Operation Midland every two weeks since my press conference in August 2015. It was nonetheless fascinating.

This is what Rodhouse wrote:

Dear Mr Gatrad,

I understand that you wrote to my colleague, DS Flynn on the 11th January 2016 seeking an update on the MPS investigations into allegations received that your client, Mr Harvey Proctor, committed offences including homicide, rape and indecent assault on a juvenile victim between 1976 and 1984.

You will be aware that the complainant in this case has also made related allegations against other named individuals. In particular, the complainant in this case has alleged that another man also committed serious sexual offences against him but that he was not involved in the murder of any young boys. The investigation into these specific allegations has also formed part of Operation Midland.

In this particular case I have concluded that all reasonable enquiries have been made but there is insufficient evidence to show that the Full Code Test can be met. As a result, unless further information arises, no action will be taken against this man.

As Mr Proctor has been the subject of allegations from the same complainant then I felt that it was appropriate for him to be informed of this development. The investigating officers are continuing to carry out enquiries in respect of Mr Proctor and are not yet in a position to apply the Full Code Test in respect of the allegation made against him.

Since Mr Proctor was interviewed on 24 August 2015, additional information has been received by the MPS. Officers are currently carrying out enquiries to understand the significance of this further information. This will be done as expeditiously as possible.

I recognise that the impact of this investigation upon Mr Proctor will undoubtedly have been increased by the media coverage of Operation Midland. The allegation received by the MPS was, in itself unusual in that details of the case were known to journalists and broadcasters prior to being brought to our attention. I would like to reiterate that the MPS has never disclosed Mr Proctor's identity to the media and does not support the practice of naming those subject to investigation prior to being charged unless there are exceptional circumstances.

The 'man' Rodhouse was referring to was, of course, Field Marshal Lord Bramall, aged ninety-two years and the only other alleged 'abuser' in the 'gang' who was still alive apart from myself. 'No further action' are the weasel words used by the police to close an investigation. It is the nearest that Lord Bramall would get to an apology – at least for the present. For more than a year, investigations had proceeded. Rodhouse made it clear that the first stage of evidential proof – whether a crime had actually been committed – had not been met in Lord Bramall's case. This is the reference to the 'Full Code Test'.

This confirmed my long-held view that 'Nick's' allegations remain false in every respect, not just in relation to me. Lord Bramall said they contained 'not a grain of truth' as far as he was aware. I am of the same opinion when it comes to his allegations regarding me, and I have no knowledge that they can be true about the others, who are now all dead.

It was no coincidence that the Metropolitan Police Service released their statement on Lord Bramall on the same day that Lord Janner's trial of the facts was concluded. It was concluded because Janner was dead. The statement was released late on a Friday night, deliberately late for the press. It was media manipulation. If the Metropolitan Police Service thought they had 'buried' what for them was 'bad' news, they were mistaken. The police 'management' of Operation Midland had taken over from the 'investigation'.

There followed another week of bad publicity for Sir Bernard Hogan-Howe, Assistant Commissioner Patricia Gallan and Steve Rodhouse and, alas, for the police generally. The constant refrain, quite rightly, was for Hogan-Howe to apologise to Lord Bramall. I even suggested he do it on his knees. In varying degrees of strength, calls for Hogan-Howe to say sorry came from the Prime Minister, the Defence Secretary, the Mayor of London, MPs, retired judges, former police chief constables, a Director of Public Prosecutions, generals – past and present – and, of course, the editorials of most of the national media, short of those newspapers who had believed that 'Nick' was 'credible and true' and who *wanted* 'Nick' to be 'credible and true'. Appeals for an apology came not for the fact that there had been an investigation but because of the unjust manner of the investigation. I noticed no such appeal for an apology came from the Solicitor General, and there was a complete silence and refusal to comment from the Home Secretary.

Under immense pressure, and scoring an own goal, on 20 January 2016 the Metropolitan Police Service issued another long, rambling statement, this time explaining why it would not apologise to Lord Bramall; it ran to 850 words. At least it made clear that 'our letter to Lord Bramall's lawyers now closes this investigation into the allegations against him'. Rodhouse's earlier statement, inferring that the investigation against Lord Bramall could be re-opened in the future, if more evidence came to light, had not gone down well. But, remarkably, Hogan-Howe left his subordinate Gallan to speak and to explain how she would meet with Lord Bramall when the police had raised the white flag of surrender over Operation Midland. Hogan-Howe obviously knew that, sooner or later, he would do to Gallan what she had done to Rodhouse – overrule her and apologise himself. He could not do this while Operation Midland was still operational.

Gallan, thinking ahead to the collapse of Operation Midland and getting her 'defence' in first, also said in her statement:

> I also accept as Lord Denning said in a famous judgment that police officers are answerable to the law and to the law alone. The government has decided to set up a statutory public inquiry under the Hon. Lowell Goddard precisely because of contemporary concerns about historic investigations. It is a powerful recognition of public disquiet about the thoroughness of attempts by the police and other agencies to investigate allegations of abuse. The inquiry has already made clear that it will be investigating cases where there are allegations of child sexual abuse and exploitation involving people of public prominence associated with Westminster. This may include Operation Midland. The MPS will, of course, fully co-operate with the inquiry and account for its actions wherever that is requested.

Gallan, by inference, blames the government and 'public disquiet' for the nature of the police investigation. She also pre-selects the manner – the forum – in which she wishes Operation Midland to be 'tried' – the Goddard Inquiry. I believe this would be entirely inappropriate for reasons I have set out earlier. It is wrong for the Metropolitan Police Service to be so considering their 'exit policy' from Operation Midland, knowing how badly they got it wrong, that they even try to determine how and by whom they and their operation, which has cost millions of pounds, should be judged. They want and are already trying to have Operation Midland investigated by the Goddard Inquiry. I think their action is unseemly. Police links with the inquiry and their interdependence make the Goddard Inquiry an unfit investigatory body to vet the police. I trust the House of Commons Home Affairs Select Committee notes the Metropolitan Police Service's attempt to circumvent them and determine who should consider their flawed investigation. The police will argue that a Commons' inquiry would be biased; I believe the Goddard Inquiry is already skewed. It is possible the Independent Police Complaints Commission (IPCC) might have a role to play. I am not sure, at present, how this impasse will be resolved, but I find it revealing that the police are already thinking in advance about these matters.

The media pressure on the police and on Hogan-Howe was immense. But so too was the investigative pressure on 'Nick'. He was being referred to by two other pseudonyms. Another complainant also alleged 'Nick' had stolen the details of his own abuse allegations and those of other complainants and made them his own.

Members of 'Nick's' family, in varying strengths of outrage at being ignored or not believed by Operation Midland detectives, revealed they too thought he was a fantasist – his mother, stepmother and stepbrother, and, indirectly, his two stepsisters – and sympathised with the plight of his 'victims'.

I could not help wondering why had the police not thoroughly investigated 'Nick's' claims and background before causing so much pain and damage to so many people. The hurt could never be assuaged. Was it the 'system' or was it the chief police officers who failed to identify the failures in the 'system' and sat back, paralysed, incapable of intelligent action to redress the injustice. Sir Bernard and his closest officers cannot absolve themselves of blame for their oversight.

So what of my position? I felt the continuation of the police investigation against me reeked of vengeance for my statement of 25 August 2015 and for setting the media loose around the phrase 'credible and true'. While Rodhouse's missive to my solicitors appeared to be extraordinarily polite, almost solicitous for my welfare and apologetic in tone, it made clear the investigation continued. It referred to 'Nick' not as a 'victim' or a 'survivor' but as a 'complainant' – terminology I had suggested at my press conference.

However, the email also said new information had been considered since 24 August 2015 and my last interview with the police. The interview was over five months ago and yet I had not been questioned about these alleged new police concerns or been told what they were; so much for investigating the matter 'expeditiously'. As Lord Bramall was not now being investigated and as apparently 'Nick' had not suggested Bramall had murdered anyone, maybe it was the murder aspects of their investigation that continued to attract police attention. But Panorama's BBC documentary had proved to any reasonable mind that one of the alleged three murders could not have taken place; that left two purported murders. Could the police have found a body or two? I doubt it; I knew there were none to be found as there had been no murders.

More likely, the new information might not even concern or be connected to me. It might concern those alleged abusers who were dead or it might even concern 'Nick'. The police did not want Operation Midland to end – well, not just yet. Could the reason have anything to do with Hogan-Howe's long-awaited renewal of his contract for a further two years? The Home Secretary and the Mayor of London still had to agree and there had been much press speculation. Could it be that the career prospects of senior officers stood in the way of ending this investigation? Could it be the police were 'managing' the collapse of their operation? Could it be they were looking more closely at 'Nick'?

Rodhouse's email to my solicitors also contained the usual nonsense about police identification, that they never released the identity of people before charge. The police appeared, quite rightly, to be very sensitive on this subject in their email to me, in their letter to Lord Bramall and in Gallan's statement, where she even accused Lord Bramall of naming himself in the media. It is as if the police do not keep pace with the veracity of their own investigation. Why can everyone else see that the police 'leak' information – whether officially or unofficially – but not themselves?

In his email to my solicitor, Rodhouse blamed the media and broadcasters for having sight of the allegations of 'Nick' before the police were asked to investigate them, as though they might not have mounted such an investigation had 'Nick's' allegations not already been in the public arena (thanks to Exaro and the BBC). There was no acknowledgement or comprehension of the damage the 'deadly' and prejudicial phrase 'credible and true' had caused in either Gallan's or Rodhouse's remarks. The police had only themselves to blame for that.

Rodhouse's comments concerning the media were very reminiscent of his earlier excuse for prolonging Lord Brittan's agony in 2014 and 2015, omitting to tell him that 'Jane's' allegations were not being pursued. Rodhouse obviously feared 'media criticism and public cynicism' if the police did not investigate my case, and that of Lord Bramall and the others, more thoroughly. If I had not been in the public limelight, I gained the impression it would have been different. It felt to me like he was adopting the same flawed manner of investigation towards me that he had with Lord Brittan and 'Jane's' allegation. The police harassed a frail Lord Brittan to his death; they were not going to do the same to me. As the Home Affairs Select

Committee report on Lord Brittan concluded, 'this is not a proper basis for police decisions on whether to proceed with an investigation, which should be considered in a wholly objective manner, based solely on the evidence'. Rodhouse has also conveniently not recalled his part in promoting 'credible and true' as a core strategy in Operation Midland. I wondered exactly what he and Superintendent McDonald had plotted before that press briefing in December 2014. Could they have taken such decisions without others knowing about it too? Could Hogan-Howe have been in blissful ignorance of their decisions in what was the highest-profile case he had to deal with as Metropolitan Police Commissioner? I believe not.

Gallan wisely said in her statement: 'The Metropolitan Police are clear that citizens are innocent until proven guilty' – if only those words had been deployed and followed in practice on 18 December 2014, and subsequently, when the police had said 'Nick' was 'credible and true'. As the week progressed I felt more strongly that those involved – Hogan-Howe, Gallan and Rodhouse – should depart. They surely would not be missed by the vast majority of good police officers looking at the harm wreaked upon the Metropolitan Police by their superiors in their search for political correctness.

Exaro remained relatively quiet about Operation Midland but tried to deflect attention away from Lord Bramall's triumph over 'Nick' by leaking a draft report of the Smith Inquiry into the BBC and Jimmy Savile. Dame Janet Smith, a retired judge and whose three-year report it was, said the Exaro version 'was an out-of-date (draft) report and significant changes have been made to its contents and conclusions' and that she was 'disappointed'. Obviously Exaro protects its sources. Could the source of the draft report have been a BBC employee? Or even 'Nick'? As he had also alleged he had been a victim of Savile, perhaps he might have obtained a draft report; or could a copy of the draft report have been sent to the Metropolitan Police Service? Could it have been an Exaro 'mole' at New Scotland Yard who thought it timely to pass on the report? Exaro were at pains to indicate the leaking of the draft report would not hamper police inquiries into Savile. Were they given a clean bill of health to publish by the police? Will we ever know the truth? It would be interesting to know who at the Metropolitan Police Service had sight of this draft Smith Report, and details of its distribution within the 'organisation'.

On my sixty-ninth birthday, 16 January 2016, the day after the police statement on Lord Bramall, a spokesman for Scotland Yard went further than before and declared, to the *Daily Telegraph*, 'There are questions as to whether Nick's claims are credible and true.' This police admission, at last questioning their own phrase of 'credible and true', was the best birthday present ever.

After nine months of constant bombardment, during which time I had rarely raised my voice in public, I decided it was the right moment to launch a further retaliatory strike. I therefore asked my solicitors to respond to Rodhouse, requesting that the Metropolitan Police Service formally to investigate 'Nick'. Nabeel wrote:

> Dear Mr Rodhouse,
>
> We write with reference to our aforementioned client, and further to your letter dated 15 January 2016, the content of which has been duly noted and communicated to Mr Proctor.
>
> In light of recent developments, our client is of the strong view that the Metropolitan Police should investigate 'Nick' for wasting police time and attempting to pervert the course of justice. Not only has Operation Midland consumed a lot of police time and resources, but the cost to the public purse has been considerable to say the least.

Our client has denied the spurious allegations against him from the very outset, and recent developments tend to support his firm assertions.

We would be extremely grateful for your views on this matter at your earliest convenience.

Should you have any queries about the content of this letter, please do not hesitate to contact us.

Yours sincerely
Mr Nabeel Gatrad

Solicitor-Advocate (All Higher Courts)
Sakhi Solicitors.

Rodhouse replied that the contents of the letter had been 'noted'.

My hopes of a quick conclusion of Operation Midland were dashed as the Metropolitan Police Service established a PR campaign to save their beleaguered Commissioner's job – well, to get his contract extended by two years – and to see how they could extricate themselves from the horrors of Operation Midland with as little egg on their faces as possible.

Sir Bernard initially wanted a three-year extension of his contract, which expired in September 2016. The Mayor of London advised the Home Secretary to grant him one year. In a week, starting on 8 February, an orchestrated campaign was launched. The Prime Minister grudgingly gave the Commissioner his support for the steps he had apparently taken to increase the number of armed officers in London in the face of the increased terrorist threat. It was announced that Sir Bernard would appear before the Commons Home Affairs Select Committee on 23 February 2016, give his long-arranged Brian

Redhead BBC lecture, a platform for a speech on the police and the press, give an interview with Mark Easton of the BBC, write an article for *The Guardian* on not necessarily believing 'complainants' and appear on Radio 4's *Today* programme. It was quite a campaign that the director of the Metropolitan Police Service and the director of media and communications, Martin Fewell, had cobbled together.

It was trumped by the Met's announcement that Sir Bernard had appointed a retired High Court judge, Sir Richard Henriques, to investigate the processes of police historical child sexual abuse operations, including Operation Midland.

In a move emulating Pat Gallan, he said Sir Richard's report would be handed to the Lady Goddard at the end of Operation Midland for the evidence to be considered by her Inquiry.

He was surrounding himself with a Teflon-like protective coating of inquiries, which Sir Bernard thought would shield him from the further onslaught of the media.

The trouble for Sir Bernard and the Met was, it did not work. The press was just as critical, called him a 'dead man walking', regarding his campaign as cynical. He now wished to receive a two-year extension of his contract. In his BBC Radio 4 *Today* interview on the morning of 11 February with John Humphrys, Sir Bernard said he wanted to serve in post for up to seven years because 'what you do in your final year is that you are dismissed'. He obviously thought he would get his two-year extension. Later the same morning, the Home Secretary disappointed him, ignored his PR self-aggrandisement and offered him only one year. Effectively, it was a well-deserved slap in the face. He had been 'dismissed'. My thoughts are that he will resign before completing his term of office.

With regard to Sir Richard's inquiry, I was invited to comment in *The Times* and on LBC. I said:

This inquiry is not independent and is part of the Met's PR strategy before closing down Operation Midland. Sir Bernard has chosen his own judge, set up his own inquiry and decided his own terms of reference. When the inquiry is over, he will decide what is revealed and what is not revealed. I have no confidence in this 'secret' inquiry and I would urge Sir Richard to resign before it starts. Sir Bernard should not be setting up an inquiry, he should be the focus of any such inquiry. It is a cover-up.

I said I would not co-operate with Sir Richard and Sir Bernard's private inquiry. As it was Sir Bernard's personal and private inquiry, he should pay for it out of his own, not inconsiderable, salary.

He said in his *Guardian* article that complainants should not 'unconditionally be believed ... A good investigator would test the accuracy of the allegations with an open mind, supporting the complainant through the process. This is a more neutral way to begin than saying we should believe victims, and better describes our impartial mindset.' Sir Bernard had listened to my arguments in my statement and, albeit belatedly, agreed with its intellectual thrust. Unfortunately, he thinks he needs the support of a retired judge and yet another inquiry before he can put this common sense into action.

With ill grace, and little by little, the truth was being established. It has had to be wrung out of the Metropolitan Police Service, but admission there had been. 'Nick's' credibility and truthfulness were finally being questioned and the philosophical argument I had advanced was being won.

I felt almost vindicated.

My thoughts were these. To prove my innocence, I had had to take on the Metropolitan Police Service. It had been a daunting task.

After another few weeks of non-stop debate and coverage in the media, I was very tired and I knew the stress was beginning to take its toll on me physically. It was not always easy to keep my composure, especially when being questioned by the media by telephone. At least they could not see my state of distress. I thought I was near the end of my personal nightmare or, at least, the beginning of the end. As James Hanning of the *Independent on Sunday* said, 'You cannot have à la carte credibility.' If 'Nick' is not 'credible and true' with respect to his allegations about Lord Bramall, how can the police consider him to be 'credible and true' over the wicked allegations he has made against me and the dead?

Let us hope we can all rest in peace one day.

AFTERWORD

I t would be all too easy to colour one's whole life by what has transpired in one part of it, or, particularly for me, in the past twelve months. That would be unfair and a travesty to a life well-lived, and I will try not to let the catastrophe that now envelops my very being flavour these final words. As I look back on my life, I recollect meeting so many good, kind and generous people of all races, creeds and outlooks; I have travelled the world and found inspiration in people, including members of my family, and I am grateful to them all for their company and comradeship, their love and affection. I have mentioned many in this book and I am sorry I have not written about them all – they know who they are.

There have been so many amusing and fun times and I am thankful for the levity that has made the bad times endurable and the good times memorable.

Helping to pass on our country's heritage at Belvoir to the next generation was an honour, and more than fulfilled my boyhood love of history and continuity and my thirst to learn the lessons of the past to better understand the challenges of the future.

For eight years it was a privilege, given to so few, to serve in the mother of parliaments. I was also delighted to serve my constituents, whom I represented and for whom I fought. It was and should be the most honourable of positions. No one can take that experience away from me.

The ability to speak for one's party, for one's constituents, for one's country and ultimately for one's self is the bedrock of our democracy. No greater faith, no greater trust, no greater honour can have been bestowed.

As I look out over a large lemon tree, heavy with yellow baubles of fruit in the weak winter sun of a foreign land, surrounded by my closest friends and my dogs, my thoughts are of experiencing the heights and depths of what has been, whatever else, an incredible journey. The ultimate destination is foreknown. I do not know how I will reach it or what will happen next, nor do I know where I will go or what I will do – it is probably for the best that I do not know.

But I do know this: I have been traduced; I am innocent.

STATEMENT

The following statement was distributed and made to the press on 25 August 2015. A full recording of the speech can be found at https://www.youtube.com/watch?v=RLm7rdRBOF4&feature=youtu.be

1. I am a private citizen. I have not held public office and I have not sought public office since May 1987. As such, I am entitled to be regarded as a private citizen. Since the general election of 1987 I have sought a private life. I have been enjoying a full life, gainfully employed and personally happy.

This all came to an abrupt end on 4 March 2015. What now follows is a statement on my present predicament created by an unidentified person making totally untrue claims against my name. Before going any further I wish to make it clear that the genuine victims of child sexual abuse have my fullest sympathy and support and I would expect the full weight of the law to be used against anyone, be he 'ever so high, or ever so low', committing such odious offences. Nobody, and I repeat, nobody is above the law.

2. However, I attach equal weight to justice for innocent people wrongly accused of child sexual abuse, especially when it is done anonymously. This is what is happening to me and many high-profile figures, many of whom are dead and cannot answer back. This statement is necessarily lengthy and detailed and at times complicated. Please bear with me and at the end I will be prepared to answer your questions.

3. On 18 June 2015, at my request, I was interviewed by the Metropolitan Police Murder Squad 'Operation Midland'. This interview lasted over six hours. At the very outset I had to help the police with my full name which they appeared not to know. It may surprise you that it was over three and a half months after my home was searched for fifteen hours and more than seven months after the most serious allegations were made against me that I was interviewed. I went on to co-operate fully with the police with their investigation.

4. The allegations have been made by a person who the police have dubbed with a pseudonym – 'NICK'. He appears on television with a blacked-out face and an actor's voice. All of this is connected with alleged historical child sexual abuse in the 1970s and 1980s. 'NICK' was interviewed by the police in the presence of a reporter from Exaro – an odd internet news agency.

5. As a Member of Parliament, I always spoke in favour of the police. I believe in law and order and I believe in equipping the police to do their job and, with my track record, it will come as a surprise that I have grave and growing concerns about the police generally and more specifically 'Operation Midland'. I have decided to share these concerns with you. I believe I am not speaking just for myself today. I hope I am not being presumptuous when I say I feel I am speaking

for those who have no voice whatsoever, including the dead, to whom
I referred moments ago.

6. Two days before my interview with the police, my solicitors –
Sakhi Solicitors of Leicester – were sent a 'disclosure' document.
It set out the matters the police wished to discuss with me. It was
the first time I had known of what I had been accused. On the day
of my interview I was not arrested, nor placed on police bail, I was
told I could leave the police station at any time and that it was a
voluntary interview. I and my solicitors had previously been told
I was not a suspect.

7. At the end of the interview I was given no information as to how
much longer the police investigation would take to bring the matter to a conclusion. I think you will understand I cannot allow this
matter to rest.

8. So you can gauge how angry I am and in an attempt to stop the
'drip, drip, drip' of allegations by the police into the media, I now
wish to share with you in detail the uncorroborated and untrue
allegations that have been made against me by 'NICK'. Anyone of
a delicate or a nervous disposition should leave the room now.

9. The following is taken from the police disclosure document given
to my solicitors two days before my first interview with the police
under the headings 'Circumstances', 'Homicides' and 'Sexual abuse'.
    I quote:

'Circumstances
The victim in this investigation is identified under the pseudonym

'Nick'. He made allegations to the Metropolitan Police Service in late 2014. Due to the nature of the offences alleged, 'Nick' is entitled to have his identity withheld.

'Nick' stated he was the victim of systematic and serious sexual abuse by a group of adult males over a period between 1975 and 1984. The abuse was often carried out whilst in company with other boys whom were also abused by the group.

'Nick' provided names of several individuals involved in these acts including Mr HARVEY PROCTOR. He states MR PROCTOR abused him on a number of occasions which included sexual assault, buggery and torturous assault. He also states MR PROCTOR was present when he was assaulted by other adult males. Furthermore, 'Nick' states he witnessed the murder of three young boys on separate occasions. He states MR PROCTOR was directly responsible for two of the allegations and implicated in the third.

The dates and locations relevant to MR PROCTOR are as follows:

Homicides

1980 – at a residential house in central London. 'Nick' was driven by car to an address in the Pimlico/Belgravia area where a second boy (the victim) was also collected in the same vehicle. Both boys, aged approximately twelve years old, were driven to another similar central London address. MR PROCTOR was present with another male. Both boys were led to the back of the house. MR PROCTOR then stripped the victim, and tied him to a table. He then produced a large kitchen knife and stabbed the child through the arm and other parts of the body over a period of forty minutes. A short time later MR PROCTOR untied the victim and anally raped him on the table. The other male stripped 'Nick' and anally raped him over the table. MR PROCTOR then strangled the victim with his hands until the boy's body went limp. Both males then left the room. Later, MR PROCTOR returned and led 'Nick' out of the house and into a waiting car.

1981–82 – at a residential address in central London. 'Nick' was collected from Kingston train station and taken to a 'party' at a residential address. The witness was among four young boys. Several men were present including MR PROCTOR. One of the men told the boys one of them would die that night and they had to choose who. When the boys wouldn't decide, the men selected one of the boys (the victim). Each of the four boys including 'Nick' were taken to separate rooms for 'private time'. When they all returned to the same room, Nick was anally raped by MR PROCTOR and another male as 'punishment'. The other males also anally raped the remaining boys. MR PROCTOR and two other males then began beating the chosen victim by punching and kicking. The attack continued until the boy collapsed on the floor and stopped moving. All of the men left the room. The remaining boys attempted to revive the victim but he was not breathing. They were left for some time before being taken out of the house and returned to their homes.

Between May and July 1979 – in a street in Coombe Hill, Kingston. Nick was walking in this area with another boy (the victim) when he heard the sound of a car engine revving. A dark-coloured car drove into the victim knocking him down. 'Nick' could see the boy covered in blood and his leg bent backwards. A car pulled up and 'Nick' was grabbed and placed in the car. He felt a sharp pain in his arm and next remembered being dropped off at home. He was warned not to have friends in future. 'Nick' never saw the other boy again. 'Nick' does not identify MR PROCTOR as being directly involved in this allegation. However, he states MR PROCTOR was part of the group responsible for the systematic sexual abuse he suffered. Furthermore, he believes the group were responsible for the homicide.

Sexual Abuse

1978–84 – Dolphin Square, Pimlico. 'Nick' was at the venue and with at least one other young boy. MR PROCTOR was present with other males. MR PROCTOR told 'Nick' to pick up a wooden baton and hit the other boy. When 'Nick' refused he was punished by MR PROCTOR and the other males. He was held down and felt pain in his feet. He fell unconscious. When he awoke he was raped by several males including MR PROCTOR.

1978–81 – Carlton Club, central London, 'Nick' was driven to the Carlton Club and dropped off outside. MR PROCTOR opened the door. Inside the premises were several other males. 'Nick' was sexually assaulted by another male (not by MR PROCTOR on this occasion).

1978–81 – swimming pool in central London. 'Nick' was taken to numerous 'pool parties' where he and other boys were made to undress, and perform sexual acts on one another. He and other boys were then anally raped and sexually abused by several men including MR PROCTOR.

1981–82 – large town house in London. 'Nick' was taken to the venue on numerous occasions where MR PROCTOR and one other male were present. He was forced to perform oral sex on MR PROCTOR who also put his hands around 'Nick's' throat to prevent him breathing. On another occasion at the same location, MR PROCTOR sexually assaulted 'Nick' before producing a pen knife and threatening to cut 'Nick's' genitals. MR PROCTOR was prevented from doing so by the other male present.

1979–84 – residential address in central London. 'Nick' was taken to the venue. MR PROCTOR was present with one other male. MR PROCTOR forced 'Nick' to perform oral sex on him before beating him with punches.

1978–84 – numerous locations including Carlton Club, Dolphin Square and a central London townhouse. 'Nick' described attending several 'Christmas parties' where other boys were present together with numerous males including MR PROCTOR. 'Nick' was given whiskey to drink before being forced to perform oral sex on several men including MR PROCTOR.

MR PROCTOR will be interviewed about the matters described above and given the opportunity to provide an account.'

10. I denied all and each of the allegations in turn and in detail and categorised them as false and untrue and, in whole, a heinous calumny. They amount to just about the worst allegations anyone can make against another person including, as they do, multiple murder of children, their torture, grievous bodily harm, rape and sexual child abuse.

11. I am completely innocent of all these allegations.

12. I am a homosexual. I am not a murderer. I am not a paedophile or pederast. Let me be frank, I pleaded guilty to four charges of gross indecency in 1987 relating to the then age of consent for homosexual activity. Those offences are no longer offences as the age of consent has dropped from twenty-one to eighteen to sixteen. What I am being accused of now is a million miles away from that consensual activity.

13. At the start of the interview, I was told that although the interview would be recorded by the police both for vision and sound, I would not receive a copy of the tapes. I asked to record the interview for sound myself but my request was refused. During the interview, to

ensure that 'Nick' had not identified the wrong person, I asked if I could see photographs purporting to be me which had been shown to him. My request was refused. At the end of the interview I was asked if I knew my eight alleged co-conspirators whose homes it was alleged I had visited. I believe I have a good recollection and the list comprised a number of people I knew, some who I had heard of but not met and some I did not know. None of the allegations were alleged to have taken place at my home and I have not visited the homes of any of the 'gang'.

14. The list included the names of the late Leon Brittan and the late Edward Heath.

15. If it was not so serious, it would be laughable.

16. Edward Heath sacked me from the Conservative Party's parliamentary candidates' list in 1974. Mrs Thatcher restored me to the list eighteen months later. Edward Heath despised me and he disliked my views particularly on limiting immigration from the New Commonwealth and Pakistan and my opposition to our entry into and continued membership of what is now known as the EU; I opposed his corporate statist views on the economy. I despised him too… He had sacked the late Enoch Powell, my political 'hero' from the shadow Cabinet when I was chairman of the University of York Conservative Association. I regarded Enoch as an intellectual giant in comparison with Heath.

17. The same Edward Heath, not surprisingly, would never speak to me in the House of Commons but would snort at me as he passed me by in a Commons corridor. The feeling was entirely mutual.

18. Now I am accused of doing some of these dreadful things in his London house as well; a house to which I was never invited and to which Heath would never have invited me and to which I would have declined his invitation.

19. The same Edward Heath's home with CCTV, housekeeper, private secretary, chauffeur, police and private detectives – all the trappings of a former Prime Minister – in the security-conscious days of the IRA's assault on London.

20. It is so farfetched as to be unbelievable. It is unbelievable because it is not true. My situation has transformed from Kafkaesque bewilderment to black-farce incredulity.

21. I have nothing to hide and nothing to fear. I appeal to any witness who truthfully can place me at any of the former homes of Edward Heath or Leon Brittan at any time to come forward now. I appeal to any witness who can truthfully say I committed any of these horrible crimes to come forward now.

22. The 'gang' is also alleged to have included Lord Janner (a former Labour MP), Lord Bramall (former Chief of the General Staff), the late Maurice Oldfield (former head of Secret Intelligence Service – MI6), the late Sir Michael Hanley (Director-General of the Internal Security Service – MI5), General Sir Hugh Beach (Master-General of the Ordnance) and a man named Ray Beech. I did not move in such circles. As an ex-Secondary Modern schoolboy from Yorkshire, I was not a part of the establishment. I had no interest being part of it. I cannot believe that these other eight people conspired to do these monstrous things. I certainly did not.

23. Yesterday I was interviewed again by the Metropolitan Police Murder Squad for one hour [and] forty minutes. It was a voluntary interview. I was free to go at any time. I was not arrested. I am not on bail. Unhelpfully, the second disclosure document was given to me some twenty minutes after the interview was supposed to start rather than last Friday as promised. My solicitors were told it was ready but had to be signed off by superior officers on Friday. The Metropolitan Police are either inefficient or doing it by design. Whatever else it is inept and an unjust way to treat anyone. During yesterday's interview, I was shown a photograph of 'Nick' aged about twelve. I did not recognise him. I was shown computer-generated E-FIT images of two of the alleged murder victims created by 'Nick'. They looked remarkably similar to each other but one with blond hair and one dark brown. I did not recognise either image. I was asked if I knew Jimmy Savile. I told them I did not. 'Nick' alleges – surprise, surprise – that Savile attended the sex 'parties'. I was asked if I knew a number of people including Leslie Goddard and Peter Hayman. I did not. I was asked if I knew well a doctor – unnamed – apparently 'Nick' alleges the doctor was a friend of mine and he turned up to repair the damage done to the boys when they were abused at these parties. I could not help there. I was asked if I could recognise images of the pen knife mentioned earlier. It was suggested it was Edward Heath who persuaded me not to castrate 'Nick' with it. I was obviously so persuaded by Mr Heath's intervention that I placed the pen knife in 'Nick's' pocket ready for him to present it to the Metropolitan Police over thirty years later as 'evidence'. I could not identify the knife. I was asked if I visited Elm Guest House in Rocks Lane, Barnes. I wondered when that elephant in the room would be mentioned by the Met. I am sorry to have to disappoint the fantasists on the internet but I did not visit Elm Guest House.

I was unaware of its existence. The so-called guest list which makes its appearance on the net must be a fake.

24. During my first interview I was told that the police were investigating to seek out the truth. I reminded them on a number of occasions that their head of 'Operation Midland', Detective Superintendent Kenny McDonald, had said on television some months ago: 'I believe what "NICK" is saying as credible and true.' This statement is constantly used and manipulated by Exaro and other media to justify their position.

25. This remark is very prejudicial to the police inquiry and its outcome. It is not justice and breaches my United Kingdom and human rights. This whole catalogue of events has wrecked my life, lost me my job and demolished twenty-eight years of my rehabilitation since 1987.

26. The police involved in 'Operation Midland' are in a cleft stick of their own making. They are in a quandary. Support the 'victim' however ludicrous his allegations or own up that they got it disastrously wrong but risk the charge of a cover up. What do I think should happen now?
Either:
I should be arrested, charged and prosecuted for murder and these awful crimes immediately so I can start the process of ridiculing these preposterous allegations in open court,
Or
'NICK' should be stripped of his anonymity and prosecuted for wasting police time and money, making the most foul of false allegations and seeking to pervert the course of justice. Those who have

aided and abetted him should also be prosecuted. 'NICK' should be medically examined to ensure he is of sound mind.

27. Detective Superintendent Kenny McDonald should resign from his position as head of 'Operation Midland'. He should resign or be sacked. But as the Metropolitan Police is a bureaucratic 'organisation' I suggest, to save face, he is slid sideways to be placed in control of Metropolitan London parking, traffic, jaywalking or crime prevention. He too should be medically examined to ensure he is of sound mind.

28. An investigation should be launched into 'Operation Midland' and its costs. Detectives' expense claims should be analysed and a full audit carried out by independent auditors.

29. Those Labour Members of Parliament who have misused parliamentary privilege and their special position on these matters should apologise. They have behaved disgracefully, especially attacking dead parliamentarians who cannot defend themselves and others and they should make amends. They are welcome to sue me for libel. In particular, Mr Tom Watson MP should state, outside the protection of the House of Commons, the names of ex-ministers and ex-MPs who he feels are part of the so-called alleged Westminster rent-boy ring.

30. Lady Goddard's Inquiry should examine 'Operation Midland's' methods so as to sift genuine historical child sexual abuse from the spurious.

31. 'Operation Midland' should be wound up by the Metropolitan Police Commissioner who should also apologise at the earliest

opportunity. On 6 August 2015, Sir Bernard Hogan-Howe shed croco-dile tears criticising the Independent Police Complaints Commission and Wiltshire Police for naming Edward Heath as a suspect. He said it was not 'fair' and his own force would not do such a thing. This is very disingenuous. When his police officers were searching my home and before they had left, the press were ringing me asking for comment. I was identified. They had told 'Nick' of the search who passed on the information to his press friends. The Metropolitan Police have also told the press that they were investigating Heath and Brittan and others. Sir Bernard should resign for the sin of hypocrisy. If he does not, it will not be long before he establishes 'Operation Plantagenet' to determine Richard III's involvement in the murder of the princes in the Tower of London.

32. Superintendent Sean Memory of Wiltshire Police should explain why he made a statement about Edward Heath in front of his for-mer home in Salisbury and who advised him to select that venue. He should also resign.

33. Leon Brittan was driven to his death by police action. They already knew for six months before his death, on the advice of the DPP, that he would not face prosecution for the alleged rape of a young woman. But they did not tell him. They just hoped he would die without having to tell him. The Superintendent in charge of his investigation should resign.

34. The police should stop referring automatically to people who make statements of alleged historic child sexual abuse as 'victims'. They should refer to them as 'complainants', from the French 'to lament', which would be more appropriate. Parliament should pass

laws to better balance the right to anonymity of 'victims' and the 'accused'. Parliament should reinstate in law the English tradition of 'innocence before being found guilty' which has been trashed in recent months by certain sections of the police, the DPP, MPs, magistrates and the courts themselves.

35. I have not just come here with a complaint. I have come with the intention of showing my face in public as an innocent man. I have come to raise my voice as an aggrieved subject now deeply concerned about the administration of justice. What has become increasingly clear about police investigations into historical child sexual abuse is that it has been bungled in years gone by and is being bungled again NOW. The moment has come to ask ourselves if the police are up to the task of investigating the apparent complexities of such an inquiry? These allegations merit the most detailed and intellectually rigorous application.

36. What is clear from the last few years of police activity driven by the media, fearful of the power of the internet and the odd MP here and there is that the overhaul of the police service up and down the country is now urgently required. We need 'super cops' who have been university educated and drawn from the professions. Such people could be of semi-retirement status with a background in the supervision of complex, criminal investigations. These people could be drawn from the law, accountancy and insolvency practices. Former Justices of the Peace could chair some of these investigations. Adequate incentives should be provided to recruit them.

37. I speak for myself and, as a former Tory MP with an impeccable record in defending the police, I have now come to believe that that

blind trust in them was totally misplaced. What has happened to me could happen to anyone. It could happen to you.

38. In summary, the paranoid police have pursued a homosexual witch-hunt on this issue egged on by a motley crew of certain sections of the media and press and a number of Labour Members of Parliament and a ragbag of internet fantasists. There are questions to ask about what kind of police force do we have in Britain today. How can it be right for the police to act in consort with the press with routine tip-offs of house raids, impending arrests and the like? Anonymity is given to anyone prepared to make untruthful accusations of child sexual abuse whilst the alleged accused are routinely fingered publicly without any credible evidence first being found. This is not justice. It is an abuse of power and authority.

39. In conclusion, I wish to thank my solicitors Mr Raza Sakhi and Mr Nabeel Gatrad and my family and friends for their support, without which I would not have been able to survive this onslaught on my character and on my life.

INDEX